Large-scale comparisons are out of fashion in anthropology, but this book suggests a bold comparative approach to broad cultural differences between Africa and Melanesia. Its theme is personhood, which is understood in terms of what anthropologists call embodiment. These concepts are applied to questions ranging fom the meanings of spirit possession, to the logics of witchcraft and kinship relations, the use of rituals to heal the sick, "electric vampires," and even the impact of capitalism. There are detailed ethnographic analyses, and suggestive comparisons of classic African and Melanesian ethnographic cases, such as the Nuer and the Melpa. The contributors debate alternative strategies for cross-cultural comparison, and demonstrate that there is a surprising range of continuities, putting in question common assumptions about the huge differences between these two parts of the world.

Bodies and persons

Bodies and persons

*Comparative perspectives from
Africa and Melanesia*

Edited by

Michael Lambek

and

Andrew Strathern

CAMBRIDGE
UNIVERSITY PRESS

PUBLISHED BY THE PRESS SYNDICATE OF THE UNIVERSITY OF CAMBRIDGE
The Pitt Building, Trumpington Street, Cambridge CB2 1RP, United Kingdom

CAMBRIDGE UNIVERSITY PRESS
40 West 20th Street, New York, NY 10011-4211, USA
10 Stamford Road, Oakleigh, Melbourne 3166, Australia

First published 1998

Printed in the United Kingdom at the University Press, Cambridge

Typeset in Plantin 10/12 pt [VN]

A catalogue record for this book is available from the British Library

Library of Congress Cataloguing in Publication data applied for

ISBN 0 521 62194 1 hardback
ISBN 0 521 62737 0 paperback

Contents

Illustrations

List of contributors

RITA ASTUTI is Lecturer in Anthropology at the London School of Economics. She is the author of *People of the Sea: Identity and Descent among the Vezo of Madagascar* (1995).

SANDRA C. BAMFORD is Assistant Professor of Anthropology at the University of Lethbridge. Her most recent work is a co-edited special issue of *Anthropology and Humanism* entitled *Fieldwork in the Era of Globalization*.

EYTAN BERCOVITCH is Assistant Professor, Department of Anthropology, Johns Hopkins University. He has carried out fieldwork among the Atbalmin of Papua New Guinea. His research interests include religion, gender, concealment and disclosure, social change, and agency and subjectivity.

JANICE BODDY is Professor of Anthropology at the University of Toronto. She is the author of *Wombs and Alien Spirits: Women, Men and the Zar Cult in Northern Sudan* (1989), and co-author of *Aman: The Story of a Somali Girl* (1994; translated into fourteen languages). Her current research is looking into attempts by British colonial administrators to "civilize" Sudanese women's bodies in the first half of this century.

ELLEN CORIN is Associate Professor at the Departments of Anthropology and Psychiatry, McGill University and researcher at the Douglas Hospital Research Center. She has co-edited with Gilles Bibeau *Beyond Textuality: Asceticism and Violence In Anthropological Interpretation* (Mouton de Gruyter, 1995). Currently, her main area of interest is the cultural articulation of psychotic experience.

RENÉ DEVISCH is Senior Professor in Social Anthropology, Africa Research Center at the Department of Anthropology, Catholic University of Leuven-Louvain. He is a member of the Belgian School for Psychoanalysis. His most recent books are *Weaving the Threads of Life* (University of Chicago Press, 1993), and *Forces et signes* (Paris, Editions des Archives Contemporaines, 1996, and forthcoming in English, Harwood Academic Publishers, 1997).

BRUCE KNAUFT is Professor of Anthropology at Emory University, Atlanta. He conducted field research among the Gebusi of Papua New Guinea on sorcery, spirit mediumship, and violence and has published *Good Company and Violence* (1985), *South Coast New Guinea Cultures* (1993), and over thirty-five articles in journals and books on a wide range of topics in cultural anthropology. His research interests include current developments in cultural theory and representation; practice, belief, and political economy; gender and sexuality; modernity; sociality and violence; and Melanesia. His most recent book, *Genealogies for the Present in Cultural Anthropology* (1996), evaluates recent developments in cultural theory and ethnography.

MICHAEL LAMBEK is Professor of Anthropology at the University of Toronto. Recent publications include *Knowledge and Practice in Mayotte: Local Discourses of Islam, Sorcery and Spirit Possession* (University of Toronto Press, 1993) and *Tense Past: Cultural Essays in Trauma and Memory*, co-edited with Paul Antze (Routledge, 1996).

EDWARD LIPUMA is Professor and Chair of the Department of Anthropology and co-director of the Center for Social and Cultural Studies at the University of Miami. He has conducted fieldwork in Highland New Guinea, the Solomon Islands, Galicia, and the Florida Keys. His most recent publications include "The formation of nation-states and national cultures in Oceania" (in *Nation-Making*, ed. R. Foster, 1995), "The cross-currents of ethnicity and class in the Florida Keys" (*American Ethnologist*), and a forthcoming book entitled *Encompassing Melanesia: Capitalism, Colonialism, and Christianity in the New Guinea Highlands*.

PAMELA J. STEWART is Research Associate in the Department of Anthropology, University of Pittsburgh and Visiting Professor in the Department of Anthropology, James Cook University of North Queensland, Australia. Her current research deals with gender issues and religious change in Papua New Guinea in addition to research on local and national identity in Scotland. She has recently coedited the book *Millennial Markers* (1997).

ANDREW STRATHERN is Mellon Professor of Anthropology, University of Pittsburgh, and Director of the James Cook University Centre for Pacific Studies, North Queensland. His most recent book is *Body Thoughts* (1996).

BRAD WEISS is an Assistant Professor of Anthropology at the College of William and Mary. He is the author of several essays on Haya (northwest Tanzania) culture and society, as well as the book *The Making and Unmaking of the Haya Lived World: Consumption and Commoditization in Everyday Practice* (1996). He is currently preparing a volume on the transnational dimensions of coffee as a consumer good.

Acknowledgments

Most of the chapters in this volume were first presented in a panel organized by the editors at the annual meeting of the American Anthropological Association in November 1994. We would like to thank Gillian Feeley-Harnik and Roy Wagner for their extremely lucid and helpful discussions of the papers on that occasion. Our thanks also to Jessica Kuper for shepherding the manuscript through the review process at Cambridge as well as to Jimmy Weiner and an anonymous reviewer for their careful reading and useful suggestions. Our deep appreciation also to Janice Boddy for taking on the role of writing an Afterword at very short notice. We invited Janice because in some respects she stands at arm's length from all the ethnographic material presented here, yet her own ground-breaking work on the northern Sudan incorporates issues of embodiment and personhood drawn from the literature of both regions.

Lambek wishes to acknowledge once again the unfailing intellectual and moral support of Jacqueline Solway and of Nadia and Simon Lambek. His work has been supported by a research grant from the Social Science and Humanities Research Council of Canada. Completion of the manuscript was assisted by a Centennial Visiting Professorship in the Department of Anthropology at the London School of Economics. Annette Chan, Audrey Glasbergen, and Carole Tuck at the University of Toronto and Margaret Bothwell at the LSE have provided invaluable backup assistance. Deirdre Rose ably prepared the index.

Andrew Strathern wishes to thank especially Pamela J. Stewart for entering into the life of this volume and jointly writing with him a paper for it. He also wishes to record his appreciation to Mrs. Patty Zogran at the University of Pittsburgh for her careful work on manuscript preparation.

1 Introduction Embodying sociality: Africanist-Melanesianist comparisons

Andrew Strathern and Michael Lambek

This volume brings together a series of intensive investigations by Africanists and Melanesianists on the relations between persons and bodies. We did not give the contributors narrow instructions but wished to discover the range of strategies and approaches they would take to this topic. Specifically we were interested in how the broad interest in the body currently evident in a range of disciplines across the academy would be refracted in the ethnography of non-Western societies, and conversely what such investigations would have to contribute to the general debate as well as to the advancement of theory within anthropology itself. Our reasons for selecting Africanists and Melanesianists are advanced below, but in brief we wanted to see how models derived from work in each area might speak to each other. An underlying aim of the book is thus to advance ethnographic comparison, a theme we take up in more general terms at the end of the Introduction.

Africanist and Melanesianist traditions: a continuing dialogue

This project developed out of a sense that close work among regional specialists, while necessary and often exhilarating, is not enough. With the supremacy of the regionalist view (as manifested, for example, in course titles or job advertisements), it has become increasingly necessary to focus one's reading on a specific geographical region of study. As the number of monographs has grown, it has been harder to keep up, and one of the things that seems to have declined is reading between regions. To the degree that this is true, one can assume that Africanist and Melanesianist scholarship have gradually begun to grow apart, their common reading situated at the level of general theory rather than ethnography. This is exceedingly unfortunate. Whatever one's view of the most appropriate mode of comparison, and the obvious value of intraregional comparison notwithstanding, it seems clear that one should draw insight from, and shed light upon, the work of ethnographers in other geographic regions.[1]

Hence in developing this book we have gone against the grain of recent collections which tend, when they explicitly consider issues of ethnographic representativeness at all, either to have a strong but narrow regional focus or to be deliberately "cross-cultural," seeking contributions from as wide a selection of societies as possible. Here we want to build on the strengths of the regional tradition of comparison while attempting to avoid the risks of parochialism. We could equally well have selected other regions and one model for continuing our work would be to add successive regions in a kind of spiraling conversation.[2]

Inevitably, given publishing constraints, our group of Melanesianists and Africanists is smaller than we would have liked. In selecting contributors we have not given great attention to trying to ensure significant intraregional "representativeness." In a continent as large and diverse as Africa that would be impossible (the very idea of speaking about Africa as a region is in some respects ludicrous[3]), and Melanesian work has also been for some time broken down into subregions not all of which are represented here. Nor is it obvious what the criteria for representativeness would be. We did consciously attempt to add to our complement of North American authors some who are European trained, thus transecting the "regional" dimension with a trans-Atlantic one based on "schools."[4] We also deliberately included a high proportion of relatively young people, fresh from the field or engaged in active field projects.

Juxtaposing conventionally labeled ethnographic regions in a comparative project and implying thereby that some privileged axis of analysis exists between them could well be considered a provocative and risky act: Africa and Melanesia? After the work of Arjun Appadurai on the dangers of misidentifying localities and mystifying maps one might question what the point is of such a comparative exercise (Appadurai 1988). There are two answers, neither of which depends on any regional or typological characterizations as such. The first is that a good deal of the kind of ethnography recognized as "classic" has been carried out in these two parts of the world, and it is interesting to see how common themes are taken up at different times in relation to "Africa" and "Melanesia." In practice, we are looking both at thematic concepts (for example, "witchcraft" and "sorcery") and at analytical ones (for example, "descent group" or "personhood") as they swing into and out of anthropological fashion.

We have to ask what the purpose of making comparisons is. Some contemporary anthropologists act as though comparisons are indeed odious and all we can do is produce specific accounts, *petits récits*. However, such a position is in practice internally inconsistent, since there is no such thing as a descriptive account that does not appeal to some general categories. Every *petit récit* draws on a *grand récit* somewhere at its back or in its words. But it is important to distinguish between such an implicit procedure of relying on comparison as classification (e.g. in sentences like "this is a descent group") and explicit procedures which attempt to construct comparison as a means of portraying and explaining difference (e.g. "descent groups in society A differ from those in B because . . . . fill in your preference").

We choose the example of the term "descent group" advisedly because it was a stock-in-trade term in the ethnography of the 1960s and 1970s and debates raged over it. In Melanesianist ethnography there was a passage of interest from descent to exchange, and thence to personhood via gender. Now all of these themes seem to crowd into the topic of the body and embodiment. "Good" ethnographies practically must say something about "the body" nowadays. It is worthwhile therefore to consider how "the body" as a topic may configure comparatively as categories such as descent group or personhood have done.

Second, it happens that exercises of "tacking backwards and forwards" have already been done between Africanists and Melanesianists. We can use such exercises as foils to the present one which deals with "bodies and persons." One thing we are *not* seeking is to provide substantive empirical generalizations (turning comparison into classification). It is rather the other way round. Starting with a category such as "body" or "person," we want to see how these interrelate *differently* across a range of cases. Here the Africanist/Melanesianist axis is useful because as it happens African models, drawn from acephalous tribal contexts, were first employed to try to make sense of group processes in the new ethnographic region of the Highlands of Papua New Guinea from the 1960s onwards. Difficulties with these applications then rebounded onto the African ethnographic contexts and the potential for a dialectical dialogue was set up. The first phase of debate was of considerably more use to Melanesianists than to Africanists. Indeed it could be argued that it led the former into exciting new theoretical terrain, if only via negation (M. Strathern 1990). It was in part Lambek's feeling that this new terrain could in turn be important to Africanists, especially when concerned with issues of embodiment and personhood, that led him to respond to an overture from A. Strathern. Melanesian ethnography is of interest to Africanists not only for the emphasis put on exchange, especially embodied exchange, but because "the manner in which Melanesian . . . relations are objectified, elicits a particular challenge to *particular* Western concepts of personhood and the nature of bonds between persons" (M. Strathern 1990:212). These Western concepts may have characterized the work of Africanists. Or, indeed, it is possible that African conceptions of persons lie closer to the Western ones than do Melanesian conceptions. Obviously these are controversial points but they are ones which bear investigation.[5]

In any case, the criss-crossing effort at making analyses with other analyses in mind went into abeyance for a while. Descent groups vanished as a focus for analysis, replaced on both ethnographic fronts by colonialism, the analysis of domination, gender, production etc. The new list of topics in turn called for a new form of integration, supplied by personhood and embodiment. Rita Astuti's paper in this volume draws attention to the ongoing potentialities inherent in making Africa / Melanesia contrasts and then subverting these on either side. Edward LiPuma's paper utilizes the strategy of double subversion in deconstructing contrasts that have been deployed between Melanesian and Western ideas on personhood (cf. Battaglia 1995b). Ellen Corin provides a remarkably complementary analysis with reference to the African context. She applies a contrast between approaches by European, primarily francophone, anthropologists that have focused on cultural categories of the person and North American concerns with subjective experiences of the self in order to undercut radical distinctions between so-called sociocentric and egocentric societies. Strathern and Stewart provide an explicit comparison of Melpa and Nuer notions of the value of human life and the histories of compensation for taking a life in the two places.

It is interesting to reflect that there are two fundamental shifts in interest here. One is from the typological to the processual. The other is from collectivity to sociality, but it should be remembered that the one does not necessarily exclude the other. They represent rather two different moments of modeling our understandings of human social life. And since it is quite obvious that personhood is partly defined in terms of group identities the levels are empirically linked also.

Nevertheless the disjuncture is there. In the 1960s social anthropologists tended to compare elements called group structures. Nowadays anthropology is faced with the quandary of not quite knowing what to compare with what and what comparative propositions, if any, will emerge from the enterprise. Bold generalizations about Melanesia done in a post-structuralist manner may arouse doubt as to their range of reference and verifiability. There is always the danger – or creative opportunity – of the ethnocentric model, the imposition or denial of difference in which we seem to be asking "why are the x not like the y?," starting out from x or y as the base, the implicit norm, a procedure that is patently arbitrary. Yet we have no other real recourse. Proceeding from the (supposedly) known to the (putatively) unknown depends always on such initial points. It depends also on the use of analytical "stretcher terms" (on which, we might say, to carry the body of theory). "Body" is one such term; it functions as an image in the production of comparative-analytical discourse in ethnography today because of its multivalent polymorphy. It evokes a transgressive image because it provocatively implies the biological while in practice it has been deployed mostly by social constructionists from Mauss through Douglas and onwards. "Body" is an operator-word used to give a layered semblance of unity to our anthropological discourse because of its supposed (etic) universality.

Why "body"?

The body is suddenly omnipresent in academic texts. The momentum of academic fashion aside, the problematization of the body is undoubtedly linked to its increased visibility and objectification within late capitalist consumer society (Featherstone 1990; Turner 1995), to feminism and the rise of feminist theory (Bordo 1993), as well as to the body's increased salience as primary signifier and locus of "home" for the uprooted, mobile, hybridized citizens of the transnational moment. Or perhaps the body is so visible now because its time is over, subject to takeover by an increasing array of technologies. Whatever the case, the new awareness of our bodies provides a useful departure for thinking about bodiliness and sociality elsewhere. However, to the degree that it is possible, we have to ensure that we do not simply rediscover or invert our own obsessions.

Within anthropology, this question, Why "body"?, has been posed, implicitly or explicitly, by many writers in the past few years, notably by Emily Martin (Martin 1987 [1992], 1994). One answer to the question, couched in terms of the history of theory, has been that "body" is a successor to "person" as a focus of interest (and some puzzlement) in our discipline (A. J. Strathern 1994). Why this succession should have occurred is not easy to say, other than by noting that there has been a strong reaction in both sociology and anthropology against mentalistic images and a powerful concern with mind/body holism issues (Lock 1993). A focus on "the body" perhaps also fits with a new materialism, disconnected from the more dogmatic side of Marxism but concerned with the domain of lived experience and the effects of the social realm on the human body. Such an emphasis easily blends further with a semiotic approach (the body as signifier), with an approach through the theory of ritual (the production by means of ritual of persons, the embodied experience of persons undergoing intense ritual processes), and with gender (the gendering of bodies and the relationship of gender to sexuality). Heuristically, therefore, "body" seems a handy term around which to organize various issues of contemporary interest in our subject.

This, however, is not sufficient for purposes of comparative work. For these, the relationship between body and person needs to be spelled out. And for writers working within the traditions of European thought, this problem obviously intersects with the older question of the relationship between body and mind although the two questions are not in fact isomorphic. The *tertium quid* here is "embodiment," which is supposed to obviate the issue of relationship by arguing that it encompasses both. Embodiment would thus be the term for a state or a process that results from the continuous interaction of body and mind or rather their conceptualization as elements in a larger unity, the body/mind manifold (Samuel 1990). Such a modeling of human life fits well enough with what is known of brain/body relationships, including those specifically that have to do with the interdependence of "the intellect" and "the emotions," looking at these as cultural categories (Damasio 1994). Neuropeptides, for example, constantly carry messages back and forth between the brain and the rest of the body that influence states which we describe as emotional.

It is important for us as anthropologists to realize that this background in brain/body studies does provide us with a universal basis for discussing some of the problems that interest us, for example certain questions of sickness and health. The widespread cultural emphasis on the influence of emotional states on illness can be referred to the new universalistic picture of brain/body interactions. However, for our own enterprises, this is only a useful beginning. If we take the sphere of culture, experience, and sociality as our domain we enter arenas that demand a relativizing perspective. The relationship between body and person thus returns as an issue of cross-cultural analysis. And here it is as with so many of our own folk concepts that we try to employ as counters in comparativist discourse: the very categories themselves are hard to define prior to such analysis, since definitions would be the result of the analysis rather than its logical precursors.

In fact, then, our approach must be resolutely dialectical, focusing on the embodiment of persons and the personification of bodies and on the ways in which these processes are differentially highlighted in different places, indeed on how different moments of these ongoing processes become objectified and singled out for cultural attention, as core symbols, foci of power, vehicles of identity, or loci of struggle. A number of basic questions come to mind. How are particular bodily practices institutionalized? In what ways is bodily experience used to legitimate authority or to subvert or challenge it? How, in a practical sense, are differences between moral and jural personhood realized and what role does the body play in each (James 1989)? How does the body serve to substantiate and to symbolize not only gender, but personhood and relationship, connection and disconnection, dependence and independence, dividuality and individuality, hierarchy and autonomy? What, if any, are the limits of the body in these tasks?

Embracing the body, therefore, we nevertheless start with a healthy skepticism toward those arguments which romanticize the body or use it simply to invert older ideas. As Novack has recently remarked, the popular notion of the "responsive body" merely emphasizes the particular opposition between mind and body or reason and emotion characteristic of North American culture. Similarly, Corin in her chapter warns of recourse to highly culture-bound notions of "empathy" and "experience," extending perhaps to "embodiment" itself. Before looking for "the body" elsewhere, we have to problematize our own local constructs, including the very opposition and its predictable sequelae, which are highly gendered (Lutz 1988; Bordo 1993). What de Coppet remarks for individualism holds equally well for the body (especially once we recognize that the body is often taken as the sign for the individual). He writes: "Those who hold individualism to be truth itself are inclined to believe that they proceed from a self-evident point of view. But this point of view is, to the contrary, sociologically determined, and, if this fact is not recognized, the object 'society' itself tends to vanish; nothing remains on either side of the act of observation but individuals in interrelation. We thus find ourselves in a situation in which humankind seems to contain only individual totalities" (de Coppet 1992).

Hence we need to start with a more critical and dialectical approach, one which problematizes the relationship between body and person or body and self in social context and which understands this as a problem for investigation simultaneously within our own thought and in the thought and practice of our subjects. As Novack says, "body must be understood as a constructed category susceptible to analysis, and it should be considered both from vantage points within the experiences of the actors in any given event and from the perspective(s) of the scholar" (1995:183). This is to suggest, however, not that we attempt to *dis*embody the body (always a risk in intellectual work), considering it only at the conceptual level, but rather that we examine how cultural concepts impact on bodily experiences and practices and likewise how our embodied condition affects cultural concepts and social practices (cf. the criticisms of Foucault made by Turner 1995). At the same time we have to be aware of how recourse to the body so often serves as a means of naturalization, underpinning some otherwise questionable social construction or systematic inequality with intimations of inevitability, weightiness, and intimacy. Marshall Sahlins (1976a) has described the process with reference to the still flourishing field of sociobiology, now flanked by an energetic evolutionary psychology.

Our first set of chapters thus each tackle a number of stubborn oppositions head on, attempting, in LiPuma's words, to "relativize relativity." To begin with, there is Rita Astuti's reinstatement of an Africa / Melanesia contrast in terms of theories of the person and descent, followed by her own obviation of the contrast in terms of recognizing elements simultaneously present on both sides of the equation. Astuti here recapitulates on a broader front the pattern of micro-conclusions reached earlier by many of the contributors to the big-men / great-men volume on Melanesia edited by M. Godelier and M. Strathern (1991). More centrally, Astuti takes on the sex / gender contrast, effectively elaborating an argument as to why we cannot collapse them, even in a society such as the Vezo of Madagascar that places so little significance on sex as a form of difference. There will always be a tension, she argues, between what is viewed as fixed in the person and what is processual or transformable; where the boundary is conceived to lie will vary from society to society. In sharp contrast to some Melanesians, the Vezo do not make a distinction between male and female substances that compose a person and this has significant consequences for the kinds of agency and transformations possible or necessary in each place.

LiPuma provides a vigorous argument about the contrast between dividuality and individuality and in addition raises important questions about the transition to modernity and its implications for notions of the person. He argues that, as the individual is the locus of desire characteristic of modernity, in order to understand recent historical change in Melanesia we must clarify our conceptions of personhood. In particular, despite its tremendous usefulness in transcending common-sensical yet ethnocentric assumptions concerning personhood, and hence in understanding fundamental differences between Melanesian and Western sociality, we must now qualify the model of dividuality (M. Strathern 1988). Conversely, we have to recognize the ideological nature of individualism and the ways in which dividual aspects of Western personhood have been masked. As LiPuma suggests, a number of questions remain unanswered by this analysis. For one, to the degree that individuality is closely connected to capitalism, are all non-capitalist or pre-modern societies alike in their emphasis on dividuality? (A more lengthy examination of definitional and analytical issues involved here is given in A. J. Strathern and P. J. Stewart in press.)

Ellen Corin addresses a remarkably similar set of concerns from the Africanist side. She provides a salutary account of the consequences of Mauss's seminal essay on the person within the francophone literature and what the concept of "individuation" would mean in this context. Although the French Africanists were not operating with the jural notions of descent theory they nonetheless appear to have had a highly deterministic view of personhood, a social determinism that marks even the work of the psychoanalysts of the Dakar school. Corin seeks alternate principles, means, and contexts for individuation that exist alongside the dominant collective forms and facilitate some perspective on them. She finds one such locus of individuation in the therapeutic rituals of spirit possession in Zaire (now Congo) and explores in great depth and with great sensitivity the symbolic contexts in which the subjective experience of patients is gradually transformed over time from subjection to new and active forms of relationship. The picture is reminiscent of that delineated earlier by Janice Boddy on the northern Sudanese (Boddy 1989), but with an explicit psychoanalytic dimension to the argument. Hence, although Corin is undoubtedly correct in her contrast between American experiential and French structural emphases overall, it is noteworthy that in this particular case her own concerns are more psychological in comparison with LiPuma's sociological or Boddy's cultural account. At the same time, Corin is careful to specify that there is more than one form of individualism; for the adepts of the Zebola ritual, she writes, "the goal is not the creation of autonomous subjects" but rather a personal "repositioning" within the collective order.

Each of these authors provides exceptionally lucid renditions of complex issues and debates. Moreover both Corin and LiPuma frame their arguments concerning the recognition of individuality with reference to the very conditions of anthropological knowledge. Similar questions are taken up in Lambek's chapter as well as in the concluding section of this Introduction. Lambek argues controversially that mind and body represent fundamental incommensurables in human experience that are everywhere transcended in practice and yet everywhere distinguished, in some form or other, in thought. Culturally diverse formulations may themselves prove incommensurable with one another so that translations of words like "mind" or "esprit" or Melpa "noman" (discussed in Strathern and Stewart's chapter) do not provide precise mappings of one another, nor could we discriminate which of them has it "right"; nevertheless they fall within the same horizon of ideas. It is important to recognize that LiPuma and Lambek differ somewhat in their understanding of incommensurability. For Lambek incommensurability does not preclude translation or comparison, but by the same token he does not expect ethnographically diverse material necessarily to fit into a single parsimonious, tidy, systematic, or overarching model. Hence while Lambek's discussion of the mind/body problem has the same general ambition as LiPuma's analysis of opening new avenues of comparison, and the same general view that "relativity must be relative," there is an interesting tension between the ways the two projects are respectively established. Lambek's description of spirit mediumship, while less complete than Corin's or Knauft's, also provides a useful counterpoint to theirs in terms of the range of subjects possession can address.

Talk about bodies and persons raises many issues. One of the more critical concerns the historical position of self-reflective thought about bodies and minds, abstracted from concrete, embodied events and practices, and how we draw the contrast between the products of Western philosophy (including our own thought as anthropologists) and those of other traditions and technologies. What kinds of lines do we draw, and where? What kind of moral do we want to draw about our story of the "invention of philosophy" and the "discovery of the soul" by the Greeks, albeit in the face of post-modern claims regarding the end of metaphysics or the spuriousness of the subject? How do African and Melanesian traditions of thought and bodies of practice (whether or not influenced by the Greek tradition via Islam or Christianity) understand selfhood and process experience? Do they distinguish a "soul" from the "body" and in what manner? Or do they simply relate to the world mimetically rather than by abstracted reason? Is mimesis as bodily practice somehow inferior to pure mentation; is the body a kind of "epistemological deceiver" as Plato thought (Bordo 1993:3); or, in somehow unifying experience rather than splitting it along the lines of self-alienating Western dualism, is it superior? Lambek tries to clarify some of the issues involved in thinking anthropologically about mind / body issues, while Devisch's chapter on a Yaka healing cult in Congo (former Zaire) implicitly raises others in its striking account of a culture which, he says (somewhat controversially), "has barely evolved a cognitive technology of 're-presentation' or of distancing in relation to bodily experience and the habitus."

Since Mary Douglas anthropologists have appreciated the body for its symbolic properties. In any given society or regional tradition we can inquire which aspects of the body or sensory experience form the prime sources of metaphor; and of which metaphors the body is also the recipient. Which features of embodied existence are singled out as primary, as metonymic of the whole (Ruel 1997), which senses tend to metaphorize each other, and what chains of precedence are thereby set up (cf. Howes 1991)? What are the consequences of starting with one metaphor or direction of predication rather than another?

One of the most basic questions concerns the use of the body to discriminate the discrete bounded ("possessive") individual. This is a central aspect of North American culture, whether we consider the body as a source of display of the self, the immensely powerful consequences believed to follow the transgression of bodily boundaries in sexual abuse (cf. Antze and Lambek 1996), or the moral disquiet at creating identical bodies (Battaglia 1995a). Yet it cannot be taken for granted; as T. Turner argues, the fact that the body surface comes to serve as "a symbolic index of the boundary between the individual actor as culturally formed subject and the external object world" (1995:149) should not blind us to the fact that "the body serves as the paradigm, not only of individuality, but of the limitations of individuality" (p. 145).[6] More generally, attention should be placed on tactility and "contact zones" (Pels and van Dijk 1995), on what happens *between* bodies and not simply on what stems from within the body seen as the single and privileged locus of experience. In this respect recent work on mimesis (Kramer 1993; Taussig 1993) is significant. Mimesis stands in contrast to a stable subject/object opposition and describes embodied imitation as a kind of psychological identification.[7] In its platonic usage it represents "both the content of poetry and that psychological condition which experiences poetically" (Havelock 1963:248–9). To the degree that, in Plato's critique, mimesis implies a whole series of disparate and possibly inconsistent identifications (Havelock 1963:202), it fits with post-structural critiques of the givenness of the subject.

Devisch's chapter is striking for the way it evokes the mimetic properties of ritual, especially tactility and the specular identification on the part of the initiate with a series of carved figurines. Like Corin, Devisch provides a psychoanalytic reading of the ritual process, drawing upon Lacan's conceptualization of the passage from the imaginary and the symbolic as well as Winnicott's notion of transitional phenomena. Yet the psychoanalysis does not come at the expense of a rich appreciation of the cultural forms of the Yaka. In theoretical terms what Devisch's study shows is the specificity of overlapping tropes regarding aspects of the body and person tied to uterine versus agnatic connections in the domain of kinship and descent and the connections made between the body of the patient/initiand and the encompassing social world by means of such tropes, for example, the image of the silurid catfish (of a special variety that breathes as lungfish do). Such a use of an anomalous creature as a central focus for religious imaging cannot fail to remind us of Mary Douglas's pangolin and her evocation of the idea of natural symbols (Douglas 1966, 1970). But the force of Devisch's treatment lies not so much in the domain of classification as in the domain of embodied experience, since the patient experiences a change in his or her condition moving from a silurid-like condition to that of an initiated human. Devisch's study also illustrates richly that the experiencing body is one that operates through its sensory apparatus and that it is this fact that makes the body "social." A prime image here is that of the "skin" and it would be very interesting to compare further Yaka notions about the skin as a locus of sociality and similar notions from Melanesia often pointed to by ethnographers (e.g. A. J. Strathern 1975). The relationship between the world, the body, and the emotions is captured neatly in Devisch's phrase "the ecology of body and affect."

In a sense the importance of the body for social and cultural theory has been the realization that we can understand the nature of such things as selfhood, practice, sociality, and religious experience only when we bring the body explicitly into the picture, stop taking it for granted, and problematize its presence both in the thought and practice of our subjects and in our own theories about them. From this point of view it is not the body or even embodiment *per se* that interests us so much as the way that bringing the body into focus can help us understand cultural practice and social process as is shown well in the chapters by Corin and Devisch. They explicitly take up classic contexts of embodiment with reference to cults of affliction and healing, associated with trancing and initiation into special associations. These topics seem characteristic of Central African ethnography, highly reminiscent of Victor Turner's work on the Ndembu. Indeed there are historical connections between the *mbwoolu* cults Devisch describes and the *haamba* rites practiced in the Luunda cultural zone.[8] It is noteworthy that this sort of cult-group that exists at arm's length from kinship obligations is in fact extremely common throughout much of Africa, while it does not appear to have a direct counterpart in Melanesia. Nevertheless, the sorts of issues addressed in the cult rituals are found in other contexts. In particular, the themes of transitionality, containment, and decontainment appear central to the phenomena described in our collection by Sandra Bamford, Eytan Bercovitch, and Brad Weiss. They help us see the ways in which the body is envisioned not only as container but as contained.

Bamford describes a Melanesian context (Kamea) in which containment and decontainment are orderly processes incorporated into the life cycle and constituted in part by practices of eating and refraining from eating, whereas Weiss describes the imagination of horrific uncontrolled flow, or as he puts it, un-making, in an East African setting (Haya) characterized by high mobility and indiscriminate contacts. In turn, Bercovitch describes the centrality among the Melanesian Atbalmin of what he refers to as dis-embodiment, namely the way in which bodies are taken apart and body parts and bodily capacities are removed from persons. Where the Kamea, in Bamford's account, eat *for* each other, the

Atbalmin imagine eating one another.[9] Dis-embodiment here is the literal undoing or inverting of the primary exchanges through which persons are relationally embodied, but it also appears more positively in the eschatological and redemptive messages of Christianity and the privileged viewing of bodily relics in the indigenous religion. Bercovitch's argument suggests an interesting contrast between the visual and hence display aspect of embodiment as opposed to the hidden, concealed quality of dis-embodiment.

Embodiment

The concept of the mindful body as laid out by Lock and Scheper-Hughes (1987) has served the field of medical anthropology well in setting up a domain for comparative work without relying on universalist definitions of either mind or body. For general anthropological theory, it is necessary now to go one step further. We need to set up an arena within which we can further integrate established domains of ethnographic analysis, such as kinship, politics, ritual, etc. (all of them also problematic of course) within the sphere of embodiment as a paradigmatic term. This implies that embodiment must have an essentially social and cultural reference, enabling us to consider it as a category of sociocultural analysis. It also means that the particular importance of the term for the study of issues having to do with personhood, structure, process, and agency needs to be spelled out. In our view, there is no doubt that the concept of embodiment does indeed provide some strategic advantages over a generalized approach to personhood. First, it indicates the intersection of the biological and the cultural in the realm of lived experience. Second, it indicates the inscription and encoding of memory in somatic and somatized forms in the manner discussed by Bourdieu (1977) and Connerton (1989) among others. Third, it is a processual term, whose locus lies in the reception of the cultural into the body but equally the work of the body in building cultural forms. Fourth, it gives us an approach to the genesis of symbolism and classification. Fifth, it implies agency in terms of the willed bodily actions of persons rather than their passive performance of roles. In all these domains the local ethnotheories of body and person are to be found woven together, and we may take such theories as a regular starting point for the investigation of embodied practices.

We follow Csordas in moving away from an anthropology "of" the body, in which the body comes to be taken for granted and objectified in its own right, toward a phenomenological focus on the condition of embodiment. As he puts it, "the point of elaborating a paradigm of embodiment is . . . not to supplant textuality but to offer it a dialectical partner" (1994:12; cf. Lambek 1993a). Subtle applications of such an approach can be found in the contributions in this volume, in particular of Corin and Devisch who interweave phenomenological with psychoanalytic insights in their examinations of therapeutic practice and of Weiss who examines the phenomenological basis of rumours of blood stealing. We want to emphasize that in this work it is the dialectical relationships between embodiment and objectification, and between embodiment and subjectification, that are critical. Hence Mauss's famous "Techniques du corps" essay (1979a) has to be placed in conjunction with his equally significant essay on "The notion of person" (1979b; cf. Carrithers *et al.* 1985). Persons (and selves) need to be understood with reference to the body, and vice versa.

Our approach, then, incorporates phenomenological insights without taking a fully phenomenological position. It is worth pointing out in this regard that attention to embodiment has not been restricted to phenomenology. In a well-known argument Geertz (1973) has shown that body and culture are inextricably linked on evolutionary grounds; the brain itself has adapted to an increasing use of culture and, in increasing our capacity for culture, has likewise increased our dependency upon it. Neither, he concludes, is imaginable without the other. From another direction, that the body is a site of political struggle is an insight recognized not only by authors such as Bourdieu and Foucault but in Anglo-American feminist practice throughout the century (Bordo 1993:16ff) as well as by women at other times and places (e.g. Ardener 1975). Indeed, if we examine the great theorists – Marx, Freud, Durkheim, and Weber – with the body in mind, we see that embodiment has a central place in the work of each. Drawing for the moment simply on the Marxian strain of thought, we take as central two key arguments, namely that the body is socially mediated and that society is informed and substantiated by the bodily practices of its members. As Haraway puts it: "neither our personal bodies nor our social bodies may be seen as natural, in the sense of existing outside the self-creating process called human labour." Moreover, "the universalized natural body is the gold standard of hegemonic social discourse" (Haraway 1991:10 and 1990:146, respectively, as cited by Csordas 1994:2). We see as one of the critical anthropological tasks elucidating the ways in which recourse to the body naturalizes social convention in the various local contexts in which we work (cf. Lambek 1992). Thus not only is the body socially mediated, but the condition of society is one of lively embodiment.[10]

Phenomenology's contribution is to overturn the dominant dualisms in which the body serves as either the passive material on which power works or the silent instrument with which it works, or in which the body is viewed more actively, as a source of asocial bestiality. It gives the body a positive and active status in social practice and hence in social theory. [11] It is here that the idea of the pre-objective is critical. The pre-objective is the realm of experience before it becomes fully "cultured" or "enculturated." It has a use in analysis because it provides for the *genesis* of phenomena, much as the idea of "the individual" can do in certain contexts. But the pre-objective is always regarded also as incomplete. It looks to objectification for its completion. Whether it is sublation, oblation, or sublimation that is involved, objectification implies the transmutation of the embodied gesture, the expressed impulse, into a form that can stand as a symbol of values. The virtue of the term pre-objective is to suggest not an evolutionary argument but an ontological one. As Csordas puts it: "Our lives are not always lived in objectified bodies, for our bodies are not originally objects to us" (1994:7). In this sense, therefore, gestures, facial expressions, and certain embodied dispositions such as the racing of blood described by Weiss, may correspond to the pre-objective; but the interpretation placed on them, and the use made of them, belongs to the realm of the objectified.

It is in an analogous spirit that we offer these Africanist / Melanesianist vignettes. What is pre-objective on one side may become objectified on the other; what is deemphasized in one may become central in the other. The aim is the dialogue itself. Yet there must be a purpose beyond the dialogue: if not classification or generalization, then at least a privileged insight that is potentially capable of being generalized. An approach of this kind was essayed long ago by Mary Douglas (Douglas 1966, 1970). In her work she often attempted explanatory comparisons in which she outlined differences between ethnographic cases and sought to explain these in terms of social factors. Douglas's basic methodology is still useful because it is capable of producing statements that are not necessarily of a functionalist cast but certainly belong to the realm of comparative "social logics." In terms of today's anthropology, we would take such hypotheses and look at them in an expanded comparative context with concern more for agency and history than for classification.

In writing this, we do not mean to imply that we need to use the same holistic concept of society that informs Douglas's models, only that social logics or logics of sociality do differ in systematic ways, as shown in Sandra Bamford's elucidation of the ideology of containment and decontainment among the Kamea people of Papua New Guinea. The Kamea concept of siblingship which is defined by originating out of the same maternal container rather than stemming from an idea of shared blood in the sense with which we are more conventionally acquainted, has interesting comparative implications. The relevance for Africa remains to be seen although on the surface it strikes a chord with ideologies of embodiment found in some of the Central African societies characterized by, as it is now phrased, matrilineal descent, as well as with Malagasy notions of kinship. The decontainment of Kamea boys, and hence their engendering, exemplifies from the Melanesian side the contrast that Astuti sets up with the Vezo in Madagascar for whom gender boundaries are far less salient and do not have to be produced out of an original androgyny. Bamford's argument is also complementary with LiPuma's in that, in a sense, she describes the regulated transition from relatively more to relatively less dividuality characteristic of the Kamea life cycle.

The next task, as we have argued, and as LiPuma also elaborates, is to set these logics into the context of history. Our model needs to be given historical force by considering "the implications of actual bodily experience for imagining and acting upon the forces of history" and hence of "bodily reform as historical practice" (Comaroff 1992a:72).[12]

The chapters by Bruce Knauft and Brad Weiss accomplish this end. Both describe the partial transcendence of older forms of sorcery by the opening up of communities and the consequent shift in attention toward new sources of potency and tension. Weiss offers an ethnographically nuanced account of how embodied images change over time, showing the mutually constitutive interplay between intimate bodily experiences and economic and social practices. The notions of blood stealing draw, on the one hand, on the importance of blood in the definition and experience of life force and kin relationships and, on the other, on the process whereby material substances may become commodities and the concerns generated by the dispersal of kin to urban centres. In this context blood is compared by the Haya to electricity. A substance of energy whose "secure containment [is] integral to viable social practice," blood is depleted by electricity, an alternate source of energy characterized precisely by its uncontainability, diffusion, and anonymity. As Weiss notes, the doors to the houses of professional blood stealers are said to be made of wood but when people touch them they are captured by electricity and pulled inside, where their blood is sucked out. Concomitantly, Haya ideas yield easily to the approach of Mary Douglas, since "blood out of place," as it is when stolen and then used for blood transfusions, is considered to be anomalous and threatening, a notion that has been amplified since AIDS became prevalent.

Knauft's chapter makes an intriguing contrast with that of Weiss in delineating a more positive initial formulation of the implications for moral personhood of the social changes entailed in wage labor and migration. Knauft shows how recent seance performances among the Gebusi people in Papua New Guinea have enabled a discursive construction of attitudes to the introduction of Western commodities and the desire for them. Wahiaw's innovative performances expressed both these desires and the new transactional contexts in which attainment of them was envisaged and also the ambivalence with which wage labor was conceptualized. Spirit possession thus became the vehicle for the articulation of a fluid, exploratory, even contradictory new form of historical consciousness that was precisely the result of, and response to, the commodification of social relations. It is also worth mentioning that while spirit possession has often played a similar role in Africa (cf. Lambek, this volume; Stoller 1995), there are some striking differences in its manifestation in the two regions. Wahiaw is more shaman-like in the way he elaborates a visualized narrative in his performance than are spirit mediums generally in Africa. A more striking contrast between Knauft's and Corin's chapters has to do with the articulation of gender and the display of sexuality.

Knauft's spirit medium Wahiaw addresses by means of the concrete images of narrative some of the same issues of changing forms of sociality in Papua New Guinea that LiPuma tackles by means of the abstractions of theory. Whereas the Kamea, in Bamford's account, continue to articulate consumption and sociality with reference to food that is ingested, Haya and Gebusi have begun to focus more on what is purchased. As LiPuma notes, there is a shift of emphasis from the relatively embodied to the relatively objectified and from the relatively dividual to the relatively individual. But this does not come unremarked; it is articulated among the Gebusi in the "privileged communication" provided by the spirit seance (cf. Lambek 1993b) and among the Haya in rumour drawing from embodied experience.

These processes are somewhat more complicated among the Atbalmin who, in Bercovitch's account, were more conflicted about change. Bercovitch shows the importance of a historical and existential viewpoint here by arguing that Christianity offered a new approach to problems of conflict and death by opposing or transcending the lethal powers of sorcery as well as the secret powers of indigenous temples. From that perspective the future held relatively little new peril. However, whereas the Church expected exclusive loyalty and the destruction of the temples, many Atbalmin saw the need for both the older and newer forms. It is noteworthy that, questions of dividuality aside, Atbalmin women seemed conscious of the gendered inequality established through the temple and hence were readier to destroy it. Bercovitch makes an interesting comparison between Christian and Atbalmin ideas, arguing that in both cases disembodiment was a precondition for varieties of "resurrection." In the case of Christian ideology, the body as a whole is subordinated to the survival of the soul; while in Atbalmin ideas, the body as flesh was subordinated to the preservation of the body as bone in terms of relics kept in the temples. The comparison is not exact, since the dimensions of disembodiment are somewhat different, but in pursuing analogies as well as contrasts, in the historically developing complex of ideas on life and death, Bercovitch shows us the intertwining between local and global social logics that is so characteristic of the contemporary worlds studied by anthropologists whether in Africa, Melanesia, or elsewhere. The representation of Christianity as "a kind of anti-sorcery system" and its attraction on that score is also reminiscent of a good deal of African material.

The shift from direct personalizing and embodying forms of exchange described by LiPuma, Bamford, and Bercovitch to commodified ones can be mediated by the sorts of compensations – material exchange for embodied persons – among Melpa and Nuer documented in Andrew Strathern and Pamela Stewart's chapter. In essence, Strathern and Stewart describe the objectification of life, following a series of transformations between humans, animals, and objects of value in cycles of exchange and following also the way these equivalences were historically transformed. Among the Melpa of Highland Papua New Guinea, colonialism, commoditization, and Christianity have each had successive and distinct impacts on the system. Strathern and Stewart also draw a number of striking parallels between the Melpa and the Nuer. In both societies the logic of redressing hostility is linked to that of marriage and reproduction; both link exchange of animals to sacrifice to ancestors; and both societies faced a crisis in the resolution of violence and compensation with the advent of guns and the indiscriminate killings they induced. They also describe the distinctions made between material and immaterial aspects of the person in each society and the fact that it is the material element – blood – that enables fluidity of social relations. The contrast returns us to the argument made in Lambek's chapter while the polluting qualities of blood that is not channeled in reproductive directions, as indicated also by Weiss, may be a widespread index of unease.

In sum, embodiment has to be situated with reference to local and translocal modes of production, kinship and exchange, gender and age hierarchies, language practices, religious and political disciplines, jural rules, pervasive metaphors, historical experiences, and mythical fantasies, in other words, with reference to all the traditional paraphernalia of the social anthropologist. Embodiment has to be understood in dialectical tension with objectivized personhood and subjectivized selfhood. The chapters collected in this volume contribute to the task of the serious investigation of the body in non-Western societies and in the heterogeneous series of historical processes we refer to as the transformation to modernity.

Our contributors address bodies and persons in various ways. Some start with experience, others with the way experience is drawn into or from collective metaphors, yet others with practice. Unlike other collections on the body, however, these chapters are not located in a specific field of medical anthropology or of cultural representation – though they may borrow heavily from such work – but address topics long central to the study of African and Melanesian societies: kinship, exchange, witchcraft, spirit possession, social change. The promises offered anthropology by a paradigm of embodiment will not be met until it is able to engage these topics fully.

What kinds of comparisons?

If this book is explicitly an exploration of embodiment and personhood, it is also an intervention in the epistemological debate about the value and means of comparison in anthropology. Here we briefly elucidate our position.

It is a commonplace of anthropology to say that ethnography has grown finer grained and more sophisticated than before. But it is also common to bemoan what is seen as an entailment of rich ethnography, namely that works have come increasingly to appear self-enclosed. In North America the individual ethnographic work is opened to readers primarily via rhetorical strategies of address (such as the invitational first person narrative) rather than by means of intertextual relations, explicit engagement with other ethnographies. Some people argue for a kind of ethnographic relativism or nominalism in which each culture is explored on its own terms, even as others challenge the very notion of cultures seen as bounded wholes. Yet others find the inability or inhibition to compare a fatal flaw in the interpretive turn and call for a return to objectivism. However there is no longer the sense that we can isolate a single dimension ("social structure") which explains the rest and hence provides the axis along which objectivist comparison could take place. Objectivist comparison is in crisis because both "variables" and "grounds" for comparison (explanatory hypotheses) have grown harder to isolate. Neither holistic presentism nor sociological reductionism is any longer in vogue (Peel 1987). Yet relativist comparison may be an oxymoron.

This collection is conceived in the firm belief that, to borrow Richard Bernstein's felicitous title (1983), we can locate comparison "beyond objectivism and relativism." But this requires us to clarify what we do when we compare. In effect, as will be seen, we are not advocating anything new so much as rendering more explicit how anthropological knowledge has long proceeded. The problems raised in the last paragraph are more apparent than real because, the claims of the "comparative method's" more vocal advocates and opponents to the contrary, they do not correspond to the main way in which we practice comparison.

The traditional reason given for carrying out comparison has been to explain the presence or co-presence of social phenomena. Explanation has moved through a number of modes from that of the development of an ideal universal history by the nineteenth-century evolutionists through the structural-functionalist paradigm in which history was ignored (Peel 1987). A marked improvement to the latter came with the development of "controlled comparison" within a specific region. While intraregional comparison emerged within structural-functionalism in order better to serve its explanatory goals, inevitably it began to bring local histories of divergence into the picture. Moreover, the procedure also proved applicable in structuralism where local models were analyzed as transformations of an underlying structure.

Holy has lucidly contrasted the role of comparison in what he calls positivistic and interpretative anthropology respectively, pointing out that among practitioners of the latter "comparative research has obviously lost the function of theory testing which it had for the positivists" (1987:8). Interpretative anthropology is interested in "culturally specific processes of meaning construction" rather than the explanation of general processes (p. 8). However, despite Holy's remark that "the line between comparativists and non-comparativists . . . is probably more sharply drawn than ever before" (pp. 8–9), interpretative anthropology is also comparative. Indeed, one could readily argue that anthropology is *always* comparative. An anthropology without comparison would be the sound of one hand clapping (Lambek 1991) since every ethnographic description minimally implies a comparison with the ethnographer's own society. Viewed simply as translation, this is challenging enough (Hobart 1987; Overing 1987). We also compare implicitly whenever we study social change, the axis of comparison being time rather than space.

The comparison practiced in this volume falls broadly under what Peel describes as the mode of comparative method in which "it is histories, or 'societies-in-change' rather than just 'societies' which are compared . . . [The] aim is to explain historical particulars through applying to them general statements, which are theories or models, rather than to move from particulars to empirical generalizations or 'laws'" (1987:109). This is more than simply "comparison facilitating description" in order to "identify or bring into focus cultural specificity" (Holy 1987:10). In the fashion of the hermeneutic circle it is hoped that the historical/ethnographic particulars and the manner in which they are worked through by our authors also contribute to the growth and refinement of our conceptual apparatus. Phrased another way, it is our expectation that the theories, models, or concepts – whether methodological or ethnographic – that emerge from the various studies in the collection might be usefully applied to each other and to additional studies. In particular, we wish to encourage a productive exchange between Melanesianist and Africanist (and other regional) anthropologies. To apply a Melanesian thought to our enterprise, we suggest that the fundamental goal of comparison is ongoing exchange, rather than the creation of distinct intellectual lineages.

Marilyn Strathern has recently remarked on the "nonsense-sounding" of "aiming for comparison with the non-comparability of phenomena kept firmly in mind" (M. Strathern 1990: 211). We think this paradox can be dissolved once we distinguish incomparability from incommensurability. Anthropology actually traffics with the latter. Incommensurability refers to a situation in which seemingly conflicting ideas are not "able to be brought under a set of rules which will tell us how rational agreement can be reached" (Rorty 1980:316). This means there is no neutral universal framework, no objectivist language into which alternative theories, paradigms, or cultures could be set side by side, point by point. However, incommensurability does not imply incomparability; to the contrary, as Bernstein argues, it clarifies "what is involved when we do compare alternative and rival paradigms" (1983:82). In particular, it implies openness and multiplicity rather than absolute and categorical discriminations.[13] Cultural comparisons are on the order of comparing art styles or, common wisdom not withstanding, apples and oranges (compared each time we select fruit to eat). To return to our Melanesianist model, what we exchange in the absence of common coin is not commodities but gifts.

It should be noted that the view here is quite different from that of relativism. Rather than seeing languages or cultures as discrete, enclosed, and entirely self-affirming worlds, we assume that language is open to the world; in conversation speakers continuously address incommensurables, making an effort to compare their concepts or thoughts, standards or problems, with those of their interlocutors even when, and perhaps especially when, they cannot be submitted to a common measure. The relativist view of bounded cultural wholes breaks down once we treat historicity seriously. When we approach our objects of comparison as "societies-in-change" their openness becomes immediately apparent. Indeed one of the chief questions for analysis becomes understanding how local people themselves address the conjunction of incommensurable discourses, with which, for example, we see the Atbalmin struggling in Bercovitch's chapter.

Finally, if earlier forms of comparison were based on an axis of social structure or mode of production, leaving "culture" as either dependent, and hence irrelevant for comparison, or autonomous, and hence the relative part that could not be compared, the recent turn to the body rearranges these relationships. It could be argued that the universal human condition of embodiment and "thrownness" in the world gives rise to certain basic existential problems (cf. Jackson 1989, 1996). Comparison then becomes the work of ground clearing in order that the various responses can speak to each other. In this view, ethnography becomes critical for philosophy, and vice versa. Philosophical questions inform our ethnographic inquiries and, conversely, the results of ethnography may speak to and perhaps even shift the terms in which questions have been traditionally phrased and answered within the Western philosophical tradition. In this collection perhaps Lambek's and LiPuma's chapters speak most directly to these issues, but in fact all the contributions can be viewed in this light.

If we can compare societies within a given region, we can also compare the *study* of society conducted in one region to its counterparts in others (cf. Fardon 1990). Here there is a shift, characteristic of the human sciences more generally, toward a study of discourse. Indeed the very constitution of "region" comes into question. The region emerges not only from geographic proximity or common historical origin, but from the act of studying it. As Fardon puts it, each ethnographer enters "a 'field' imaginatively charted by others" (1990:24–5). Whether or not one believes that "Africa" and "Melanesia" form real subjects suitable for comparison with one another, it is undoubtedly the case that the anthropological scholarship conducted in and about each of these places falls into roughly comparable units.[14]

In distinguishing regional traditions of study, Fardon provides a cogent critique of those who distill the anthropologist's object to a single abstract Other. "The regional specialist is aware," Fardon writes, "that research has not consisted of an encounter between a fieldworker and 'the Other', but the nuanced continuation and modification of a relation between an approach delineating a region and the people who live within it. The tenacious character of these regional nexuses is decidedly double-edged: they institutionalize the potential for developing criteria of specific regional competence in an area, monitoring the work of others and cross-referencing between individual bodies of work" (1990:25).

The present work can be said to partake of both inspirations; we leave in play both the comparison of "African" societies and ideas with

"Melanesian" ones and the comparison of "Africanist" approaches with "Melanesianist" approaches. Indeed, we think this is the only way comparison can reasonably be done; as Fardon remarks, "region, problem, and descriptive values are established intertextually" (1990: 22). Our goal is neither general explanation in the sense described above nor text or discourse analysis but to enable African(ist) and Melanesian(ist) cases to speak more easily to each other.

We said above that ethnographic work minimally entails implicit comparison between the society being studied and the society of the anthropologist. At times this becomes explicit, the ethnographic Other becoming a vehicle for auto-critique. Thus, for example, in studying emotion in Ifaluk (Micronesia), Lutz (1988) discovered she first had to take apart what emotion meant in Western discourse and begin to distinguish an analytic language from the everyday (local, American) one that, she argues, passes for scientific knowledge in fields like psychology. In comparing African and Melanesian concepts and practices to one another we are, of course, doing so not directly but through our respective translations into our shared analytical language. We think that the explicit expansion of translation to include a "third" may provide an interesting way to address the problems of translation from a single source.

It is the presence of this "third" which ultimately enriches the language we compare into and distinguishes it – anthropological knowledge – from our common everyday speech. We would thus expand Fardon's point: not only does anthropology face more than one Other, but there is always at least the shadow of other Others present in every ethnographic encounter. In fact, although ethnographic production entails translation from one language to another, this is never simply binary comparison. The language we translate into has itself been constructed in part from previous translations from other ethnographic sources. Words in the anthropological repertoire, like "kinship," or "witchcraft," in contrast to their use in everyday speech by "the man on the street," are a product of this continuous explicit process of triangulation and resonate with connotations from diverse ethnographic sources.[15] Thus, with each new ethnographic study of emotion, we can expect the existing conceptualization of "emotion" which Lutz found wanting to be refined.

The common body of anthropological knowledge grows in this way, each significant new study repositioning our central concepts. Interregional comparison provides a triangulation that lessens the kind of *folie à deux* possible between an areal tradition of scholarship and the ethnographic material it reports on. It should have the same salutary effects on regional analysis that the study of a single society, like that of Lutz, can have on thought at home. A direct example of triangulation is to be found in Delaney's discussion of the virgin birth debate (1986), specifically her challenge to the way we have understood the Trobriand material, by means of her own ethnographic work from Turkey and what it says about anthropologists' own cultural "conceptions." In the same way we hope the Melanesianist interventions can disturb the habitual way Africanists translate African terms and practices into "witchcraft," "sorcery," "spirit possession," and the like; likewise the Africanist interventions may challenge or enrich elements of what becomes the "culture" of Melanesianist writing. It is the very incommensurability of the constructs and concepts that makes the comparison interesting, requiring ingenuity in the carrying out and producing unexpected outcomes.

The point of this is not to argue that ethnographic comparison leads us step by step toward a final truth (say, about "kinship" or "the body") but that it continuously enriches and refines our language, reshaping it to new contexts of debate. We are always working at our language, opening it out and challenging it by means of ethnography, even as we use it to push our understanding of ethnography further. The language of anthropology in this sense is not neutral or objectivist, standing outside the phenomena studied, but continuously forged in the crucible of our inquiries as we confound it with new realities. Comparison is not a matter of standing back and coolly observing but of wading in and putting the concepts derived in one study to work in another. The result is not a fixed language of theory any more than everyday language is fixed, but like the latter, something supple and always changing to meet the needs of new conversations and new contexts.

Put another way, one of the things that most distinguishes anthropology from the opinion of the day is the earnest efforts we make, within our own tradition of knowledge, to enlarge our horizons and confront our prejudices. Comparison is a chief means by which we do so, both in the practice of fieldwork, and then in the use of ethnography to engage and enhance our own tradition of thought, i.e. anthropological knowledge, and finally in our critical reflections on our own social and cultural milieu.[16]

NOTES

1 Werbner (1989) and Bloch (1992) provide recent examples of vigorous thinking about the body grounded in comparative ethnography.
2 Other conversations that have taken or are taking place are those between South Asianists and Melanesianists; between Melanesianists and Amazonianists; and between specialists on regional cults and trading systems in Australia and Melanesia.

3 However, questions about the cultural unity or divisions within Africa, while frequently the subject of political discussion, have hardly been adequately treated in the anthropological literature, at least in English.

4 Of course, these are not entirely independent variables. It is no accident that our two Belgian anthropologists (one long resident in Québec) report on work conducted in Zaire (now Congo).

5 See also Morris (1994). The effect of his discussion is to show similarities between African and Melanesian ideas of the self rather than between African and Western ones.

6 Turner (1995) himself provides a paradigmatic elucidation of the dialectics of embodiment and objectification among the Amazonian Kayapo.

7 Lambek is grateful to Nancy Lewis and George Ulrich for elucidation of this point and direction to Havelock.

8 For other outstanding analyses of embodied ritual in this area see De Boeck (1991, 1994).

9 This is an image which, to be sure, is also found in Africa. See, for example, Wilson (1951), a classic piece of anthropological comparison.

10 Berger and Luckmann (1966) provide a notable attempt at synthesis of phenomenology with sociological theory.

11 However we are reluctant to go the next step and refer to "the body as an experiencing agent" (Csordas 1994:3). Bodies may have agency, but it is embodied persons or selves who are agents.

12 For recent collections that provide historically located accounts of spirits in Oceania and witchcraft in Africa, see Mageo and Howard (1996) and Comaroff and Comaroff (1993), respectively.

13 These brief remarks concerning incommensurability are drawn from Bernstein's extensive discussion of the development of the concept in the works of Kuhn and Feyerabend (Bernstein 1983). See also Lambek (1993a:ch. 12). It is significant that in developing his argument Feyerabend draws explicitly on his understanding of anthropological method.

14 In Fardon's collection on the regionalization of ethnographic accounts (1990) Africa and Melanesia are even placed within a single section. At the same time, the discrepancy of scale is manifest. "Africa" is divided into four subregional chapters (which by no means cover the whole continent) while "Melanesia" stands alone in a single chapter.

15 Following Bakhtin's notion of polyphony we could say that everyday language is characterized by resonance and perhaps an implicit triangulation as well.

16 This discussion and some of its language draws from the work of Gadamer (1975; cf. Bernstein 1983; Wachterhauser 1986). For an earlier and somewhat more extensive attempt to grapple with anthropological comparison from a hermeneutic perspective see Lambek (1991).

Part I

Transcending dichotomies

2 "It's a boy," "it's a girl!" Reflections on sex and gender in Madagascar and beyond[1]

Rita Astuti

The reflections on sex and gender presented in this chapter were set in motion by the experience of giving birth to my son four years ago in London. Under the influence of the National Birth Association, I was determined to have a "natural birth," free of any unnecessary medical intervention. Accordingly, one of my requests was that the midwife should refrain from telling me the sex of my baby, for I wanted to be allowed to register it "in my own time," and to decide for myself whether the fact that the newborn was male or female should be of any relevance at all.[2] At the time, I imagined that my Vezo friends in Madagascar,[3] unlike some of my British and Italian friends at home, would have no difficulty in understanding why I did not want the sex of my baby to be the first thing to be uttered about him or her, only seconds after the birth. I thought they would understand my attempts to escape the strictures of the dominant "gender system of the west" (as in Errington 1990), in which a person, from the very beginning, cannot be anything at all if it is not sexed.

I thought they would understand because the Vezo with whom I had lived and worked for almost two years had impressed me for their lack of interest in the difference between people with male and female genitals – a difference which, in many contexts, appeared to make very little difference (Astuti 1993). In good Southeast Asian fashion (Errington 1990; Karim 1995a, 1995b; Carsten 1995b), the Vezo were more prone to downplay the difference between the sexes than to dwell on it, stressing complementarity and similarity in gender relations rather than difference and hierarchy. From what I knew about the Vezo, I could easily imagine them to be like the Balinese who, when a child is born, make "no special point . . . as to whether the infant is male or female" (Errington 1990: 2, quoting Belo 1949).

But I was wrong. When I returned to my adoptive Vezo village for a short period of fieldwork a year after giving birth, I discovered that the very first thing a Vezo mother is told by the woman who has helped her in the delivery is the sex of the baby: "it's a boy!" (*lehilahy io!*), "it's a girl!"

29

(*ampela io!*).[4] Indeed, inside and outside the home where the delivery has taken place, this is just about the only thing that is ever asked and discussed about the new birth: whether the baby is a boy or a girl.[5]

Needless to say, I was taken aback by my misjudgment, and by the realization that I had tried to out-Vezo the Vezo themselves. It is my "surprise" at finding the Vezo different from what I had imagined them to be that generated the question I will be addressing in this essay: why do the Vezo make a point about the sex of their new-born babies? If the reader finds this question absurd (as my Vezo friends certainly would), let me clarify at the outset that I use it as a rhetorical device to focus my analysis on the inconsistencies and contradictions that lie at the heart of the "gender system" of the Vezo.

The argument is organized as follows. I start by reviewing the reasons why I thought that the Vezo might wish to ignore the sex of their new-born babies. I do this in the first three sections of the chapter, on Vezo identity, on the yet unformed and indistinct nature of small babies, and on the constitution of the Vezo person, both within and through its relations without. In every case, I shall conclude that it would make a great deal of sense for the Vezo to take little notice of whether their babies happen to be boys or girls. It is against this background that I return to my point of departure, namely the fact that the Vezo, contrary to my expectations, classify every baby, from the moment of birth, as male or female.

I will argue that in order to understand what is being said when the Vezo announce: "it's a boy," "it's a girl," we need to salvage, against recent and insistent calls for its dismissal (e.g. Yanagisako and Collier 1987; Butler 1990; Moore 1994), the old dichotomy between "sex" and "gender," originally used in anthropology to distinguish between what is "biologically intractable," to use Butler's formulation (1990:6), and what is culturally constructed. In the case of the Vezo, the analytical distinction between sex and gender resonates usefully with local understandings of the person, which centre on the tension between what in the make-up of the person is "intractable," and what is "negotiable."

To illustrate the tension between "sex" and "gender," I will introduce a new category of people, who, in a sense, are the alter-egos of the new-born babies I discuss at the outset of this essay. These are men who, in the course of their childhood and throughout their lives, become "images" of women (*sarin'ampela*, men who are "images of women"); that is, men who choose to become women and shift their gender identity. The reason for discussing *sarin'ampela* together with new-born babies is that these two sets of people illustrate the extremes in the dialectical interplay between sex and gender: while the first ones are all gender, even against their sex, the second ones are, as it were, all sex and no gender.

However, the "intractable" limits to the transformation of men into women, as are expressed by my Vezo informants, will serve as a reminder that what babies are born with – a sexed body – can never be entirely re-constructed: hence, the unresolved tension between sex and gender.

As will become apparent in the conclusion, the argument developed in this chapter recapitulates my previous analysis of the coexistence among the Vezo of two contrasting and apparently incompatible forms of identity (Astuti 1995a): one which is achieved through activities performed in the present, the other which is given as an essence inherited from the past; one which is transformative, non-primordialist, and non-essentialist, the other which is rooted in, and determined by, the unchangeable order of descent. The Vezo resolve the tension between these different ways of being a person by assigning one to the living and the other to the dead. In other words, while the living create their identity through performance, the dead are identifiable only by the essential and inherent qualities inherited through descent. Through their rituals, the Vezo endeavor to raise a barrier (*hefitsy*) to separate these two types of existence, for "the dead and the living are not together, they are not the same" (*ny maty ny velo tsy miaraky, tsy mitovy*).

In the context of the comparison between Africa and Melanesia advanced in this volume, it is notable that each of the two forms of identity known to the Vezo appears to fit neatly into well-established "localizing strategies" in ethnographic writing (cf. Fardon 1990). Looked at from a purely Austronesian perspective, the Vezo would find their place in a world where persons and groups are fluid and boundless, and where identities are non-primordialist and non-essentialist (cf. Linnekin and Poyer 1990); looked at from a purely African perspective, the Vezo would belong to a world where the person is determined by membership of bounded and divisive descent groups (cf. Fox 1987). To a certain extent, the distinction between Austronesian and African ethnographic concerns reflects the separation that the Vezo endeavor to establish between themselves and the dead, as they labor to raise a solid barrier between life and death, between the village and the cemetery. The academic division of concerns fails, however, to render adequately the continuity that also exists between the indeterminacy of the living person and the determinacy of the dead, between the fluidity and malleability of Vezo-ness and the fixity of descent – a continuity which the Vezo are forced to recognize by the indisputable fact that living people die, that the dead were once alive, and that the living were generated by those who are now dead. It is by laboring to establish the discontinuity that the living Vezo also acknowledge that a continuity exists: the one is achieved dialectically by denying the other.

The Vezo, therefore, are caught in the middle of our regional comparison, as they live and die in a world in which the person is "Austronesian" in the present and "African" in the future, in which identity is performative among the living and essentialist among the dead, and in which the separation between these two types of existence is only temporary and never conclusively realized. The analysis of sex and gender which will occupy us in the remaining sections of this chapter will reveal the same unresolved tension between the same irreducible aspects of human existence: between what in the nature of human beings is processual and transformable and what is categorically fixed and unchangeable.

The non-essentialist nature of Vezo identity

During my first period of fieldwork among the Vezo, my informants, who later became friends and relatives, took the initiative of teaching me what it means to be Vezo. The thrust of their lesson was that Vezo identity is not a fixed state of being which people are born into, but is a way of doing which people perform in the present and which makes them Vezo contextually and contingently. To be Vezo means to know how to swim, fish, sail, make canoes, and so on; in more general terms, the Vezo define themselves as "people who struggle with the sea and live on the coast," thereby stressing that it is what they do and the place where they live that makes them what they are.[6]

The non-essentialist nature of Vezo-ness, an identity that does not stem "from within" (from blood, or bones, or any other inherited substance), but is acquired "from without" (from one's interaction with the environment, defined in its widest sense), explains why any stranger can be transformed into a Vezo, while Vezo people can be transformed into something else (typically into their inland neighbours, the Masikoro, who are cultivators and cattle keepers): for in both cases, what one "is" depends on what one does, rather than being predicated on inherent qualities of the person.

The fact that Vezo-ness is not inherent in the Vezo person does not mean that it is less identifying or differentiating. The list of Vezo "ways of doing things" (*fomba*), as opposed to Masikoro "ways of doing" the same thing in a different way, is almost endless – how women braid their hair, how men wear their blanket, how children dis/obey their parents, how people walk, how softly or loudly people speak, for how long corpses are kept in the village before burial, how much or little money people are able to save, and so on.

The significant point, however, is that Vezo and Masikoro people *become* different from one another by doing all these different things, rather than *being* different prior to doing them; the absolute difference between Vezo and Masikoro lies in the different things they do, and not in the people themselves. For the Vezo difference, like identity, is performative, not essentialist; so that, prior to the enactment of their respective identities (their different "ways of doing things"), Vezo and Masikoro can actually be assumed to be *identical* people.

Elsewhere, I have used this argument to make the point that Vezo-ness is not an ethnic identity, for it is not based on intrinsic, in-born, natural, or naturalized traits of the person (Astuti 1995b). In the context of the present discussion, the most striking expression of this alternative theory of identity is the Vezo's perception of the making of their body.

It has been argued by those who regard ethnicity as a "primordial" attachment, that the body is the most obvious and uncontroversial locus of one's identity. This is because one's body, from the moment of conception, encapsulates one's true heritage, all of that which comes, uncontaminated, from one's ancestors: "in the streams of the blood" as Morgan would have put it, or "in the genes" as contemporary writers are now able to say. Thus, a "primordialist" like Isaacs wrote that "the body is the most palpable element of which identity – individual or group – is made. It is the only ingredient that is unarguably biological in origin, acquired in most of its essential characteristics by inheritance through the genes" (1975:36).

This "ethnic body" is an obvious and perfect example of "mythologizing" (à la Barthes), a case of making appear natural what instead is cultural and historical (cf. Errington 1990:15). The Vezo offer an obvious and perfect counter-example: for them, the body is most definitively a cultural artefact, and not a biological given.

In this respect, the Vezo body is just like Vezo identity: it is made processually through practice, its distinctive features being the contingent result of one's activities, rather than the predicted outcome of one's inheritance from the ancestors. The Vezo are proud of what they call "the signs that one is Vezo" (*famantaram-Bezo*); these are traces which their activities at sea leave on their body, such as the whitish scars that the fishing line leaves on men's fingers and, sometimes, on their waists; or the lack of a callus at the base of the thumb of women's hands (Masikoro women develop this from the daily pounding of maize or rice); or the particular build of men's bodies (small hips, broad shoulders and the absence of over-developed pectoral muscles) and women's bodies (slim and tough), that comes from sailing (as opposed to cultivating), and from eating a lot of fish (as opposed to a lot of starch). Another significant "sign" of Vezo-ness is not so much "on" the body as in the movements that bodies make, in particular in the way people walk. The Vezo adopt a special technique in walking so as to avoid getting stuck in the sand, and it is their distinctive rotating movement of feet and hips that is yet another "sign that one is Vezo."

What is significant about all these different "signs" is that they are on people's body only as the result of their active and sustained engagement with the environment. This means that people are not born with a Vezo body (as they might be born short or tall, with darker or lighter skin, with a squint eye or a club foot), but only acquire such a body – a significant marker of their identity – through the practice, enactment, and embodiment of Vezo-ness.

Now, if Errington (1990:15) is right in saying that one of the most important sets of meaning which bodies are asked to bear in any given culture is the culture's gender ideology and its "mythologies" of the person (by which she means the process through which cultural and historical differences between men and women are made to appear natural), the fact that the Vezo "*de*-mythologize" their bodies, and their identity more generally, can also be expected to make a difference to the way they think of *gendered* bodies and identities. In other words, the non-essentialist nature of Vezo identity and the resulting features of the Vezo person and body – made from without rather than determined from within – can be expected to offer an ideal background for thinking of gendered bodies and identities in similar non-essentialist terms: a background against which people could easily be imagined *not* to be born gendered but to *become* so, in the same way in which they are not born but become Vezo by, among other things, fabricating for themselves a Vezo body.

This prediction is not simply the result of abstract reasoning. It is noticeable, for example, that the way the Vezo talk about the difference between men and women resonates with the way they talk about the difference between Vezo and Masikoro, in so far as the emphasis is always on what men and women *do*, rather than on what men and women inherently are, prior to what they do.

But then: *if* people are not born Vezo; if bodies are perceived as artefact rather than as natural givens; and *if*, following the same "de-mythologizing" approach, gendered identities and gendered bodies are also not simply and "naturally" born as they are, but are created, "culturally" and "historically," through practice – *then* it would make sense for the Vezo to take no notice of whether their babies are born male or female.

It would make sense. But, as we know, this is not what they do. Instead they exclaim: "it's a boy!," "it's a girl!"

Are babies fully human?

Something I learned from talking to pregnant women, to women who had given birth several times, to midwives, and to old ladies surrounded by shoals of grandchildren and great-grandchildren, is that new-born babies are so incomplete, so fused with their mothers, so malleable and so vulnerable, that they can barely be considered fully human beings. In this sense, at least at one level of discourse, people not only are not born Vezo: they also are not born human.

One way of considering the less-than-human nature of Vezo babies is by appreciating that the boundary between mother and baby is rather fuzzy and ill-defined, so that it is not always clear where one begins and the other ends. The fusion between mother and baby is most obvious during pregnancy when the two often act as one person, the mother for the baby and the baby for the mother. For example, the baby will make the mother crave special foods or will "make trouble" (*miola*), kicking violently and making the mother bleed, when the father comes home after sleeping with a lover; only when the father, advised by a diviner, admits his fault and pays the wife a fine does the baby quiet down.

While during pregnancy the mother is a vehicle for the baby's desires, and the baby guards the mother's interests, at the moment of birth it is of great concern that the separation between mother and baby and between the mother and the placenta take place swiftly and successfully. Once more, the baby may "make trouble" and refuse to emerge, if the father has "dirty things" (*raha maloto*) to confess. The main anxieties, however, are aroused by the placenta, which is considered the eldest sibling of the baby[7] and is referred to as a "killer" (*mahafaty io*): the stuff which kills women if it does not detach itself properly and completely.

The wound left on the mother by the birth of the placenta is likened to the wound left on the baby's body, the navel; both are referred to as *fery*. Both bodies are in danger of being penetrated by "air" (*iliran'tsioky*), an event which can result in death. To avoid this, mother and baby have to be kept hot and wrapped up securely in several layers of clothes and blankets. During the first few weeks after the birth, the new-born baby is hardly visible, buried as it is in a bundle of synthetic blankets, themselves part of the bigger bundle of heat and sweat which envelopes the mother. In a sense, the separation which has occurred at the moment of birth is also the cause of this prolonged symbiosis, for it is the lack of strong and clearly defined bodily boundaries (which the baby never had, and which the mother has lost as a result of giving birth) that requires mother and baby to remain fused with each other.

Another reason why mother and baby must be close to each other[8] at all

times during the first couple of months after the birth, is that the baby is
so susceptible to outside influences that its face will change completely if
left alone for even a few minutes. My Vezo friends could hardly believe
that Europeans keep their babies in cots, soon after the birth, often in
separate rooms; with Vezo babies, I was warned, this would be just
impossible: didn't I see how their eyelids often tremble, or how their eyes
roll sideways? This happens every time an *angatse* (a rather ill-defined
kind of spirit, of which there are always many around) flies over the baby
and frightens it. The problem is that if the baby is left alone, any passing
angatse will be able to get hold of it (again, in a rather ill-defined manner),
which will result in a change of features. *Angatse* are able to reshape the
face of an unprotected baby[9] because babies are still extremely malleable
and plastic;[10] they gradually become less so with time, so that when they
are old enough to sit up by themselves, their eyelids will no longer
tremble, their eyes will no longer roll, and their features will no longer be
in danger of transmutation.

The possibility that a spirit might take hold of new-born babies is just
one example of their vulnerability. Babies are soft and weak (*malemilemy*),
and boneless (*taola tsy misy*),[11] and their ability to survive and to hold on to
life can never seem to be taken for granted. People seem only too aware of
the many things that can go wrong in a baby and which, in the absence of
Western medicines (*aolim-bazaha*),[12] can easily result in death; moreover,
babies are particularly exposed to the possibility of acts of reprisal from
easily angered ancestors – it being much easier for a vengeful ancestor to
kill off a "boneless" baby than a strong and "fully-boned" adult.

It is precisely at the time of their death that babies' malleability and
vulnerability turns most clearly into an assertion of their less-than-human
status. For babies who die before they are one year old are not buried in
their parents' ancestral tomb, but are laid without a funeral in an unmar-
ked grave in the forest. Although I was once told that there would be no
point in burying boneless bodies in tombs whose purpose is "the gathering and preservation of bones" (*fanajaria taola*), the most common explanation for excluding small babies from ancestral tombs is that they are not
yet people / human beings, they are "animals" (*mbo tsy olo fa biby*[13]).

It is perhaps too easy to take this statement excessively literally. I do not
think that any of the people I talked with ever wished to suggest that their
babies were "animals." If babies were said to be *biby*, what was being said
was that nobody could predict their chances of *becoming* human beings: a
chance to acquire bones and clear (if perhaps only temporary) bodily
boundaries; a chance to consolidate their facial features; and a chance to
become strong and invulnerable to *angatse*, and a little more resilient to
bad-tempered ancestors.

This, however, should not be taken simply as a commentary on the uncertainty of survival; it is also an acknowledgment of the relative insignificance of birth in the making of full human beings. From a different perspective, I am restating a point previously made by Bloch about birth among the Zafimaniry of Madagascar: namely, that in this part of the world – as also occurs in Austronesia[14] – birth is a relatively unimportant event for "creating" the social person (Bloch 1993:120).[15] hat is born among the Vezo is merely a potential person, still closely fused with its mother, in need of constant protection from outside influences, still wholly pliable and, especially, utterly vulnerable – a *biby* who "is," but who still has to *become*. The significant point is that everyone's attention, among the Vezo as much as among the Zafimaniry, is focused on this crucial process of becoming, rather than on the somewhat incidental moment of birth.

But then: *if* birth is relatively insignificant in the creation of the person; and *if* what is being born is a shapeless being, a weak and vulnerable creature who is uncertain to survive and may or may not become human – *then* it would make sense for the Vezo to take no notice of whether their still unformed babies happen to be born male or female.

It would make sense. But, as we know, this is not what they do. Instead they exclaim: "it's a boy!," "it's a girl!"

Ungendered persons within and without

So far I have discussed only what mothers do with their babies, while completely ignoring the position of fathers. This reflects what the Vezo regard as the fundamental difference between men's and women's contribution to the making of children: that men simply "throw away" their semen inside the woman's body, while women are left with the hard work (*asa mafy*) of carrying and nourishing their babies, both before and after birth. Although men, thanks to their semen, are said to be the "origin" and "source" of pregnancy (*lehilahy ro fotoran' ateraha*), women, thanks to their physical effort, are considered "the real source - origin - hence the owners of the children" (*ampela ro tena tompony*).

I have discussed elsewhere the complicated ritual process through which the difference between men and women in procreation is transformed into sameness, thereby creating a system of relatedness in which gender difference makes no difference: a bilateral system in which relatedness traced through women and through men is absolutely identical, in which women's children and men's children are the same, and in which mother's side and father's side are indistinguishable (Astuti 1993).

A crucial aspect of this transformation of difference into sameness is the fact that the Vezo are remarkably uninterested in translating their (admittedly rather vague) theory of procreation into a model of the person where gender differences are traced "within" bodies rather than "between" them (as in Moore 1993b and 1994). In other words, women's and men's different roles in the creation of children are *not* used, as they are in other parts of the world, to draw a distinction between female and male substances.[16]

In this respect, the Vezo could not be more different from the Melanesians, whose model of the "partible" person is predicated on the possibility of sorting out a whole history of past relations which have "conceived" – and are "de-conceived" by the repeated actions of – each person (Strathern 1988). In Melanesia, since each constitutive relation is gendered, the resulting person is not only "partible" but androgynous: made up of both male and female relations. In substantive terms, this means that, as in Tubetube, the person is composed of female bones (formed by the maternal breast milk) and male flesh and blood (formed by paternal foods and substances) (Macintyre 1989:138); or, as with the Mekeo, it is composed by an equal share of male-derived blood (semen), and female-derived blood ("womb-blood") (Mosko 1983: 25). The crucial fact is that at any point in time (and, most dramatically, at the moment of death), what is female and what is male is clearly distinguished and distinguishable *within* the person.

Busby (1997b) has noted that because in Melanesia the separate gendered substances brought together in procreation remain identified thereafter with "partible" and distinct parts of the body, the resulting person, whether a man or a woman, remains "a mosaic of male and female substance." Consequently, "there is *an equivalence* of men and women as both mosaically constructed, at the same time as there is *a radical distinction* between (gendered) male and female body parts" (emphasis added).

Busby rightly emphasizes how in Melanesia gender as related to men and women is contingent and fundamentally unstable. This stems from the fact that men and women are essentially similar in their androgynous make-up, and it is therefore only as a result of transacting in male or female things that cross-sex can be turned into single-sex and gender can be made manifest (but only momentarily, before reverting back to cross-sex). While the lack of "cumulative sedimentation" of gender through performance is a striking Melanesian feature, of equal significance is the second, complementary feature noted by Busby, namely the *radical distinction* between male and female substance on which the partibility of the Melanesian person is predicated.

It is on this point that the Vezo differ most markedly from the

Melanesians. There is no sense in which the Vezo person could be imagined as androgynous (or in which gender differences could be imagined as being traced "within" bodies), because the Vezo do *not* draw the radical distinction between male and female substance which underlies the androgynous character of the Melanesian person. Gender among the Vezo appears to be far less contingent and fluid than in Melanesia, but this is so, paradoxically, because deep down in its make-up – in the bones and in the flesh, in the blood and in the marrow – the Vezo person is *not* gendered.[17]

In some respects this is also what happens in South India, where male and female substances are merged and are thus indistinguishable in the final substance of the body (Busby 1997b). In the Dravidian system people, like the Vezo and in contrast with the Melanesians, do not divide up the body internally into distinct male and female parts. However, they do distinguish relationships on the basis of the different ways in which parents of each sex transmit their male or female substance to their children. To take the primary example,[18] mothers are considered closer to their daughters and fathers to their sons, because daughters have received from their mothers the female substance (milk) which they will in turn transmit to their own children, while sons have received from their fathers the male substance (semen) which they will in turn transmit to their own children. The significant point is that although in this system people are born with their male and female substances fully merged in a unitary body, the relationships in which they are involved are marked categorically by gender:[19] because of the substantially different ways in which men and women are related to their children.

Here the similarity between Vezo and Dravidian examples ends. For in the case of the Vezo the emphasis is on the *sameness* of the relationship that each parent has with the children of either sex.[20] It is true that women, because of their hard work, are considered "the real source - origin - hence the owners of the children," and that unmarried men – who throw their semen away and have nothing more to do – may not even become fathers of their offspring.[21] But if a man accepts (and is accepted) to join his wife in generating children and in creating new relatedness, then they will do so together with no distinction being drawn between them:[22] they jointly create a system of relatedness in which the difference between them makes absolutely no difference.

It is for this reason that, in light of the comparison with Melanesia and South India, the Vezo person turns out to be strikingly ungendered: not only ungendered within, but also in its relations without.

But then: *if* the Vezo person is ungendered within, deep down in its constitution, and is ungendered without, in the relationships it has with the people who have generated it and in the relationships it will generate in its turn – *then* it would make sense for the Vezo to take no notice of whether their new-born babies are male or female, since this will make no difference to their place in the network of relations that has produced them and which they will contribute to produce.

It would make sense. But, as we know, this is not what they do. Instead they exclaim: "it's a boy!," "it's a girl!"

And so: why do the Vezo make a point about the sex of their new-born babies?

If I were to ask one of my Vezo friends this question, I would probably get another question back: Don't you, Europeans, also make a point about the sex of your new-born babies? If I were then to ask, What do people mean when they say "it's a boy!" or "it's a girl!"?, men would probably not answer at all; women, on the other hand, would explain with a rather puzzled look on their faces,[23] that they simply mean that boys have a penis (*misy latake*), girls a vagina (*misy lity*). And this is, on the face of it, all that there is to it. Except that, by saying that some babies are born with penises and others with vaginas, the Vezo effectively say that babies are born *sexed*. To say this, I suggest, is to say very little and a great deal at the same time.

It is to say very little, because to be born with a penis or a vagina is in no sense the end of the tale. The most significant part of the story will unfold as these babies grow up and gradually acquire what, at birth, they still lack: a "gender." This will happen through the process of acting as a boy or a girl, and of learning and doing boys' as opposed to girls' things – a process similar to the one through which they will also acquire Vezo identity. Boys and girls are said to be just the same (*mitovy avao*) in their character and disposition (*fanahy*), and in the ways they do the things appropriate to a baby (*fomban-drozy*): crying, sleeping, sucking, peeing and pooing, and so on. The only difference occurs at the moment of birth, when boys appear facing downwards, and girls appear facing upwards. This is because boys must avoid looking up at their mother's vagina, which will be taboo (*faly*) when they grow older; but girls have none of these problems, since mothers and daughters are made in the same way (*sambility iaby*, they all have the same vagina). As they come into the world, boys and girls behave in a manner that is appropriate to their gender, and they do so as a matter of fact, although nobody quite knows how it actually happens! Later on in life, these boys and girls will have to become wise (*miha-mahihisty*) in order to behave in discriminating and appropriate ways according to their and other people's gender. And as they become wise, they also become increasingly different. They play different games, do different things, learn different tricks, forge different friendships, and have different nocturnal lives: the boys wandering around the village wrapped up in their blankets, waiting to be let in by one of their lovers; the girls, inside their houses, deciding who, if anybody, they want to let in. It is this playing, doing, learning, knocking on and opening of doors, which transforms what at first were sexed babies into gendered persons.

From this perspective, the previous point that the Vezo could ignore the sex of their new-born babies because their babies are shapeless, unformed, weak, and vulnerable, can be turned on its head. For to say that a new-born baby is a boy or a girl, that it is sexed, that it is born with a penis or a vagina, is actually *the only* thing that can be said about it: the only thing which is given at the moment of birth, when *everything else* has still to be made and created processually through time and "wisdom."

And yet to say that babies are born sexed is also and at the same time to say something far more significant. By attributing a sex to their babies at the moment of birth – a sex in the absence of gender – the Vezo construe sex as a categorically fixed and "intractable" trait of the person, even of such unformed persons as their babies are perceived to be. By making a point about the sex of their new-born babies, the Vezo acknowledge that sex, contrary to gender, is not and does not need to be made, but is given.

If we refer back to the several good reasons why the Vezo could be expected to ignore the sex of their new-born babies, the fact that they do not reminds us that the *processual* nature of gender identity coexists with the *categorical fixity* of sex – with the "intractable" fact that some babies are born with penises and others are born with vaginas.

Thus, although it was factually wrong to imagine that the Vezo would take no notice of the sex of their new-born babies, it was nonetheless analytically appropriate to be surprised that they did. For there is a real inconsistency here between what is categorically fixed and what is processual: an unresolved tension between sex and gender.

The existence of a tension, and the fact that it remains unresolved and unresolvable, becomes clearer if we turn our attention away from new-born babies towards the *sarin'ampela*, towards people who, by acting and doing, acquire a gender which contradicts their sex.[24] As already suggested, babies and *sarin'ampela* illustrate two opposite extremes in the dialectical interplay between sex and gender; it is with this contrast in mind that I present my still tentative understanding[25] of what it means to be born of one sex and become an "image" of the opposite gender.

Sarin'ampela: men who are "images of women"

I first heard about *sarin'ampela* when I met one in a Masikoro village during an expedition to the interior. She[26] was sitting among a group of women gathered around her *hotely*: a little table on which she had laid a few pieces of boiled manioc, some rice cakes, and a couple of small cups with which clients could drink coffee. The Vezo friends I was with told me that she was a *sarin'ampela*: a "man" who is "an image of a woman."

Sarin'ampela are "men" who "like women" (*tia ampela*). "Liking women" in this context is different from "looking for or wanting them" (*mila ampela*), which is what other men do when looking for sexual partners; *sarin'ampela* "like" women in the sense that they would prefer to be women. When they put this into practice, this results in the creation of an "image": the "image" of the woman they would like to be.

My informants described how one starts becoming a *sarin'ampela* from an early age. As young children, *sarin'ampela* prefer to spend time with girls rather than with boys, and learn to braid their friends' hair, carry water on their head, search for head lice, and so on. As adults, their identity is defined most crucially by the fact that they perform "women's jobs" (*asan'ampela*) and adopt "women's ways of doing things" (*fomban'ampela*).

Sometimes my (mostly female) informants mentioned that *sarin'ampela* have sex with men, although there was a certain degree of confusion about this, especially as to whether *sarin'ampela* have sex among themselves or with other men who are not *sarin'ampela*. In all cases, sexual preferences seemed strikingly unimportant in defining what kind of people *sarin'ampela* are. Although it does not mean that sexual preference is irrelevant or secondary to the experience of *sarin'ampela*,[27] it is nonetheless significant that, unanimously and consistently, my informants agreed that practicing of a "woman's job" or adopting a female "way of doing things" is of primary importance in transforming a man into "the image of a woman."

Despite the crucial importance of *sarin'ampela*'s productive activities in creating this "image," it is rather difficult to specify what it is exactly that *sarin'ampela* do. This is because the definition of men's as opposed to women's jobs is highly localized and rather fluid. As one moves along the coast, people's livelihood varies greatly: in one place, people specialize in line fishing and sell their catch at the market; in another, they employ fishing nets and barter dry or salted fish for maize and manioc with the Masikoro; in yet another, they rely on the seasonal catch of lobsters sold to outside traders; and so on. In each case, the specification of men's and women's jobs will vary: for example, in one setting men's job is to fish and women's job is to trade at the market; elsewhere, both men and women are involved in net-fishing, women are mainly in charge of drying and salting the catch, while men do most of the travel inland for bartering.

The distinction between men's and women's tasks is nonetheless never rigid: where the men's job is to fish, women join in when necessary; where the women's job is to dry and salt the catch, men can be asked to help. Similarly, although cooking and fetching water for the kitchen are everywhere "women's jobs," men can also perform these tasks and do so more than occasionally.[28]

When it comes to "ways of doing things" (*fomba*), male and female distinctiveness is more marked. For example, women carry heavy loads on their head, while men will always carry them on their shoulders; women let their hair grow and have it braided, while men have theirs cut short; men and women tie their sarong differently at the waist, and men never wear it, as women do, high around their chest; when women are in groups, chatting and gossiping among themselves, they can be heard making a distinctive kind of laugh (*mitohake*, generally understood to be occasioned by sexual joking), which is never heard among men.

Hence, whereas men who perform "women's jobs" – selling fish at the market or washing clothes – are not regarded for this reason alone as *sarin'ampela*, men who carry a bucket of water on their head or do *mitohake* with other women will most certainly be considered such. However, these actions alone are not enough; they must be accompanied by a clear and unambiguous performance of recognizable "women's jobs." *Sarin'ampela* cannot simply intrude incidentally upon the women's domain of activities, as other men do. In order to be credited with their identity, they have to present a much more coherently gendered "image" than is ever the case with other men or women.[29]

Doing is therefore essential to how *sarin'ampela*'s identity is defined – whether it be how they tie their sarong, or how they make a living.[30] This raises an important point about the processual nature of gender identity among the Vezo. For it is clear that the existence of *sarin'ampela*, like that of the famous American Indian "berdache," is predicated on the distinction between what Whitehead called "anatomy and physiology" on the one hand, and "behaviour and social role" on the other (1981:86): in Vezo terms, between what people are born with – a penis (*misy latake*) or a vagina (*misy lity*) – and the "image" they construct for themselves. This distinction and, most crucially, the fact that one's "image" can be at variance with one's sex, account for the way some people *become sarin'ampela*: they do so by *creating* their gender against their sex.[31] *Sarin'ampela* are unique only in so far as the "image" they create for themselves is at variance with the shape of their genitals; if it were not for this, they would be like any other Vezo person, actively engaged in the process of gender creation. What *sarin'ampela do* is what all Vezo people *do*: having been born sexed, they *become* gendered by way of acting and doing. In this respect, the example of those few men who become "images" of women proves that for all Vezo people, whether *sarin'ampela* or not, "gender" is no more and no less than an "image" – something that is *created* through what one does and does not do; something that one *becomes*.

If the example of the *sarin'ampela* highlights the fact that gender identity among the Vezo is made as an "image" rather than being given as an essence, it also raises the question of how far the disengagement of one's gendered "image" from one's sexed body can be sustained. When discussing *sarin'ampela*, my friends would often remind me, with the help of vivid gesturing, that although these men perform women's jobs and adopt women's "ways of doing things," they still nonetheless have a penis between their legs: they carry water and firewood on their head, they go to the market to sell fish, they wear earrings . . . "*kanefa, misy latake io*" (and yet there is a penis down there).

The fact that, as with the American Indian "berdache," "the sheer fact of anatomic masculinity was never culturally 'forgotten'" (Whitehead 1981:86), but was in fact insisted upon (at least by my informants, whose "image" did not contradict their anatomy), made me ask how far *sarin'ampela* are actually able to claim that they have become women. In a context where death is ritually constructed as the limit of a person's transformability (Astuti 1995a), one way of formulating this question is by asking what happens when *sarin'ampela* die.

My informants had no doubts: *sarin'ampela* will never be treated as women when they die. There are three instances when the sex of the deceased clearly affects funerary procedures. The first is when the body is washed, dressed, and laid on the bed where it remains during the wake; the second is when the body is put inside the coffin before being carried to the cemetery. In both cases, only people of the same sex as the deceased are allowed to handle the corpse. The third instance is when the deceased is buried in either male or female sections of the tomb: a man among men, a woman among women. People told me that no living woman would dare handle the corpse of a *sarin'ampela as if* it were "really" that of a woman, "for there is a penis down there" (*ka misy latake io*). And it was similarly suggested that there would be no question of burying a *sarin'ampela* in the female section of the tomb, for this would cause serious trouble with the ancestors, who would want to know why the body of a man was buried among the women.[32]

During funerals, then, the "image" of *sarin'ampela* is undone and fundamentally negated.[33] At this point no living person is prepared to recognize the "image" of a woman in the body of a man: regardless of how much *sarin'ampela* are transformed by what they do and by the way they act, the shape of their sexed body (the existence of a penis) remains unchanged.[34] A fundamental distinction seems to be drawn here, between a person's "image," which is changeable and transformable because it is constructed through practice; and a person's sex, which is unchangeable and categorically fixed – from birth, through to life, and beyond death. On the basis of this distinction, the corpse of a *sarin'ampela* is treated for what it is: a sexed body, albeit dead.

On "sex" and "gender"

Throughout this chapter, I have used the dichotomy between "sex" and "gender," at times explicitly, at other times implicitly, to refer to the difference perceived by the Vezo between what people are born with and the identity they create for themselves through their lives. I began by outlining why I originally thought that the Vezo might wish to ignore the sex of their new-born babies, and I sketched a "gender system" in which gender identity is de-mythologized and is shown to be culturally and historically created through practice. Against this background, I suggested that when the Vezo announce the sex of their babies, they complement (rather than contradict) their "gender system" by acknowledging the "intractable" nature of sex. In the Vezo "gender system," the categorical fixity of sex coexists with the processuality of gender. The same conclusion was drawn from the discussion of *sarin'ampela*. Whereas the *sarin'ampela*'s gender is constructed, like an "image" fabricated through a careful choice of "jobs" and "ways of doing things," their unchangeable sex determines them in the way their transformation is perceived by other people, and in the way they are treated at their death.

The validity of the dichotomy between "sex" and "gender" has, it is true, been radically challenged. Yanagisako and Collier (1987), for example, have advocated the analytical disengagement of gender from sex. They have argued that we should question what we have always taken for granted, namely that gender, as we have "invented" it, is the cultural elaboration of sex: of the biological difference between men and women. Thus, while gender was originally a liberating category, for it freed "culture" (gender constructs and gender relations) from biological determinism, Yanagisako and Collier suggest that we should now make the further step by defining gender as "pure" difference, no longer connected to, as the cultural elaboration of, biological difference. And although Yanagisako and Collier admit that it is impossible to know what gender would mean if it were to be disconnected from sex (1987:34; cf. also Errington 1990; Stolcke 1993; Howell and Melhuus 1993), they also believe that the only way to explain, rather than assume, the *difference* between men and women is to transcend the dichotomy between sex and gender.

As a leading representative of the theory of performativity which defines gender as the effect of discourse and sex as the effect of gender (cf. Morris 1995), Judith Butler (1990) has also argued that we should dispense with the distinction between sex and gender. "Sex" and "gender" can exist as two separate analytical entities only if they differ from one another, in other words, only if "sex" can be shown to be "natural," given, and intractable, and "gender" to be cultural, constructed, and variable. Butler's argument, inspired by Foucault, is that "sex" only appears to be natural, given, and intractable as a result of a specific discursive practice which constructs it in this way. And this in turn means that "sex," instead of being the raw material over which culture imposes its meaning, is in fact as culturally constructed as gender. Hence, "the distinction between sex and gender turns out to be no distinction at all" (1990:7).

Henrietta Moore, combining both of the above positions,[35] has also urged feminists and anthropologists to free themselves of the sex/gender dichotomy (1993b, 1994). It has been too easy (i.e. under-theorized) to go around the world searching for the many ways in which "sex" is culturally constructed and is transformed into gender. For Moore, as for Yanagisako and Collier and for Butler, "it is the pre-existing categorization of sex . . . which is the stumbling block" (1994:23). On the one hand, it prevents us from asking, instead of assuming, how different cultures actually construct the difference between men and women, and on the other, it blinds us to the fact that the categories of sexual difference are as culturally variable as gender constructs.

Why, then, have I chosen to rescue the old dichotomy between "sex" and "gender"? At one level, my answer is a localized one: I wish to retain and to use this dichotomy because it captures, if only approximately and rather clumsily, a prominent cultural theme which engages the Vezo of Madagascar.

There is no doubt that "sex" and "gender" are analytical categories that would make no sense to my Vezo friends. When I write "sex," they talk about penises and vaginas; when I write "gender," they talk about how men and women tie their sarong, about different ways of carrying heavy loads, about the nocturnal movements of young men and the choice girls have of opening doors or keeping them shut.[36] Yet, the difference anthropologists have perceived between what is biologically given (according to their definition of biology) and what is culturally constructed (according to their definition of culture) is not so remote from the difference the Vezo perceive between what it means to be born with a penis or a vagina, and what it takes to become a woman, a man, or a *sarin'ampela*, as the case may be. In this respect, our "sex" and their penises and vaginas share a fundamental feature – that they are categorically fixed and "intractable"; while what our "gender" shares with their ways of tying a sarong, of carrying heavy loads, and of behaving at night, is that they are processual and negotiable features of the person.

Like other peoples in Madagascar, the Vezo are deeply engaged by the tension between malleability and fixity, indeterminacy and determinacy, processuality and stasis which marks their existence. I indicated earlier that the Vezo resolve this tension, if only temporarily, by drawing a sharp distinction between the living – who create their identity through activities performed in the present – and the dead – whose only identity is given as an essence inherited from the past. In their rituals and in their fraught interactions with the ancestors, the Vezo negotiate the boundary between life and death, between processuality and fixity, between what human beings create and make of and for themselves in the course of their lives, and what they are given as irreducible features of their personhood. Their efforts provide only tentative and temporary solutions to the tension between these two fundamental aspects of human existence.

In this chapter, I have discussed another version of the same unresolved tension. It is that gender identity is created processually and is acquired through practice, but that people are born, live, and must also die with their intractable sex. To retain and to understand this particular "problem,"[37] we must be able to distinguish, as do the Vezo, between the fact of being born with a penis or a vagina, and the process through which one becomes a man, a woman, or a *sarin'ampela*. One convenient, if only approximate, way of retaining this distinction is to maintain the dichotomy between sex and gender.[38]

Besides suggesting that we should continue to use this dichotomy because it applies rather well to the Vezo, I wish to claim something rather more. In so doing, I aim to extend Michael Lambek's argument in this volume that we should salvage another currently unpopular dichotomy: that between mind and body. Lambek suggests that far from being the expression of a peculiar Western obsession, "what we call the mind / body problem (at its most general level, whether a valid distinction can be made between the mind and body) may be but one particular historical expression of what are universal existential conundra rooted in the human capacity for self-reflection" (Lambek, this volume). Thus, while "mind" and "body" are obviously not universal categories, the conceptual distinction drawn by the Cartesian terms between two incommensurable areas of human experience appears to be so, rooted as it is in our embodied existential condition. Lambek lists a variety of "fundamental tensions of human experience" onto which the dichotomy between "mind" and "body" can be mapped: connection to and separation from others, the boundary between the subjective and the objective, the relation of concept and objects, experiences of the voluntary and the involuntary, morality and desire, being and becoming, active and passive, male and female (Lambek, this volume). Similarly the dichotomy between "gender" and "sex," while clearly pertaining to the Western tradition and a product of a specific "discursive practice," speaks to the same fundamental tension: the unresolvable tension between what in the nature of human beings is processual and transformable – what one becomes – and what is instead fixed and unchangeable – what one is.

Thus, although Butler may be right in claiming that the pre-discursive nature of sex is the effect of a discursive practice (in other words that "sex" looks "natural" and "intractable" only because it has been constructed in this way), I would suggest that this discursive practice is not peculiar to the West, but is grounded in the shared human experience of discovering the limits to the transformation of one's sexed body,[39] and of exploring the potential for creating one's gendered "image."

NOTES

1 The field research on which this chapter is based was supported by grants of the British Academy and the Centro Nazionale delle Ricerche (Rome). I wish to thank these institutions for their support. I would also like to thank Charles Stafford for seeing me through the various stages of thinking and writing about babies and *sarin'ampela*; Maurice Bloch, Cecilia Busby, Janet Carsten, Jennifer Cole, Lorenzo Epstein, Michael Lambek, Karen Middleton, Mila Rosenthal, Jackie Spector, and Paola Tabet for reading and commenting on earlier versions of this chapter.

2 In the hospital where I received ante-natal care, I was not given the choice of finding out my baby's sex through scanning. In any case, the rather predictable advice of the Natural Birth Association was to avoid scanning as much as possible and to postpone finding out the sex of the baby until the birth, when this can be done "naturally" rather than through the aid of technology.

3 The Vezo are fishing people who live along the western coast of Madagascar.

4 Throughout this chapter I shall use "boy" and "girl" as an approximate translation of the terms used by the Vezo. In the Malagasy language, there are no distinct terms for "boy" and "girl," but only ungendered terms such as *anaky* (son / daughter), *zaza*, or *aja* (child). When people want to specify that a child is a boy or a girl, they "genderize" the term *anaky* by adding that it is male or female (*anaky-lahy*, *anaky-vavy*, or *anaky ampela*). In some cases, when the child's gender is the primary focus of the conversation, people refer to the child with the gendered terms used for adults: a "man" (*lehilahy*, *johary*), a "woman" (*ampela*).

5 It is not my intention to suggest that by announcing or asking about the sex of their new-born babies, the Vezo attribute ontological priority to sex over everything else that they do *not* announce and do *not* enquire about. It could indeed be argued, as I shall do later, that the Vezo dwell on the sex of their babies because this is the only feature which, at birth, *can* be discussed, in the absence of other distinguishing features of the newly born but yet unformed person which will require time to develop. But there are also cases when even the question as to whether the baby is a boy or a girl becomes irrelevant, and is only asked as an afterthought, if at all. This is when the most important thing that can be said is that "the baby was not OK" (*tsy nimety ny zaza*), and that, unfortunately, the mother has not managed to keep it (*tsy nahazo*). In a sense, then, when people announce that a baby is a boy or a girl, they are also stating something far more crucial than its sex: that the baby, thanks to *Ndrañahary* (God), is alive.

6 For a fuller discussion of this aspect of Vezo identity, see Astuti 1995a, 1995b.

7 Throughout Southeast Asia, baby and placenta are regarded as siblings (cf. Carsten 1992:25–6). As is common in that region, the Vezo, like other peoples in Madagascar, devote special attention to the correct disposal of the placenta so as to prevent the child from becoming ill or crazy.

8 More specifically, the baby must always be facing the mother.

9 A few days after the birth, on a propitious day chosen by the diviner and in the presence of all their relatives, mother and baby are allowed to step out of the house for the first time. After this, the mother will be able to leave the house to relieve herself, and during these short absences she will make sure to leave the baby next to a sharp piece of metal or a special medical wood (*sañatsy*) which are said to keep *angatse* away at least for a little while.

10 As they were when still in uterus. Many factors can influence and contribute to shape a fetus: if a person sits behind the back of a pregnant woman, the baby will in some ways resemble that person; if the mother takes a dislike to someone (normally a close relative) when pregnant, the baby will most probably resemble the detested one; if a lover has sex with a pregnant woman, he will "steal" (*mangalatsy*) some of the features of the baby's face, which will resemble his instead of his father's; if a white person spends a lot of time with a pregnant woman, the baby will have very light skin (a desired quality, especially in girls). Cf. also Bloch 1993.

11 Depending on the context, people also say that small babies have bones, but that they are extremely soft and not yet fully formed (*taola fa misy avao, fa malemy, tsy henja*).

12 I was often told that the reason European women are free to disregard all the restrictions (*faly*) which affect Vezo women after delivery is that they have access to strong and effective medicines. For example, European women and their babies need not be kept hot and wrapped up in layers of blankets because a "good injection" (*pekira soa*) received by the mother immediately after giving birth safely seals her and the baby's body, freeing them from the danger of being entered by "air."

13 "Animal" is only an approximate translation of *biby*, which has a wider range of meaning than the English term. *Biby* designates what is not human,

including animals, people who behave inhumanly, ancestors, and various creatures of the sea and forest.

14 As pointed out by Fox 1987; see also Carsten 1995a.

15 In contrast to the general assumption in traditional kinship studies that birth and biological parentage are the determining factors in creating relatedness and personhood.

16 I believe this would apply to the whole of Madagascar. The obvious exception can be found in Huntington's analysis of the Bara (1988), a pastoralist group in the south of the island. Huntington derives Bara notions of the make-up of the person directly from their theories of procreation (semen and bone are male; blood and flesh are female), and he proceeds to claim that "for the Bara, male and female are the primary categories of human existence" (1988:16). The problem with this interpretation is that there is in fact no evidence that the Bara construct of the person may be grasped through such a simple and rather crude translation of their understanding of physiological reproduction (which in any case is probably far more tentative than Huntington makes it out to be).

17 In this respect, as I noted elsewhere, the Vezo person remains whole and undivided (Astuti 1995a:92).

18 From which, as demonstrated by Busby (1997a), the distinction between cross-sex and same-sex cousins also follows.

19 Hence Busby's point (1997b) that in South India gender is "more fixed and essential" than in Melanesia.

20 And in the next generation, on the *sameness* of the relationship between cross- and same-sex cousins, who are all considered as full siblings.

21 Children born out of marriage (which can take place either before or well after their birth) are considered to be related only to their mother and not to their "biological" father (*tsy mana baba*, the child does not have a father); cf. Astuti 1993. It is interesting to note, however, that later in life the child will be made aware of the identity of his/her biological father (*baba niteraky azy*), so that s/he can avoid having sex with people who, although not recognized to be so, are in fact related to him/her.

22 This assertion is correct with a proviso: that a distinction between mother's and father's side will be made at the time when the children's place of burial is decided upon, for they will be buried either in mother's or in father's tomb. It is only in death, in other words, that a categorical distinction between mother's and father's side becomes not only relevant but unavoidable (see Astuti 1995a:ch. 6).

23 In many instances, when discussing sexual matters, I felt that my informants had to make an effort to believe, or pretend, that I did not already know the answer to the questions I asked them. Thus, when I returned to the field as a mother, one of my woman friends jokingly told me that either she was the one responsible for teaching me how to have babies, or that I must have known about it already!

24 For the purpose of this chapter, I will limit myself to the discussion of *sarin'ampela* (men who become "images of women"). I will not deal with the case of *sarin'johary* (women who become "images of men"), whom the Vezo say are only known to exist among the Masikoro, their neighbors who live in

the interior. When asked about *sarin'johary*, my informants would define them in the same way as *sarin'ampela*: people of one sex who have become of the opposite gender through doing certain things and acting in a certain way. They also recognized, however, that it is much easier for a man to become a woman than for a woman to become a man. My data at present do not allow me to address the question of why, here as elsewhere (cf. for example White-head 1981 on the American Indian "berdache," or Atkinson 1990 on the Wana), there is a marked prevalence of male to female gender shifting.

25 The main limitation in my enquiry is that I never directly talked to any *sarin'ampela*; I therefore present here the "image" of an "image": what my informants (especially women) who are *not sarin'ampela* make of this category of people. *Sarin'ampela* (or *sarim-bavy*, as they are known in other parts of Madagascar) have been mentioned and described in several early accounts by travelers and colonial administrators; a useful review of this literature can be found in Allibert (1994).

26 In recognition of her change of gender, I shall use "she" when referring to a *sarin'ampela*.

27 On the other hand, it is equally possible that the fact of having homosexual relations is not enough to be defined as a *sarin'ampela*; it is possible, in other words, that there are many more homosexual men than there are *sarin'ampela*.

28 Canoe-making is a significant exception. All stages of this activity are very clearly defined as exclusively men's work: women can be present (*tsy falin' ampela*, it is not prohibited to women), but they never participate in the actual construction.

29 As far as I know, *sarin'ampela* or *sarin'johary* do not have ritual prerogatives of any kind.

30 Although, following my informants, I here emphasize what men and women *do*, it is possible that what men and women do *not* do is as important in constituting their gendered identities (cf. Lambek 1992).

31 I borrow this formulation from Mathieu's (1991) discussion of the contrast between "identité sexuelle" and "identité sexuée." The former is a type of "naturalistic" identity whose primary referent is "sex," while the latter's primary referent is "gender." Thus, while in the first instance a person's gender must adapt to its sex (and if it does not, sex will be refashioned to fit gender), in the second one a person's gender can be at variance with its sex.

32 I never thought of asking whether *sarin'ampela* would be allowed to handle the corpse of a woman.

33 My informants' assumption was that *sarin'ampela* would like to be treated as women when they die, but that this treatment is denied them. Since I never discussed this matter with *sarin'ampela* directly, I do not know whether this assumption is correct.

34 As far as I am aware the Vezo do not speculate, as the Wana are reported to do (Atkinson 1990), about the possibility that by changing one's gender one may, as a result, also change one's sex. Interestingly, in the case of the Wana, people only contemplate the possibility that women may acquire a penis when they become men, while they never consider the opposite instance: for no man in becoming a woman would be so foolish as to sacrifice his penis, which is said to be "hard and brave" and which, as Atkinson puts it, is "a badge that

empowers its owner to exceed the limits of Wana communities to confront the dangers and to obtain the advantages that lie in the realms beyond" (1990:93).

35 Cf. Moore 1994:18 for a critique of Butler's "radical social constructionist position."

36 One could argue that the term "*sary*" (image) used in *sarin'ampela*, comes very close to the meaning of the term "gender" as the "cultural construction of sex." As I pointed out above, in the case of *sarin'ampela*, the Vezo explicitly and linguistically recognize that a person's gendered identity is an "image" – constructed through a careful choice of behavior and productive activities. For "*sary*" to be translated as gender, we would need the Vezo to use this term also when talking about men and women whose "image" does not contradict their sex.

37 For another version of this same "problem" as it relates to the relationship between brother and sister among the Karembola of Southern Madagascar, cf. Middleton ms.

38 My argument here is not very different from the one advanced by Thomas Laqueur whose work has been widely and enthusiastically deployed to make the point that sex is discursively produced. For although his book *Making Sex* does indeed provide an excellent example of the discursive construction of the sexed body, by demonstrating that "the content of talk about sexual difference is unfettered by fact, and is as free as mind's play" (1990:243), Laqueur is also at pains to draw and to retain a clear distinction between "language" and "flesh," between "the body and the body as discursively constituted, between seeing and seeing-as" (p.15). Just like the Vezo, Laqueur draws a distinction between what is constructed and what is given, between "images" and "flesh." And like the Vezo, who are unable to treat the corpse of a man – with its "unforgettable" penis – as if it were that of a woman, Laqueur is unable to reduce the dead body he finds on the dissecting table to a cultural construct: "For all my awareness of how deeply our understanding of what we saw was historically contingent . . . the flesh in its simplicity seemed always to shine through" (p.14).

39 It could be argued that my use of the sex / gender dichotomy does not apply to the Melanesian world, where sexed body parts appear to have no limits to their transformation; for example, breasts can be phalluses, penises can be birth canals, and this in turn means that "what differentiates men and women . . . is not the maleness or femaleness of their sexual organs [for how do we know what is 'female' and 'male' in the first place?] but *what they do with them*" (Strathern 1988). The crucial point, of course, is that the limitless transformation of breast into phallus, of penis into birth canal, can only be achieved symbolically and ritually (most famously, through the androgynous flutes of the Gimi). While the Melanesian material proves the limitless possibilities of transcending sex through gender, it also points to the "intractability" of sex: for the immense ritual efforts devoted to the creation of the Melanesian androgynous person can only be understood as attempts to transcend the irreducible "problem" that, outside their initiation huts, men and women have different sexed bodies and no choice at all as to what they do with them.

3 Modernity and forms of personhood in Melanesia

Edward LiPuma

Introduction

The insurrection on Bougainville, the cascade of new types of commercialism, mass media advertising, the continuing admixture of "Western" and local forms of medicine, the expansion of the public sphere, the penetration of the state into the recesses of domestic life, the reshaping and abstraction of labor, the use of education as an instrument of civic integration, and much else summarized by the term modernity underline the need to grasp the redefinition of local epistemologies brought about by the continuing encompassment of Melanesia by its "Other" – the West. At issue is how indigenous categories of knowledge and ways of knowing the world are not only transformed but permanently set in motion by the political economy of capitalism, the rise of the nation-state, the internationalization of the public sphere, the infiltration of Western popular and scientific cultures (from Christian religions and electronic media to medicine and anthropology), and interstate organizations such as the World Bank. In this context it is necessary to shape an ethnography of modernity that goes beyond an account of manifest change (e.g. adoption of Western religion, the advent of new practices of production and exchange, the implementation of a Western schooling system, the inscription of English) and grasps the transformations in knowing, agency, and subjectivity wrought by encompassment – the interplay among structures of different orders of magnitude, power, and intelligibility.

The construction of the "person" figures centrally in any such analysis because the concepts of personhood indigenous to Melanesia and Papua New Guinea in particular are significantly different from those embodied in Western practice and texts and presupposed by the colonially inspired political institutions that define the emerging states of Oceania. Especially concepts such as nationhood, liberal democracy, civil rights, and electoral politics presuppose at least a Western-like image of the individual (ideologically defined as an autonomous, self-animated, and self-enclosed agent). The emergence of the nation-states of Melanesia, oriented toward and encompassed by Western culture and capitalism, entails the evolution of Western-like conceptions of the individual (embedded, for example, in World Bank policy about how these nations should organize their economies in terms of a free market [LiPuma 1996]). To so speak of modernity is to place the construction of identity in the path of desire, not least being the desire of Melanesians to internalize the modern, to consume and be consumed by the goods and services of the capitalist economy, to entertain "rights" not known or needed before (e.g. the right of privacy), and the desire to redefine the political so that the polarity of power reverses course and flows back from the white West to black Melanesia.[1] All of these motivate the emergence and increasing visibility of the individual facet of personhood because *the individual is the main and mythologized locus of those types of desire particular to modernity*. To connect the study of the person to the evolving of modernity and the larger set of forces reshaping life throughout Melanesia is to carry the ethnography of personhood on to a terrain rarely visited by anthropology and certainly not by the anthropology of Melanesia – which in theory and description has long been bound to the local level. To approach the construction of the person in the context and conflicts of modernity is to problematize the interpenetration and interfunctionality of levels: for the people of Melanesia, the ongoing dialectic between the construction of subjectivities at a local level and the encompassment of Melanesian societies by the nation-state, capitalism, and the other modalities of Westernization.

More than anything else, such an account of personhood requires a sense of proportion. Studies that overemphasize or underestimate relations of sameness and difference between Melanesian and Western societies will hobble our efforts to understand how the dynamics of encompassment reconfigure local forms of personhood. The necessity is to clarify the character of relativity. And, also to relativize relativity: for what is considered (and contested) as "local" today has been influenced by Western presence and pressures, just as what is considered Western (parliamentary-style government, capitalism on Bougainville, the use of all-purpose money in bridewealth payments) bears an indelible Melanesian imprint. In other words, a theory of relativity is crucial because all scientific and most public-sphere discourse about Melanesia (even when Melanesians are themselves the authors of such discourse) is comparative.

The concept of the person also has another and different hold on anthropological understanding. The reason is that ethnography – and one could go back to Malinowski and the mythological origins of fieldwork –

has always held, indeed been founded on, if not an overt contradiction, then two positions that want careful negotiation and management of perspective. Subsuming itself to the universe of the Other, anthropology has argued for the unique and special character of each and every culture. At least in part because the genesis of anthropology was inseparable from the encompassment of the Other by the "West," anthropology has positioned itself against all versions of ethnocentricism (including in-house varieties) which would otherwise reduce the others to some version of the West. And, as I have argued elsewhere, this defense of the "otherness" of the Others led ethnographers to ignore precisely those conditions of encompassment that made their own enterprise possible. Within the academic field of anthropology, a much more positive political value was placed on an ethnography of difference than on sameness. Certainly a primary trope of anthropology is to criticize others' studies (specially by the preceding generation of ethnographers) on the grounds that they have been compromised by ethnocentric presuppositions. This is the basis, for example, of M. Strathern's critique of Leenhardt's study of New Caledonia; namely, that though Leenhardt recognizes that the person is highly relational / dividual, he cannot break free from his Western bearings, leading him to posit a residual individual aspect or center (M. Strathern 1988:268–70). For Melanesia and beyond, there has been imagined a theory of anthropological "progress" based on increasing epistemological awareness of the uniqueness of other's cultures.

In the same breath or at least the same texts, anthropologists have been making equally strong claims for the psychic, linguistic, and biological unity of humankind. The foundational claim is that whatever differences may exist, however much indigenous notions and practices were bound to their context of production, no matter that local cultures had their own epistemology, ethnographers could work their way into the habitus of the other, could understand what lay behind local practices,[2] and could translate and reproduce this for a Western audience of, minimally, peers.[3] No less a student of otherness then Stanley Tambiah began his Morgan lectures (1984) with the statement that the ethnographic project begins in the understanding that there are human "continuities of experience" as well as common "existential problems" (e.g. death) that engender a "psychic unity" across time and culture (Tambiah 1990:1). If the rationale for an anthropology rested on the first claim, the possibility of a viable ethnography adequate to its task rested on the second. In practice, anthropological claims of distance and the "uniqueness" of cultures coexist with claims of proximity and sameness (although the latter claims have not been the subject of the same theoretical reflection). In the absence of these claims, anthropology would be drained of purpose,

ethnography of meaning: the enterprise would be nothing more than
self-analysis exoticized. Nowhere are these twin claims brought into relief
or contested more than in reviews of the character of persons. In sum,
there is no way to grasp the journey toward modernity by the nation-
states and cultures of Melanesia or the anthropological project itself
without clarifying the character of personhood. Moreover, the two are
linked inseparably because an account adequate to an understanding of
modernity in Melanesia must be able to grasp the conditions of its own
construction.

Reconceptualizing personhood

I would like to begin by setting out the primary argument, not least because
of the complexity of engaging an issue that crosscuts so many dimensions
(e.g. linguistic, political, juridical, medical) and social levels. The perspective developed here takes issue with theories of personhood which posit the
self as fully individualized and defined in terms of internal attributes,
thereby presuming that the "individual" is an ontologically privileged
transhistorical and transcultural (which is to mean, non-cultural) category. From this viewpoint, the difference between persons in Western
and Melanesian societies is a function of the content given this category.
Though this view dominates Western social science, it is a minority report
in the anthropology of Oceania which has progressively stressed the
difference between our images of the person and those indigenous to
Melanesia. In this light and against this background, I would also like to
take issue with the view that Western and Melanesian images of personhood are fully incommensurable because the West constructs individuals
while the societies of Melanesia construct dividuals or relational persons.
Though this theory is politically appealing to an anthropology that
fetishizes difference, it is ethnographically, theoretically, and in the context of the emerging nation-state also politically troubled. In making this
argument, the analysis cannot help but promote a dialogue with the
relational position staked out by M. Strathern (1988; 1990) and others.
The intention is to clear a theoretical space better to explore the conceptual and historical relationship between Western and Melanesian persons.

In all cultures, I will argue, there exist both individual and dividual
modalities or aspects of personhood. The individual facet emerges in the
use of language (insofar as speech metapragmatically[4] centers itself
through the use and/or presupposition of an "I"), in the existence of
autonomous physiological systems of the human body, and by the fact
that the body serves as the ground and signifier of the person, most
importantly as the locus of an intentionality that is shared between, and

thus presupposes, agents (Lambek 1992). By equal account, all societies encode relational, dividual aspects of personhood. This is true insofar as the identities of subjects and objects vary across contexts (e.g. domesticated animals can both be treated as members of the family and be "put to sleep," eaten, used in medical experiments, etc.), each language inscribes the use of a "you" as well as an "I," and identity and self-construction are the result of socially created relations (e.g. ethnicity, ritual, etc.). The foregrounding and hence transparency of individual and dividual aspects of personhood will vary across contexts for action within a given culture. More, cultures differ critically in the ontological status, visibility, and force granted individual / relational aspects of persons, especially as these appear in the construction of their own comparative discourses about persons, such as justifications or explanations for actions. From this view, it is a misunderstanding to assume either that the social emerges out of individual actions, a powerful strain in Western ideology which has seeped into much of its scientific epistemology, or that the individual ever completely disappears by virtue of indigenous forms of relational totalization (such as those posited for certain New Guinea societies). It would seem rather that *persons emerge precisely from that tension between dividual and individual aspects / relations.* And the terms and conditions of this tension, and thus the kind (or range) of persons that is produced, will vary historically.

In this regard, encompassment and the progress of modernity in Melanesia simultaneously create and capitalize on the foregrounding, affirmation, and promotion of the individual aspect of this tension, thus leading to a greater visibility and public presence of persons as individuals (see Foster 1995). To assume, in other words, that there exists an opposition between societies based on substance and those based on relations, cultures of fully dividual persons versus a Western world of individuals, is not only to accept Western ideological notions of the person (which sees the person as undividedly individual), but to use that ideology to construct the Other as its opposite image. Indeed, a general problem in the conceptualization of the relation between Melanesia and the West (taken collectively) is that accounts of Melanesian thought and practices are contrasted not with equivalent accounts of Western notions of personhood, but with Western ideology. And because our understanding of Melanesian persons takes place in that field of contrasts with Western persons (in theory and in the practice of ethnography) an adequate analysis of Melanesia is inseparable from an adequate account of the Western construction of persons. Unfortunately, I would argue, many recent analyses define the Melanesian person against an inadequate account of the Western person which leads them to overstate the differences, a failure that, quite consonantly, is most apparent in the contexts of ethnography and of modernity.[5]

Those who hold a relational view of Melanesian personhood, who in Josephides (1991) words practice the "new melanesian ethnography," read the following contrasts from the ethnography.

Contrast of Western and Melanesian personhood

Western

Melanesian

Persons are conceptually distinct from the relations that unite them and bring them together.

Persons are the compound and plural site of the relations that define them.

Grasps and symbolizes collectivity as a unification of pluralities. Singular person is an individual.

Defines collective sociality / life as an essential unity. Singular person is composite.

Society and the individual are in a relation of opposition, contestation and hierarchy.

The social and the individual are homologous, parallel, and equivalent.

Social life consists in movement from one internal / external state to another.

Social life consists in movement from one mode of sociality to another.

The person is the subject of an explicit and visible ideology – individualism.

There is no explicit ideology of persons, only contextually situated images.

An individual's behavior and intentions are interpreted as the public expression of inner qualities (honesty, greed, etc.)

An individual's behavior and intentions are interpreted in terms of his / her actions in context.

Persons mature biogenetically as a consequence of their own inner potential.

Persons grow transactionally as the beneficiary of other people's actions.

Persons depend on themselves for knowledge about their internal selves, i.e. self-knowledge.

Persons depend on others for knowledge about themselves, and they are not the authors of this knowledge.

A person's power lies in his / her control over others; power is a possession.

A person's power lies in his / her ability to do and act; power is a relation.

Persons are axiomatically same-sex; social identity should fully replicate one's natural physiological state.	Persons alternate between same-sex and cross-sex identities; social identity is detached from physiological state.
Society stands over and against the individual as an external force that imposes norms, rules, and constraining conventions.	Society runs parallel to the individual; it is embodied as dispositions to think, believe, and feel in a certain way.
Its commodity logic leads people to search for knowledge about things and to make an explicit practice out of knowing the nature of objects	Its gift logic leads people to search for knowledge about persons and to make a practice out of knowing the person-making powers of objects.

The contrast here is between the West's own self-understanding, which exists both ideologically and normatively (e.g. as embodied in constitutional and statutory law, ethnoviews of aesthetics, economic reasoning, the relation of individuals to the government, etc.), and an account of the foregrounded elements of personhood in traditional, nonencompassed Melanesia. The Western notions of the person against which the Melanesian ethnography appears are ideological inasmuch as they privilege and foreground individual elements of Western personhood while masking, subordinating, and sublimating the more dividual facets. For the West, the notion of the person as wholly individual (as an autonomous, self-contained, self-moving agent) is constructed historically, contested, at best a partial description, and critical to forms of "misrecognition" (Bourdieu 1984) and abstract domination (Postone 1993) common to capitalism. Although I can only gloss here at what is implicated in the Western production of the person, it is nevertheless necessary at least to locate the Western person because it constitutes the background and presuppositions for our discussion and ethnography of the Melanesian person.

The person in capitalist society has two defining features: (1) the person is composed, historically and culturally, of dividual and individual aspects; and (2) paradoxically, the person appears as the natural and transhistorical individual. The double character of the person is intrinsically bound to, and homologous with, the character of commodity-determined labor. Unlike Melanesia where products are distributed by ties of kinship and community, and overt relations of power and domination, in capitalist societies "labor itself replaces these relations by serving as a kind of objective means by which the products of other are acquired [such that] a new form of interdependence comes into being where . . . one's own labor or labor products function as the necessary means of obtaining the products of others. In serving as such a means, labor and its product preempt that function on the part of manifest social relations" (Postone 1993:6–7). So it is that commodity-determined labor is mediated by structures such as that of personhood (and also class) that it itself constitutes. The social relations of capitalism are thus based on a quasi-independent structure that stands apart from, and opposed to, persons understood as individuals. Labor, here, as socially mediating activity creates relations among persons which, though social and containing dividual elements, assume a quasi-objective and individualist character. And as capitalism develops, as it is doing throughout Melanesia, the mediating function of labor slowly, but inevitably, reshapes the cultural form of the person.[6] The person becomes progressively reified as a self-contained, self-shaping, independent agent. What this means is that a defining feature of capitalism is that the ontological forms, such as labor and the individual, that appear to underlie the social ones (individuals' actions) are not only themselves social but have their sociality disguised. The extension of this view is that an ideology of the person as fully individual is a necessary feature of the form and reproduction of the person in capitalist society. Certainly one of the major features which distinguishes Melanesia from the West is the absence of a sanctified ideology of persons that is necessary to their construction. Nonetheless, the ideology of the Western person as fully individual only partially conceals the reality that Western persons are interdependent, defined in relation to others, depend on others for knowledge about themselves, grasp power as the ability to do and act, grow as the beneficiary of others' actions, and so forth. Most of the features of Melanesian personhood cited in the list above also apply to the West, however much they may be misrecognized or pushed into the background.[7] It is at this depth of sociohistorical construction that we discover that the true ontological form is not, as the West would imagine it, the individual; it is the dual person delineated by both dividual and individual facets – the basis of what anthropology knows as the psychic unity of humankind and which opens the possibility of an ethnography of Others.[8] Simply phrased, it is because persons are inherently dual that an ethnography of Melanesia is possible.

Once we grasp the character of personhood in societies defined by the commodity form, it becomes evident that our real danger is in understanding the inventory of differences as a totalizing opposition: as indicative of two incommensurable forms of personhood and sociality, rather than as two socially and historically variable ways of relating dividuality to individuality. The contrast between the West and Melanesia is telling because along this epistemological divide Western cultures place the greatest emphasis on individuality whereas Melanesian cultures stress dividuality. My argument is that we should not replace the "ethnocentric" notion that Melanesians are sovereign unified subjects who operate as causes of sociohistorical effects with the idea that they are partible subjects who operate as effects of multiple lines of determination because neither notion is a productive description of personhood either for Melanesians or for Westerners. The ethnographic goal, I would argue, is to uncover the conditions (e.g. encompassment by the West) under which dividual and individual aspects of personhood emerge and are hidden.

Ethnographers, of course, have assumed all along that whatever forms personhood may take there are sites of commensurability and the possibility of translation. The very practice of description assumes that between we and they, Westerners and Melanesian / others, there is never absolute separation of substance and agency, individuality and dividuality. No matter what is argued theoretically, ethnography as intercultural communication and experience presupposes at least the partial unification of person and agency. To juxtapose a theory of Melanesia that separates the person and the agent to a Western image (ideology) of the unity of person and agency is to render these two forms of society incommensurable, to push relativity to the point at which ethnography is no longer possible. It is to say that there is no point of essential similarity, no sameness between Melanesian personhood and Western personhood that would allow translation: the "I" of the Melanesian sentence would have no translation into English or any other non-Melanesian language for that matter. Perhaps the case that ethnography as anthropology has known and practiced it is truly impossible, and perhaps the sadness that understanding is a function of the encompassment of others by the West: that "we" can understand others only to the extent we make them like ourselves. But I think and would argue not, one key reason being that a too-strong claim of cultural relativity is politically disabling and disempowering (e.g. to Melanesian women, rural populations forced to deal with mining or logging operations, etc.). Because such relativistic positions rely on a positional epistemology, they shear away the ground of critique itself, a crucial political point that many anthropologists in their desire to honor difference seem to overlook.[9]

Ethnography and the person

Though an earlier anthropology assumed that Melanesian cultures were comprised of Western-like individuals and a later anthropology denied the existence of such individuals, ethnography all along has presupposed both a critical element of difference and a fundamental sameness. For however cultures construct intentionality, and those of Oceania clearly imagine intentionality differently from the West (LiPuma 1994), they must always link agency to personhood. That is, the sentence must always have a speaker, the agent must always have a name (even if that personal name is fully bound up in a system of relations),[10] and bodies perform acts (e.g. observe taboos), acquire habits and language, and undergo changes independent of one another (e.g. birth and birthing, illnesses, and death). What I am getting at is that a Westerner can have access to Melanesian intentionality and a Melanesian can have access to Western forms of intentionality because both operate in terms of dividual and individual aspects of personhood. Whatever else ethnographers have said in statements of theory and method they have always presupposed (1) that persons are the locus of intentionality, (2) that every agent (the ethnographer especially) has an identity that is neither reducible to nor wholly predictable from his/her position in a system of relations, and (3) that a person's identity is more than culturally constructed; it is continually reshaped in a life world that is never itself reducible to a fixed system of social relations and values because people are confronted with, and encompassed by, unpredictable circumstance and foreign phenomena (like colonialism and capitalism) which transcend the limits of understanding of local epistemologies. Ethnographers have assumed this to be the case in a double sense.

The first is that every ethnography presupposes the conditions and possibility of coordinated intentionality. This is the premise that the people with whom ethnographers live and interact have beliefs, desires, and judgments, that is to say, intentions to act, and that we as ethnographers have access to those beliefs, desires, and judgments. Sufficient access that we can grasp and understand the action of others as deliberate and meaningful. For example, if an ethnographer witnesses a curing ceremony (a Maring shaman places leaves and water in a bamboo tube, bespells it, and then passes the tube over the body of the ill) the ethnographer must presume that those involved hold global beliefs about the form and value of curing and specific beliefs about the form and efficacy of the particular cure; that they have the desire to cure the ill individual; and that they have made the judgment that this curing ceremony is appropriate to the illness in question. Even the simple and seemingly transparent act of watching a woman and her young daughter plant taro, which we may take as commonsensical and demanding no explanation (or even a note in our field diary), presumes beliefs (about the value of taro and when it should be planted), desires (to be productive, help and support kinsmen, etc.), and judgments (that this is the appropriate time and place to plant), and takes as axiomatic that ethnographers can and do have access to them. Ethnography is founded on the idea that a coordination of intentionality is cross-culturally possible; that a person from one culture has the bases to grasp and interpret the actions of a person from another culture.[11] The actions may be no more or less than a report about the past action of other agents or what ethnographers do when they interview someone about what has happened previously. To put this differently, ethnography rests on the assumption of the ontological existence of the person; an agent defined minimally by the fact that he / she has beliefs, desires, and judgments, thereby constituting intentions and thus the possibility of coordinated intentionality or shared meanings (with, for example, the ethnographer).

The second premise of ethnography is that it can be transcendent in a social sense. That ethnographers can overcome both the social and the epistemological separation that almost all ethnography, the study of New Guinea societies being where such separation is at its zenith, is condemned to. The premise is that the accounts produced by ethnographers will not simply be an objectification of their own culturally and individually defined beliefs, desires, and judgments. On one hand, they simply will not understand, thereby reducing, the Other's categories to their own epistemology. The idea is that the ethnographer can find points of convergence which allow him / her to determine, explore, and relate the shape of indigenous epistemology in a way that does not do violence to that epistemology or the acts and events that presuppose it. On the other hand, ethnography must assume that its agents, by virtue of taking up a position analogous to local agents, or capitalizing on indigenous means of integrating strangers, can make a place for themselves (social position) in the societies they study. The integration of the ethnographer into any society, even those with highly relational images of the person, is possible only through the space of individuality, precisely because an ethnographer has no socially, locally created identity. In this respect, ethnographers resemble, at least for Melanesia, big-men or chiefs: namely, agents who possess the power to express and enforce their individuality. In terms of modernity, the ethnographer (like the missionary and the health official) is a locus of individuality and an instrument and index of historical change. Or, to note this a different way, the dividual is to the individual as culture is to nature, as the social / ritual order is to entropy, as the clarity of custom is to the epistemic murkiness of modernity. For Melanesians and others, the conundrum is that Western notions such as democracy, freedom, and civil society (because they are founded on the concept of individual rights) foreground the individual facet of personhood in societies in which culture, social orderliness, and epistemology have been mostly (though never exclusively) defined in terms of the dividual facet of personhood.

What this means is that ethnography as social action presumes the existence of an intrinsic connection between individuality and social dividuality. Ethnography in Oceania has long been based on, and taken advantage of, the fact that the very incorporation of a Western ethnographer into a society that privileges the relational aspect of personhood is itself a privileged position from which to see social life. In other words, ethnography not only presupposes an individual aspect to Melanesian personhood but uses that aspect as an entrance point into indigenous lifeways. This individualist aspect would be much more transparent if anthropologists routinely deconstructed the space of being an "informant" in a society which does (or at least did) not recognize such a "role." Certainly, in the era of modernity what needs to be analyzed is the construction of the practice and position of information mediation and mediator (i.e. informant) in the face of requests for social information by anthropologists, colonializers, missionaries, government officials, and other emissaries of Westernization.

This chapter has made two interrelated arguments with respect to Melanesian personhood. The first is that there has always been an individual aspect of personhood, even if this aspect was traditionally in the background and on the margins of practice. The second argument is that this individual aspect is becoming more important, visible, and foregrounded with modernity. In the remainder of the chapter, I seek to illustrate these twin arguments by turning to the Maring materials.[12]

The person in Maring exchange

The assumption, long made by ethnographers, that there exists a necessary and universal connection between substance and agency, dividuality and individuality, is more than a methodological trope or a descent into ethnocentricism. For most ethnographers, it has its basis in their ethnographic experiences. We could retrace our steps back to Leenhardt and the founding of comparative studies of the person (1947) to see that even, as he explores the character of relationality, he is aware that there must be a connection between agency and cause. The connection becomes apparent when we examine the construction of persons in, and across, practices and contexts for action, which are also instances of self-(re)presentation. To do this, I would like to explore the Maring concept of the person; specifically in the context of exchange which appears to exemplify the relationship between dividual and individual aspects of personhood. The evidence suggests that the "person" in exchange emerges precisely from the tension between dividual and individual aspects and that is particularly true in instances where the exchange goes awry and there is no coordination of intentionality. Moreover, I would argue that tension between dividuality and individuality has long been a common refrain in Melanesian society (see Kulick 1992) though it goes under other names (such as the contrast people make between agents whose intentions are transparent and who act openly and in public versus agents who operate secretly and privately and whose intentions are easily imagined as nefarious).

The Maring concept of truth holds that truth has an inner and outer dimension and that it is inscribed in the act itself, an idea that has been explored in the context of "veiled speech" (A. Strathern 1975). The surface or appearance of an action, its skin to use the Maring's own metaphor, characteristically manifests deception, lies, and dissembling. Its aim is to manipulate the beliefs, desires, and judgments which surround the presentation and reception of the gift. By contrast, the inner core of the action is its truth and power to pull or bend others. Language is thought to lie on the skin of the action; it is the primary (though not only) means of disguising the "true" intentionality of an actor. In this respect, the importance of exchange lies in the virtue that gifts are indexical; they are a part of that which they express. Nevertheless, the social practice of gift-giving is still infused with manifold intentions and active dissembling. When agents evaluate a gift, they expect a difference between its surface or "skin" and its more "interior" truths. This inside-outside schema is the Maring way of organizing the hierarchy of intentions that will be embodied in a given action. For example, the presentation of a gift will include a verbally stated intention (e.g., the gift is because you are my affine), a presupposed though unstated intention (e.g., the gift helps to discharge my outstanding bride payment debt), and a disguised intention (e.g., the gift will be followed by a request for use of your garden lands). Conversely, every request for a gift can be seen as the maintenance of a social relation, as repayment for a gift given previously, or as an extortion based on power, such as the power to harm through sorcery and magic. The intentionality of a gift is such that the beliefs, desires, and judgments of the recipient concerning that gift are often read onto the donor. If a recipient "feels" subjugated by a gift, he/she may well interpret the subjugation as intrinsic to the gift-giving, and thus part of the intentionality of the act itself.

Maring locate intention in the relationship between an action and its influence rather than in the "mind" of the agent. There is no means in Maring to speak about someone's intentions or judgments apart from what they do and other people's experience of those acts. There is no way to differentiate between the mental dimension of an act and the act itself; rather the action is understood to embody a hierarchy of intentions. Determining the meaning or intent of some action, "digging out its root" to use local metaphor, is a function of understanding and assessing its inner and outer layers. In this respect, the agent is the fulcrum of the relationship, the cause of a specific response inscribed in the relationship itself, such that the agents appear passive in the sense that they are constituted by that momentary crystallization of relationship – what we refer to as an event. The actions of agents appear to be sucked out of them by the complex of relationships with others in terms of which they act (M. Strathern 1988:272–4). Agency and cause appear to live separate lives.

At the same time, however, agents are also aware that nothing can guarantee the execution, meaning, interpretation, or aftermath of a specific act of exchange. The structure of clan affiliations, relations of affinity, the history of exchange between the parties involved: none of these relations can guarantee the actions of the participants, and, more precisely, the unfolding of intentionality. There is always a possibility that one of the agents will back out of the exchange or interpret / intend the gift as an act of violence or extortion. There is always the possibility that the agents, as the body and embodiment of intentionality, will tell (cause) a lie or dissemble. There always exists a degree of uncertainty that is at least partly brought under control by representing persons. So it is said of certain persons that they "see gifts badly," meaning that they often ascribe malevolent intentions to the donor; other persons are portrayed as tolerant and inclined to be generous. In the same spirit, some ancestors are portrayed as generous, to look favorably on the gifts (of pig) offered to them and to reciprocate by helping the living; a smaller number of ancestors, by contrast, are depicted as ungracious and unwilling to help their descendants. And, just as a man will cut off an exchange partner who sees gifts badly, so he will refuse to propitiate an ungenerous ancestor. In this respect, people classify the behavior of others. They create a comparative discourse about interpretation of the intentionality of gifts that is inflected by, but never reducible to, the complex of relations shaping the event. The "scandal" of the gift is that there is a thin subjective line between generosity and treachery – even in some cases between brothers, what Maring ideology lauds as the most presupposed and predictable of kin relations.

The Maring not only think and talk about people comparatively, they also create and recognize persons' biographies. How a person exchanges – simply and practically, that person's pattern of action over time – is a central element in the biography. The performance of giving objectifies the affinity between exchange partners. But the act of objectification, that performance, is undertaken by the "singular subject." This is exemplified by the language of giving which centers itself indexically in the I. Thus, the presentation of a gift will use such ritualized phrases as: "I give this to you for nothing" (i.e. without expectations). No matter how set the field of relations, no matter how regimented the exchange context, the inscription of intention / meaning is not necessarily transparent or predetermined. The individual aspect emerges because performances are individuated, and the history of these performances generates a person's biography, name, reputation. And the history of people's performance is circulated, becoming part of collective memory such that the memory itself becomes an aim and presupposition of future exchanges (e.g. raising one's name). Though, according to Maring, the reasons why others are the way they are can never in principle be known, and those I talked with were unwilling even to speculate about why some agents often "see gifts badly," there is always the possibility that a person will be the basis of his / her own actions, and that some agents are comparatively more likely to be the basis / cause of their actions than others. There is always a possibility that individuality will help to shape the meaning and implications of an exchange event. So it is not only that the person comes into being in the context of relationships: to some degree agents always act as their own cause because they always have the option of doing so or not. It is not just that agents come into focus with respect to their relationships to others but that they do so as a matter of choice, however presupposed and overdetermined this choice may be.[13]

Within Maring society, the individual aspect of personhood has little visibility in many contexts for action, such as exchange and production. There is no ideological endorsement of individuality – as, for example, occurs in the West generally and especially in the United States. People do not simply valuate others by the ways that others activate relationships (i.e. successfully or unsuccessfully) though this is surely critical; people evaluate others also through their personal biographies of activation of relationships. And the difference between the way different persons activate relationships, and more precisely, the memory of these differences as instantiated in people's comparative discourse about action (e.g. the way people are represented by others), *is* their individuality. For the Maring, there is always the presence of individuality, though this presence is masked by a notion of unknowableness. One way to interpret this evidence is that the difference between the West and Melanesia lies not only in the respective emphasis they place on individuality versus dividuality, but also on the way in which they objectify and represent persons' actions. The objectification of behavior in the West converts acts which are both dividual and individual into pure individuality, whereas the objectification of behavior in Melanesia converts dividuality/individuality into a knowable set of relations and unknowable reasons for action.

The corollary to the involvement of persons in exchange is the relationship between these persons and the things that flow between them. The possession of an object, like a bird plume, engenders a partial and contextualized identity (affiliation) between the owner and that object owned, a partiality that is revealed in the reality of the enjoyment of its use values, even as that object is destined to be alienated by decay, loss, theft, or sale. The product can be separated from its producer, the plume from the man who captured it, with a partial though recoverable loss of self. For Maring, as for Westerners, there is never a one-to-one correspondence between owner and object, producer and product, although in certain situations it may appear that way. What distinguishes Westerners from Maring, and from Melanesians more generally, is that Westerners presume ideologically that there is an identity between an agent and what that agent owns and that persons are the sole authors of their own actions, whereas Maring presume, but do not submit to ideological reflection, that a partial connection exists between owner and object, and that agents author their behavior in relation to, and with, others. For Maring and for Westerners, persons are least like what they are, have, and do in the domestic sphere and more so along the avenues of exchange and circulation. The error here would be to assume that the one-to-one relationship between owner and object, the necessary and highly inculcated form of capitalist epistemology, accurately reflects the structure of Western life, and then to conceptualize Maring society as its opposite, thereby ignoring or having to "explain away" those instances where Westerners act as if no correspondence existed, and Maring act as if it did.

The direction of an intention away from the "self" reveals the intention in the act (of giving) and the coordination of intentionality, each agent acting as the other's effects. The gift a person creates is evidence of his/her effort in relation to an "other" who in that sense incorporates that effort. At the same time, however, the form of the gift (e.g. its size, quality, form of presentation, etc.) and therefore its intentionality is never fully predetermined (meaning that the gift is indexical and hence a statement about the current state of this relationship). The result is that in the act of exchange the person emerges – becomes visible – as dividual and as individual because that effort both belongs to the recipient and is never totally predetermined by virtue of existing relations.

This tension reveals itself when there is an absence of a coordination of intentionality. Donor and recipient may have different interpretations of the gift: the beliefs, desires, and judgments of one may be very different from the other. The attempt to reproduce or grow relations through exchange may or may not be successful. A clear example is a case described by Riebe (1987) where an exchange misfired owing to a lack of a coordination of intentionality, leading to accusations of sorcery and an eventual murder. Similarly, it is sometimes the case that a gift earmarked to support one relation is redirected toward another. Here is an example.

Yingok has three wives, the middle wife having been with him for seven years and the youngest wife two years. The kin of the youngest expect a payment of cooked pork from Yingok and indeed Yingok seems to have intimated that two of his larger male pigs are destined for them. However, he slaughters the animals as part of a ceremony for his second wife's clansmen, in payment, he says, for her children. The relatives of the youngest wife are miffed at the outcome and threaten to take him to court. Yingok readily acknowledges the claims of his youngest wife's clan, but disparages them as greedy and says that they did not "hear him properly."

The case in question clearly indicates that the gift or effort cannot be self-consumed, but also that its destination and thus its intentional effects are neither preordained nor free from ambiguity. The problem with a purely dividual reading of this event is that it leaves no room for contingency or creativity. Interestingly, given the fact that the Maring have a rather deterministic ideology, this event, when recounted in the past tense, is portrayed as inevitable and very presupposed, as though Yingok's decision was simply called forth by the relational field in front of him. Just as a "Western" ideological reading would see only the individual – Yingok trying to maximize his resources strategically, to improve his social status – so Maring grasp his behavior as predetermined by obligation toward his affines. Analysis is lost here if it forgets that the power of these ideologies to construct reality is simultaneously their power to disguise it, to produce forms of misrecognition essential to the reproduction of that reality.[14]

The practice of the individual

If local representations of exchange mask the presence of the individual, there is another practice in which the individual facet of personhood could not be more transparent. Indeed, it is the one local practice defined by its expression. The practice in question is, of course, sorcery.[15] Whereas other local practices presuppose constraining relationships which consume and devalue the individual, sorcery devalues the social through the wanton consumption of other members of the social body. It can be said that until the progress of Westernization sorcery was the indigenous name for instances and acts of individuality. So a person who was inordinately successful in relation to others (in hunting, pig-raising, etc.) was suspected of sorcery. And just as sorcery is the expression of individuality so those persons who rise above others could only have managed this through some form of sorcery. The argument is that the Maring know the individual element of personhood in two ways: in practices such as exchange in which the individual element is ideologically masked and in the practice of sorcery in which it comes to the fore and in this respect challenges the indigenous image that the social is the paramount cultural value. Further, I would suggest that one reason that the advance of modernity is being accompanied by an upsurge in the practice of sorcery (LiPuma 1996) is that they share the same underlying epistemology.[16]

For the Maring, sorcerers are as powerful as they are marginal. They express that facet of all of us that is better left sublimated and mute. While ethnographers frequently grasp sorcery in terms of cause and effect, viewing it as the prosecution of physical ends by symbolic means, the Maring focus much more on the personhood of the sorcerer. They speak first of the sorcerer as someone who wantonly disregards the limits of kinship and thus of morality. All social relations have the propensity to be violent or peaceful, reciprocal or non-reciprocal, mutually beneficial or predatory. A moral person is someone who modulates and controls these propensities in respect to social distance. But the sorcerer cannot. Greed overcomes him, envy "eats" him, and so he turns on his own kin. The sorcerer does not "walk on the road" – a description that is equally a metaphor of the public and visible paths that join residential hamlets. Rather, the sorcerer "walks in the bush," hidden and hiding from the comings and goings of everyday sociality. Where normal people make "noise" to announce their presence, the sorcerer treads silently to conceal his movements. Sorcery is selfishness carried to its most profane result.[17]

Sorcerers think only of themselves, casting aside their social obligations to others. They "want things only for themselves," thus expressing a possessiveness, a sense of greed, that is the opposite of sharing and reciprocity. The sorcerer "throws away" the kinship relations that define him in social space, and becomes the sole and only cause of his own behavior. The intentionality of the sorcerer is opaque and unfathomable because he acts only in his own interest. Whereas the ancestor spirits (including nowadays Jesus) may attack a wayward man to punish him for having spurned his social commitments – not least the imperative to share food with kin – sorcerers attack their own kind for self-aggrandizing and malevolent purposes. They act without regard for the wellbeing of their community and in this regard define themselves in opposition to it.

For this reason, the sorcerer must be stopped at all costs and indeed he is the one type of person who may be killed, and killed justifiably, by his own close kin: for his uncontrolled individualism threatens the nature of the social itself. A sorcerer's *nomane* (meaning: sentience and culture brought about by the socializing influence of kin) is "twisted" and "crooked" (see Strathern and Stewart, this volume, for the parallel Hagen concept of *noman*). So the Maring say that "sorcerers are not part of us though we know they live among us" – or so at least it is told in indigenous ideology.

But this is only one of a number of stories that people relate about sorcery. They also know that it is very reckless to discount the reality that someone living nearby, even though they may appear oh so normal, may be deeply engaged in sorcery. In this sense, the sorcerer as a "species" of person is an abstract personification of a set of actions and relations. And so people admit that anyone, a man, a woman, regardless of age or social position, may and can use sorcery if they are overcome by greed, anger, or envy. The sorcerer leads a secret double life. My housemate Gou put it this way: "You believe all along that this man you know, even one of your own near kinsmen, respects the customs of reciprocity, but actually he wants to take and destroy what's yours without giving anything in return." Sorcerers almost always "see things badly" although they pretend to "think straight." The duplicity lies in the fact that the "skin of the behavior" of someone who practices sorcery simply disguises its twisted intentionality – an intentionality defined by possessiveness, a quest for accumulation at the expense of reciprocity, a disregard of kinship in one's own interests; in short, the sorcerer takes himself as the primary value. Note that what the Maring perceive to be the worst traits of the sorcerer – such as his compulsion to possess power, accumulate things, and live in privacy – the West understands as the natural and universal attributes of persons qua persons. In acting as agents, sorcerers internalize or consume the relations of which they are composed. They literally cannibalize the life force (*min*) of their own kin. In this respect, sorcerers exhibit only in the most false way known to Maring, the knowledge of their internal compositions and capacities in the response of others.

What Maring say about sorcerers indicates that they were, and to a great extent still are, the most visible, telling, and forceful expression of the individual aspect of personhood. Though markedly antisocial, sorcery was the exemplar and name for the articulation of unbridled and transparent individuality at the expense of social relatedness. It was the surfacing of the should-be-sublimated dimension of the human psyche. In this regard, the Maring have always had much more than a casual acquaintance with the individual aspect of personhood.

Politics and the emergence of the individual

Within those societies that privilege the dividual dimensions of person-hood, the individual has a critical political moment, not least as a resource of negativity. Even before the arrival of the colonial officials and missionaries people imagined the individual as the obverse of dividuated person-hood. And especially since the advent of modernity (read encompassment), agents have been enabled to protest the "traditional" order by organizing action around the individual aspect. Modernity has allowed the individual to become visible, the tension more explicit, and the expression of individuality more legitimate. In the pre-colonial epoch, there were two recognized sites for the emergence of the individual facet: common acts of sorcery and rare cases of "wild man" behavior.[18] In other words, the other transparent form of individualism was insanity or *pym* in which a person, for no apparent reason, became disconnected from his social moorings. Both were instances in which a person's secret or unknowable individual desires overpowered his/her sense of social limits, leading to the inward direction of violence against their own kin. The encompassment of Melanesia has generated a new and much more powerful context for the expression of individuality. This individuality is personified by missionaries, anthropologists, and local "informants"; it is objectified in new institutions such as schools, tradestores, and courts; it is broadcast by television, radio, newspapers, and other forms of mass media as well as by the constant migration of people between town and hinterlands. Indeed, what modernity has in common with the traditional contexts for the expression of individuality is that it also involves violence.

Maring society, inscribed in ethnographic history on the basis of its indigenous practices (e.g. *kaiko*), has since the mid-1960s been the scene of profound and accelerating changes. Contact with the capitalist economy has animated the opening of tradestores and the sale of services (e.g. helping the local mission), panning for gold, cash cropping for coffee, and contract labor jobs on coastal plantations. The emerging generation now is fluent in Pidgin (and in many cases English), attends the Anglican-run school, cherishes imported consumer goods, and uses the health clinic as the primary source of medical service (LiPuma 1989). Political offices at all levels are won through elections and most disputes and infractions are resolved in local and district courts. In what Maring portray as the modern time or new road, the public political sphere within which clan members exercise power now extends well beyond the clan and clan cluster; in some cases, like the struggle over where and who will construct he road from district headquarters at Tabibuga, it embraces all Jimi Valley Maring. The enlargement of the public sphere shapes and motivates new social strategies like implicating the Anglican church in what were historically intraclan disputes. The expansion of the public sphere opens new opportunities for the representation of action, and also for discourse about action that presupposes that the local community depends on, and is subordinate to, external sources of power and authority, such as the church or the state. And, moreover, these penetrating forms of power presuppose the individual as the paramount social value.

In a series of articles, Robert Foster (1992, 1993, 1995) has examined the structure of media and communications at the national level. His analyses underline the extent to which the politics and practices of modernity stress individuality. In a similar though more muted and retarded sense the same thing has been happening at the local level, and for a longer time. The persons and practices of Westernization motivate more than merely institutional changes, they inaugurate a transformation in the social epistemology of the indigenous world. Perhaps the most subtle and powerful change has been the creation of contexts for the expression of the individual aspect of personhood, and the legitimation and empowerment of that aspect and its expression.

This begins with the arrival of the "white, European, Western" person, and permanent contact with such Westerners in the guise of district officers, missionaries, medical personnel, ethnographers, and sometimes their families. More than anything else, what characterized these Westerners was their clear willingness to step outside of social relatedness, and inhabit a world where they had little or no connectedness to anyone. From the Maring slant, they appeared to be beholden to, and trusting, no one. Many Maring, in fact, found it hard at first to believe that the Westerners on the Koinambe mission station (Jimi Valley) – the VSO nurse from County Cork, the Anglican priest from San Francisco, the former policeman from Newcastle, the Summer Institute Bible translator from Western Australia, as well as the anthropologist who lived with them – were not somehow related. They believed there must be some kinship and community connection not because they were all "white" – the Maring were more than aware that all similarly colored people do not have a kinship relation – but because no one would be so individualistic. Such people seemed to approach the world as if it were a canvass for the achievement of their own desires.

The lesson, inscribed in Western practices and embodied by its agents, a lesson that time and experience would reinforce over and again, is that desire is personal. The mission school, the nature of Christianity with its belief in a one-to-one relation between a person and God, the behaviors and sermons of the Anglican minister, an introduced system of trials which focused on the culpability or guilt of specific persons, the operation of the mission tradestore and other agents of capitalism (e.g. coffee buyers) have gradually created the understanding that the individual aspect of personhood and its expression is what modernity is all about. It is persons as individuals who receive grades in school; God saves individuals not whole clans; it is the person who committed the crime who must pay for it: all these reinforce the concept and legitimacy of the individual facet. There is no small irony in the reality that the "progress" of modernity has coincided with a growth in sorcery and sorcery trials (LiPuma 1994), a critical reason being that sorcery was one of the primary traditional sites for the expression of the individual aspect of personhood.

The pressure brought to bear on the local notion of the person is remarkable for its unevenness, with the consequence that agents must necessarily practice, if not endorse, a bivalent epistemology, using one image of the person in rural settings and another in the context of urban, capitalist, Western-like interactions. But even in the rural locale, there is a dynamic between not only urban and rural notions, but also between the ways in which different aspects of Westernization intersect variably and contingently with indigenous practices and are imbued with variable degrees of legitimation. Indeed, if we take the Maring as an example, an implicational logic runs from the appearance of the tradestore to the emergence of the individual aspect of personhood. The tradestore implies the right of private property, exemplified by a decline in the obligation to share, and private ownership in turn is a metaphor for privacy, or the self-containment of the person that is an index of individuality. The emergence of a notion of private property is exemplified by the emergence of intraclan and even intrakin (e.g. between first parallel cousins) trials for property theft. In such trials, it was typical for defendants to claim that they were only sharing/borrowing the object in question whereas the plaintiffs argue that certain forms of sharing are no longer possible. So one plaintiff argued that "the time when no one cared who took what is over; now is a time of business, a time when individuals own things and have a final say in who can and cannot use them." What is increasingly clear is that, under the conditions of modernity, different levels of epistemology become metaphors for, and speak on behalf of, each other, thus opening the way for the construction of a new politics of personhood.

Conclusion

The Gender of the Gift is a milestone in Melanesian studies, being the culmination and synthesis of analyses of the person that began with Leenhardt. For the first time, the total extent of the dividual aspect of personhood is set out. And thus M. Strathern's account is both the culmination of previous ethnography and one of its highest achievements. After half a century, we finally have an account of dividuality worthy of its object. But the strengths of the analysis are also its weakness. For the project to relativize our own metaphors can too easily be carried to the point where the relations between Melanesia and the West appear so incommensurable that we have no way to account for the possibility of ethnography and the emergence of the individual person in the modern era. It thus seems that if the notion of the composite person or dividual is to be integrated into the modern history of Melanesia, it needs to be relocated or repositioned in ethnographic space.

I have argued in a preliminary way that studies of personhood in Melanesia (and one could also include Africa, the Amazon, and a good deal of Asia) which posit an indigenous concept of the person fully incommensurable with its Western counterpart are problematic on a number of grounds. First, they compare Melanesian notions of the person not to the Western reality of personhood but to Western ideology, itself a highly contested product. Second, they tend to see Melanesian notions as the inverse of Western ideology, thereby winding up defining the former as the negative image of the latter. Third, to argue that these forms of personhood are incommensurable rules out the possibility of ethnography which presumes that there are points of commensurability. Most importantly, there are basic primitives of human action – beliefs, desires, and judgments bound pragmatically into intentions – that are cultural universals. This is part of the central core, I would submit, of what ethnographers call the "psychic unity" of humankind. So ethnography as a way of knowing the social world presumes that ethnographers can grasp the intentions of the agents they encounter and that this relationship is reciprocal (i.e. coordinated intentionality). Fourth, to argue for total cultural relativity is politically disempowering insofar as it undercuts the ground of critique. And finally I would argue that a relational theory of the person cannot grasp the conditions of its own construction or possibility.

My reading of ethnographic theory and methods indicates that the ontological form is the dual person delineated by dividual and individual facets. Universally, then, the person emerges from the tension, itself always variable and culturally/historically shaped, between these two aspects of personhood and the ways in which they are objectified and embodied. And further, the marginalization of individuality in Melanesia and the sublimation of dividuality in the West are necessary for the creation of the kind of person that each of these sets of societies attempts to produce (LiPuma 1995). It is precisely this individual dimension of Melanesian personhood, traditionally subordinate to the dividual image of the person, for the most part ideologically unarticulated, almost invisible in the context of "traditional" social practice, that is now beginning to emerge with modernity. A critical reason for this history is that individuality is central to modernity not only conceptually but as the locus of the forms of desire that define the modern. The true irony is that overemphasis of the individual that was the hallmark (and error) of the original encounter between Western ethnographers and Melanesians has turned out to be an omen of things to come.

NOTES

1 I mean this distinction between white and black metaphorically as the simulacrum for a raciology that is intrinsically intertwined with colonialism, power, and production and validation of regimes of subjectivity.

2 In Marilyn Strathern's words, to understand local practice, we need to adopt techniques that permit us to overcome the "tenacity of our own intervening metaphors" (1988:175).

3 This includes, of course, (partially) Westernized others such as non-Western academics and scientists.

4 See LiPuma 1990 for a discussion of the linguistic terminology used here.

5 This goes a long way in explaining why studies of personhood in Melanesia (such as Munn 1986) sidestep the issue of modernity and attempt to bracket the contexts and effects of the encompassment of Melanesia by the West, one of the primary effects being that Melanesians are the subject of Western understanding.

6 See LiPuma and Meltzoff (1989) for a more detailed description of the relation between culture and capitalism as well as the very theoretical work of Postone (1993).

7 Analysts who think an incommensurability exists between Melanesia and the West cannot help but overestimate difference. For example, in *The Gender of the Gift*, M. Strathern notes that "gift exchange has always been a conundrum to the Western imagination [because it is] the circulation of objects in relations in order to make relations in which objects can circulate" (1988:221). But while this is certainly the culture of gift exchange, it is hardly unimaginable for Westerners such as ethnographers. Suppose, for example, I rewrote her sentence to read: dinner parties (among colleagues, members of a family, etc.) circulate foods and words in relations in order to create relations in which foods and words can circulate. There is little here that is mysterious or hard to imagine. The difference between gift- and commodity-based societies, I would submit, is not (perhaps never) absolute; they do not rely on fully incommensurable epistemologies. The difference is that in gift-exchange societies, commodity-like transactions occur only on the social margins (with, for example, Westerners), where in commodity exchange (capitalist) societies, gift exchange is reserved for the small, nonpublic, and intimate spaces where kinship and community still have a voice.

8 Such duality is an inherent aspect of any social practice that objectifies persons

through objects produced. This is as true for the anthropologist as for the Melanesian gift-giver. For instance, the paper which an anthropologist presents at a colloquium, though presented individually and bound by the norms of individual responsibility, embodies the labors of others, directly and / or indirectly. The paper is detachable and publishable under the sole name of the author because the author has extracted him / herself from the set of social relations without which that paper could not have come into being. So, what I write here inscribes not only my own labor, but that of numerous others, in the absence of whose labor in relation to me my paper would look very different. In the ideology of the commodity-form, this matrix of relations is externalized under the euphemisms of "influence," "assistance," and other things which, conventionally, appear in footnotes, brackets, and prefaces – lest the individual and individuality of the author be compromised. In this way, our commitment to the ideology of the individual and the commodity-form guarantees that this product (the paper) will appear to be extrinsic both to its producer and to the set of relations that produce him / her. From the standpoint of the audience that focuses on the content of the paper, "what it has to say," the meanings of the paper for its author (e.g. the memories of the "field" that it arouses) and the set of relations it embodies are tangential. So much so that this is hardly obligatory or presupposed information. The paper comes to the audience as evidence of its author's intent, knowledge, ethnographic research, analytical insights, etc. For the audience, it is the author's prestige, or intellectual capital, that is at stake. By reverse action, what an author derives from the presentation (besides a small amount of money) is the author transformed in regard to others which the author attaches to him / herself as prestige and intellectual capital. The author thereby depends on others for evidence of his / her own fame and intellectual identity. In this respect, the dividual aspect of the person can be uncovered, buried as it is beneath the ideology of the fully individual person and the paper as a pure commodity.

9 For example, it is more than possible to conclude from a truly relativist viewpoint that it is impossible to make any independent determination of a person's rights. On this view, there is no critical position or leverage from which to conclude that a person from another culture has been deprived of his / her rights since the notion of right itself is culture bound. This is the case whatever these rights may be (e.g. right to life, right to be free of foreign domination, right of freedom from slavery, etc.). Thus, there are no grounds to conclude that the Western colonization of Africa and Latin America, policies of apartheid, enslavement, and genocide by a nation against one of its ethnic or religious minorities, and so on, abridge these victims' "rights." Truly relativistic positions are ultimately politically highly conservative even if they appear to be scientifically rather than radical. And two disturbing (at least for me) consequences follow from this relativism. First, we have little or no obligation to help members of other cultures since we do not know if they have rights to violate; second, the "truth" of a position is ultimately no more or less than the power to enforce a particular image of reality. The very notion of "human" rights or "women's" rights (as opposed to culturally specific rights such as Enga, Catalan, Ndembu, Apache, or Kurdish rights) presumes that there are sites of commensurability of personhood across cultures.

10 In fact, the status of names in a given society is a critical index of the relationship between dividual and individual aspects of personhood.

11 It should also be observed that cross-contextual regularities in ascribed intentionality are inseparable from the metapragmatic regimentation of speech. The reason for this is that what I call metapragmatics is nothing more than the system of signs for stipulating the use and meaning of signs in context. That is to say, we know that the use of language to convey an intention in social context A (e.g. a shaman's intent to heal) is the same as in context B (e.g. a nurse's perceived intent to heal) because the metapragmatics of the language stipulates that the use of certain speech forms in A can carry the same meaning when used in B.

12 See LiPuma 1988 for a general description of the Maring.

13 Other Melanesian societies also create comparative discourses about persons. The Paiela, for example, characterize some people as having spirits that are straight and good and others as having no spirit or bad spirit, with the result that these agents act crookedly and badly (Biersack 1991:234).

14 The vision of misrecognition entertained by M. Strathern in *The Gender of the Gift* is rather problematic. She asserts that the Western notion that society is authored is an "illusion" but she fails to ground her account by articulating the character of illusion or misrecognition. In fact, the whole tone of the word "illusion" would seem to be a mistake in that it suggests simply a false belief, a sensory error correctable by sight and insight. In my view, a theory of the appearance and power of forms of misrecognition in social life should move along the following lines. It must begin in the understanding that these forms are socially constructed. That is, they are genuine cultural products having as much ontological authority as any others. Further, the forms of misrecogition are socially necessary. That is, the way that the forms inflect social action is essential to the reproduction of a society in its current, specific historical form. Hence, a given way of misrecognition will transform only when the society of which it is a part also transforms. And finally, analysis is able to grasp the genesis and source of misrecognition (and also establish the ground of social critique) through the analysis of the contradictions within the sociocultural system. Failure to come to terms with the terms of misrecognition forces the writer to adopt a universalizing logic in order to shape a relativistic position – which is precisely what M. Strathern does (Josephides 1991:148–9 drives home this point).

15 There are analogues to sorcery in other societies that stress the dividual element of personhood. In Hindu and Buddhist cultures, for example, world renunciation and other forms of ascetic retreat permit persons to declare their independence from society and thus express their individuality in respect to the social body. To put this another way, societies that feature the dividual facet of the person can permit the full-fledged appearance of the individual only on the margins of society – that is, as either profane or sacred.

16 Weiss (this volume) notes that Haya notions of the practice of sorcerers have changed in respect to capitalism, specifically that family farms, where the dead are interred, can now be bought and sold for cash. So Haya sorcerers are now more likely to disinter and cannibalize corpses than in the past. Indeed, I would suggest that it is possible to construct, for both Melanesia and Africa, a

model of contemporary sorcery as the reconstruction or reimagination of "tradition" in the context of the modern.

17 Those who opt for an unalloyed theory of dividuality forget that many Melanesian societies have a conception of selfishness, meaning situations in which a person remains unpartible, refusing willfully to give in to the pull of the relations in which he / she is enmeshed (e.g. Biersack 1991:248).

18 I was only able to get four or five known cases of "wild man" behavior in which a person runs amok striking people irrespective of kin relation or distance.

4 Refiguring the person: the dynamics of affects and symbols in an African spirit possession cult

Ellen Corin

Persons and selves: the politics of representation

Throughout history, the description of other cultures has been shaped by a politics of representation which can be neither dissociated from nor subjected to the relationships of power and domination constitutive of the colonial order. Travel narratives and ethnographic descriptions of explorers, missionaries, and merchants are permeated by the unusual super-position between a referential use of language, supposed to provide a precise description of an objective reality "out there" to be described, classified, categorized through language, and the oniric representation of the world in which the Other becomes an imaginary screen for projecting the hidden fantasies, desires, anxieties, and the dark side of our own being (Obeyesekere 1995; Taussig 1987; Zavala 1989). Post-colonial criticism has dealt with both of these aspects, but behind the power politics of the colonial encounter, we can see that this problematic representation of other cultures reveals the difficulties and limitations of the encounter with the Other and the danger of drifting toward objectification and subjectification when minimizing or absorbing the alterity of the Other within the illusory continuum of an immediate understanding. Solutions proposed by contemporary anthropology to the aporia of the encounter with the other are often unsatisfactory since they themselves are embedded within a North American ethos organized around notions of "empathy," "feeling," and "experience".

The first travel narratives described other customs, ways of being, and beliefs from a natural history perspective with the intention of creating a taxonomy of non-human and human objects and species. The violence permeating colonial writings has already been denounced; the use of the colonizers' language and politics of representation was a central pillar on which the cultural, political, and economic hegemony of the European countries over the new world was built (Jara and Spaduccini 1989). The construction of the colonial subject through writings not only served to justify the discourse of imperialism but was also instrumental in its implementation. The theoretical anthropological construction of other cultures has not been immune to this process. It could be argued that the main schools of anthropology represent different ways of dealing with the paradox inherent to a colonial anthropology. In defending the idea of the natural ordering of societies along an evolutionary axis, evolutionism has created a hierarchization between societies and contributed to the legitimization of the Western domination of the world. Conversely, other schools of anthropology have tried to soften the harsh reality of the violence of the asymmetrical encounter between colonizing and colonized societies, either by emphasizing the coherence and internal unity of societies, or, on the contrary, by diluting them into infinitely permutable structural pairs of opposites which transcend societal boundaries.

While the representation of the Other remains inescapably framed by our vision of ourselves and the world, the anthropological project has been constantly haunted and animated by the desire to have access to the Other's alterity and to transcend the contingencies and boundaries of our own cultural condition (Wagner 1975). Moreover, cross-cultural comparisons have been used as an instrument in the ethic of "decentration" (leaving one's perspective behind) and cultural criticism to gauge the contingency and relativity of our construction of reality and ourselves. Descriptions of other worlds have introduced imaginary variations within our representation of ourselves and have led us to explore latent possibilities of our common human reality (Shweder 1990). This can be traced back to Jean-Jacques Rousseau's fantasy of the "good savage" in denouncing the alienating potential of his society, or to Mead's and Benedict's proposition of cross-cultural comparisons as a "social laboratory" where the cultural relativity of Western notions of normality, life stages, gender relationships are tested. This process of critical decentration is built on two basic tenets: the acknowledgment of similarities in what appears to be different in Others, and the revealing of a dimension of strangeness to what we consider familiar. Vehement criticism directed at the ethnographic project ultimately deals with the possibility of decentration from one's own world towards the role of the Other in the construction of oneself. Contemporary anthropology tends to be very radical in its criticism and concentrates almost exclusively on the deceit involved in the pretence of gaining access to the Other's alterity. Ironically, this stance leads to two conflicting views often expressed by the same author: the deconstruction of the very notion of culture and denouncing it as one of the processes contributing to essentializing Others; and the emphasis on the radical cultural relativity of notions such as "person," "emotion," "self" and the inherent need to understand these concepts from within the cultural world to which they belong. This apparent contradiction is overcome by an approach to culture as that which stands out, and is indissociable from interactive practices, as an essentially fluid, shifting, elusive reality. The problem remains as to how these interactive, informal realities can be interpreted without projecting one's own premises and postulates on the Other's world. Taken to the extreme, there is a risk that the cultural alterity of the Other would disappear, to be replaced by a pretense to communicate from experience to experience; cultural differences would be relegated to an external, non-significant appearance in favor of the concrete reality of life. The feeling of cultural difference expressed and experienced by the actors themselves is denounced as an illusion created from within and from outside the society, in order to serve the interests of certain classes of people and to reinforce the hidden play of power relationships.

However, one cannot help but wonder whether that criticism of anthropology, necessary as it is, does not reflect the evolution of Western societies, their inability to come to terms with their identity, the disappearance of cultural bench-marks and values which lead to the understanding of one's place within the world. Far from freeing itself from the shackles of historical determination, the contemporary critic would participate in the universe of post-modernity, which is normal, and project it on the Other, which is much more problematic. It is difficult not to view the current fascination of anthropology for "shifting selves," "embodiment," "subjectivity" as a reflection of the inward, narcissistic turn of contemporary Western societies.

Some authors have argued that the notion of culture which is being deconstructed by critical anthropologists is in itself a construction at odds with a more polysemic and dynamic understanding of culture in classical anthropological studies, as if the implicit project were to caricature culture in order to legitimize its destruction (Brightman 1995). In order to escape the contingencies of our specific collective and individual positioning within a post-colonial order where intercountry domination remains the rule, we could then deny the existence and meaning of cultural differences, and simultaneously ease the tension toward the alterity of the Other and the power of criticism attached to making the detour by the Other. We have difficulties imagining differences which would not represent inequality and conceiving forms of heterogeneity which are both irreducible and constructive.

Anthropological studies of the person reflect analogous debates. They can be tentatively organized around two poles which correspond to different kinds of questioning and to different approaches to culture. These two poles appear to have been differentially influential in North

American and in European anthropology, which is reflected in their relative importance in studies conducted in the Pacific and in Africa. At the one hand, authors attempt to describe "lived worlds" and the experiential, subjective dimension of human life. On the other, authors focus upon the cultural coordinates of the notion of the person and upon what the person's position towards culture and the society is founded on.

The first set of studies tend to refer to "selves" rather than to "persons". The key words are those of intentionality, emotional expression, cognition, will, action. Culture and society are conceived as exercising their influence through concrete interactions; their influence is captured through the details of interpersonal practices and through the analysis of critical events. Papers collected by White and Kirkpatrick on *Pacific Ethnopsychologies* (1985) are a good illustration of this approach. The term ethnopsychology emphasizes the need to understand subjective phenomena from within particular cultures and from how they conceive the person and self–other relationships. At the same time, culture remains an elusive reality derived from recurrences and convergences in discourses, narrative forms, exchanges, or conflicts. The centrality of the work on emotions and embodiment in North American anthropology reflects a similar perspective; however, in the case of embodiment, it is enriched by Bourdieu's and Foucault's analyses of the role of the body in mediating the imprint of the social order and of power relationships on individuals (Lock 1993).

The second set of studies, which have been more influential in European writings, unfold the frame outlined by Mauss in his classical essay on the notion of Person considered as a category of the human mind rather than approached through subjective experience (Mauss 1985). Mauss's essay reviews the various forms of the notion of Person across societies and through time. The analysis is framed on an evolutionary perspective which describes a progressive transformation from a person-character (*personnage*) organized around ascribed roles, to a person-subject of rights and duties, and to an autonomous self-centered individual. Some authors have reframed Mauss's analysis around the distinction between "sociocentric" and "egocentric" societies. Modern Western societies are considered the paradigm of egocentric societies but the current literature tends to recast this feature as an "anomaly" rather than as the ultimate term of cultural evolution (Shweder and Bourne 1991). African (Collomb 1965) and Asian (Shweder and Bourne 1991) societies are presented as typical examples of sociocentric societies but this second model would in fact be much commoner than the first model.

Stereotyping of this kind has been denounced and most recent anthropological studies prefer to point to the presence of both dimensions in societies and their complex interplay. Authors have described cases which do not fit the supposedly dominant model (Holland and Kipnis 1994); more interestingly, they have also shown that both dimensions are intertwined in language, folklore, and tales (Lienhardt 1985). Dumont (1985) introduces another interesting distinction within individualism itself when he contrasts the notion of the individual associated with the modern ideology of man and society with that in holistic societies; India, with the figure of the renouncer, and early Christianity are examples given of this second setting. The category of individual has to be qualified in relation to a larger cultural frame.

The notion of "individuation" therefore appears as a central issue in the studies influenced by Mauss's thinking. It refers not to the concrete subjective experience but to the structural possibility, framed from within the culture itself, of distancing *vis-à-vis* the defining power of the social and cultural order. This implies a shift in focus from the description of concrete interactions to the identification of spaces where the cultural coordinates of the person are made explicit. One such privileged space is the ritual scene, as it punctuates and marks the life cycle, or as it clarifies and reworks the meaning of illness and misfortune.

The principle of "individuation" in African societies

Papers published in 1973 on the notion of the Person in Black Africa (Centre national de la recherche scientifique 1973) are clearly situated within the second frame outlined here. Most papers approach this notion through the analysis of categories and representations through which a society elaborates its image of Man, its constitutive elements, and its place within the world. The person is defined in terms of a series of components which relate her to a genealogical frame and to the social and cosmological order through notions of entourage, heritage, and "innateness" (Cartry 1973). Although these essays leave open the degree to which mythical categories are experienced and actually frame everyday life, they illustrate the presence of two apparent "anti-principles of individuation" in African societies: the plurality of the elements which make up the person, and the merging of the individual with his environment, his alterity (Bastide 1973).

This vision of the African person as being essentially embedded within a collective framework has been reinforced and legitimized by the work of two psychoanalysts, Marie-Cécile and Edmond Ortigues (1973) in their description of an African version of the Oedipus complex. Their book is based on data collected from a psychoanalytically oriented clinical practice with children consulting for school and emotional problems, and from discussions of a multidisciplinary team of anthropologists, psychologists, psychoanalysts, and psychiatrists. The Ortigues consider the Oedipus complex from a perspective which emphasizes the need for the child to detach himself from the mother's world and to become integrated in society's symbolic order, through processes of identification, opposition, internalization. According to the authors, this process is significantly influenced by the fact that in African traditional societies, the Father merges with the figure of the Ancestors with which no competition or opposition is possible; aggression toward the Father is therefore deflected to the Brothers and, repressed by an imperative of solidarity, comes back to haunt in the guise of ideas of persecution which have been shown to dominate African psychopathology. The Ortigues view beliefs involving sorcery, witchcraft, and spirit possession as collective constructions of this process and as further indication of the depth of the person's dependence on a relational and collective field.

Not all authors have subscribed to this vision. For example, in his analysis of African oral literature, Lienhardt (1985) describes a more fluid notion of "self" which is simultaneously conceived as "apart from others" or "separate from others," self-interested and self-indulgent, and which is determined by outside references to clans and divinities which add to, rather than detract from, their individuality.

In the series of essays published on the notion of Person in Black Africa, authors attempted to describe a specific form of individuation framed from within the culture. For example, Héritier-Izard (1973) describes how, among the Samo, the idea of "individual destiny" emerges at the interface between two radically distinct worlds: that of men, dominated by social rules, principles, and customs within the framework of agnatic principles of descent, and that of women escaping the boundaries of the male social order yet with its own rules of transmission and solidarity beyond lineage. In a theoretical paper, Bastide outlines the specific features of an African principle of individuation in response to the question regarding the degree to which the African person is defined by events, personages, components, or unifies these elements from within herself. According to Bastide, individuation in Africa must be conceived as a balance between different principles or forces: it represents a dynamic formal unity which expresses the person's position within a symbolic order; attributes derived from the person's participation in various systems of classification define her singularity: "Singularity results from the formula, which differs from person to person, of her *appartenances*."

In his description of the Melanesian notion of person, Leenhardt (1947) had already described how, in a context of culture change, the structure of person is released from the breaking up of mythical social domains. The person, however, cannot be confused with actual individuals and encompasses the broader human reality of participation, sociality, communion and depends on a mythical basis. Contrary to the individual, the Melanesian person could be enriched by an indefinite assimilation of outside elements. This process would itself be grounded in the unconscious debate in the person confronted with the mythical world of traditional society; it would also be foreshadowed by the positioning of heroes or heroines who have rejected the constraints of their social role.

I have also recognized the presence of a principle of individuation culturally embedded within the formation of the collective identity within a traditional matrilineal society of Zaire (Corin 1995). I was interested by the cultural framing of becoming a person and by the structural differentiation culturally established between the figures of maternal uncle, father, and grandfather who are symbolically introduced into the universe of the child through a series of rituals in the first two years of life. My analysis focused on life-cycle rituals and funerals, the representations associated with witchcraft, and the discussions where the contingencies of life, disease, and death are interpreted. Data reveal the parallel functioning of two principles of reference involving different dimensions of the person. On the one hand, various indices point to the preeminence of a matrilineal ideology with a social identification with the maternal uncle, the absolute preeminence of his authority grounded in the world of ancestors, an important dependence on the lineage for asserting one's social identity, and the transmission of official functions and status through the matrilineage. This evokes the Ortigues's description of the African person. However, I also observed the existence of another less important principle of reference involving chains of father–son identifications, including reciprocal and symmetrical relationships between alternate generations, and associated with issues of life, fertility, fulfillment, and individuation. I hypothesized that patrilateral references allow the matrilateral prescriptive structure to be infused with actuality and performance. Chains of father–son relationships not only indicate the limit of the matrilateral principle; they also enable the escape from and balance of its constraining power through the intervention of a concurrent principle of legitimacy.

Some authors have gone further in attempting to understand how cultural signifiers are used to articulate particular personal and collective experiences. In a seminal paper, Ortigues *et al.* (1968) applied the principles of a clinical approach to cultural phenomena in order to understand how cultural representations and practices are mobilized in particular ways by individuals or groups, with regard to their position within the social and cultural field. This requires that cultural phenomena are subjected to structural analysis for the identification of the internal articulation of representations; it breaks down a belief into its formal elements and brings out a multiplicity of associated relationships that can be used in different ways. These associative chains link to other chains through which they are connected to the larger social and cultural context. The clinical approach attempts to reveal the particular valencies and associative connections used in particular cases by groups and individuals.

Zempleni applied this perspective in the reconstruction of the life story of Khady Fall, a priestess of a possession cult in Senegal (1977). The narrative shows the parallel evolution of the priestess's way of referring to different segments of her spirit world, and of her position toward matri- and patrilineages throughout her life. The analysis also shows how the idiom of the spirits enables the woman progressively to affirm and articulate her own difference and individuality, as she comes to accept her father's heritage. In a clinical setting, Ortigues and her collaborators (1967) described how individual patients use cultural signifiers through time and then discussed the clinical implications.

In this paper, I will pursue the idea that African traditional societies have a potential for individuation which is freed and enacted in particular settings or circumstances. I will focus on the potential for individuation structurally inscribed within a particular idiom of spirit possession and its ritual enactment. I will therefore attempt to bring out the significance of representations and rituals from the perspective of the person initiated within the ritual and discuss its articulatory potential with regard to personal experience. Rather than addressing this issue from the analysis of case histories (Crapanzano 1977; Zempleni 1977), I will analyze the structure of the ritual idiom itself. I will try to understand which particular notion of individuation is involved and how it relates to individualization associated with culture change. My reflections are based on several years' fieldwork in various parts of Zaire (now Congo), Central Africa, and on extended contacts with several spirit possession groups. Each group elaborates the relationships between the person, her social environment, and the spirits in its own way which is characterized by contrasting forms of body language (Corin 1985; 1995). I will focus here on the Zebola, a female spirit possession ritual originating among the Mongo, in northwestern Zaire but which is also very popular in the large city of Kinshasa where it attracts women from various ethnic backgrounds.

For a long time, spirit possession seems to have captured the imagination of a wide range of scholars interested in African societies. Accounts and interpretations have varied according to researchers' personal inclinations or perspectives, to disciplinary stances and to general changes in ideas and fashions on the academic scene. This process of constant reinterpretation is certainly not limited to spirit possession, but it is intensified by the fact that spirit possession straddles the boundary between the corporal, the cognitive, and the symbolic; between the private, the social, and the spiritual; and between reality, imagination and fantasy. Polysemy and multi-referentiality could be intrinsic to spirit possession and seem to defy a priori total interpretation.

The heuristic potential of spirit possession for understanding the notion of person is based on the fact that a diagnosis of spirit possession indicates that the person's problems are understood as involving the person's identity and her permeability to some kind of Otherness which has come to dominate her. In the Zebola, as in most spirit possession rituals in Zaire, spirit possession is always revealed through the presence of mental or physical health problems; initiation has always a therapeutic dimension.

The paradoxical figure of spirit possession

Approaching the notion of person through spirit possession may appear paradoxical, as possession implies that the person is de-possessed of herself and controled by an external force or agent. For a long time, this feature, far from being perceived as a potentially productive paradox, tended to reinforce the idea that the African self is sociocentric, essentially defined by its interpersonal and social embedding.

Recent studies on spirit possession in Africa have emphasized its collective significance and its counter-hegemonic character; authors have argued that far from serving ultimately to reinforce the traditional structure of power, spirit possession simultaneously enacts and challenges conventional cultural codes, in a process which introduces a dialectic tension within culture and society (Boddy 1989; Corin 1981; Lambek 1981). Yet there is on the collective scene a paradox analogous to the one observed at the level of the individual, as the control by an external agent or power is analyzed as a form of resistance to objectification and subordination; subjection therefore would serve as an idiom for expressing resistance and subversion. I will argue that this paradox cannot be reduced to a strategy for concealing rebellion or for forcing one's way through the barriers of cultural norms. Rather, I will use my fieldwork experience in Zaire to demonstrate that it is inherent to the specific process of transformation of individuals through spirit possession rituals.

Instead of concentrating on the theatrical aspect of the spirit possession dances, I will consider spirit possession as a process which takes shape and evolves along a temporal dimension throughout initiation which, among the Zebola, lasts several months. I will show that the initiation ritual performs a structural rearticulation of personal space and of its relationship with the cultural order, but from within the cultural scene. My argument is that spirit possession releases and articulates a potential for individuation and sustains a position of subject in African traditional societies; at the same time, spirit possession redefines the foundations of the relationship with the cultural order and, more generally, creates a new dialectic at the individual as well as at the collective level. I will argue that this dialectic is of the same order as the one involving *"la parole"* and *"la langue"* in the area of linguistics and that it tends toward the development of the second historicization alluded to by Lacan in his early writings (1966). Throughout my analysis, I will refer to concepts developed in adjacent fields which "resonate" with what I understood of the work accomplished by the Zebola ritual. I refer to these in the perspective proposed by Canguilhem (in Missenard and Gutierrez 1989) when he suggests putting concepts to work (*faire travailler les concepts*) by uprooting them from their place of origin to alter their extension and comprehension.

My analysis will be centered on the structure of the Zebola idiom of spirit possession and on the role played by the body in the initiation process. In fact, the very notion of possession indicates from the outset that the body is the locus of negotiation between the spirits and the initiate and of the redefinition of her identity. In his description of the ceremony of initiation in the *rab* spirit possession cult in Senegal, Zempleni (1987) described the symbolic function played by the parallel manipulation of the bodies of the initiate and of the sacrificial animal, as an icon of the subsequent healing process. The dressing of the animal's inverted belly and intestines on the head and around the initiate's body symbolically transforms the possessed person into a sacrificial victim and accomplishes a spatial and temporal inversion which expresses metaphorically the process through which "what was acting diffusely and continuously from within" (the illness) "returns, and has to return, violently and periodically from outside" (ritual possession). In his work among the Yaka of Zaire, Devisch (1993b) preferred to accentuate the emotional dimension of the work on the body. In his analysis of the *mbwoolu* therapeutic initiation for the physically handicapped, for humoral disorders, and for some forms of insanity, he hypothesizes that initiation reenacts the process of gestation, reconnects the person to the uterine sources of life, and reintroduces her progressively in the social order regulated by the laws of patrilineage. It is through her reanchorage within the traditional sources of life that the person can be reinvigorated.

In the Zebola initiation, I will argue that the work on the body mobilizes emotions and affects and ensures the full involvement of the person into what is accomplished. Notions of embellishment, seduction, and

pleasure are central in the process of initiation and infuse the transformation with emotional energy. Music, songs, and dances constitute a
sensory environment which contributes to accentuating the subjective
participation of the initiate in the healing process.

Reframing a personal space: a process of de- / re-capture

The Zebola spirit possession initiation is therapeutic insofar as it is always
through an illness that the spirit manifests its presence in the woman. All
kinds of physical or mental health symptoms may be interpreted as a sign
of spirit possession; they generally arouse anxiety because of their dur-
ation and resistance to treatment. Women are often involved in a long
quest for therapy, consulting many traditional and modern medical practitioners before turning to a Zebola healer. Trembling and dizziness often
signal the likelihood of spirit possession. In the rural region where the
ritual originates, the woman often becomes withdrawn, with a fleeting
gaze and typically – but not nearly always – she may suddenly escape into
the forest where people have to look for her.

By the time the family brings her to consult the Zebola healer, the
woman is therefore generally permeated by an ethos of suffering and
discouragement; she appears immobilized in a status of patient. The
diagnosis of possession is the first transformation in the meaning of the
symptoms which come to signify the spirit's presence in the woman. This
process however is more complex in the Zebola than in other spirit
possession groups. In the Zebola idiom, the spirit's intervention in a
person's life always occurs in the second stage of a disease process. Illness
preexists possession and is ultimately attributed to the malevolence of
others or to a punishment for the transgression of a law. The spirit
transforms the disease into a spirit illness which can then be cured
through initiation. It invades the woman's body and life in order to
protect her and creates a distance between her and the threatening power
of the disease. The change in the meaning of the symptoms (from disease
to indication of possession) accomplished through divination therefore
mirrors a deeper change which has already occurred.

However, early on, the spirit's presence is marked by analogously
threatening connotations. Its love is demanding and intransigent and if
the person refuses to be initiated, or is prevented from doing so for
whatever reason, she is likely to become insane or die, causing her
descendants to be struck by the spirit. If the spirit acts as a mediator
between the woman and the disease-causing agent, it remains situated
within a register of immediacy and capture from which there is no escape
at that point.

Initiation in the Zebola ritual reverses this process. It allows the person to de-capture herself from spirit domination and to reframe her relationship so that the spirit remains with her as a protector. This is accomplished through the mediation of a healer and the group who support the process of "recapturing" the spirit.

After divination during which the spirit manifests its presence in the woman's body, the healer "binds" it with herbal laces and headband; the spirit should no longer entrance the woman. Any symptom of trance or dissociation is immediately suppressed with very strong and painful eye drops. The spirit's presence is then experienced through milder forms of trembling or dizziness. Unlike other spirit possession rituals where possession-trance is periodically provoked, progressively tamed, and culturally shaped, in the Zebola, the possession-trance which inaugurates the initiation is reshaped as possession, i.e. as an interpretative device. The woman's body is transformed into a kind of shrine for the spirit; it is embellished, cared for, and animated day after day, for its pleasure. Some more direct spaces of contact are created when the woman begins daily fumigation wrapped up in mats and blankets, with another initiate beating the drum to please the spirit.

The main part of the lengthy initiation involves taking care of the woman's body, learning the Zebola dances, and controlling the spirit's presence through medication. Immediately after initiation, the healer anoints the initiate's body with a red paste to please the spirit. The woman spends a large portion of her days grinding bark to a fine powder, through constant rubbing, and transforming it into a paste with which she anoints her whole body, several times a day. In this way, she embodies the reference to the spirit while at the same time revealing her special status to others. Dances for the Zebola spirits are exceptionally beautiful, fluid, nimble, demanding great flexibility of the body. Initiates exercise daily in groups and learn to untie their body to the rhythm of the drum. Medicines penetrate the body through the eyes, nostrils, and scarifications on the articulations, the forehead, the chest; some of them help tame the spirit and bind its manifestations whereas others are related to symptoms experienced by the person.

This set of bodily processes is intended to please and seduce the spirit and thereby recapture it, so that another kind of relationship, grounded in the person's own involvement toward the spirit, can be created. This can be seen as a second inversion within the initiate–spirit relationship itself. The person is transformed from a passive – chosen – object into an active object-subject of the relationship. The spirit's first desire is echoed, interiorized, and then appropriated by the woman. In this way, a first embodiment responding to an external force, the possessing spirit, is complemented by a second embodiment, deliberately shaped from within. As she engages in active communication with the spirit, the woman moves from a relationship trapped in an imaginary and unmediated world in which she feels captured by the others' power (people or spirit), to a position of dialogue in a symbolic space where she becomes the subject. Connotations of spirit possession switch from intrusive-threatening to allied and protective. The link however never loses its menacing character completely since the initiate can always fall ill again if she transgresses the spirit's rules.

Parallel to this, all the care and treatment undertaken involves the body surface as experienced sensorially and as seen by other people. Anzieu (1985) has described the importance of the body envelope in the development of an "ego skin" (*moi peau*) whose basic function is to hold affective and psychic contents and to protect from the outside and to mediate the contact with the external world. This would provide a sense of security which would allow the child to represent herself to herself, from her experience of the bodily surface. Anzieu also describes how sounds, warmth, and odours can create other envelopes which may contribute to strengthen the sense of self. As mentioned above, in the case of the Zebola, initiation often takes place after a long period of suffering, of uncertainty, and of shopping around for treatment. The work done on the body during initiation may be interpreted as reshaping several corporal and sensory envelopes and as participating in the recreation of a sense of self; its reconstructive value should be enhanced by its symbolic reference to loving and protective spirits who are the real recipients of what is done to the body.

The family group of the initiate is submitted to a parallel process of distancing, reshaping, and reactivation. Family members must be present at the two divinations which open and close the initiation; they have to express their consent to the process of disclosure of the etiological frame which triggered the spirit possession. Once the presence of the Zebola spirit is confirmed, a family member entrusts the woman to the healer; at the end of the initiation, the healer publicly and symbolically returns the woman to her family. For the months in between, she lives at the healer's place, separated from the outside world by various interdictions. She cannot shake hands, eat food from outside, or sit on modern chairs. She is bodily marked by her clothes, her make-up, and various signs of belonging to the group. In the healer's house, she lives with other initiates undergoing treatment, in a warm and friendly atmosphere. Former patients and other healers come to visit; they attend ceremonies conducted by their healer or in the house of other Zebola healers. Initiates therefore become part of a tightly knit group to which they will remain attached after initiation. The potential conflict between these two frames of references is represented and played out in the dances which terminate the initiation. The requirements and rules associated with the status of spirit possessed will later allow the woman to negotiate a certain degree of freedom within her family environment. The family will have to agree to her regular, sometimes frequent, attendance at Zebola ceremonies, or risk her falling sick again. At the representational level, the possessing spirit's demands fulfill the mediating function acted out implicitly, but very efficaciously, by the group of initiates in everyday life.

The discursive transformation of the person

Contrary to what has been described in other spirit possession cults, Zebola spirits are not associated with particular characters appropriated by the initiate while possessed. They pronounce their name through the mouth of the woman during divination but this is to signify the passage from an anonymous relationship of grip to the establishment of a more reciprocal exchange link. Zebola spirits appear as symbolic operators who reshape the person's experience and position toward the social and cultural. In fact, particularly where the ritual originated, the intervention of the spirits is often sought by deceased people who love the woman (like a mother, an aunt, a stepmother, rarely a close friend) and who ask the spirits to protect her from death. This mediation anchors the action of the spirits in a familiar setting and adds to its legitimacy. It also contributes to the creation of an area of security and confidence rooted in the ascendency. It may also reinforce the emotional involvement of the woman in her relationship with the spirit and strengthen the therapeutic dynamics at play in the ritual.

The most striking feature of the Zebola divination is its discursive character and the fact that the spirit speaks through the mouth of the woman. The healer traces marks on her body in order to protect her from the intrusion of evil spirits; she also traces circles around her eyes to represent the "second look" she will acquire, while entranced, as to what really caused her disease and triggered the spirit's intervention. The woman enters in trance and her voice is used by the spirit to identify the chain of causes which led to their intervention. The diagnosis takes the form of a narrative which has every chance of sticking close to the woman's subjective experience of the world. The divination is repeated at the end of the initiation. Its public character is then emphasized. The initiate is no longer seated, leaning over a bucket behind mats and blankets. She climbs onto an elevated bed of sticks under which herbs and leaves are thrown on a fire, producing a thick smoke. She is sprinkled with palm wine and with the blood of a sacrificed chicken whose neck was wrenched by the healer. She is then covered with blankets and the entranced initiate acts as a medium for clarifying her own situation and that of other participants. We will see that this transformation of the woman's illocutionary position is an icon of a deeper change which occurs at the level of personal identity. A comparison of the narratives in the two divinations, which are several months apart, gives us an idea of the degree to which the initiation modifies the woman's perception of her world and of herself.

Narratives from the first divination often reveal the woman's global impression of being in a hostile and threatening environment where "people talk too much about her." This refers to gossip, complaints, and jealous comments which are believed to have the power of making the person vulnerable to the intrusion of evil spirits. A negative intentional quality of the world echoes the woman's perceived vulnerability to a threatening illness which expresses her "atmospheric understanding" (Tellenbach 1983) of her situation within the world; this special kind of understanding is based on the overall intuition she has of her situation from various indices pertaining to the multiple levels of that situation. In revealing the presence of the spirit in the affected woman, the divination accomplishes a transformation of this atmospheric quality of the perceived world; the woman now feels protected and reinforced by the spirit's presence. In fact, Zebola healers say that divination is the first step in treatment.

The divination narrative also enunciates more specifically the etiological chain of events which led the spirit to intervene. It mentions conflicts, events, and transgressions which appear to have set the process in motion. In the region where the ritual originated, disobedience of rules of sharing, the transgression of laws, and lack of respect for authorities are central to the narratives and reflect the difficulty women have in finding their place in a world regulated by norms and values set by men; it speaks of their subjective anxiety. A woman's problems can also be caused by her standing out from the group. One of the founding stories of the ritual relates how Madjika, the first Zebola possessed, was the target of other people's jealousy because of her beauty; people kept talking about her, repeating her name so that the evil spirits entered her body and carried her into the water.

Two examples will illustrate the complexity of the etiological chain revealed through the woman's narrative. In a first one, a young woman did not send her father her first salary. The father felt offended and walked into the forest "repeating her name." Evil spirits heard the name and entered her body, making her sick. Her deceased mother took pity on her and asked the Zebola spirits to save her. In another example, the entranced woman revealed that her father and his kin wanted to take revenge against the mother who had "refused the father's love." They also complained that their own children and kin were dying; therefore she also had to die. On the other hand, the family of her maternal grandfather wanted to sacrifice her for catching more fish and because they were jealous that she had more money. The woman concluded: "We are attacked from all sides."

Without challenging the legitimacy of social rules and values, the Zebola spirit de-captures the woman from their overwhelming authority and suspends the rigor of their application. The spirit stands up for the woman even if she placed herself in a fragile and transgressive situation. This process of distanciation parallels, on the social scene, that accomplished toward the disease.

The Zebola divination therefore invites the woman to express her problems in narrative form and to situate them within a reconstructed historical frame. The fact that it is through the woman's voice that the etiological diagnosis is made could allude to the progressive recovery of a position of subject within society, not in the woman's name, but as supported by the spirit's credentials.

The first divination must be confirmed and expanded at the end of the initiation. The second divination marks the entrance to a series of festivities; they prepare the person's return to the community, just as the first divination inaugurated her entrance into initiation.

A comparison of the two sets of narratives reveals that, contrary to what may be expected and what has been described in other settings (Piault 1975), the narratives do not progress toward greater coherence or stereotyping. Rather than greater emplotment within a preconstructed frame, the initiation seems to liberate chains of associations and sustain a further analysis of the complex tensions which contributed to frame the initiate's daily life. The Zebola idiom, interiorized and embodied during months of treatment, provides a framework for reassessing the situation.

The second divination can pick up and expand upon the first diagnosis by adding details and circumstances. It can also mention additional causes not necessarily part of the first story. This adds to the intricacy of the world where the person felt trapped within the lines of conflicts which went beyond her own responsibility.

The mother and her daughter have both been ill and submitted to the Zebola divination. The entranced daughter incriminates the defunct maternal grandfather who is angry against her mother because she did not wait for the closing grieving ceremonies to resume her life. This is confirmed at the second divination. This time, however, the mother also accuses the wife of her husband's brother of bewitching her daughter; the daughter complains of her father who "discusses" and wants to reduce their period of seclusion in the healer's house: "He has to refrain discussing and murmuring: evil spirits and witches are listening."

In another case, the first divination incriminates a deceased friend who wanted to take the woman to death for love. In the second divination, the spirit also reveals the responsibility of other persons: the husband who "speaks too much about her" because she refused to make love with him even though they had several children together, and her husband's brothers and sisters who "speak too much about her."

The flexibility of the Zebola idiom allows the formulation of very complex patterns of vulnerabilizing and protective factors which express various levels of demands and claims.

The diagnosis given at the first divination is confirmed and amplified the second time: It is the husband's second wife who speaks too much about her and wants her to die. The woman then adds that her husband's kin also speak too much about her. They do not like her. Evil spirits were transmitted to her by her husband when they made love together: "He is too hypocritical. He does not believe in witchcraft. He has to be washed with very strong medication; too many doubts; too many doubts."

In this case, the interceding spirit is the deceased stepmother. This time, she is the one who speaks through her stepdaughter's mouth: "Thanks to me she cannot die. She gave birth to a daughter who bears my name. Moreover, if she dies, members of the maternal family will come to kill us; other people's child is the child of these persons."

As illustrated in the previous and the following examples, the identity of the spirit speaking in the divination can contribute to reinforce a position perceived as fragile.

Divination reveals a series of conflicts which culminate in an accusation of infertility: "She dies because of her marriage, because of her husband: his parents and brothers speak too much about her, they speak her name; his children hold it against her that their father sent their mother away and she came to replace her." On her side also, they accuse her of being infertile, not giving birth: "This child does great work in her husband's house and no one congratulates her."

The spirit stands up against these accusations with all its authority: "I, Elima Ekolo, I am dangerous and she will give birth. I, you know me, I am from my village Mbayo Ikolo. I tell the truth. I, I turn pirogues upside down in water. I am always in the whirl of water. In her house, from the time of her ancestors, there has been no infertility, until now."

I alluded to the transformation of the illocutory position occupied by the initiate between the first and second divinations. This is echoed in the content of the second diagnosis. As a matter of fact, the entranced woman can also add normative comments to recall the need to follow certain norms and traditions. These admonitions can be directed at family members whose failure to follow customs endangered the woman's life or threaten their own lives, as in the following three cases:

After having confirmed the first diagnosis which incriminated a woman with whom the initiate had quarrelled, the second divination expanded the interpretative frame and identified people living in "the village": "In the village, they speak too much about her. The father's brothers and sisters wonder why they left for Kinshasa. She has to come back to the village. Since she grew up, since she had children, she never went back."

The spirit incriminates the husband who had an affair with a woman initiated in another ritual and then wanted to break up with her. She took revenge on his wife. The spirit adds: "This woman's kin and younger father are taking sides with that woman because you, the husband, and your wife did not send them money or clothes."

The first divination revealed that the woman's sister, who died while under Zebola treatment, wanted her to organize a dance for the Zebola spirits, under her name. In the second divination, the deceased sister confirms her request and adds that the sorcerer who killed her continues to be with her family which lacks protection because of its failure to follow the rules of exchange. The possessed woman addresses her family: "Your father does not take care of you because you do not help him when he needs it; you only send money to your mother. Moreover, your aunt did not give birth but you do not help her. She speaks too much but she does not bewitch you. Big sister must pay attention; she has already lost a child, she could lose a second one. She only has to give something to the aunt." The aunt who is present then confirms that she feels rejected by her family.

In some cases, the second divination gets totally absorbed by this normative function. The possessed woman can successively address family members and comment on their behavior, acting as a genuine family leader.

(To a cousin): "I congratulate you. You support your children and family very well. Your paternal uncle (the speaking spirit) tells you: go also and claim your uncle's pension money for his children."

(In response to the cousin's questions about his own children): "They are well but you have to make a protective horn for the oldest one."

(To an attending woman): "You were forbidden to marry your husband. You see what happened? He prepared fetishes so that you remain a slave while he lives well with his second wife."

(In response to her cousin's question about his older brother): "Members of my family do not come any more to clean my grave. Why?"

As illustrated by the latter example, the woman does more than enlightening her own situation. In fact, she also clarifies other people's problems and difficulties. In the last part of the seance, she acts as a medium for members of the audience or other initiates who come to consult the spirit speaking through her voice.

It is fascinating to observe the degree to which she has changed since she arrived as a distressed, suffering, uncertain, and anxious person. Two days after the second divination, the unfolding of the last great possession dance in some way renders visible and recounts this process. The initiate enters the dance area between two Zebola healers or senior members of the group. They perform a few dances together; the initiate appears to be very shy. She then starts singing songs which other Zebola members pick up as she dances the very beautiful Zebola dances, alone, for hours; she appears to be increasingly self-confident. In a particular dance, she challenges members of the audience and invites them to dance with her in the middle of the circle and to give her money. Toward the end of the day, the audience participates in collective dances: either Zebola dances or traditional dances of the initiate's home region; family members either join the members of the group or dance together.

I would suggest that the work on the body which takes place throughout the whole initiation period is redoubled by the work accomplished on the subjective experience of oneself. The two divinations provide a framework which permits the construction of what Ricoeur (1988, 1992) calls a "narrative identity" which is grounded in the linkage between history and fiction in the framing of personal identity. In fact, the Zebola divination leads to the clarification of the woman's sense of her position within the world through the elaboration of narratives which express the woman's interpretation of herself in relation to some objective events, inscribed within a specific history. I would go on to suggest that by the end of the initiation, the woman has broadened her initial understanding of her situation and infused it with subjectivity and variation. When consulting a Zebola healer, the family expects to be provided with a reason for the cause of the disorder. The Zebola idiom allows the woman to respond through narratives which work and rework the past, introducing in her account what may appear to be fictional or imaginative variations but which in fact express the truth of her subjective history. It could be said that reference to the Zebola spirits serves as a heuristic device to allow flexibility in the unfolding of the person's life. The woman's present state (disorder) was the manifestation of external forces which came to disrupt her life. Zebola spirits introduce a second-order change which reopens and reorients the deadly effect external agents may have on her life.

Reworking the collective frame

The Zebola ritual is a female ritual. Although I have stressed its potential transformative action on personal experience, its impact cannot be reduced to it as it also involves the women's position within the cultural frame.

One could hypothesize that the personal impact of the ritual is permitted and reinforced by its action at the collective level.

The mediating function of the Zebola spirits regarding a particular woman's position toward her social and cultural environment is grounded in the specific representation of the spirits' world within the Zebola idiom. Zebola spirits are thought to be the spirits of deceased Mongo women but their association with existing lineages remains unspecified. They are therefore associated with the world of male ancestors yet differentiated from it: they are female; they are not related to the living beings through a lineage line; they inhabit forests, springs, and whirlpools whereas the altars of male ancestors are situated in the village where prayers and sacrifices are regularly offered. The Zebola spirits' social and physical exteriority can be seen as an icon of the particular stance they occupy toward the cultural order.

This situation on the outer limits of the male cultural world on the side of the wild is paralleled by the concrete and symbolic place awarded in the Zebola ritual to everyday female behavior and gestures which can be seen as defining the internal borders of the social world. During the long months of treatment, the initiates' time, when not taken up by pleasing the spirit, is punctuated with chores of preparing meals, washing clothes, perhaps taking care of infants, in a very convivial female atmosphere, activities which weave the daily life of women. This quality is also symbolically introduced into the ritual itself through the dances for the spirits, which often imitate women's activities: emptying river holes with baskets to fish in the mud; killing fish; doing themselves up; looking in the mirror; chatting with other initiates. The challenging power of the Zebola ritual seems to be anchored in these two spaces, on the inner and outer boundaries of the male-regulated social world.

This anormative dimension of the Zebola ritual scene is also expressed at a stylistic level by the parody of some dances which mimic typical male activities, such as hunting or even ludicrously portrayed sexual relationships. When a male is invited to join the initiate's dances in the middle of the circle, it is not unusual to see other Zebola initiates coming to dance with him. They cling to him, pressing their pelvis against him, sometimes to the point of overturning him. The audience then bursts out laughing.

More generally, the convivial nature of interpersonal relationships during initiation and the playful style of the dances for the spirits create a transitional space of play which could contribute to mobilizing creative forces at the personal and collective level. In fact, the objective of the ritual is not to contest the legitimacy of the cultural order, as seen in the second divination, but rather to introduce an element of suspense, comments, and distancing toward its application. In Babcock's discussion

(1978) of the cultural function of symbolic inversions, she notes: "it is through various forms of symbolic inversion that culture frees itself from the limitations of 'thou shalt not's,' enriches itself with the subject-matter without which it could not work efficiently, and enables itself to speak about itself" (p. 21). This playful aspect of the ritual may be interpreted as a form of liminality (Turner 1978) congruent with the general orientation of the ritual. It also echoes the role that Winnicott (1971) attributed to transitional phenomena, simultaneously part of the person and of the world, in the framing of symbols. Cultural phenomena are present, independent of the person, and recreated, hallucinated, and enriched by our own projections, discourses, and desires. The Zebola ritual appears to produce such a creative, transitional space which infuses the existing social and cultural worlds with new meanings, at both personal and collective levels.

Refiguring a world

The Zebola idiom consists of a series of inversions which parallel and reinforce each other and which allow the multiple levels of its sphere of action to be traced: on the body, diseased / chosen by the spirit; on the relationship to the spirit through a process of de / recapture; on the atmospheric quality of the women's world; on the relationship to oneself, endangered / protected; on one's subjective history; on gender and family relationships. These various inversions can be subsumed under a process of *dégagement* which, without rejecting the external world, allows distancing. This would characterize the specific form of individuation accomplished by the Zebola ritual.

The goal is not the creation of autonomous, emancipated subjects, but to rework the relationships of *appartenance* of the person to her world. The issue is to find a new inscription within the collective order, where traditional references are both interiorized and reshaped in the context of a new personal and collective repositioning. The transformation of the illocutory position of the initiate during initiation then blends with the playful and emotional quality of the ritual space in order to create a new way of presenting oneself to oneself and to others. The framing of the person's identity from the outside by the social and cultural rules is complemented by a repositioning from within the person and the women's world. In a distant analogy with Lacan's discussion of psychoanalytic treatment (Lacan 1966), it could be said that a primary historicization, which determines the subject from the outside by placing her within the field of language and culture, moves toward a secondary historicization which is part of a projection toward the future where *la parole* is enunciated in dialogue with cultural signifiers. This must be understood in light of the double aspect of language itself. On the one hand, language is by essence an alienating structure which can never express the ineffable totality of the experience. Moreover, it imposes violence to the person forced to use words and expressions already predefined by a network of associations (Derrida 1967). On the other hand, it defines a framework of signification which lends meaning and relevance to the individual experience and permits communication through which we can discover ourselves as personal and collective subjects. The Zebola can be said to create a space of *parole* from within the field of language.

Zebola spirit possession can be understood as articulating a potential for individuation and allowing the construction of the position of subject in African traditional societies. This potential for individuation is expanded and strengthened in the new urban spaces of modern Africa.

In Kinshasa, the Zebola ritual attracts many women from all classes and various ethnic origins. It competes with other kinds of possession rituals which are structured differently to work out the relationship between spirits and humans. They also differ in the way they involve the body in the initiation process. The popularity of the Zebola ritual could be believed to derive from the extremely beautiful and spectacular nature of the initiation dances and from the minimal importance attributed to trance phenomena which seem to take a more alien character in an urban environment where the presence of spirits no longer permeates the daily approach to life. I would hypothesize that the specific kind of individuation associated with the discursive nature of divination contributes to reinforcing its potential impact in an urban environment and its role in the process of individualization associated with modernity. Even if the Zebola ritual has kept its essential features in Kinshasa, a few transformations have appeared, resulting from less familiarity the city dwellers have with the spirits' world and from a greater individualization of references (Corin 1979). For example, the typical nature of the possession disease or of the accompanying signs tends to disappear; a woman may ask another initiate to replace her for the first divination (never for the second) because she is unable to enter trance or is afraid of the spirit, or she would like to attend the divination and listen herself to the spirit's diagnosis. The intercession of deceased people tends to be eliminated and the spirits' choice is then directly based on their own attraction for the woman. The preeminence of the transgression of traditional behavioral rules in the etiological process tends to be displaced by feelings of jealousy and malevolence by others. Nevertheless, traditional signifiers are still used to support this general movement toward individualization lending it cultural legitimacy. I would suggest that in Central Africa, the process of individualization associated with modernization and triggered by post-colonial circumstances is not a wholly new phenomenon and that it coincides with an already existing principle of individuation. One of the main issues facing contemporary Africa is for the people to be able to infuse their own sense of inserted individuation into the post-modern decomposition of social and cultural life.

It is possible that the importance of spirit possession rituals in modern Central Africa – like, at another level, that of the numerous prophetic churches flourishing throughout Black Africa – could provide an escape from some of the dehumanizing features of (post-)modernity and contribute to the creation of an African version of the Melanesian "Person" described by Leenhardt (1947) some decades ago.

5 Body and mind in mind, body and mind in body: some anthropological interventions in a long conversation

Michael Lambek

> The traditional antithesis of the body and soul is not a vain mythological concept that is without foundation in reality.
> (Durkheim, *The Dualism of Human Nature and Its Social Conditions*)

> I have not elucidated that the soul and the body are identical, I have not elucidated that the soul is one thing and the body another . . .
> (The Buddha, *Majjhima-Nikaya Sutta* 63)

It is with some trepidation that I enter the long conversation on mind and body, a conversation that has included many more strong and subtle positions than I can possibly encompass. This chapter is not an intervention in philosophical arguments so much as an exercise in anthropological ground-clearing; I have no pretensions about resolving philosophical debates between monism and dualism. I take these debates to be constitutive of our philosophical tradition rather than assuming that one position must be foundational and others wrong. What is of equal interest is to start with the philosophical problems – not solutions – of our tradition and then to extend the horizons of these debates to include, in a Gadamerian sense, the philosophical conversations, explicit and implicit, of other societies. It is my suspicion that both monistic and dualistic experiences are inherent in the human condition and hence that mind / body and perhaps even monism / dualism are oppositions like nature / culture and male / female which all cultures, hence all anthropologists, must encounter. In sum, my position is very much like the famous wit who claimed that there are two kinds of thinkers in the world, those who divide the world into two and those who do not. To raise the paradox is perhaps already to take sides. Less comfortably, the position might be described as having my cake and eating it too.[1]

Since the reflections that follow are ethnographic in inspiration, it may help to provide some background. Much of my fieldwork has been concerned with spirit possession as I encountered it among Malagasy speakers on the French-controlled island of Mayotte in the Mozambique

Channel and among Sakalava in north-west Madagascar. Spirit possession has to do with intimate relationships that, in Malagasy understanding, particular spirits engage in with particular human hosts. At some times, while the host is in a state of dissociation, the spirit speaks and acts through the host's body, temporarily taking it over, in a manner that one spirit medium, seeking the means to make me understand, described as a *coup d'état*. But between such moments of manifest possession, a long-term relationship between host and spirit continues to be recognized and is marked by such things as the attribution of particular dreams or illnesses to the spirit and by certain actions, notably adherence to specific taboos, on the part of the host. On-going social obligations are acknowledged between host and spirit and with other parties.

Spirit possession is widespread, across not only most of Africa but the globe, although the Malagasy are perhaps at one end of a continuum in emphasizing the distinctiveness of host and spirit as discrete, alternate voices and persons. Spirit possession is a complex phenomenon, integrally related to many other aspects of society and culture in Mayotte and Madagascar and it is of great interest to local people themselves. Much intellectual, creative, and emotional energy is invested in it and generated by it. But spirit possession is also, I think, intrinsically interesting – it raises questions that are provocative for all of us as human beings, questions pertaining to such things as the sources of human agency, or the relationship between action and passion, or autonomy and connection, in selfhood. One of the questions it inevitably touches on has to do with the relationships between mind and body.

In this chapter I explore the directions to which my thinking on mind and body via spirit possession has led me. The attempt is to clarify the bases on which references in the anthropological literature to mind and body arguments rest. I am responding to a general trend in contemporary anthropology and to some degree going against it, but I hope the direction of my arguments will also reveal some of the kinds of connections that can be made between anthropology and philosophy. To put this more specifically, how anthropology might continue to bring cultural difference to the attention of philosophy without advocating a simplistic relativism.

The body is currently a topic of great interest. But, it is anthropologically relevant only in its relationship to other significant categories: body and person, body and self, body and mind, body and memory (and so on). Anything less is simply biology. In question is, first, the relations through which the body helps constitute, express, and ground such things as experience, meaning, reason, identity, value, vitality, continuity, transformation, relationship, agency, and intentionality; and second, how these relations are configured in local thought (including, naturally, our own).

We tend sometimes to suggest that mind/body dualism is peculiarly Western and that we can turn to other cultures for the solution of our "mind-body problem." It is my contention that body/mind or body/person distinctions are widespread, and probably universal, although obviously they need not take the same form, divide the terrain in the same manner, or reach the same proportions or significance as the Cartesian version. My argument is that mind/body dualism is at once everywhere transcended in practice yet everywhere present, in some form or other, in thought.

In other words, we have to attend to body and mind in body (embodiment), and also to body and mind in mind (imagination). I note in passing that this distinction may be a way to characterize the shift of emphasis between the phenomenologists, like Csordas (1990) or Jackson (1989), who are interested in mindful bodies, and the cognitivists, like Lakoff and Johnson (1980), who are interested in embodied minds.

Whether these propositions – that mind/body dualism is at once everywhere transcended in practice and yet everywhere present, in some form or other, in thought – prove true or not, I believe they provide an interesting space for comparative work. They alert us to the fact that in making cross-cultural comparisons we ought not to be comparing embodied practice in one society with concepts or theories in another, but practice with practice and thought with thought, or moving up a level of abstraction, their suitably historicized mutual constitution and interrelationships in the societies in question. Moreover, insofar as the mind/body contrasts we find in different societies do not map directly onto one another, but leave problems of translation, these discrepancies should themselves open up new avenues for investigation.

More generally, my discussion speaks to the fact that philosophy supplies interesting questions for anthropological investigation. And if anthropology can intervene in philosophical debate that is surely to the good as well. Such intervention was a matter of course for writers such as Durkheim and Lévi-Strauss. It is all the more critical today that we contribute to the task of widening the horizons of academic philosophy, providing diverse cultural material to think about and with. At the same time, philosophy can help reduce anthropologists' naiveté and both refine and expand the questions we ask of our material. Together we ought to be able to move beyond both ethnographic particularism and academic philosophy's arguably ethnocentric embeddedness in Western concepts. Despite the long-standing existence of Asian philosophies and the recent emergence of a vigorous professional African philosophy (e.g. Kwame

1995), the questions – can there be a transcultural or pluralist philosophy (not to speak of a global one) and, if so, what would it look like? – have hardly begun to be addressed.

Body and mind in mind

In a recent article on taboo as cultural practice (Lambek 1992) I attempted to demonstrate a dialectic of embodiment and objectification in which the body serves to substantiate and legitimate certain cultural ideals, identities, and relationships. I congratulated myself for showing how taboos, identifiable by means of both explicit, objectified rules and embodied practices – avoiding certain foods or sexual engagements – as well as visceral reactions to their violation – nausea, rashes, and so on – transcend the mind/body opposition. But by the time I had completed the paper I was disconcerted to realize that my analysis had, in fact, proceeded by means of a discussion of similar dual oppositions salient among speakers of Kibushy, the northern Malagasy dialect spoken in Mayotte. Thus, although spirit possession in Mayotte, as over much of Africa and parts of Asia and Oceania, is a highly embodied cultural phenomenon, it is equally grounded in a conceptual distinction – and quite a radical one at that – between particular minds and bodies. Simply put (and over-simply glossed), possession is constituted by the occupation of one body (*neñin*) by more than one person (*ulu*) or mind (*rohu, fañahy*).

Thus I discovered that while I had attempted to deploy theoretical vehicles that would transcend Western dualism, I was actually making use of the dualistic categories of the people I was studying. That such dualism is present in the semantic area of mind/body, even if the Kibushy terms do not correspond exactly to Western ones, and in fact differ from them in interesting ways (Lambek 1992), suggests that dual or possibly multiple categories might be common or even necessary for apprehending this area of human experience. In other words, while "mind" and "body" may not be universal categories, it is striking that people seem to need more than one term to talk about the domains covered by their referent/s. I am not making the strong cognitivist claim that the inferences people make distinguishing what pertains to mind and what pertains to body will be the same everywhere; research on this question is under way (Bloch, pers. comm.). I am saying that what we call the "mind/body problem" (at its most general level, whether a valid distinction can be made between the mind and body[2]) may be but one particular historical expression of what are universal existential conundra rooted in the human capacity for self-reflection. I emphasize that the point of cross-cultural comparison is not to seek solutions to a reified "mind/body problem," but to contextualize a component of Western thought and hence to clarify its very constitution *as* a problem. The assumption is emphatically not that others have "solved" a problem.[3]

The body is good to think with, as we know from countless studies of symbolic dualism or the work of Mary Douglas (1966) on boundaries and transgressions. Indeed, bodily registers have long been prevalent in Western European culture to represent social distinctions (Stallybrass and White 1986). Lakoff and Johnson go further: the body is *necessary* to think with. They appear to suggest that the body (via image schemata) underlies all metaphor and that metaphor, in turn, underlies many of our basic concepts (Lakoff and Johnson 1980; Johnson 1987). For example, to speak of a moral person as upright, or a clever argument as insightful, makes use of prevalent metaphors – so prevalent that they are largely unremarked – metaphors that draw upon sensory or proprioceptive aspects of our embodied condition. But studies of metaphor or of bodily symbolism rarely move beyond the corporeal to examine the way the contrast between the body and something "other" to it (whether glossed as "soul," "spirit," or "mind") is expressed. I suggest that some kind of a mind/body dichotomy marks, and indeed helps constitute, such pervasive oppositions as those between animation and inertion, choice and necessity, "consciousness" and "unconsciousness," and even the transcendental and the mundane (cf. Bloch 1992), as well as providing an idiom in which to address questions of accountability. Of course, the particular ways in which the dichotomy is expressed, the kinds of relations posited between mind and body, the places where boundaries are drawn, even which terms will appear on which sides of the analogies posited above, will vary from place to place and over time. This is the case if only because there is no single or final exclusive, comprehensive, and parsimonious way available for humans to comprehend the human situation.

"Mind" and "body" speak to fundamental tensions of human experience: connection to and separation from others, the boundary between the subjective and the objective, the relation of concepts to objects, or reason to sensation, experiences of the voluntary and the involuntary, morality and desire, being and becoming, active and passive, male and female, the transient and the enduring, culture and nature, life and death. Phrased as "mind" and "body," the opposition and the concerns just listed may appear specific to Western metaphysics. However there are roughly equivalent sets of terms, such as Kibushy *rohu* and *neñin*, addressing roughly similar oppositions, though not necessarily all of them at once, characteristic of the thought of other traditions (cf. Gyekye 1995). These terms and oppositions will not be identical to each other, any more than Plato's mind/body dualism is identical to that of Descartes. In Mayotte, as I elaborated in the earlier article, the body substantiates socially significant distinctions and relationships, for example between kin, manifest in the maintenance of specific taboos or the effects of ignoring them, thereby serving as a primary means to articulate person-hood. Individual preferences that are socially insignificant, or indeed antisocial, are attributed to mind. This is in contrast to the Western picture as articulated by Durkheim, in which "Passion individualizes, yet it also enslaves. Our sensations are essentially individual; yet we are more personal the more we are freed from our senses and able to think and act with concepts" (1965 [1915]:307–8). Durkheim associates the universal with reason and the individual with the body whereas the ideology I heard expressed in Mayotte did something different (Lambek 1992:258; cf. Parry 1989).

I do not mean to suggest that usage in Mayotte is fully consistent. Although the mind/body distinction is evident from spirit possession, the fact that two persons are thought to share the same body complicates the way the body personalizes. Thus the partition of particular attributes, such as skill at dancing, or sensations, such as hunger, pain, exhaustion, or too much liquor, to one person or the other, is not entirely straightfor-ward, any more than we ourselves are fully clear whether to attribute these traits, or others, such as emotions, to body or to mind.

Although in each case, Mayotte and the West, the distinctions premised on mind and body are relative rather than absolute, the lack of identity between cultural models creates a translation problem. There are two things about this problem that may look contradictory but in fact, I will argue, are not. The first point is that the translation problem is not radical; it is possible to see that both inheritors of the Western tradition and the Malagasy speakers are addressing similar kinds of problems or issues even if their phrasing means that they are not identical; they can be placed within the same horizon. The second point is that translation problems may be intrinsic to the subject matter, that is to say that the very irresol-ution of mind/body issues within any given tradition is part and parcel of what makes full and complete translation impossible between traditions.

The argument that "mind"/"body" distinctions address basic dimen-sions of human experience has some affinities with structuralism, specifi-cally Lévi-Strauss's understanding of culture (myth) as the unending attempts to resolve conceptual "irritations" and the displacement of abstract oppositions by sets of concrete signifiers (1963, 1971). My argument about analogy owes much to him. However I do not suggest that the categories function in the formal way some followers of Lévi-Strauss have sought to understand binary oppositions of the left/right, hot/cold variety. The more interesting sets of terms are those that are composed not of logical opposites (good and evil) or empirical contraries (life and death) but of *incommensurables*. These provide genuine conundra. Mind and body, I claim, refer not to contraries or opposites, but to fundamental incommensurables in human experience. Incommensurables (by definition) are not susceptible to measurement by a common yardstick. In this way they are radically different from binary oppositions whose very definition, in the phonological prototype, is relational and constituted by their commensurability.[4]

For this reason, transposition of their terms into the register of the concrete does not provide a very satisfying or neat form of resolution. Moreover, what is at issue is in part the relationship between the concrete and something different from it. The field that the terms cover is inherently messy and complex. Incommensurables do not exclude each other, but by the same token they cannot readily be mediated since they share no common measure along which an intermediary position could be staked out. There is no place half-way between mind and body. Similarly, neither suffices, neither can cover the ground alone. Water may be hot or cold and food raw or cooked, but what could it mean to say of a living human being that they were all body or all mind? Robert Murphy (1987) may have come close, but one of the points of his story of his paralysis is surely how he could never escape the limits of his embodied, albeit bodily silent, condition. Neither "body" nor "mind" is sufficient to describe human experience yet they are not simply additive either, since each is somehow implicated in the other.[5]

Incommensurables are not logical or empirical opposites; in fact, there is no single way in which their connection can be definitively and parsimoniously described. They simply fail, in Kuhn's words, "to make *complete* contact."[6] Mind/body is our expression for one such area of fundamental incommensurability, with no possibility for "resolution." Mind is not simply the absence of body, nor body the absence of mind, though this is one coordinate along which their relationship might, to a degree, be fruitfully explored. Some attempts to mediate the terms, some conversations, may mistakenly assume or try to establish an exclusive, foundational logic. To the degree that we can be said to have a mind/body *problem*, it is precisely this. I mean first, the assumption that we can clearly establish, as Descartes may have asserted, a real distinction between two essential, stable phenomena. Second, then, are the attempts to establish whether there are definitive relations between such discrete substances.[7] Similar pairs or sets of pairs can be found in other traditions, but without the sense of urgency regarding precise clarification of the points of separation or connection.[8]

In sum, the mistake of Cartesianism lies not in its dualism, not in distinguishing mind from body, but in assuming that the relationship between them is one that can be definitively and unilaterally established. The mistake lies in trying to reach conclusion; in Weberian terms, in trying to rationalize the boundary.

In suggesting that mind and body are incommensurable I am extending the understanding which Kuhn (1970) applied to successive paradigms in science and Feyerabend (1975) to distinctive art styles and societies (as studied by anthropologists) to outlooks and even individual sets of terms that are found within a single society or language. Hence my point about body and mind is part of a broader argument about culture. Culture does not rest exclusively on a unitary bedrock of axioms or a primary set of logical oppositions. Rather than being built entirely from logically related categories, systematic propositions, or relationally constituted terms in a structural set, culture is equally constituted from incommensurables and the diverse series of tropes, statements, practices, and interpretations to which they give rise, situated in local "conversations" in which the participants inevitably talk not only to each other but past each other, and which in turn shape experience, although never fully systematically or conclusively.[9] Mind and body must be located in such long, indeed, interminable conversations.

My argument is heavily indebted to Bernstein's discussion of the distinction between incommensurability and both incompatibility (logical contradiction) and incomparability (Bernstein 1983, esp. 79ff.). The incommensurability argument claims neither that there is an overarching framework in terms of which mind and body can be measured against each other point by point such that contradictions can be established, nor that each is encased in a radically different framework such that no communication between them is possible. It is thus neither objectivist nor relativist. Instead, Bernstein emphasizes the open-endedness of incommensurability. Rather than ruling out comparison, it implies that the forms of comparison (or interpretation) will be multiple and not anchored along some fixed grid.[10] A good illustration is the comparison of art styles; just as there is no single or final axis of comparison between two styles of representing the body artistically, so too with thinking about the human condition by means of "body" and by means of "mind." Hence, the lack of resolution between mind and body is not a negative thing but generative of potentially lively cultural production and debate. Indeed, the very incommensurability between mind and body suggests that both monist and dualist ideas will be produced.

I have been arguing that real incommensurables of human experience (including, in this case, the very incommensurability between representational language and experience itself) elicit the production and use of incommensurable categories. Rather than the cross-cultural evidence suggesting that the Cartesian form of conceptualizing the opposition is simply false, it suggests that it is one contingent way of thinking about an issue that does not permit a single "true" representation.[11] Not only is any local formulation likely to be composed of terms incommensurable with each other, but we can expect this to be the case in any comparison of terms drawn from different cultural loci. The different ways in which the primary incommensurability is phrased may have distinctive local consequences which we will want to pursue. However, it follows from my argument that once we have passed the first round of describing local concepts (African, Melanesian, etc.) and of demonstrating that they fail to make "complete contact" with Occidental "mind" and "body," as they surely will fail, we will nevertheless find ourselves within a common horizon of ideas, enabling multiple forms of comparison and directions for conversation. Comparing the alternative formulations should raise many questions and, at the very least, speak to the broader significance of the Western constructions.[12]

In other words, cultural comparison serves to enlarge the discussion of mind and body that is carried on within any given culture or tradition. The discrepancies between some of the terms used in one tradition and those used in another are of the same order (though not the same degree) as the discrepancies between some of the terms used in any given tradition.

It is worth mentioning in passing a problem which my argument raises, namely why, if "mind" and "body" do not emerge from a logical discrimination or a relational paradigm, they are represented by pairs of concepts rather than any other number above one. The empirical question is whether the terms genuinely appear in pairs cross-culturally. In their chapter Strathern and Stewart offer three terms for the Melpa of Highlands Papua New Guinea and Strathern suggests (1996) that we often encounter a triad of mind, spirit, and body. Among another Highlands group, the Paiela, the distinction between a working, active body and a stationary, vegetative one is extremely significant, although the ethnographer (Biersack 1996) provides no specific lexical terms for the contrast. Thus it may be that the collapse of "more-than-two" into "two" in my presentation is simply a rhetorical product of cultural bias, a distortion produced by centuries of attempting to argue within a framework in which the terms are assumed to be commensurable. The alternative, of course, is that human *experience* does have something genuinely dual about it, a matter which comparative work can surely address. If the roots of mind/body *dualism* lie in our embodied existential condition rather than more narrowly within human language there is all the more reason that the terms to express it be incommensurable.[13] A compromise position would be to suggest that the terrain is transected by multiple incommensurable pairs. Indeed, I think it likely that the domain for "mind" will be constituted by multiple terms which arise in different historical circumstances (viz. the Arabic origins of Kibushy *rohu*) but which, since they are not commensurable, never quite displace each other. Thus body may be opposed to soul in some contexts and to mind in others. The foreign anthropologist who attempted to organize the English terms "mind, "soul," "spirit," "self," "ego," etc. into a paradigmatic set would have a difficult time of it.

Body and mind in body

I now turn, in equally condensed fashion, to practice, that is, to body and mind in body. If, from the perspective of mind, body and mind are incommensurable, from the perspective of body they are integrally related. The view that I present here is not (I hope) in contradiction to the previous discussion, but rather incommensurable with it.

Bodies serve as icons, indices, and symbols of society and also of individuals and of the relationships between them. But they are also something more. At the most basic level, in posture, adornment, and so on – but also in touching, in relative positioning, in gathering together, in coitus, in feeding and being fed, in working cooperatively and in consuming together, and again in refusal of engagement or consumption, in the maintenance of taboos, in all these situated practices – persons and ongoing social relationships are not simply signified but actively constituted. Their development is simultaneously established, enacted, charted – and naturalized or challenged, celebrated or mourned as well. If sociality is embodied, conversely human bodily activities are culturally mediated, hence infused with "mind."[14] At the same time, bodily action is critical to the constitution of the perceiving and thinking person.

In one of his formative essays, Mauss (1985) derived Western notions of the person from two sources, the dramatistic or performative and the jural. Unlike Mauss, we can take these to represent less distinct traditions, successive historical phases, or discrete types (status and contract; oral and literate; cold and hot; pre-modern and modern) than two poles of an ongoing dialectical relationship between embodiment and objectification which is operative in any society. In saying this I am drawing on the model so memorably developed by Berger and Luckmann (1966) but with a greater emphasis, deriving largely from Bourdieu, on the embodied, performative, mimetic nature of the internalization pole (1990).

Too often the person (and culture itself) has been identified uniquely with the objectifications, especially the mental ones encoded in language. Yet to have a social identity, as Fortes (1983) argued, requires embodying it in actions, putting your body where your mouth is, so to speak. Being a person requires in Bourdieu's phrase, a "feel for the game";

the values given body, *made* body, by the hidden persuasions of an implicit pedagogy which can instil a whole cosmology, through injunctions as insignificant as "sit up straight" or "don't hold your knife in your left hand", and inscribe the most fundamental principles of the arbitrary content of a culture in seemingly innocuous details of bearing or physical and verbal manners, so putting them beyond the reach of consciousness and explicit statement. (Bourdieu 1990: 69)

The habitus, Bourdieu tells us, is "embodied history, internalized as a second nature and so forgotten as history" (p. 56). At the same time, he makes a different point: this habitus is a locus of "dispositions . . . predisposed to function as structuring structures, that is, as principles which generate and organize practices and representations" (p. 53).

Elsewhere I have examined the way in which cultural rules, values, and social relations are embodied and thereby ostensibly naturalized by means of spirit possession (1992, 1993a). Following the lead of van Gennep (1904), I argued for the centrality of practicing and internalizing taboos in delimiting, differentiating, and thus ultimately constituting social persons, as selected aspects of the context are alternately incorporated or repulsed. As Alfred Gell put it: "outside the specific acts, obervances – and taboos – which specify a self as *my* self, there is nothing for an emblem of the self to be an emblem of." And further: "To observe a taboo is to establish an identifiable self by establishing a relationship...with an external reality such that the 'self' only comes into existence in and through this relationship" (1979:136). Moreover, if such acts constitute selfhood, they also, as Rappaport saw (1979), instantiate morality.

These arguments refer to the embodiment of selfhood and society. Here I want to turn to the other swing of the dialectic, the way embodied dispositions may "generate and organize" objectified representations, or as Jackson puts it, how "persons actively body forth the world" (1989:136). As Merleau-Ponty, from whose inspiration this position is derived, is a good deal more opaque to me than Malagasy spirit possession, I turn to an anecdote, drawn from my fieldnotes, to illustrate.

However in arguing that embodiment entails the conjunction of mind and body, I want to resist a completely smooth picture. Embodied practices are carried out by agents who can still think contemplatively; nothing "goes without saying" forever. The relation between conceptual objectification and embodied practices is always dynamic; there is always something that escapes or exceeds what is given from either side. The body provides objective limits to what can be embodied, and embodied performance provides more than the thought alone would. Yet as my vignette indicates, thought, too, pushes beyond the limits of the embodied performance, linking alternate embodiments.

French or Creole sailors from the pre-colonial period form one of the kinds of characters manifest in spirit possession by means of which the northern Sakalava of Madagascar imaginatively re-present and quite literally re-embody their history. The sailors are neither the most common nor the most important type of spirits in the city of Mahajanga, but in some mediums they serve as popular diviners and consultants, characters with whom one can chat more comfortably than the complex and powerful deceased Sakalava monarchs who comprise the main spirits.[15] In 1994 I visited a male medium whom I will call Ali who has a sailor spirit among the many spirits who possess him. Through his performance Ali brilliantly embodies the French sailor or bodies forth his world. When possessed by the Sailor (as I will refer to the spirit) he switches from Malagasy to a pungent, idiomatic, properly accented French. He changes into a blue and white striped sailor's shirt and jaunty blue hat with a red pompom. In contrast to the older Sakalava spirits who chew tobacco and drink rhum from the bottle, the Sailor chain-smokes cigarettes (sometimes he asks for menthol), and drinks his rhum from a glass. His bearing shifts as does his whole demeanor. The mimetic performance engages the entire body of the medium, drawing upon and transforming the senses, and constituting a new habitus. The bodily habitus in turn generates thought.

Let me quote an edited excerpt from my fieldnotes (July 27, 1994).

A young man accompanied me to the medium's house, ostensibly to show me the way, but also, it turned out, in order to pose his own question. The Sailor spirit lit up a cigarette and addressed my friend, Richar', in French. Thereafter their conversation was largely in French; Richar' indicated he was able to follow, but his own contribution was limited to monosyllables.

The Sailor began by remarking that we can only pray to God for what we want. He added that while religions are many, there is only the one God, le Bon Dieu. [Both Ali and Richar' are nominally Muslim.]

Richar' explained that he was having difficulty finding work on one of the small transport boats that ply the west coast of Madagascar.

The Sailor inquired whether he had his work papers, then picked up a deck of playing cards in order to perform divination.[16] "*Votre nom, monsieur?*" he asked politely.

"Richar'."

"Nothing more?"

"Théophile."

"*Ah, vous avez un joli nom* [You have a nice name]," opined the Sailor. He shuffled the cards, asked Richar' to cut, and then laid them out in a pattern. After a few more comments and questions he concluded, "You have luck. Wait a little and you'll have work." He added, "You think too much about your future, but one of these days it will come."

After a pause the Sailor suggested, this time in Malagasy, "You have a child out of wedlock (*bitiky an tany*)?"

"No. . . . Well, I might, but I don't know," said Richar' somewhat lamely.

"You must use a condom," responded the Sailor. "It's the fashion in Réunion."

"Corn silk (*volovolo n'tsakotsako*) worked as a medicine for syphilis," the Sailor went on, "but it won't work for AIDS (*SIDA*)." Offering us another drink of rhum and another cigarette, he began reminiscing about his ostensible experiences in the good old days. "Working in the boats, you travel. I have visited Singapore and Johannesburg when I was a sailor. Single men . . . one knows the malady . . . " But the Sailor's point was the radically changed implications of sexually transmitted diseases and the necessity today for proper protection against AIDS.

The Sailor made these observations in a droll French accent, but seriously, a little world weary. He continued that he was young himself [spirits remain the age at which they died, in his case around 35], but that he saw how young people today tend to forget the customs of their ancestors. "One must respect the ancestors. People here disrespect the [Malagasy] spirits, yet look at all the Comorians who come to them for advice."

Somewhat nonplussed by the direction of the conversation and hampered by his lack of facility in French, Richar' kept replying, "*Ah oui, c'est vrai.*"

The Sailor said, "I am more intelligent than my medium. (*Je suis plus intelligent que saha nakahy*)." He explained that the senior spirits [i.e. those from earlier times] could never understand about *SIDA* and condoms, whereas he warns people to stay with their spouses due to the spread of AIDS. Most people in Madagascar now use condoms, he observed. The other "sailors" also spread the warning.

Richar' then said he had been sick. At night he feels something moving up and down inside his body.

"You can't just eat anything or with anybody. . . Your stomach cannot support every kind of liquor. People can't drink like spirits. *Nous, c'est autre chose*; we drink and don't get drunk. The odor lingers but the effects disappear. . . [This is a salient means for expressing the local distinction between the host and spirit, hence between mind and body, while also illustrating for us their connection such that the meaning imposed on the context of drinking can offset the hangover.] *Rapellez les ancêtres. C'est eux qui étaient içi avant nous* (remember the ancestors; it is they who were here before us)."

Richar' brought the conversation back to his main concern, entreating that he might find work on a boat and that things would turn out well for him.

The Sailor replied, still in French, that this depended on "*la volonté de la personne, la volonté de Dieu* (the will of the person, the will of God). If you strive with your force, aim toward your goal, God will help you. You must not be jealous of other people. Do your own work, and you can succeed with the force that God has given you."

Warming to his subject and broadening the argument, the Sailor continued, "Malagasy shouldn't think they are better than each other. Malagasy tend to be competitive." He turned to me. "It's not like that between Toronto and Montreal. . . or Paris and Marseilles. That's why this country is in trouble."

"You young Malagasy are lucky; this is a good country (*vous avez [de] la chance; c'est un bon pays*)." He compared it with Kenya where people don't understand each other's languages and have to use English or Swahili. "But here in Madagascar, everyone can understand each other . . . "

Before we left the Sailor provided Richar' with more specific assurances about his future and further warnings about his behavior. Richar' having drunk several glasses of the rhum that was offered freely during the interview (and that, as was customary, we had provided to the spirit at the outset), the Sailor observed that he should watch his drinking.

Although a surprise to both of us, the lecture to Richar' embedded in the consultation appeared to be a natural pronouncement from the person of the worldly spirit. Indeed, a discussion of sexually transmitted diseases could have found no more appropriate spokesperson since, as his conversation made explicit, the Sailor was someone once associated with promiscuous sexual exploits himself. It is striking that this discourse was pronounced specifically by a sailor spirit rather than any other kind. The representation of AIDS appears to emerge directly from the habitus of the Sailor, the embodied condition or pre-objective giving rise spontaneously to the objectified discourse or at least having tremendous affinity with it. Yet at the same time, the Sailor's own experience is of a maritime culture that has largely passed. It is remarkable that any of the Sakalava spirits have begun talking about AIDS, keeping up with the times despite being voices from the past.

In a similar vein one can note how the embodiment of the Sailor's persona enables him to speak about "Madagascar," to construct "the Malagasy" as an object; he speaks of the nation from the perspective of a partial outsider. The Sailor also reflects on race (at one point he remarked "God created us all the same except the colour of our skins"); on ethnic politics (in his view the critical problem in Madagascar, despite the fact that people are closer linguistically than in many African countries); on religion (every religion has its forms of worship, its own sacred day, etc., but God is really One); and formulates a work ethic. It is ironic that his discussion of the fact that the Malagasy, unlike the Kenyans, do not need a lingua franca was conducted in French. As a voice of modernity, the Sailor is reminiscent of the Gebusi spirit described in Knauft's chapter. Regarding religion, the Muslim spirit medium can take on the voice of Christianity from within the Sakalava idiom of possession. His ecumenical point is prefigured in his practice.

The Sailor's ability to objectify was also apparent in a conversation we held the year before. On that occasion he explained how the Sailor spirits were all pro-French in their politics and had helped ensure the victory of the pro-French forces in neighbouring Mayotte.[17] "But then," he said, "I'm only a sailor (*un marin*) and don't mix in politics . . ." He went on to mention the malagasization policy in national education with reference to a female client who had come for assistance in passing her *bac*.

There is a wonderfully imaginative weaving of politics, positionality, and French culture in the Sailor's talk. To my ear he seemed to have the tone exactly right and he is also extremely charming in the role, exuding a confidence and a sparkle that are absent from Ali's ordinary speech. Indeed, the Sailor went on to apply his insights to the medium, saying that he [the Sailor] had taught Ali some French. Ali had been an art student in Antananarivo in his youth. The Sailor took down Ali's portfolio. As we looked over the rather mediocre drawings, the Sailor said of Ali, "*Il n'avait pas de talent, peut-être, mais il s'amusait* . . . (He had no talent, perhaps, but he enjoyed himself)."

We see in the performance a unity of mind and body, exactly the sort of *savoir faire* and feel for the rules of the game that Bourdieu describes or the bodying forth that Jackson makes claims for. The spirit's speech seems intrinsically connected to the embodied comportment, emerging from the habitus established by the state of possession. Yet there are several qualifications. First, it is not trance *per se*, trance viewed as an abstract physiological state, but meaningful possession by a particular kind of spirit, a garrulous French one, that establishes the spirit's discourse. Had Ali been possessed by one of his other spirits, the politics expressed would have been of a rather different order.[18] Second, whatever may be pre-objective *vis-à-vis* what is enunciated is at the same time post-objective, as it were, *vis-à-vis* the cultural model of the sailor that Ali embodies. What bodies forth is in relation to what has been embodied – the persona of the Sailor himself. Moreover, the body from which the Sailor speaks is not the body that slept with prostitutes across the ports of the Indian Ocean. The mimesis of alterity, to recombine Taussig's terms (1993), is not a quality of the "mindful body" (Lock and Scheper-Hughes 1987) alone. While mimesis, in Plato's formulation, is opposed to contemplative reason (Havelock 1963) and, in arguments like Stoller's (1995) or Taussig's, to purely discursive reason, we see here that possession enables Ali to take a more distanciated position *vis-à-vis* society and the self (see also Corin's chapter for a similar point). To put this in Weberian language, it is from the very position of enchantment, that the rationalized discourse of modernity emerges. The Sailor declares himself more intelligent than his medium and in commenting on Ali's art career engages in remarkable self-objectification; he comments reflectively on contemporary politics and religion; with the cosmopolitanism of a French sailor he can refer with ease to the anthropologist's home in Canada; and he makes a specific and quite deliberate intervention with regard to his client's sexual practice.

It is quite right that it should be the sailor spirit who propagates AIDS prevention, even though "in our day the problem was only syphilis and there is medicine for that." The worldly cosmopolitanism of the Sailor contrasts with the fear and chauvinism of several of the older Sakalava spirits. Yet Ali also embodies some of these other spirits and thus at times speaks in different voices. Possessed by a spirit from an earlier epoch I once heard him stumble playfully over the word for a cigarette lighter. Each voice emerges from its habitus and is closely connected to it. But too great an emphasis on the smooth unfolding of embodied dispositions would be to underplay the agency, acuity, and artistry of the particular virtuoso.

Stepping back from this case, and even from the entire subject of spirit possession, it is the particular constitution of the dialectic of body and mind in practice, the means, performative obligations and possibilities, and the particular dynamic trajectories they establish in a given society that are of interest; the ways in which they shape experience, model personhood and social connection, and underpin political, moral, religious, and therapeutic agency and institutions and their changing relations. Persons, and ultimately society itself, are the product (even as they are also the producers). But embodied personhood always leaves open the possibility, via one cultural medium or another, for self-reflection and for grasping the implications of such possibility.

A further implication is that the dialectic of embodiment and objectification is critically implicated in the production of social difference and hierarchy, even as distinctions of gender, class, and nationality can be temporarily transcended or reversed via media such as spirit possession. The question then arises, as contemporary feminist thought well recognizes, whether and in what manner mind / body issues, problems, and practices are themselves gendered, racialized, etc. One might also want to investigate comparatively the ways consistency and redundancy of metaphoric predication (Fernandez 1974), pervasiveness and scope of liturgical order (Rappaport 1979), coherence and integration of habitus (Bourdieu 1990), or cultural (over)determination of embodied selfhood (Boddy 1989) are implicated as well as how they are undermined or offset by commoditization, heteroglossia (Besnier 1996), fragmentation (Mageo and Howard 1996), indeterminacy and conjunction of disparate or incommensurable forms (Lambek 1993a).

Conclusion

I have tried to clarify recent discussion by distinguishing arguments about mind and body from the perspective of mind from arguments that begin with the body. Regarding the former, I have argued that dualism ought to be understood in terms of incommensurability. Regarding the latter, I have argued that monism needs to be opened up by means of a dialectic of objectification and embodiment.

In distinguishing mind and body in practice from their place in thought I have, of course, merely been repeating the mind/body opposition at another level of abstraction. Paradox remains intact, only redescribed. My point, once again, is that the focus on practice and the focus on thought are neither mutually exclusive nor redundant, but incommensurable with one another, covering the ground in different kinds of ways. It is as misleading to try and understand thought and practice in isolation from one another as it is to attempt this with mind and body. But, by the same token, it is misleading to attempt to conflate them or to imagine one could capture them within the same structure. While the turn to practice theory has been tremendously important in transcending certain stubborn oppositions, notably between materialist and idealist and between objectivist and subjectivist positions, it would be a mistake to use it to conceal or deny the relevance of Weber's basic insight concerning the ubiquity of rationalization (as understood in its most general sense as contemplative reason). To depict a pre-rationalized, seamlessly embodied world of practice – whether it be that of the Kabyle or Balinese, of Bavarian peasants, or of any group of pre-colonial Africans or Melanesians – is a tremendous intellectual and literary feat, but it is also to risk a serious romanticization. Despite their convergence in practice and occasionally in non-Western poetry (e.g. Weiner 1991) or philosophy, mind and body (in their various cultural transmutations) also remain distinguishable in thought.[19] Such thought is not only characteristic of modernity, though heightened and given precedence here; it is not simply the distinguishing feature of some great divide between the West and the rest, but fundamentally characteristic of the human condition.[20] Indeed for Weber, rationalization may be a product of the very mind/body split (in his particular formulation) that we have been addressing.[21] I am partial here to Gadamer's "conviction[s] that philosophy is a human experience that remains the same and that characterizes the human being as such, and that there is no progress in it, but only participation" (1986:6).

If personhood, selfhood, and sociality impart meaning to the body, its components and substances, forces and capacities, and enable the body, following Durkheim's classic argument, to transcend itself, the reverse is true as well. Embodiment surpasses language, rules, ideal models; the performance is always more than the script. The richness of embodiment is perhaps only now being grasped and celebrated in anthropology. And yet one can go too far. The very emphasis on the body risks reproducing, and possibly even exaggerating, the Cartesian dualism that proponents of theories of the body have set out to transcend. The task is not to reverse the values of the equation, to celebrate body at the expense of mind – though that is perhaps something to attract deskbound intellectuals – but to see them always in light of each other. In the end it is not to transcend dualism at all so much as to see it as endlessly rich and productive of a central dialectic in the ongoing constitution of human culture, society, and experience (and hence of anthropological theory).

It is relevant in this regard to note a curious feature of current debate. Anthropologists who oppose dualism do so in order to challenge reductionist conceptions of the body, whereas philosophers who defend dualism do so in order to challenge reductionist conceptions of mind. In a sense, both have a common enemy, namely physicalism (Smythies and Beloff 1989; cf. Searle 1997). Thus when anthropologists advocate monism, the monism they have in mind is certainly not the monism of contemporary materialists characteristic, for example, of much of the work in artificial intelligence (and which, I assume, they would see as a pathological consequence of Cartesian dualism). The question, however, is whether they can transcend dualism in a nonreductive way.

Finally, the very success of the Artificial Intelligence paradigm and of neuroscience suggests a possible note of historical irony regarding my own argument. Nineteenth century anthropologists such as Tylor discovered the soul as the defining feature of "primitive religion" at the very moment the soul and the discourses of theology and philosophy in which it was embedded were being displaced in Europe by the psychological sciences of memory (Hacking 1996). The concept of the soul came thereby to stand for the specifically "pre-Cartesian" nature of primitive thought (just as "mind" may invoke a specifically Cartesian view) and hence was defined with reference to the very opposition it was claimed not to have understood. It could be that once again ideas that are out of use in the hegemonic disciplines get displaced onto anthropology and projected outside the West. Anthropology is notorious for seizing hold of things only at their point of vanishing (Ivy 1995). But whether or not this is to anthropology's discredit is another question.

NOTES

1 My thanks to Paul Antze, Laurie Arnold, Maurice Bloch, Jackie Solway, Andrew Strathern, George Ulrich, and Anne Vallely for incisive, extremely helpful, and justifiably severe comments on various drafts. Doubtless there remains much that would leave them unsatisfied in this one. Versions of the chapter were presented at the annual meeting of the American Anthropological Association, November 1994, and as a public lecture at the London School of Economics, May 13, 1997. I first heard the joke from my colleague Tom McFeat.

2 The depiction is from Shaffer (1967) who provides a useful overview of Western philosophical thought on the issue.

3 We need also to allow for multiple formulations within any given society and the effects of their institutionalization in domains such as medicine. Likewise, we have to distinguish, at the very least, between the formulations of people when they are thinking more reflectively and when they are simply trying to get something done. The debate between Gyekye (1995) and Appiah (1992) on the presence of dualism among the Akan is relevant here (cf. Kwame 1995).

4 Commensurability lies at the heart of what Lévi-Strauss means by a structure. We can argue about *what* the common measure is – in the case of death, cessation of breathing, heart beat, brain waves, etc. – without doubting that there is a binary distinction. It is possible that nature / culture provides another example of an incommensurable pair.

5 What Murphy's account illustrates is neither the exclusion of mind from body nor a fundamental opposition between them, but rather the breakdown of the socially relevant dialectic of embodiment and objectification.

6 Kuhn (1970:148) as cited by Bernstein (1983:81), Bernstein's italics.

7 For Descartes mind and body are nonidentical and the content of each might be described as incommensurable with one another. But the tendency in post-Cartesian thought to emphasize the exclusive properties of each presupposes incompatability (rather than incommensurability), while attempts to characterize the boundary between them in positive and unilateral terms, whether to shore it up or to conflate or substantively mediate it, assume commensurability. However, it is not my intention here to depict the bulk of Western philosophy since Descartes is mistaken or naive on this matter. Shaffer ends his review of the philosophical literature with the remarkable comment that: "It may well be that the relation between mind and body is an ultimate, unique, and unanalyzable one. If so, philosophical wisdom would consist in giving up the attempt to understand the relation in terms of other, more familiar ones and accepting it as the anomaly it is" (1967:v, 344).

8 The urgency derives, of course, from the culture of Occidental science with its assumptions about nature. "Mind" presents an unstable category for science. Claims that the objects of science are all reducible to number or measure – commensurability in the most literal sense – transform the study of soul or mind into "behaviour." My thanks to Paul Antze for this point.

9 This view is elaborated in the conclusion to Lambek (1993a). It should be noted that I use incommensurability somewhat differently from LiPuma in the present book.

10 Hence the criticism of "comparing apples and oranges" is misphrased; we compare them all the time (for example, when we choose what to eat). What is invalid, however, is submitting them to a single common measure (cf. Lambek 1991).

11 This point can also be made by comparison of the historical transformations of the issue within Western philosophy (cf. Taylor 1989).

12 There is a parallel with "nature / culture" (and also, as Astuti suggests in her chapter, with sex / gender) although the debate about these terms foundered in relativism when, in response to Ortner's formulation (1974), it was discovered that the terms did not fit precisely onto each other in other cultures (MacCormack and Strathern 1980). It is only from an objectivist perspective that one would ever have expected them to.

13 Conversely, if mind / body dualism is rooted in language I am more likely to be wrong in claiming incommensurability. Here my position is doubly removed from that of Lévi-Strauss since he begins with dualism as a property of mind or language, rooted in binary oppositions, rather than of the phenomenal world (1963), and since he then assumes, at least in some places in his work (1972), a parallelism or consistency between the structure of language and the world of which it speaks. I assume an initial and fundamental incommensurability between language and world.

14 See Geertz (1973) for an evolutionary argument establishing that the human brain is culturally mediated and Sahlins (1976b) for the demonstration that practice is culturally mediated.

15 The sailors appear to be from Ste. Marie, an island that long saw the intermixing of French and Malagasy, producing a sort of Creole culture. According to an account that Ali gave me on another occasion they were under the employ of a nineteenth-century Sakalava king (Ndramañavaka) when their boat was wrecked and they drowned between Madagascar and Mayotte. The sailors are also found on Mayotte as the *changizy* spirits (Lambek 1981).

16 Divination by means of playing cards is a common practice, not limited to the sailor spirits.

17 This refers to struggles over three decades in Mayotte to ensure special status with France rather than incorporation in the independent republic of the Comores (cf. Lambek 1995).

18 There is a kind of spirit for virtually every political persuasion, though the spirits are not the direct product of political interest. That possession does not merely enumerate ethnic or historical types, but appropriates their voices and their perspectives on politics and history thereby constructing a complex heteroglossia and multi-levelled historical consciousness, is the subject of my ongoing work in Madagascar (Lambek in press).

19 Weeratunge-Starkloff (pers. comm.) has cautioned that the characterization of South Asian thought as monist is a form of orientalizing. See also Parry (1989).

20 I draw here on the fundamental (profound and necessary) ambiguity of Weber's concept (cf. Lambek 1989). It is perhaps for *individuating* minds rather than in simply distinguishing mind from the more manifestly individuated body that Occidental modernity ought to be acknowledged, less the

mind/body opposition than its containment within highly individuated, internally complete, and unique beings, a process whose development Mauss briefly charts (1985). Taylor's lengthier account of the emergence of the inwardness of the modern self (1989) is complementary to this, while Leenhardt provides a suggestive formulation of the emergence of the individuation of the Melanesian body (1979 [1947]). See also LiPuma this volume. Another trail would pursue the shift in the balance of authority placed on knowing *how* (both *techne* and *phronesis*), knowledgeable practice, relative to knowing *that* (*scientia*), abstract knowledge. Foucault (1980) makes suggestive remarks along these lines that perhaps have not yet been sufficiently explored by anthropologists.

21 My thanks to Anne Vallely for the point.

Part II

Transitions, containments, decontainments

6 Treating the affect by remodelling the body in a Yaka healing cult

René Devisch

It is in the interplay of physical links and individualizing relationships a person weaves through the mother's lineage with the *uterine* source of life and the primary and fusional object that the Yaka culture in Kinshasa and south-west Congo (formerly called Zaire) localizes the origins of serious illness, infirmity, and also madness.[1] By contrast, links of *agnatic* filiation issuing from the founder ancestor of the patriline define the social identity and norms: it is before the fathers and the paternal ancestry that the ideal versus deviant traits of the social subject are being defined. The social role and the identity processes are elaborated in the centre of public life and are conducted by the male patriarchs. They ensure that the social subject is assimilated into a system of filiation and seniority, most particularly through the ritualized imposition of a name, circumcision, and initiation into adolescence, as well as through political power (palaver, jurisdiction, and enthronement), marriage and bereavement, and the practices of competition, solidarity, and exchange (Devisch 1988).

The interweave between body and culture, the body's contact or experiencing zones and the cultural modelling, is studied here in the context of a therapeutic cult that operates and is transmitted through links of matrilineal or uterine descent. This initiatory therapy is organized on the margins of the established society (Devisch 1993a). Such therapeutic cults reenact, so to speak, the birth of the initiated into physical and social life: they reelaborate his various forms of contact, envelopment, and exchange on the sensory level. They take the individual back to the point of emergence from the primary processes and reweave his or her most vital links, such as those between mother and child, brother and sister, uncle and nephew / niece. They envelop the patient in a feminine, uterine, mothering universe, while bringing into play a concentric and cyclical time-space. This regenesis and resourcing of the "person" takes place, then, on the margins or in the background of daily community life and is elaborated at one and the same time on the bodily level, on the group level and in relationship to the world. In contrast, it is in public time-space, before the agnatic ancestral authorities and within relationships of seniority and masculine power, that the roles of the "social subject," the discourse of authority and the gaze appropriate to "super-vision" are brought into play.

There are among the Yaka some fifteen great cults (*phoongu*) or thera-peutic brother- and sisterhoods more or less equal in scope, half of which are at the same time possession cults. These therapies proceed like passage rites, ritually inducing the ill person to die in his former condition and be reborn into a new one. Following a fusion with the group, accomplished with the aid of vibrations, rhythms, music and culminating in a trance-possession, the patient undergoes a seclusion lasting from one week to several months, in the presence of a dozen or so statuettes or figurines, which lie on a bed parallel to his own. The play of mirrors between the figurines and the patient mobilizes his sensory perceptions and body movements. The figurines therefore take on the function of doubles that the patient incorporates[2] or inscribes in his bodily envelope that serves as his interface with others (Csordas 1990). Through a verbal liturgy that evolves to the rhythm of the initiation, the initiate begins to incorporate – and to some extent decode, although without knowing it – the traces of the imaginary or collective unconscious conveyed by these figurines and this liturgy. Thus the figurines serve increasingly as poles of specular identification.

The *mbwoolu* figurines enact a cosmogony, intimately associating the patient with it throughout. This phylo- and ontogenetic evolution fo-cuses on the gradual transition from the silurid to the complete, sexual-ized and adult human being, founder of family and generations, and vested with social roles. By manipulating these objects, and covering them with red paste before coating his own body with this substance, as well as by addressing a ritual discourse to them that becomes ever more elaborate, the ill person incorporates the form and the "in-formation" of these traditional figures. At the same time, he associates himself with the phylogenetic passage from the imaginary to the symbolic, as well as from the sensory to the verbal and the tactile to the figurative. Similarly, he associates himself with the ontogenetic passage from a fusional state toward a sexualized identity with precise contours, situated within a social hierarchy and a historicity of generations and of roles. It is in relation to this central theme that I will describe first the ethnography of the cult.

It remains to sketch out the status of representation and discourse in the oral-based or non-literate culture of the Yaka. The culture has barely evolved a cognitive technology of "re-presentation" or of distancing in relation to bodily experience and the habitus. In such a culture, speech is as much a set of acquired skills, as the province of a "creative bricolage" (to paraphrase Lévi-Strauss) of meaning, using the means at one's disposal. At the commencement of their gatherings, family patriarchs define the art of palaver, saying: "We are here to produce in speech the way of things / the new social reality" (*Thuna ha muyidika maambu*). In oral culture, it is in the very saying of things that they are done and they are done by no other means: speaking is doing. Speaking, then, has its own finality, whereas in written culture, speaking – like writing itself – is often only instrumental in nature: speech expresses information, a point of view. Unlike in written cultures, orality rarely leads to "representation," that is, the introduction of some sort of project, intention, or scenario for an objective re-presentation between the experience of a thing and the saying of it. What is more, it is the modality of the spoken – who is speaking, to whom, when, under what modality, according to what order of priority – rather than the objective information itself that counts and that is, when appropriate, the object of sanction. Speech weaves a tissue of life, rather than an exchange of information. The untimely, offensive, over-excited utterance, or one spoken in anger, is a symptom of folly. In pursuing their routine duties of wickerwork or hut building, and most especially hunting, or in relating their exploits, the men rarely express themselves in referential representations. Moreover, in the context of therapeutic cults, speech is very symbolic and fixed in character. Just as the traditional therapies themselves accord only a very limited place to speech – which is, furthermore, very codified in the rite – the patient is reticent about verbalizing his actual experience in referential representations. Hardly fifteen days after the therapy, the therapist, finding himself now out of context and out of practice, is unable to explain what he did; he either has to return to the scene, or repeat certain gestures and reproduce something of the rite's mood before being able to communicate the details. In therapy, it is neither the representation nor the narration that predominates, but the interweaving of practice, meaning, the imaginary register, and libidinal forces: that is, the "inter-animation" of body, group, and world.

The identity composed of knots and weavings

In the light of the underlying metaphors, to become a person (*wuka muutu*) is to enter an interplay of multiple sensory, sexual, and verbal tissues. It is to knot those transmitter exchanges of life, emotion, forces, knowledge, and this essentially between agnatic and uterine parents, between the living and the ancestors, between human beings and the water and forest spirits, between man and environment. Paradoxically, a person's center of gravity is formed not starting from the individual and his deepest self, but essentially in the practice of exchange and "inter-animation." The individual's center of gravity (*muutu*) is to be found on the skin level, with its capacities for sensory and sexual contact, that is, at the interface (*luutu*) of all exchanges with the other and the world. He becomes a person who is successful in the hunt, who excels in the physical and social reproduction of the group, and whose appeal when met, as well as whose knowledge and authoritative speech, ties in, bonds, and stimulates. To become a person is to be connected, bonded, and tied into and with those multiple forms of reproduction and exchange that give form to the Yaka universe. Yaka culture regards such reciprocity as an extremely vital tissue of ties or articulations in and between the spheres of body, family, and the world. The more the individual enters into these multi-relational spheres, the more he constitutes an identity known to many, the more their gazes and their words refer him back to himself and reaffirm him in his identity as it evolves from sociocentric to egocentric. The Yaka identity is structured as an envelope and a link, that is, a knot (*-biinda*) in a weaving of superimposed layers. The Western perspective that situates the identity in a nucleus derived from an internalization, introjection, and projective identification does not accommodate the Yaka perspective.

Everything harmful to life is conceived in terms of thievery or sorcery, themes that serve in fact to conceptualize the origin and nature of numerous illnesses. The effect of a theft or a spell, as well as of an illness, is associated with a knot tied too tightly or too loosely. Illness is seen, just as is madness, either as a kink (*yibiinda, -biindama*) or binding that blocks (*-loka*) vital links, or as an untied knot, a tangled interlacing that impedes the exchange between body, group, and world. Illness is seen either as a torsion, as something that obstructs, encloses, enlaces, or as an intemperance, a dissolution, a dispersal, an effusion (*n-luta, phalu*), or again as an inversion of the normalized movement of the transactions of the bodily orifices (for example, vomiting, ejaculation outside coitus, fellatio, flatulence during a meal). All serious perturbations in the exchanges normalized by the culture can be symptoms of madness; for example, when the boundaries of the body are compromised or eradicated by the effects of an oral or sexual "bulimia," or when the body closes in on itself ("when the heart shuts up on itself like a bundle of cassava paste"). A chaos-generating confusion (*mbeembi*) evoking madness can result from an intrusion of the sexual or the anal into the sphere of nourishment. Sexual allusion during the preparation or consumption of family meals, the act of cooking during menstruation, obscene attitudes and gestures are all the more polluting and pathological when they occur in the zones of transition themselves. Adultery in the conjugal home, or the placement of excrements at the entrance of a home (a maternal space), as well as any other obscene act in this place (particularly on the part of a man who, for example, exhibits his bare bottom) signals the irruption of something that falls short of the social, of an alarming, chaos-generating power; these are the acts of an individual not in possession of himself, who is outside himself, ensorcelled, psychotic. Numerous metaphors concerning knots, the action of tying, interlacing, and weaving, are the basis of many Yaka therapies and rituals aimed at intensifying life, fecundity, the wellbeing of the group. Thus, for example, a course of therapy normally ends by a reknotting of conjugal ties, called "mutual incitement to an interlacing of legs."

The *cults of affliction* (*phoongu*) aim at reweaving the interanimation between body, group, and world (Devisch 1990). These cults pertain to translineage and interregional traditions in the Bantu cultural zone. Some cults have spread from the equator down to the Cape of Good Hope (Balandier 1965; Buakasa 1973; Janzen 1982b, 1991; Lima 1971; Turner 1968; Van Wing 1959; Yoder 1981).

Here, I will deal only with *mbwoolu*, one of among the some fifteen affliction cults to be found in Yakaland. It is a major possession (*phoongu yakhaluka*) and healing cult (*phoongwa mooyi*). I am drawing on my own observation in rural northern Yakaland (in 1972–4 and 1991), and on annual sojourns of some four to seven weeks, since 1986, in Kinshasa. Here the *mbwoolu* cult also remains popular among the older population. Both its ritual tradition and the ills it addresses are transmitted along uterine lines.

Mbwoolu addresses primarily a set of symptoms of "lack of form," "not fully shaped," and forms of anxiety and nightmares related to haunting rivers, that is to the primary fusional object. It first concerns the disabled and rehabilitation patients, particularly those new-born whose "skull is considered too weak (*bula*)" or children who "fail to crawl or stand upright" at an appropriate age. It may also be sought for the healing of motor problems due to birth or misfortune, such as growth defects, polio, anemia, accidents, stiffness or pains in the joints, and lack of erection. The *mbwoolu* cult is secondarily invoked in the treatment of grave and chronic fevers, particulary those occuring in children or due to sleeping sickness (*maniimba*) or malaria. In these cases it seeks to stabilize forms of serious humoral disequilibrium, to regain a balance of the wet/dry elements of the body. The symptoms of such an imbalance may include exceptional emaciation, especially in women, and/or chronic diarrhoea accompanied by bleeding and white stools, black urine, a chronic and productive cough with fever, and river blindness (literally "eyes that died out"). Thirdly, the cult seeks to heal persons suffering from a major "implosion," namely who have lost self-esteem or feel as if living outside of themselves. They may feel engulfed by frightening nightmares related to some "White Man" ("from across the ocean"), to dark ravines and haunting rivers, or to having capsized in a pirogue and thrashing helplessly about in deep waters. Such recurring nightmares may variously depict ominous encounters with snakes in the bush or the house, or being struck by lightning.

Mbwoolu proves itself to be very popular for it is practiced in almost every village of northern Yakaland as well as among the older generation of Yaka who have emigrated to Kinshasa. I was informed that the *mbwoolu* was initially known to the Mfunuka, Huumbu, and Zoombu populations to the north of the Yaka from where it dispersed over the whole of the Yaka region; this corroborates information supplied to Bourgeois (1978–9), De Beir (1975:46), Huber (1956), and Vorbichler (1957).

Mbwoolu is considered closely related to the *khita* cult (Devisch 1993a). The latter provides for the initiatory treatment of gynecological difficulties (including amenorrhea, dysmenorrhea, barrenness, premature birth, still-birth or the repeated death of unweaned infants) as well as the permanent congenital anomalies of the deformed, albinos, dwarfs, and twins. *Mbwoolu* is similar to the *(ma)haamba* rite practiced in the Luunda cultural zone of Angola, Congo, and Zambia (Lima 1971; Turner 1968; Yoder 1981). Another major possession-cult is that of *ngoombu*. It is practiced in view of curing patients prone to hysteria and epileptic spasms, crises which frequently manifest an individual's vocation as medium or diviner. Several other cults, like *khosi, mbaambi, haamba*, and *n-luwa* address symptoms of mental illness. More than the other spirit cults, these are invoked for the purposes of cursing and effecting extrahuman retaliation. Apart from these possession cults, there exist in the Yaka therapeutic traditions the *phoongu zan-niku*, literally the "healing cults which basically rely on the use of medicinal preparations"; these involve both the use of medicinal substances and the transmission of initiatory knowledge and skills. It is the *n-khanda* which, of all the cults, offers the most elaborate ritual constellation. This is particularly evident in the circumcision ritual practiced there, along with the subsequent parade of the masks, and in the treatments offered for impotence or broken limbs. There are, moreover, minor forms of therapeutic assistance, e.g. those of reconciliation and purification which aim at rendering harmless those forces that are attributed to sorcery, curse, or infringement. There are countless medicinal preparations, some of which involve medicinal incantations to invoke the powers of the ingredients.

The social context

Approximately 400,000 Yaka presently inhabit wooded steppes and savannah land of the Kwaango region of western Bandundu, an area of
southwestern Congo bordering Angola. Yaka culture is partly the outcome of a prolonged interplay of Koongo domestic traditions and Luunda
feudal political institutions above the village level (Devisch 1988). In rural
Yakaland women practice subsistence agriculture, whereas hunting is
men's most prized productive activity. In Kinshasa, the Yaka population
is estimated at some 300,000. The rich cultural and artistic traditions of
the Yaka people are well known, and in particular the healing cults.

Yaka society is organized in segmentary patrilineages (Devisch
1993a:115 ff.). The individual inherits his or her social attributes, i.e.
name, status, and privileges, through his or her agnatic ascendants.
Extended families live as corporate groups which are formed according to
patrilineal descent and patrilocal residence. A single village may number
from one to two hundred adults and children. They are usually divided
among three to six extended families, each of which is headed by an elder
whose authority derives from seniority.

The northern Yaka recognize uterine descent as well, however. It is
believed that physical and innate characteristics, such as health, blood,
and inborn capacities (*yibutukulu*), are passed on to the individual primarily through maternity and the uterine line. These attributes originate
from a source of life conventionally associated with the individual's
matrilateral great-grandmother. The Yaka in fact express uterine descent
relations in terms of an idiom emphasizing the corporeality that characterizes the mother–child relationship. Siblings "coming from the one
womb" share privileged bonds of warmth, trust, and mutual help in the
household, together with their genitors and dependants. Maternal relations delimit and found relations in the domestic realm as well as in the
seclusion phase of the rites of passage. They therefore govern principles of
bodily contact, food supply and cooking, commensality, and so on.
Uterine relations and co-initiates may thus share their vital force, weaken-
ing or strengthening each other, through the exercise of these same bodily
activities. Personal skills as well as aptitude for the roles of divination and
healing are also believed to be passed down through the uterine line.

The healing: a sequential and semantic approach

The *mbwoolu* therapeutic treatment entails seven sequences evolving as a
rite of passage. Although it is agreed that "there are many ways of
organizing the same therapeutic initiation" (*tsakulu tsakulu*), I will first of

all attempt to disclose the overall pattern of the *mbwoolu* ritual of initiation.

Sequence 1 : The etiological diagnosis and the arrival of the maternal uncle and the healer

Inasmuch as the Yaka consider prosperous health as a quality of good kin ties, ill health is similarly seen as a problem among consanguines. Symptoms of physical disorder, bodily deficits, and other alterations of health become socially alarming when they begin to hinder the individual in the accomplishment of his or her tasks. This occurs, for example, when bodily impairments exclude the patient from appropriate social interaction and involvement in the sphere of daily life.

The uncle, the husband, or the father and occasionally also other kinsfolk examine the family history, the fields of extrahuman forces, and authority relations within the kin susceptible of having caused the affliction or of being disturbed by it. If the illness is lasting or severe, family elders will call upon a mediumistic diviner to divulge the origin and meaning of the affliction in the family history (Devisch 1991). This enterprise is paradoxical: it is the diviner's task to situate the origin of the client's affliction in a field of extrahuman forces, notably of sorcery and spirits, while at the same time unmasking the complicity and disastrous effects in the fabric of family relations. The diviners interpret *mbwoolu* illnesses primarily as forms of retaliation relative to an attack on the underlying social order. This attack may be defined as theft or more commonly as an "intrusion upon conjugal rights" (*yidyaata*), which are protected by *mbwoolu*. The misdemeanor itself usually has been committed by one of the patient's uterine or agnatic ascendants. Elders of the patient's family subsequently invite a therapist, who himself once suffered from the same ailment, to organize the very *mbwoolu* treatment by which he was initiated into the art of healing.

Before turning the patient over to a *mbwoolu* therapist, the family group invites the patient's maternal uncle to participate. In his position as the one who has given his sister for marriage, and in relation to her offspring, the uncle represents the relations of descent between the generations, as well as the tie between brother and sister, ascendant and descendant, mother's brother and sister's children. Having liquidated the tensions and significant problems within the group concerned with the afflicted person, the family heads offer the uncle a payment in order that he remove all possible obstacles to the cure. This event is usually planned for a new moon and is held in the presence of the whole village community that has assembled near the house of seclusion.

A therapist, chosen from outside the circle of close kin, has meanwhile been invited to organize the cure. He only treats the ailment he himself or his mother before giving birth to him once suffered from; this is of course the very treatment that initiated him or his mother into the therapeutic art. (Although all initiated therapists in the rural areas are masculine, several Yaka women beyond child-bearing age act as therapists in Kinshasa; this is possible since the therapeutic treatment in the healing cult is the equivalent of professional initiation.) When arriving on the spot, the therapist may, in a trance-like manner, display the symptoms that led to his mother's or his own initiatory treatment. He thereby displays a concrete model for the symptoms and the initiatory cure. For the time of the cure, the therapist assumes a transitional and emancipatory role of the maternal uncle of the patient, literally of "male mother, male spouse, male source" (Devisch 1990). Just as the uncle, he symbolically integrates a double, hence androgynous function. In his *maternal* function, the therapist represents the patient's genitrix, as well as the group which has married off the genitrix. He thereby offers an individualizing identification model and assumes the patient's desire for symbiosis with the uterine source of life. The ties he sets out with the patient are playful and intimate, as for example through touch and massage.

On the other hand, the therapist shows his more virile and *paternal* function, his professional competence and the norms and their sanctions transmitted in the uterine line that he exemplies. To testify to this, he holds in his right hand the insignia which recall his initiation, namely his pharmacopoeia witnessing to his initiatory knowledge and his prerogatives. The therapist undertakes the healing as a representative of an ancient therapeutic tradition or of a venerable and sacred healing cult. As such, he is able to provide protection against particular contingencies and whims.

Sequence 2: The installation of the initiatory house

The therapist's activity occurs in and around the seclusion house, called *luumbu*: it is either the patient's dwelling, or a hut built or transformed specifically for the cure. On the eve of the initiation and in the presence of the patient's uncle and family, the therapist begins to "bound off" (-*siinda*) and to "protect" (-*sidika*) the ritual space against sorcerers and malefic influences. The therapist acts here as a hunter or a trapper, taming and trapping the evil or the disease in a way analogous to the snaring of a wild animal in a trap, the greed or envy of the evildoer – alike of the game – being the very trap. With this in mind, a long liana vine is hung along the front and back walls of the dwelling and attached to the centre pole supporting the roof. A second vine is attached to the roof and side-walls perpendicular to the first. The vine transforms the hut into something of a mortuary house, since it is the same liana, of the species *n-singa phemba*, which is laid in a similar manner over the corpse wrapped in the mortuary cloth. The therapist plants the *khoofi* in front of the dwelling while "reciting the ancestral origin of his art" (*-bula n-taandu*). The *khoofi* is essentially a bundle of three sticks of different species to which is added at the base some riverplants, old palmnut pits, nailclippings from the respective initiates and some *khawa* ("explosive elements used in ritual arms"). This device is intended to declare to all living above and below the earth that an initiation is about to commence; it equally prevents any ill-meaning interference.

It is on the morning of the intiation that the therapist digs out the so-called *mbwoolu* pits (*mawulu mambwoolu; myeewu*), but not before having planted the ritual cane (*mbvwaala* or *khuumbu*) at the centre of the site. This cane is actually a savannah liana which often binds one tree to taller ones or holds a tree at an inclination. The therapist adds some stimulants and food offerings (*ndzaku ye bikwaama*) to the hole left as he plunges the cane in the ground and withdraws it. He repeats this gest three times in anticipation of plenty of blessing. The therapist then digs a pit, some four or five feet in width and four feet deep, close to the eastern wall on the outside of the seclusion house. The pit is surrounded by a high circular or rectangular fence of poles and palm leaves extending from the hut. The therapist then sets about making four niches, literally mouths (*n-nwa*), to the centre of each wall at the bottom of the pit. He there conceals *mbwoolu* figurines with the aid of vegetation from the river. The figurines have either been freshly carved by one of the patient's kinsmen or some may have been renewed following their inheritance from a deceased *mbwoolu* initiate. The initiate will be able to squat on another large figurine from the *mbu*-series (see below) which has been laid in the middle of the pit. The cane, to which has been added the ritual arms (*mateenda*) by attaching a liana to its upper end, is planted to the southern and frontside of the pit. The therapist's incantations, the statuettes, and the cane with its ritual arms all work to transform the pit into a protected or sacred space (*-siinda mawulu*).

Sequence 3: The initiates' river journey

The initiation ceremony itself commences only in the afternoon when "the sun anoints itself with *khula*-red"; this takes place around five o'clock. All of the participants congregate around the entrance to the seclusion house. They include the *mbwoolu* therapist of course, known by the ritual name of *n-luula*, and a young male or female servant, whose respective titles are Mapolu or Matsaayi. The patient is referred to as *n-twaphoongu*, literally the cult's head or face. A title is also given to the husband or father of the patient as "the person responsible for the afflicted" (*n-kwambeefu* or *taa khuula*). One other important relative is in attendance: the owner or lineage representative responsible for the cult, *pfumwa phoongu*; this is the patient's mother or brother representing the line of descent, usually matrilineal, through which the *mbwoolu* is active. These key participants are joined by many other family members who take up chanting initiation songs, some of which are common to various cults (De Beir 1975: 56ff., Devisch 1993a).

The patient enters the pit; sometimes the lineage head, along with the mother should the patient be female, and a servant also join in. Each of them squats on the bottom facing a niche as the therapist makes an invocation for the protection of the initiates. He then commences an incantation, keeping time by stroking a notched wooden instrument, whose refrain is gradually taken up by the group of villagers who have gathered round. At nightfall, the therapist may suddenly begin to fill the pit with water which he pours over the initiates' heads. The water has been brought from the river in earthenware jars the same morning by women relatives. It is intended that the pit be filled in order that the patient's illness would be drawn down with the flowing water and leap onto the figurines, so that the pit thus filled may "enter in gestation" (*-bukwala maamba*). The ritual bath (*buka dyaphoongu*) is considered complete when the figurines begin to float and the initiates appear to be bathing. At this point the pit is covered with a white cloth. Pouring water over the initiates and the singing of songs induces in the initiates, and particularly in the patient, a shaking and trembling which leads to the *mbwoolu* trance-possession.

Sequence 4: Seclusion of the patient

As darkness falls, at bedtime around nine o'clock, the therapist aids the initiates to climb out of the pit all the while maintaining his chant. One by one he anoints their arms with kaolin. It is usually the left arm which is anointed, for the disease is more commonly believed to be inherited through the uterine line. Should the ailment be diagnosed as having passed down through the agnatic line he will anoint the right arm. The therapist secludes the initiates in the house of seclusion. They are put to rest or sleep (*-niimba*) on the bed placed there, a procedure which is called *-buusa khita*, "to be lain down for initiation." It is said that the statuettes remaining in the pit undergo a similar form of seclusion-mutation. This initial phase, organized when the waxing moon is just visible at sunset, reaches its peak either the following morning, or after three nights with the installation of the statuettes in their transitional function.

Protections such as fences and traps (*n-kiindzi*) are placed around the entrance, walls, and roof of the hut as well as next to the posts which support the bed. Along with the spells pronounced by the therapist, these protections "transform the seclusion house into a screened-off space" (*-siinda*), a protected (*-saka*), almost sacred space. The bed on which the patient lies throughout the seclusion is made from wood of the parasol tree (*n-seenga*: *Musanga cecropioides*, Moraceae) and river plants (specifically *mangangatsaanga*: *Selaginella scandens*, Pteridophyta). The parasol tree is the first plant to grow high on land left fallow as it reaches its full height in only three years. Its straight trunk branches out only at the top. These and other plants, animal articles, and the ritual carvings and objects brought into the seclusion house principally symbolize forms of life which interconnect the various cosmic habitats, viz. the zones above and below the forest treetops as well as those of soil and water. These symbolic articles may also refer to the predecessors of man (the *bisiimbi*, who are portrayed by the twisted shapes of worn river-stones), to the origin of birth and the succession of generations, to culture heroes, and to the domestication of fire.

Sequence 5: *"Winning hold over the anomaly"*

At the termination of the so-called "three-day" initial seclusion period, the therapist leads the initiates to a nearby river where they must undergo a test. They are made to enter the water and are then told to literally "eat things from the shore" (*-diila mayaanga*) by somehow transforming themselves into scavengers or predatory fish. When this task is completed they return to the seclusion house where the therapist "decorates the initiates' faces" (*-sona yiluundzi*), in order to show that each has acquired a new bodily form. The patients are then led out of the ritual compound and dance around the village, moving from house to house "collecting offerings" (*-seenda; n-seendu*). The villagers offer the patient some coins or agricultural products; these gifts are thus transformed from being harmful fruits of theft, which cause illness, into productive goods which the patient may put to use in fulfilling his or her rightful domestic role. This whole procedure serves to exhibit how well the patient is actually acquiring a new social status.

On this evening a legal proceeding takes place during which "a charge is brought against the source of the illness" (*-fuundila fula*). During this trial ill fortune is overcome and turned round into a process of recovery. The ritual cane is planted firmly into the ground. The pharmacopoeia (*yihalu*, usually wrapped in a monkey-skin) of both the healer and the initiate is attached to the top along with a small bag containing *fula*, the bits of agricultural and other offerings collected by the patient during the afternoon. The patient's own pharmacopoeia is in fact partially made of ingredients taken from that of the therapist. The *mbwandzadi* (literally "river-dog") statuette and a "knife without a hilt" (*n-seengedyambeedi*), to which a fowl is tied, are placed close to the cane. The patient, the husband or wife, the uncle, the lineage head, and the therapist then all simulate a struggle to grasp hold of the cane and thump it on the ground. In time with this rythmical movement, they chant several songs:

> Yilaala, eh eh maama. (bis)
> Yilaala, batoka mbaka, luwakya. (bis)
> Yilaala, kutsaangwa pheni, luwakya. (bis)
> I am vanishing (i.e. copulating), oh mother.
> I am vanishing; some ichtyotoxic is being pounded, do you notice it?
> I am vanishing, at the vaginal entrance; do you notice it?

A particular chant develops a litany of social relations and type of wrongs which may have been associated with them (Devisch 1993a: 208 ff.). The patient's past and his or her problems are reflected in the charges thus made and when the chant evokes the origin of the patient's misfortune the latter usually falls into a state of trance. Once the patient has succeeded in winning hold of the cane he or she is urged to "reveal the origin and circumstances of the sickness and suffering" (*-taaka mafula; lutswa lwaphoongu*) or of the grievances held. While this cathartic indictment is called *fula*, it is clear from the ritual and social context that the struggle portrayed is in fact an enactment of the unmasking and arrest of the "origin of the anomaly," also called *fula*. The trance thus allows for the expression of new meaning within the context of a ritual re-creation. At the outset, the cane signifies the anomaly (e.g. the failure to stand upright) and its origin (*fula*); this symbolism of misfortune is inverted such that it now denotes rehabilitation, good fortune, and hence recovery. The caprices of ill-fate and evil, of which the patient has spoken during the indictment, and their homeopathic inversion are given further material expression through other life-forms, specifically in the *lukobi* calabashes or in small baskets containing kaolin, mud, water-plants, and water-animals.

The healer will likely be busy during the night teaching the patient, mainly through songs, the curative use of plants and the various prohibitions which the patient will be required to respect during the initiation period and for the rest of his or her life. At sunrise the lineage head reappears and "buys back the ritual cane" from the therapist, offering him several lengths of cloth in exchange. The therapist has prepared a potion from leaves gathered indiscriminately near a busy path and from old palm nuts. The initiates then free themselves of any unknown evil by rubbing their bodies with this "mixture of leaves" and throwing the remains into the pit.

Before filling in the pit the healer plants the *n-saanda* tree of life (*Ficus thonningii*, Moracae) in front of the seclusion hut. He performs the same offerings in making this hole as he did previous to digging the pit. He erects a forked pole to the right of this life-tree. The pole will support the earthenware pitcher filled with the *zawa* – used to "sprinkle oneself" (*-dituuba*) in ritual and therapeutic ablutions – in which the statuettes have been cooked (see below). A hooked branch, called *kuundzi* or *yikata*, of the *n-heeti* tree (*Hymenocardia acida*, Euphorbiaceae) is placed alongside the life-tree. Because of its form, its whitish sap, and its whitish trunk, whose bark has been stripped off by termites and yet which has been left untouched by the annual bush fire, the *n-heeti* tree portrays the "turning of the patient's ill fate against itself autodestructively" (*-kaya*). The parasitic plants (*yikhundakhunda*; *Pragmenthera capitata*, Loranthacae) which are added to the top of this branch express the hope that disability will give place to ability. Once the seclusion site has been thus outfitted the therapist may finally fill in the ritual pit.

Sequence 6: "Cooking the statuettes"

The investiture of the freshly carved *mbwoolu* figurines in their symbolic role, like the patient's cure itself, is associated with the transformative process of cooking (*-laamba biteki*), and more implicitly of gestation. The patient, from disabled or incomplete as he or she was, undergoes a gestation and remodelling in ways prefigured or exemplified by the figurines. As a sign of their undergoing incubation, both the statuettes in the pit and those in the cooking vessel, literally are "put to rest," namely positioned upside-down. The pot is covered with a white cloth and contains a mixture of river water and poisonous plants in which the figurines bathe. The toxic concoction, called *zawa*, symbolizes the killing of those fish-like agents which have caused the patient's disability. It usually contains bark, leaves, and remnants of the following plants or objects or of their symbolic equivalents: *fuula dyatseki*, a savannah suffrutex (*Lasiosiphon kraussianus*, Thymelaeceae) whose woody base is used as a poison in fishing dammed-up streams; *mbaka fungununu*, an ichtyotoxic forest shrub (*Thephrosia vogelii*, Paplionaceae); *kusukusu*, an ichtyotoxic fruit; particles taken from the picket or the liana used to moor a pirogue, literally "the pirogue's paw" (*siimba dyan-diimba*). To this mixture may be added some bark from an uprooted tree or one struck by lightning, some *khawa* (i.e. explosive ingredients used with ritual arms), and even bone remnants from dangerous river animals. By the use of this mixture, whose preparation is accompanied by the incantation of a powerful spell, the healer aims at "uprooting the evil" and at "turning it back against itself autodestructively" (*-kaya*).

On their return home from a bath at the river, the therapist anoints the initiates and the figurines, first with the mixture taken from the *zawa* pot in which the figurines have bathed, and then with a red paste (which may be prepared either of *muundu* clay or of the *khula* tree) thinned with palm oil. The therapist spits chewings of kola nut (*-seengula*) or aphrodisiac (*tseengwa*) on those areas of the patient's body which are considered the source of great vitality: the forehead, temples, heart, shoulders, and the back of the loins. The lineage member responsible for the cult in turn spits kola nut on the *mbwoolu* figurines. The initiates are then invited to sit together on a mat laid close to the house of seclusion and alongside the ritual cane and statuettes.

At this point the therapist "sacrifices a fowl" (*yimenga kyafuula kuphoongu*), the same bird provided by the lineage responsible for the *mbwoolu* cult which has been tied since the previous evening to the "knife without a hilt." He breaks the legs of the chicken and draws it around the legs, arms, and head of the initiates. Tearing open its beak, the healer kills the fowl with his teeth. This manner of killing the bird emulates that of a rapacious animal seizing and devouring its prey, or the way in which a riverine bird might snatch a fish from the water. He then sprinkles the blood over the initiates' limbs, the statuettes, the pharmacopoeia, and the pit. These gests are accompanied by the recitation: "Feed yourself from the chicken's blood, keep away from the blood of men." The spiral movements with which the healer draws the fowl around the initiate's body indicates a disentangling (*-biindulula*) of whatever may be binding and disabling the body of the patient. The chicken is thereupon prepared for a common family meal by the female servant, *matsaayi*. Apart from its clear homeopathic reference to the disorder and its cause, the sacrifice and the sacrificial meal intend to underscore the "foster" relationship (*-tsaatsila*) between the patient and his or her family. The initiate will thereafter keep one of the chicken's legbones in his or her personal pharmacopoeia. It may then be used by relatives suffering from the nightmares or illnesses characteristic of *mbwoolu* to "bring bad luck on the misfortune" (*-beembula; mbeembi*). By rubbing the bone against the heel they will "disperse the ill fortune into anonymity," as it is said. Relatives having received this treatment may also wear a small *mbwoolu* figurine taken from the initiate's shrine.

Sequence 7: From seclusion to reintegration

The initiates return to seclusion following the sacrificial meal. They must there respect a number of dietary and behavioral restrictions. The initiate is, for example, required to hide under a white cloth whenever he or she leaves the seclusion house during the daytime. Initiates are otherwise forbidden to walk around or participate in conjugal life. A specific treatment is also prescribed. The patient applies an ointment to the body; the process is referred to as "washing with a mixture to gain weight" (-*yebala boondu dyawutooka*). The lotion is a mix of river vegetation, moss, and mud taken from the river. Other *boondu* salves are concocted from *khula* and the bark from poisonous or uprooted trees, or from those manifesting various deformities. Their application thus evokes a homeopathic or self-destructive action upon the patient's own impairment. Patients suffering from chronic diarrhoea or emaciation may similarly be prescribed enemas (-*soobuka; yifutu*) prepared with plants of the same type.

The *mbwoolu* figurines also play an important role in accompanying the initiates during this phase of seclusion. The statuettes are placed on a bed made from the parasol tree. This bed is either placed next to that of the patient or is attached to the western wall of the hut and elevated parallel to the patient's bed. This period may stretch from one week to two or more months, depending on the time needed for convalescence, or that required for the patient's kinsmen to produce the fee demanded by the healer. On the last night of seclusion, the initiates, therapist, and family elders all wake and sing, again "bringing a charge against the source of the illness." They thus lead the initiate once more into a state of trance. The therapist at this point may transmit more of his "art of healing" (*buti; luphati*), and especially of his knowledge of herbal medicaments. The initiate then bathes in the river.

The healing cult is not complete until the patient is made capable of fulfilling his or her conjugal and parental roles. The avuncular ties made with the therapist during the treatment must be loosened in favor of a form of exchange relation, such as that between wife-taker and wife-giver. The patient is then free to take up normal social life and rejoin the conjugal dwelling. The initiation has, however, led to a permanent consecration to the *mbwoolu* cult which is now centered around the shrine of statuettes and continues to involve various dietary and behavioral prescriptions. The initiate is fully invested (*yiyaalu*) into the *mbwoolu* legacy when the lineage member sponsoring the cult helps the initiate to bound off and regain autonomy: he "dresses the initiate up with iron (or copper) armrings which prevent seizures" (-*viika n-tsunga myavila-vila*), or sometimes provides a woven band to be worn round the ankle. The initiation culminates with dancing and singing. The initiate resumes the responsibilities of family life and the next child born to the couple will be named *Mbvwaala*, after the initiate's ritual cane.

Metabolising the passion of forces and signs into concord

Looking at the initiate and the way he is led to participate in the ritual, we see to what extent *mbwoolu* has a *transitional* function and is astonishingly *paradoxical* and *trangressional*. *Mbwoolu* addresses a relatively specific complex of symptoms of "lack of form" coded in terms of a humoral logic and an essentially spatial image of the body. The syndromes that form the objects of the other cults are specified in this same humoral logic and through this attention to the boundaries of the body and its orificial transactions. In addition to this focus on the body and recourse to multiple bodily techniques, each cult brings into play and manipulates the imagination, and of course a whole group dynamics. Initiation into such cults unfolds in an atmosphere where the ludic and the serious, licentiousness and a call to the norm, overlap. The therapeutic cult brings to the fore the body's drives and forces, as well as the imaginary register, as distinct from representation or reflection. These zones are mobilized through the rhythm, the gestures, and the themes of the dances, the fittings of the ritual house, the prayers, the massages, and many other activities. Thus are brought into play the functions, qualities, and transitional spheres of that libidinous and subjective dimension in the person to which are tied the social and ethnic logic. Indeed, each cult draws its inspiration and spirit from an extremely vital, imaginary, untamed, and energetic universe that the Yaka culture relegates to the domain of the collective phantasms related to the night, the forest, and the water spirits, to death throes, orgasmic communion, gestation, parturition, the bonding of the mother and her suckling, as well as to trance-possession. These untamed sources of energy from which the subject can draw, constitute the Yaka culture's specific idiom for dealing with the zones of the unconscious, or rather the imaginary, and expressing to what extent the self is experienced "as if on a stage on which is performed a pantomime directed elsewhere on Another stage" (Florence 1987:155). It is as if the ritual embraces such an imaginary and transgressional excursion not only for the purposes of a resourcing, but also with a view to a discovery, a ramble through the intra-uterine experience and the earliest infancy. In parallel, the therapy tries to (re-)knot ties with the norms and attributes of the external world, that is, with the established social order and adulthood. The therapist aims, then, to elevate the collective imagination into a symbolic order and governable practices, and this by articulating yet further the border between life and death, pleasure and displeasure. In order to so manipulate it, he projects temporal order – the time of the prelineal ancestors and of uterine filiation – into the common space of the rite: the time of origins, as well as the matrilineal past of the group, coexists in the space of the ritual scene; the ancestor and the spirits are there; the beginnings of society and of the genealogical origins of the patient are etched into the setting of the rite.

Theme 1: The riverine origins of mbwoolu: from silurid to human being, from phylogenesis to ontogenesis

The initiates as well as the texts, chants (De Beir 1975), and exegesis all affirm explicitly that "*mbwoolu* originates from the water/river." It is reported that the Mfunuka and Huumbu populations living along the Waamba river in northern Kwaango were responsible for the spread of the cult. *Mbwoolu* apparently experienced a revival and intensive propagation in northern Kwaango around 1910. In the interests of their long-distance commerce (*wusa muyikhita*), Mfunuka and Huumbu traders were criss-crossing northern Yakaland to sell rubber latex in the river ports of Popokabaka and Lukuni controled by European administrators and merchants. Eventually a "White Man" was added as "the master figure of the shrine" of *mbwoolu* statuettes. In this way *mbwoolu* practitioners aimed at domesticating the disruptive presence of the European colonizer. The figurine of the White Man draped in white cloth has incorporated several connotations: (i) *mbwoolu* is variously a spirit or a deficiency, as well as a cult; all are understood as having originated from the river; (ii) The Europeans were thought to have come from over the "water of salt," i.e. via the ocean, from *Phutulukeesu* or *Phutu*, a local rendition of Portugal which also stood for Europe. These first Europeans controlled the portuary trade along the Kwaango river; (iii) Kwaango people wrap a deceased member in white cloth for burial, a gest which is meant to facilitate taking on the white colour proper to the condition of the ancestor in the after-life; (iv) the ancestor is joined to *kalunga*, the cosmic womb separated from the this-worldly sphere, by an underworld river; this river parallels the Kwaango which drains most of the Yakaland basin.

In the esoteric language of the cult, and particularly in its chants, the patient's illness or deformity is compared to "a tree trunk stuck in the mud which hinders the ferryman from passing" (*kuka dyandzadi n-koonda babaangu*), or similarly to "a pirogue that keels over or floats adrift" (*mbaangu watika*). The initiation process itself is correspondingly referred to as a river-crossing, and the therapist as a ferryman. So it is that the *mbwoolu* shrine generally includes a pirogue with a miniature oar or paddle. It is possible to ascertain the latent models of identification as much for the illness as for the cure from the linguistic and dietary prohibitions imposed on the initiate. This is particularly the case when the person goes into a trance of a psychotic nature upon hearing or seeing the prohibited and identificational animal in question. For *mbwoolu* initiates, these prohibitions apply principally to a suborder of silurids or fresh water catfish, *leembwa*, *yikhaaka* (Cypriniformes, Siluroidei), as well as *n-tsuka* and *ngaandzi* (Cypriniformes, Percoidei). To my knowledge they are equipped with lung pouches and therefore may be considered air-breathing fish. The first three species mentioned, at least, are scavengers who feed on almost any type of vegetable or animal matter. They are also nocturnal predators, and have been nicknamed *mbwandzadi*, literally river dog. Both the species *leembwa* and *yikhaaka* are scale-less with small fins. The prohibitions may also, however, refer to hippopotami, snakes, underground rodents, fungi protruding from rotted wood, and even two animals commonly associated with sorcery and vendetta, the pig and the white chicken.

The silurid inspires a basic metaphor in the *mbwoolu* cult, rendered artistically by the twisted statuettes and the stridulator made from a notched bamboo slat. The silurid offers a latent model of identification for the patient seeking deliverance from physical handicaps (developmental problems, stiffness, sexual impotence) as well as from forms of madness. Silurids possess a substantial number of human characteristics: they breathe air, detect and emit sounds, have a mouth located on their ventral side, do not have scales, have a skeletal armor that becomes more and more visible with growth; they are omnivorous predators, protect their eggs, and are even capable of leaving the water. It is said that their armor gives them an "erectile strength." It protects them from other predators and retains its form even after desiccation, attributes that furnish a transformational metaphor in the treatment of impotence or lack of erection. The silurids habitually build their nests in the mud and hide their eggs under leaves. (We may recall that the figurines in the initiatory wells are covered in riverbank vegetation before the patient gets in.) During the night, silurids may leave the water in search of food, slithering on the humid earth. They bury themselves in the mud when the river dries up. Like many openwater species of fish, these catfish have developed a contrasting coloration of light belly and dark back. This counter-shading allows them to blend into the darkness of the river-bottom, or to reflect the whiteness of the water's surface if observed from below. The catfish's coloration, however, is opposite to that of the other openwater fishes as its ventral surface is darker than its dorsal side; it is apparently the only exception to this rule of camouflage. Since the mouth of the catfish is located on its ventral side it must swim upside-down in order to feed on surface plankton.

Certain species of silurids, and in particular *ngaandzi*, a species of "electric fish" (*Malopterurus electricus*), are capable of paralyzing their victims. These last detect sound and produce strident sounds themselves. The low humming note they emit is so loud that it can be heard at some 100 feet distance when the fish is out of the water. This same sound is reproduced during the rite by means of the stridulator. These silurids are artistically represented in the twisted figurines.

All references, accidental or otherwise, to the silurid can incite a trance-like outburst on the part of the initiate. Flexing his elbows and clenching his fists, he strikes his sides convulsively with his elbows. To me, this entire mimic enacts in succession not only the movements and sounds of the silurid, but also those of a person thrown into the water, or having a harrowing nightmare. The initiate emits anguished cries that confirm that the patient or initiate is possessed by *mbwoolu*:

Brr, brr . . .	Brr, brr . . .
aa mé, ngwa khasi	poor me, Uncle
aa mé	poor me
aa mé	poor me
aa mé, ngwa khasi	poor me, Uncle
brr, brr . . .	brr, brr . . .

The initiate may then collapse and remain immobile for some time.

Theme 2: Choice of identity by incorporating transitional qualities

The patient is incited to make identity choices by incorporating the transitional qualities of rhythm, a shower of water amidst a trance-inducing resonant envelope, a sacrifice, the cult house and danced chants, as well as through the anointing in mirror-image of the figurines and his own body.

During this ritual a shift in transitional functions takes place. The intermediary space is set up successively by the relations responsible for the patient and especially the uncle, by the therapist and then by the altar of cult figurines. These are so many transitional qualities and creative sources in the midst of which the patient – and any other participant – may deposit the non-differentiated. A progressive shift occurs. First there is the fusional absorption in the rhythm and the music. Then tactile, olfactory, and auditory contacts develop, and are finally interwoven into an increasingly elaborate utterance, by the mirrored gaze. Thus the patient progressively converts the primary fusional object, into processes and phenomena of identification by incorporation. The patient converts a sensory, pathic relationship with the other into a more gnosic one of symbolization in language (Maldiney 1973).

The shrine of figurines

The *mbwoolu* shrine generally contains some eight or more statuettes, 20 to 40 centimetres in height, slender, about the thickness of a branch. They are sculpted in *n-hala* wood from the savannah shrub that bears poisonous ichtyotoxic fruit (*Crossopteryx febrifuga*, Rubiaceae). Their stylistic characteristics have been described by Bourgeois (1978–9). Certain figurines are said to be accompanied by a young wife, children, and / or colonial soldiers. Each figurine in the cult is invoked separately and accredited with personal names. The series presents a partial version of the family and clan structure. It appears that this series portrays the cosmogony of the emergence of the human from the silurid. This development figures initially as an exvagination, the boat being considered as the first of the figurines: it is a cavity or uterus filled with red paste – symbolizing the maternal blood – that the initiate uses as an unction. The internal differences in the series mutate as if by an enacted or exemplified myth in relation to the gradual morphogenesis of the human being, that is, relative to its phylogenetic development from a formless, memberless ichtyoid existence, to one with a bony structure endowed with members; or again, from a being with a single leg, arm, or breast, or from an asexualized, deformed state, characterized by handicaps and deficiencies in development, to a state of accomplishment and autonomy, marked by full feminine or masculine sexualization. (The attributes of the silurid are the most pronounced in the slender memberless figurines as well as in the twisted figurines and / or those surmounted with a muzzle.)

When speaking to the statuettes the initiate addresses them with the title *bapfumu*, a term of reverence denoting chiefs, and refers to them by the term *makuundzi*, protectors or supports (i.e. that shore up, for example a bed, a roof, a banana tree, a disabled human body). In a show of deference to the chiefs the initiate kneels before the shrine and claps the right hand in the left and vice versa. He or she then presents the palms of the hands and leaning forward presses the knuckles to the earth as a sign of homage and submission. Taking a statuette in each hand, the initiate then strikes his or her shoulders, arms and sides with them, and spits kola nut on the heart of each figurine.

The statuettes are loosely divided into three groups or bands (sing. *buku*). Each group embodies different aspects of both the gradual

phylogeny into a fully abled human and of the disorders which characterize *mbwoolu*. These typical characteristics have been neatly described by
Bourgeois (1978–9: 60–1). Although the following classification may be
somewhat tentative, it seeks to emphasize the individuation of the statuettes: each is invoked separately, bears an individualized name, and is
credited with personal attributes.

(i) *Buku dyambu*, the first of these groups, includes some twisted or
spiral-shaped (*-zekula*) figurines and others which express grave congenital deformities (*lukata, n-kata, yikata*) such as the absence of limbs.
Another characteristic of this band is that it always includes its own
lukobi, a calabash or wooden tube with mud, vegetation from a ravine,
and rotted pieces of pirogue or driftwood. The initiate may thus carry out
his or her own treatment in the case of persistent nightmares or chronic
anxieties and pain. The miniature pirogue (*n-diimba, mabwaati*), filled
with kaolin and rivermud and equipped with paddle (*khafi, pawu*) or pole
(*ndaangu*), belongs to this unit as well. The pirogue and paddle are most
likely fashioned from the *n-seenga* parasol tree. The initiate makes offerings to the pirogue as it represents a pre-ancestral spirit (*yisiimbi*).

(ii) The name of the second unit, *buku dyavula biteki*, literally translates
as "the band that soaks up or engulfs many figurines." This group deals
with a large variety of *mbwoolu* afflictions, such as the nightmares spoken
of above, accidents in the river, encounters, with serpents, stiffness,
impotence, serious fevers, chronic diarrhoea, emaciation and productive
cough. Most of these figurines possess limbs and marks of sexualization.
This group finally includes one or another animal figure which the patient
has been dreaming of; this might be a pigeon, a lizard or a monkey for
example.

(iii) *Buku dya pfumwaluumbu*, or "band of the head of the shrine,"
completes the series. There is in each shrine a master-figure which is
accorded a status similar to that of a paramount chief. It is represented by
the tallest statuette in the series which often bears a notched head-
covering. This dominating figure is variously named *N-ndedi* (White
Man), *N-ndedyaphutu* (White Man from the rapids / the ocean), *N-ndedi
mosi Luaanda* (White Man from Luanda), or *N-ndedyathoyo* (White Man
commanding a battalion). It is draped in white cloth, wears a European
hat on a white-painted head (Huber 1956:279), and is often accompanied by a wife and / or colonial soldiers (sing. *mbulumbulu*).

Transitional qualities

(a) The fusional bath of rhythm and sounds, as well as the shower,
establish the transitional function. They allow the patient to fuse with all
around him and reinforce his experience of the skin and of the sense of

hearing as zones both of contact and of separation serving as a base for the blossoming of the self.

It is at the boundaries between village and bush, at the turning point of day into night, that the initiates enter their seclusion in the pit near the initiatory house. The drums and the chants offer a bath of sound and melody enveloping the self and bearing it along on the rhythm, the flow of sounds, the modulations and harmony of the drums and chants in unison. The patient finds himself untangled, unfettered, unbent, unlaced as much in his enlacement (isolation, handicap) as in his pathological un-tiedness: in a state close to trance, the patient vibrates at one with the collective rhythm. So operates a dedifferentiation between the world of self and the world of the other. The numerous participants generate a ludic, carnivalesque, and transgressional atmosphere.

Taking their inspiration from relationships of badinage and dream phantasy, the chants, dance, and body language recall the games of seduction and erotic banter that occur on the outskirts of the village in the evening, or at the carnival-like celebrations that bring an end to bereave-ment. These chants treat thematically how such interplays and relation-ships are bathed in ambivalence, creating at once delight and disappoint-ment, relaxation, and mischief. The participants are submerged in an ambience of vibrations, sounds, rhythms, and melodies, all emanating from the body of the other; it is as if the drummer, perched on his drum, forms a single body with his instrument. This sensual and enveloping resonant bath leads to an experience of plenitude and enchantment: it is the illusion of an outpouring or fusion that erases the separation between the self and the environment.

At nightfall, after an hour and a half to two hours of dance and chant, this fusional resonant bath is transformed for the initiates in the pit by a shower that articulates in a thermo-tactile manner both separation and oneness. The water poured in abundance onto the bodies of the co-initiates crouched in the pit stimulates their perception of the frontiers of the body as a contour that both envelops and separates them, and as a medium for the exchange of sensations and emotions among themselves and with the group. But at the same time, the patient finds himself partially thrown back into the limits of his own body by this shower. He is seized by a dread of annihilation, and enters into a convulsive trance. The trance is a process that negates the time rhythmically punctuated by the group. Those witnessing the trance, the family and community members gathered at the site, amplify their rhythms and melodies for a while as a sign of an enveloping, reassuring, understanding presence. A white sheet spread over the patient and the pit articulates a separation and an elemen-tary point of contact.

For his part, the therapist seeks to domesticate the eruptive manifestations of the *mbwoolu* spirits by forming a sort of alliance with them. In his avuncular role, the therapist acts as one giving away the bride, as he who introduces the patient into a relation of alliance or marriage with the spirit. The cult figurines serve as the recipients of the *mbwoolu* spirit in its positive capacity. Next, the animal *sacrifice*, standing in for the sacrifice of the possessed / ill person, is intended radically to transform the originally morbid relationship with the spirit. The beneficent capacity of the spirit is transferred to the shrine: the spirit becomes a tutelary. By killing the sacrificial chicken with his teeth, the therapist reelaborates the meeting between the spirit aggressor and its victim, whose negative aspects he inverses by redirecting them in a positive healing sense. The origins of the illness, as indicted during the simulacra of a trial and struggle, are transferred to an object introduced into the pharmacopoeia which assumes the function of a non-human receptor: this receptor is composed of an amalgam of signifiers, handicaps, and illnesses, which the therapist must take care to tie up by means of various ligatures in order to enlace the binding evil in its own entanglement, that is to say, twist it in an autodestructive or homeopathic fashion against itself.

(b) During the ritual, the music and dancing evolve in a playful and transgressional mood. For the patient, the initiandi, and the public, they fulfill a transitional function, operating at once union and separation. The rhythm and the resonant bath cause the patient to go into a trance. They interconnect into an articulated whole the idiosyncratic body and the socioculture. The initiation chants sung to dance rhythms are those that mothers and grandmothers have so often sung in the form of lullabies. The dances have been given their rhythms in the period of the full moon with which the mother is linked, her child on her breast or later on her back or arm. In other words, the music and the initiatory songs arouse traces of sensual and sensory childhood experiences engrafted in the bodily envelope: they are sensual experiences of socioculturally encoded harmony, fusion, and variation. The themes of the chants and the swaying movement of the dancers introduce an important erotic element. This is to say that in a latent, sensory, sensual, and vigorous fashion, the rhythm, dance, and chants tie in body, affect, collective unconscious, and emotion, while linking them to the sexualized and social body and the order of the world (the cosmological body). These dances take place practically every night during the initiation.

(c) Metaphorically, the house of seclusion is a womb and the seclusion a fetal condition. The fittings of the ritual house and the dictates governing the seclusion reinforce this significant dimension. Indeed, the door of the ritual house and the mode of entry have a genital connotation. A curtain of raffia palm hides the entire entranceway, which is called *luleembi* or *masasa*, a word that in Koongo – which is very close to the Yaka tongue – means pubic hair. The use of raffia palm is hardly surprising when we know that it served formerly for the weaving of raffia grass skirts for the initiandi. As night approaches, and they are on the point of entering the house of seclusion, the therapist and the patient chant: *Kongoongu a mwaneetu*, "In this primordial womb, let us lay our infant down." The initiate lives in a relaxed and warm body to body contact with his co-initiates.

The seclusion reenacts the cosmogenesis of *ngoongu*, that is, that primal cosmic emergence in the universe of generating powers, renewing themselves endlessly at their point of issue: the original uterine or gestational space. These cosmic metaphors, "which signify and bring about the change that must take place" (-*saka*), intertwine the processes of gestation and regeneration on the levels of the body, the group as well as the world (Devisch 1988). The device of the house and its function as a container gives the patient the possibility of displacing partial objects of the self onto the figurines or ritual objects, and this within an interplay of interactions and a framework of containment. The figurines evoke a relationship with the time of origins, evolution, and reiteration, whereas the ambience of relaxation and rest, as well as the supine position throughout the daytime, evoke the time of hatching and euchronic time.

During the seclusion, the presence of the therapist is low key, but reassuring and containing. The therapist brings bouquets of fresh plants to the initiate daily so he can take decoctions or enemas. As he keeps watch on the seclusion, his activities and rules offer the patient a container, a transitional zone. The therapist does not seem to engage in a role of healer or any other messianic role intended to save the initiates from suffering.

(d) The unction in a play of mirrors between the patient's own body and the figurines performs a transitional function. The unction affirms the boundary or the bodily envelope as a source of comfort and as a mirror. By the daily unction of his entire body, the patient stimulates his body tone, and the sentiment of being intact and cohesive. By inflecting the source of smell and limbering up the skin, the unction awakens tactile receptivity, adaptive permeability, or a predisposition to stimulation. It articulates the *skin-self* ("le moi-peau," as coined by Anzieu 1974) as a faculty of regeneration, confidence, indeed, of communication with the world of the water spirits and the unconscious. The skin has a function as intermediary, as go-between, of transitionality (Anzieu 1985:17).

By applying the red powder first on a few figurines, then on his own body and then on the remaining figurines, as in a play of mirrors, the patient regains the sense of touch and the skin-self as linked to a sensation of comfort. This takes place in a mood of relaxation. The red powder, a symbol of uterine blood and fusion with the mother, is above all an unction bringing into play a sensation of surface and volume. The ill person has the thermotactile experience both of a sort of life in unison with the figurines and of a division by the skin. In other terms, the unction contributes to the "acted upon" or "acted by" appropriation of the articulated, membered, sexualized body, both as surface and as volume, and that in a process of mirror effect. Through this reflexive unction, the *mbwoolu* spirits acquire a tactile body and the initiate begins to incorporate them, incarnate them, and no doubt desire that these objects reproduce their qualities within him. By the unction first of these figurines and then of his body, the patient can only beautify and further incorporate his mirror image as constituted by this game of delegation, transfer, and recognition. This is where the metaphoric transpositions of phylo- and ontogenesis that activate individualizing movements of identification tie in and are reinforced.

Each figurine is a program, a code. To enter into the skin of these figurines is to shed one's skin and turn over a new leaf: "The massage becomes the message" (Anzieu 1985:38). The figurines form an external skin, so to speak, that is socialized, idealized, and protective. One's own skin becomes the internal, receptive, or "invaginated" layer of the identity in formation. The fantasy world that these figurines trigger and incorporate offers to the initiate an imaginary and differentiated space that allows him to form his identity. Through the interaction with a series of identificatory cult figurines, the patient develops his identity as a unity of social and individual skins. Thus, what arises in the figurines arises also in the patient, that is, a relationship to the body as a source of comfort, confidence, reciprocity, and social distinction. This relational boundary offers to the hatching self the possibility of an ulterior evolution. The play of identification and differentiation leads to a number of delegations, transfers, and in- or ex-corporations. The figurines and the *mbwoolu* spirits stimulate, among other things, a flux, a coming and going between body image and fantasy, as well as between childhood reminiscences, the history of the family and the group mixed with all sorts of conventional images on the one hand and individual and unconscious fantasies on the other hand. These figurines have great transitional power, an intermediary function capable of evoking all sorts of sensations and affects of earliest infancy, of the biographical and family history and, by association, all kinds of social conventions. These sensations, affects, fantasies, and associations of images, are activated on the level of the liminal zone formed by the embrocated skin of the patient's own body and the "acted upon" surface of the figurines. In the eyes of the Yaka culture, the structure of the self is one of an envelope and of exchange, of tie and interface: the self does not develop in isolation. We can perhaps say that in this exchange, the figurines become the external, protecting, and mediating layer (the surface of excitation), whereas the patient's own body is the internal, receptive layer (the pocket or surface of inscription) of the identity in elaboration.

In other terms, unable to turn the body of the possessed/ill person inside out to extract the evil, disability, or persecuting spirit, the cure effects a symbolic turning inside out, an invagination of the body by a mirror-image unction of the figurines and the initiate's skin. The patient's outside becomes his inside, the form of the figurines' messages becomes the patient's container – "the social skin," as it were (Turner 1980); in other words, their form becomes information. Upon this, is superimposed the transforming effect of the animal sacrifice and the sacrificial blood on the patient's body: the patient also takes on a new skin thanks to the sacrificial dynamics that transform death into regeneration, sacrificial blood into uterine blood.

Theme 3: From incorporation to incorporated decoding

The cult figurines offer and model an *ecology of body and affect*. Through the cult and the cult utterance, the patient decodes the archaic-mythic message relayed by the figurines. This message takes on an oracular value, transforming a fate into a destiny, while prompting specular identification.

During the first trance-possession, speech is but a murmur, a hardly articulated guttural cry, an inchoative phonation, a sonorous vibration, a basal manifestation, so to speak, of animal, ichtyoid life. At the beginning of the seclusion, the therapist talks to the figurines, and thus little by little the patient learns the cult utterances to address to each figurine or *mbwoolu* spirit: they are so many mythical fragments that suggest that all is proceeding as if one were in the time of origins. It would appear that the initiate enters progressively into a dialogue with an interlocutor who is doubtless a figment of fantasy, but who is no less real or tangible for all that, that is to say a water spirit. Through the effect of the prayer, these spirits transform the initiate's *needs* – his troubles or handicaps – into *demands* addressed to the initiate. No doubt we can see in this phenomenon a mirror experience that introduces the self into the chain of intentions. The figurines and the cult language represent a potential capable of metaphorically transforming traces of the archaic and unthinkable. At the same time, the patient hatches in a new identity, that is, that of the initiated. Although very codified at first, the initiate's prayer can take on a certain improvised and personalized character at the end of the initiation. This prayer is essentially a route of initial identification as a process of self, allowing the initiate to assume his biography and his multiple social roles at the heart of a drama that is partially extrahuman, paranormal, outside the normal and sacred. In this respect, his biography participates in a pantomime being played out in part on "Another stage," and of which he is not the author even while being the protagonist. By means of the unction and the prayer, the cult figurines acquire an oracular and authoritative value. They emit messages concerning the healing of the patient or his biography: to be healed, he must obey certain rules; will he become a parent, an elder, or the chief himself? Through the cult prayer, the figurines relate the story of the cosmogenesis and reflect on human development and, above all, account for the unity between the individual, social, and cosmological orders.

The cult seeks not only to confirm anterior identifications. On the contrary, it aims for an expulsion, literally a "dénouement." The evil is transferred into a sacrificial animal, the figurines, and the pharmacopoeia, which assume the functions both of receivers of the illness and as "good objects." *Mbwoolu* that enlaces the ill person is also capable of disenlacing him, unknotting him; having been persecuting spirits, the *mbwoolu* spirits become protecting genies, benevolent receptacles of identification. The figurines and the pharmacopoeia contain the memory of the transferential relationship maintained with the therapist ("if I don't persevere with the cult, misfortune will befall me"), and socializes it or attenuate both the expectation and the illusion. The cult invites the subject to keep open a window of disbelief ("is this a game?") and to postulate a superior truth or wisdom accessible only through the acts of initiation. Without them, this truth remains indefinable. It can only be secured by the accomplishment of the rite itself.

Mbwoolu is poles apart from the social initiations at the center of the social order. These include circumcision and the initiation of boys. Such celebrations are held at the centre of the village and in full daylight, in the presence of elders and the village community. They draw on a sort of narration concerning the origins of society and of various prestigious aspects of its social and political order (Devisch 1988, 1993a). *Mbwoolu* is worlds away from this: in the intimacy of the night, the initiatory pit and the house, in that transition from village to forest, death to renaissance, prehuman forms of life to human development, the *mbwoolu* figurines portray a progression of multiple identifications, in that evolving and negotiable process by which are incorporated identificatory forms. There is the development of embryonic, prehuman forms, then the emergence of sexualization and of hierarchy leading to the valued identities of parent, elder, or chief. To this multiplicity of forms are further added basic collective phantasms, which are evoked in an esoteric language and thus hidden from common language, as well as dreamlike images and fragments of esoteric myths.

In his interaction at once tactile and corporal, as well as verbal and visual, with these cult figurines, the patient explores a multiplicity of human figures and specular modes of identification. In this cult, sensation, phantasm, affect, emotion, the association of ideas, and representations of family and networks and interactions blend with identification in the formative process of the self. Indeed, be it through the injunctions and the unction, by specular identification or by metaphorically projecting himself in the figurines, the patient is led to explore and incorporate the affective modalities of the senses just as they are found in condensed form on these sculptural figurations. Thus the initiate is moved to incorporate the essential dimensions of the Yaka culture. We are dealing in short with a kind of metamorphosis, an incorporated trance-possession, a transfiguration, an incarnation of forms and of itineraries, indeed with a transcorporeality (a term I have borrowed from Julia Kristéva 1987:63). Inducing and modelling culturally determined affects, the forms of the figurines and the unction in the play of mirrors anticipate and inform, or orient by sensory and sensual channels and by unconscious representations or imagos, the representations and the behaviors to be adopted in society.

Theme 4: The heart as the centre of the person in a state of becoming

At the close of the unction, the initiate chews a cola nut and spits some on the various figurines in the region of their hearts. In an esoteric language, he utters the particulars of each figurine and issues injunctions to them. The initiate repeats this ritual every time he feels himself in distress or when he seeks to structure the turmoil provoked by his dreams, or, again, by the initiatory chants he hears around his house in the evening. By transferring this intermingling of tonic and injunction onto the hearts of the figurines, the initiate fortifies the heart as a centre of listening and of interiorisation, and as the seat of knowledge and of the choices that inform one's deeds.

The Yaka say the cola nut has the form of a heart. This tonic nut is the privilege of the elders, and in particular, of those who safeguard "the heart and the unity of the hearth, concord and cordiality" (*yibuundwa*). The heart constitutes the capacity to balance ancestral tradition and the messages of others (received through the ear, the eye, or in dreams) and emancipate them in cordiality. The heart is the hearth of the person in the image of the family hearth, that is, it is the source of harmony and concord (*mbuundwa mosi*, literally "a single heart") between parents and children. According to the Yaka, the heart is the site of the capacity to balance the ancestral tradition and the messages of the others with a view to promoting them in "con-cordia" within the family. The heart is not especially regarded as the organ of blood, passion, attraction, or repulsion, which are affects deriving much more from the fields of the olfactory, and of ludic and generating sexuality. The heart is the centre of the inner, gnosic, or representative gaze (Maldiney 1973) of the person (*muutu*), which assures the unity of his multiple involvements, and his multiple pathic implications on the level of the orificial and sensory body (*luutu*). The heart is the organ that receives the messages decoded by hearing or sight, taking them in and mulling them over, that is, visualizing them by projecting their content onto scenes of the past or the present world. The heart is as much a screen as it is a source and a form of knowledge, virtue, discretion, moral judgment, choice, conscience, communication, loyalty, and pride or remorse. In touch with the drives, the heart "reflects" and revitalizes the wisdom and words of others. Thus the heart is the basis of the mutual inclusion of the social and individual identities, of the social subject and the person in progression and transformation.

ACKNOWLEDGMENTS

The research among rural and urban Yaka has been financed by the Belgian National Fund for Scientific Research, the European Commission (DGXII B4 STD2 0202 B), and the Guggenheim Foundation. It was carried out in collaboration with the IMNZ (Institut des Musées Nationaux du Zaïre/Congo), as well as with CERDAS (Centre de recherche et de documentation en sciences sociales desservant l'Afrique sud-saharienne) based at the University of Kinshasa. I thank Mrs. Ann West for her editorial help.

NOTES

1 I was privileged to live as a guest of the population in the Taanda village settlements in the north of Kwaango, about 450 kilometers south-east of Kinshasa, from January 1972 to October 1974. It was as a participant in everyday life there that I had many close contacts with five diviners and some eighteen therapists. I was able to witness two *mbwoolu* initiation rites, visit some eighteen *mbwoolu* shrines, and maintain intimate contact with three *mbwoolu* therapists. During my annual six-week sojourns in the Yaka milieu in Kinshasa (since 1986), and / or in the north of Kwaango (since 1991), I could interview at length eight *mbwoolu* therapists practicing in Kinshasa, as well as observe that the great therapeutic cults remain popular in the city, although their cosmological dimension is somewhat diminished.

2 By the term "incorporate" – which I do not use in its accepted psychoanalytic sense – I seek to render a Yaka perspective that situates the formation and the constitution of the individual identity on the level of the sensory envelope of the relational body, that is, on the level of the skin, the orifices, the senses, and exchanges between one individual and another. This identity is not conceived as an introjection in one's inner core or heart of hearts. Thus I will also avoid the terms internalization and introjection, mainly out of respect for the Yaka genius. In any event, these notions derive from an intersubjective context, whereas the *mbwoolu* cure operates principally in a liturgical sphere where gesture, esoteric utterance, and cult figurines with benevolent natures and esoteric names serve as mediums for fantasy and inner emotion.

7 To eat for another: taboo and the elicitation of bodily form among the Kamea of Papua New Guinea

Sandra Bamford

Meyer Fortes once wrote about the privileged place that food taboos occupy in the discipline of anthropology. Eating, he argued, is a uniquely individual act in that each person must eat for her or himself – it is not an activity that one person can undertake for another (also quoted in M. Strathern 1988:20). Furthermore, eating is both "organic" and "social": "it is a means by which we are not merely made aware of an external reality but take permitted parts of it into our [body] . . . " (Fortes 1966:16). This being so, it is not surprising that food taboos have captured the imagination of anthropologists. Not unlike Lévi-Strauss's (1949) leitmotif – the incest prohibition – dietary restrictions tease and titillate us with the possibility of casting light on some of the West's most persistent analytical dilemmas: the relationship between mind and body, and the individual and society.

I am not in this chapter going to offer up a new theory of taboo. Nor will I enter into some of the more specific debates which have surrounded how anthropologists have approached the subject (see Lévi-Strauss 1962). Instead, I want to examine one feature of taboos which has received scant analytical attention: their capacity to image the apparently contradictory states of unity and disjuncture. Most anthropological treatments of taboo have taken the issue of boundary maintenance and disjuncture as their point of departure. Taboos, we are told, are about preserving the integrity of a classificatory system – they have to do with keeping certain categories of people and things apart (Douglas 1966, 1979; Leach 1964; Tambiah 1969). Pollution results when the dividing lines between classes have been breached: when what is distinct threatens, because of contagion, to become an undifferentiated mass. To follow a taboo, then, is to shore up a system of cultural distinctions and to prevent connections from forming between cultural domains that must not be mixed (Schieffelin 1976:71; Wagner 1987:235).

Among the Kamea of Papua New Guinea with whom I conducted research, taboos frequently *do* mark off categories of persons and things. But they are also a means by which such distinctions are constituted in the first place (cf. Wagner 1977; Lambek 1992), and they furnish a background of similarity against which such acts of differentiation take place. Melanesianists have long noted that the "work" of most New Guinea cultures is not centered on reproducing a formalized model of "society" as such, but rather is geared toward creating particular kinds of social relationships (Wagner 1975, 1977; M. Strathern 1988). This "work" is ongoing in the sense that what was once differentiated inevitably slips through time back to a position of unity requiring that further acts of separation take place. It is this need to *keep* differentiating against a countervailing pull of similitude that gives New Guinea cultures their forward-going momentum. Unity and disjunction become twin moments in the ongoing flow or elicitation of social life. The taboo conditions that I discuss are noteworthy in that they capture both of these processes simultaneously: on the one hand what they "differentiate" is a moment of unchecked similarity, and on the other they become a venue through which such differentiation is carried out. Through an examination of these taboos, I hope to capture something of the ethos of Melanesian "embodiment," and to ask what it might mean to our understanding of the body were it possible to eat for someone else after all.

Ethnographic setting

The Kamea are a Highland people who number some 14,000 and occupy the heavily forested interior of Gulf Province, Papua New Guinea.[1] Linguistically and culturally, they belong to the Angan ethnic group, who are perhaps best known to anthropological audiences through the ethnographic writings of Maurice Godelier (1982, 1986) and Gilbert Herdt (1981).[2] Like most of their neighbors, the Kamea derive their living from a combination of shifting horticulture and the raising of pigs. Their main agricultural crop is the sweet potato which is cultivated in family plots at elevations ranging between 610 and 1850m. Hunting and gathering contribute only minimally to the diet, but figure centrally within the context of social and ritual prestations (cf. Godelier 1986; Herdt 1981).

The research upon which this chapter is based was carried out in the northern Kamea region, approximately 30 km to the north of the government station at Kaintiba. At the time of my fieldwork (September 1989 to February 1992) there were no roads leading into or out of the region. From the late 1960s onward the state, in both its colonial and nationalist guises, has declared that one of its top priorities lies in establishing a system of roads that would connect the district to one of the ports on the Papua or New Guinea coasts. Thirty years later, this network of roads is still completely absent and the area remains accessible only by foot and small aircraft. In the absence of access to outside markets, opportunities to earn cash within the district are severely constrained. Those who reside in the immediate vicinity of the government station derive a small but steady income from the sale of fresh foodstuffs to station staff, or by signing on as casual wage laborers for the occasional government-spon-sored project. A notable few have achieved some measure of success by owning and operating small tradestores, while others have sought work outside the district at the goldmines in Wau or on one of the coastal plantations in New Ireland or New Britain. They have taken away from these experiences a sense that much of the world around them has undergone a series of remarkable transformations, while their own par-ticular segment of it has remained largely unchanged.

Like other Angan groups, the Kamea practice male initiation which is organized on the basis of a two-stage ritual sequence. Entry into the men's cult begins when a boy is ten or eleven years old and is brought to the bush to have his nose pierced by an older, initiated man. Along with his age mates, he will remain in the cult house for a number of weeks until the sores have healed after which time initiates are permitted to return to the house of their parents. Several years later, boys will be fed marita[3] – the fruit of the pandanus tree – in a secret cult ceremony which marks the final grade of the initiatory sequence. Passage through both these stages is marked by the disclosure of secret narratives, including detailed knowl-edge of how to conduct oneself in matters pertaining to warfare and women[4] (cf. Blackwood 1978).

Embodied consumption: eating for self and eating for others

Food is an important nexus of cultural value for the Kamea and its consumption furnishes the Western observer with an analytic spring-board into the multiple arenas within which indigenous views of the body acquire meaning. The types of food that a person can eat are tabooed or restricted in accordance with a wide variety of events and conditions such as pregnancy, death, illness, and the like (cf. Schieffelin 1976; Gell 1979; Meigs 1984). The vast majority of these restrictions are voluntarily undertaken and are terminated without undue fanfare as the individual sees fit. A man may avoid chewing certain types of betelnut (kabibi), for instance, as an expression of grief over the passing of his father's sister. Against this background of casual and predominately idiosyncratic interdictions, one taboo complex stands apart from the rest both in terms of the rigor with which it is observed and by its capacity to knit boys and women into a single cultural image.

I first became aware of these prohibitions soon after settling at Titamnga, the Kamea village where I conducted the bulk of my fieldwork. One morning, not long after I had arrived, I was invited to accompany a small group of women and children to hunt rat (*mataka*) along the forest edge. After several hours work, we had managed to "bag" a tiny handful of the rodents before beating a hasty retreat back to our house to avoid the late afternoon rains. Later that evening, Kokoban – one of the women in our party – dropped by my house where she launched into a detailed account of how she had distributed her share of the spoils to kinsmen. Everyone in her immediate family, it seemed, had received some portion of the game, although I noticed that she failed to mention her younger brother Drinda as having eaten any. When I asked Kokoban about it, she explained that rats were taboo to him. Were Drinda's mother dead, the boy could eat them without fear, but for the time being at least, they were forbidden until he was initiated.

Rats, as it turned out, were not the only item prohibited to young boys. As I pursued the topic of food taboos in greater detail, I soon learned that boys were also barred from eating a number of other mammalian species, including several varieties of marsupials and bats. Many of these animals live on the ground, others in trees, and they are indigenously recognized as having highly variable habits and appearances. What these different species have in common with one another is that they are all said to emit a particularly strong odor when cooked.[5] While "smell" is a highly salient quality of experience for the Kamea, my concern in this paper lies less with analyzing the semantic content of these prohibitions than it does with explicating the specific form which they take.[6] As I hope to demonstrate, meaningfulness for the Kamea resides less in a system of positively defined concepts than it does in the cracks and crevices which exist between them.

At the time it struck me as rather ironic that the more I struggled to learn about rats and boys, the more my friends at Titamnga wanted to tell me about the life-cycle of women. Unlike boys, who labor under an onerous array of dietary restrictions, Kamea girls are free to eat virtually anything they please. Indeed, some women will enjoy a taboo-free existence until the day they die; the determining factor is the sex of any offspring they may carry. Should a woman give birth to a child of the same sex as herself, her life will continue pretty much as before: both she and her daughter are free to consume all varieties of "smelly" game. If she carries a son, by contrast, her eating habits will eventually change. From the time that her son has his nose pierced onward, all of the food items that were previously taboo to him now become taboo to his mother as well. When both stages of the initiation sequence have been completed, the boy can begin to eat these foods for the first time in his life, but they will remain taboo to his mother until her dying day. Should a woman violate these taboos, it is said that her "backside would break," and she would be forced to remain in the house, lonely and sapped of her energy.[7] A woman thus afflicted eventually dies of a wasting disease.

So far, the taboo conditions I have discussed appear to fall quite neatly within the scope of the existing structuralist paradigm. A mother and son will never be eating precisely the same foods at the same time: what is permitted for one is taboo for the other.[8] As Douglas (1966) has argued, food taboos are acts of separation which define discrete identities through a system of negative differentiation. The situation at Titamnga, however, is somewhat more complex. We have seen why a mother abstains from eating certain varieties of game – she follows these taboos to protect her health and physical wellbeing. But it remains to be seen why her son, prior to being initiated, should do the same. Although a few Kamea told me that boys avoid these items because their consumption may lead to a scabies-like condition, this was seen as a relatively minor consequence: certainly a small price to pay for a tasty mouthful of much-prized game. Instead, the principal reason for eschewing these animals is that were a boy to eat them, they would have an adverse effect *not on himself, but on his mother.* As one boy explained: "If I ate these things, my mother wouldn't be able to leave the house. She couldn't go to her garden, collect firewood, or care for livestock. She would sit in the house all day long where she would eventually die."

For the Kamea, then, what the initial taboo conditions mark is not a *singular* but rather a *conflated* identity. In a recent paper that deals with the Malagasy-speakers of Mayotte, Lambek discusses one of the more common features of taboo: "a taboo clearly differentiates between those who practice it and those who need not" (1992:249). For the Kamea, as we have seen, this is not necessarily the case. The taboo conditions which operate between a mother and son do not simply mark the two as distinct, but also establish their *essential similarity.* Taken together, they present an image of a singular body wherein the eating habits of one directly affect the health of the other. But the fact that only one half of this dual entity actually follows the taboo also has an *anticipatory* value – it anticipates the differentiation that will take place through the men's cult and its associated rituals. Prior to being initiated, a young boy is said to be "female-like" (*apaka*)[9] (cf. Herdt 1981, 1987; Godelier 1986): indeed, he continues to wear the style of grass skirt that is characteristic of women.[10] It is only through participation in the men's cult that a "masculinized" (*oka*) form of being is created. At initiation, the previously conjoined identity of the mother and son is disarticulated, thereby marking the point at which gender is created (cf. M. Strathern 1993). The taboo conditions emphazise *both* phases of this process and shifting them becomes a means whereby the state of disjunction is achieved.

I have described the intersection of cult life and taboos in terms of their capacity to call forth different types of culturally recognized identities. It should be stated, however, that Kamea ideas surrounding the efficacy of initiation translate only awkwardly into the categories of Western social science. While we are prone to see initiation as being constitutive of gender (M. Strathern 1993), the Kamea are more apt to view it as a process of "decontainment" – a process which carries with it a decidedly temporal dimension. Kinship at Titamnga is bilateral. Social relationships in this system are organized along two planes: the lineal (generational)[11] and the lateral (sibling) (cf. LiPuma 1988; Tambiah 1969). Conception is said to take place when a man's reproductive fluids (*iya coka* – literally "penis juice") both mix with and are encompassed by the fluids of his wife (*pango coka* – literally "vaginal juice"). The essential equivalence which goes into the making of a fetus is recognized in the means by which social ties are conceptualised after birth. A continuity with past generations is seen to adhere in the male line and becomes the basis through which claims to property are activated. Land, paternal names, and modes of ritual competence are all transmitted through men, from a father to his son (Bamford 1996b, 1997). Siblingship, on the other hand, derives exclusively from women and is spoken of in terms of an idiom of "one-blood" (*hinya avaka*). Any children that a woman bears, regardless of who their father might be, are said by the Kamea to be "one-blood" with one another. The same, it should be pointed out, does not hold true of a man. Should a man have more than one wife during the course of his life[12] any children that he has with these separate women will *not* be spoken of in terms of the "one-blood" relationship.[13] Only persons born of the same womb (*awtwa*) are *hinya avaka*. To be "one-blood," then, is to have originated from the same maternal container.

This same notion of "one-blood" groupings effectively *separates* rather than connects a woman to her offspring (Fig. 7.1). I initially confused the notion of "one-bloodedness" with our own ideas concerning the inheritance of biogenetic substance and assumed that the expression referred to the cultural fact that blood is the female contribution to conception. The Kamea, as it turned out, did not share my fascination with genealogical connections. *Neither a woman nor a man is considered to be "one-blood" with their children: the term refers exclusively to having issued from the same prenatal*

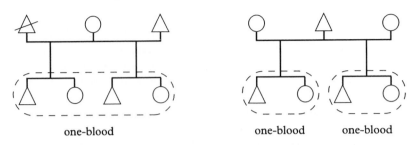

Fig. 7.1 The Kamea concept of one-blood

receptacle. Thus, one's mother, for example, would be "one-blood" with
her own "true" (<u>tru</u>) siblings, but not with any person in the ascending or
descending generation. Women bestow upon their children a "horizontal" type of relatedness which is imagined in terms of "containment"
rather than the lineal transmission of substance.

This carries with it a number of important implications. Much of the
published literature on Highland initiation systems takes the existence of
a substance-based universe as its analytic baseline (see Herdt 1984a,
1984b). Rituals like bloodletting and insemination are frequently understood to "remove" the maternal (i.e. feminine) part of the individual and
to replace it with a masculine counterpart. Initiation becomes a kind of
"gender surgery" (Herdt 1981) which acts on identity by manipulating
the alchemy of bodily substances. The Kamea, as we have seen, do not
understand the tie between a woman and her offspring as being primarily
substance-based. Indeed, as I have argued, substance disconnects rather
than connects persons in proximate generations. This is not to say that
the tie between a mother and her child is not embodied – rather, it is
based on that very act which brought the relationship into being in the
first place: the act of containment itself.

Until he is initiated a boy is, in a sense, still "contained."[14] During the
parturition process, what the mother eats affects the health of her child.
Pregnant women, for example, are enjoined not to eat either sago or
watercress because both have deep root systems which will fasten the
child to the uterus and prevent an easy birth. The taboo system marks an
extension of this process in that the eating habits of one directly affect the
wellbeing of the other. It is only through initiation that a woman's son is
finally "decontained." He and his mother are no longer joined as a single
entity, and the consumptive patterns of each no longer affect the other.
What was once perceived as a moment of similitude has become differentiated. What was once "one" is now free to enter into a *relationship.* The

son can now take a wife of his own and in the process he becomes another peg in the vertical line of male enchainment.[15]

This process of decontainment is played out as a concrete image within the context of last-stage initiation. When the timing is right and sufficient quantities of food have been amassed to support prolonged absences from gardens, initiates and their kinsmen assemble on a designated patch of ground which has been cleared of all vegetation for the occasion. The ensuing rites may last up to a month or longer, during which time anyone who cares to join the celebrations is free to do so. Beginning at dusk and continuing until dawn each night, novices are instructed to stand at the centre of the dance ground with their hands supporting an immense wooden post which stands in the middle. They are surrounded by men who dance in a circle about them, and on the outskirts of the clearing move the mothers of boys, who by their placement, collectively envelop the bodies of others. A cult house stands several hundred feet away from the dance ground, and it is here that boys will be given pandanus fruit by older men. On the appointed day, just as dawn casts its pale light over the serrated landscape, the older men will arrange themselves in a straight line and break through the women who continue to dance in a circle. The men collect up the novices amid a chaotic mock battle and spirit their charges away to the cult house on the hill. The "containment" of women is thereby broken (both literally and figuratively) and is replaced by a lineal use of space whereby men hold the cult house and women the dance ground (see Bamford 1997 for a more detailed discussion of Kamea initiation).

If the mother of a boy is no longer living, he need not adopt the dietary restrictions which prohibit the consumption of "smelly" game. Safeguarding the health of his mother has ceased to be an issue, and he can eat the tabooed items without fear of ill-effect. The son has, by his mother's death, already been decontained, and this state has important consequences *vis-à-vis* cult life. While living at Titamnga, I had the opportunity to befriend a young boy whose mother had died several years earlier. Habipu was approximately 10 years old, and like most boys his age, he had yet to be initiated. However, unlike other boys, he was well versed in the goings-on of the men's cult, and was given to turning the bullroarers whenever the opportunity presented itself. When I expressed surprise that a child such as Habipu had any knowledge of the bullroarers given that they were normally hidden from women and children, I was told that motherless boys are not barred from the secret male proceedings but are free to take on many of the rites of older men.[16]

I have argued that Kamea rites of initiation separate what is otherwise a conjoined entity: the inherent singularity of a mother and son. Up until the time that he is initiated, a boy's identity is fully enmeshed with that of his mother. The nature of this attachment is revealed in the consequences of their respective eating behavior: more specifically, by the capacity of each to influence the corporeal state of the other. Bodies are not perceived by the Kamea in exclusively individual or relational terms, but pass back and forth between singular and composite states. Unity, rather than differentiation is taken as axiomatic, and it is only through human effort that discrete social identities and relationships are achieved. One of the key ways in which bodies are brought together and taken apart is through being gendered – a process which eventuates, in part, through the performance of the initiation / taboo complex.

If initiation (decontainment) is seen to elicit a male form, the agent so defined is now in a position himself to elicit the capabilities of others. Until recently, it was inconceivable for a boy to marry unless he had been initiated into the male cult. Most men took a wife shortly after completing their final initiatory grade and married a second-degree cross-cousin on either the mother's or father's side. At marriage, a woman's child-bearing capabilities are obtained by a man through the payment of bridewealth – the game and garden produce that he gives for her as a wife. But more than simply *acquiring* her fertility, a woman's husband-to-be and his family effectively *creates* it. The Kamea say that girls mature more quickly than boys because they are eager to find a husband and bear children of their own. "Women think only of men and of getting married – this makes them grow quickly." A girl's kinsfolk are given food by the groom and his family over several years and this is also seen to hasten the maturation process. The idea seems to be that having enjoyed a particularly bountiful diet, the growth rate of a girl rapidly outpaces that of a boy.

The main, and certainly the most important, constituent of bridewealth prestations is game: an item which men collect from the surrounding forest environment. Hunting is the productive activity of men *sui generis*. Although men help their wives with the initial clearing of garden plots, their own productive labor is defined in large measure through their hunting activities. When a couple heads off to the bush to stay in their gardens, the daily round generally consists of women going off to their gardens each morning while men traipse off to the bush in search of game. Indeed, so close is the association between men and hunting that a boy's umbilical cord is cut with <u>pitpit</u> (*hapianga*), a type of cane which is used in the manufacture of arrows, while that of a female child is cut with bamboo (*haka*), a woody perennial that is used by women as a cooking vessel and water container. The intended productive domains of men and women are inscribed on the body from the moment of birth onward. As one woman explained it: "If we cut the navel (*pe'a*) of a boy with bamboo, he would carry a digging stick to harvest sweet potatoes when he grew up. If a girl's umbilicus was cut with <u>pitpit</u> she would always favour hunting over garden work." In the Kamea scheme of things, hunting falls squarely within the domain of men.

It is significant that bridewealth prestations are given to the mother of a girl: that is, they are given to that very person whose own "containing" capacities one hopes to elicit in her daughter. The bride's mother will share the food that she receives with those in her immediate family with one notable exception: much of the game that is presented to the mother as brideprice is taboo to young boys while they are growing up because of their "smelly" qualities. Hence, a distinction emerges early on in the eating patterns of "one-blood" siblings. A little girl is fed all varieties of game in copious amounts while the same food is prohibited to her male "one-blood" sibling. By eating brideprice, a girl's body comes to contain items of male production (in this case game), just as she will later contain her husband's sperm and finally any offspring that the marriage produces. A girl's capacity to act as a "container" is gradually drawn out through these prestations.[17] The payments made to a girl's mother become a compelling force which genderizes the female aspect of the "one-blood" tie.

Kamea interpretations of childlessness play off of this association between bridewealth and fertility. The men and women of Titamnga contend that it is impossible for a single woman to become pregnant. An unmarried woman can engage in repeated acts of sexual intercourse, but unless brideprice has been paid in her name, she will never conceive. Similarly, barrenness on the part of a married woman is often attributed to the working of a type of sorcery (*pa'a*) by the bride's kinsmen over their displeasure at having received what they consider to be inadequate brideprice. Seen in this light, a husband and his kin effectively bring about the possibility of the woman's conceiving. By acting as appropriate affines *vis-à-vis* the parents of the wife, they constitute her capacity to act as a container and in so doing bring the cycle of social enchainment full circle.[18]

Conclusions

New Guinea scholars have always been impressed by the fact that Melanesian peoples appear to make considerable use of gender imagery. Male and female appear as polarized beings who are not only different from but anathema to one another. Their distinct sexual substances and physiological processes are seen to have adverse effects on members of the opposite sex. The existence of a gender dichotomy is also reflected in a strict division of labor where males and females are not only assigned to different productive domains, but are believed to be incapable of carrying out the work of the other.

Most interpretations of male initiation in Melanesia have taken the existence of this dichotomy as their analytic baseline and have attempted to document how it is reproduced through time. The men's cult is seen as the principal means by which a male identity comes to be stamped on the body of a boy. But more than the creation of a gendered being is at stake. In many accounts, the rituals of the men's cult emerge as a political weapon through which men instantiate and perpetuate their political domination over women. Many anthropologists have claimed that through initiation men usurp the powers of women to give birth (Herdt 1981; Read 1952) and, in so doing, assert their autonomy and political ascendancy.

At the heart of the issue is the denial of the importance of women in the process of the reproduction of life in the enforced separation of sons from their mothers. Baruya thought is accordingly obliged, in the imaginary world, to dispossess women of their creative powers and to transfer these to men. (Godelier 1986:146)

Initiation emerges as a war between the sexes: one which pits men against women and reproduces a system of unequal power relations.

I have argued that Kamea initiation is not about reproducing a hier-archy of gendered states. Here the world is not seen to rest upon a ready-made system of cultural distinctions in need of being perpetuated: it is the act of constituting those distinctions in the first place that is the primary aim of social action. The practice and the symbolism of the initiation / taboo sequence reflects this difference in emphasis. Kamea women are intimately involved in the initiation of young boys – indeed, it is the mother–son relationship which stands at the heart of the initiation sequence. Here, men do not reproduce other men independently of the world of women: both sexes engender the social world through their mutually elicitive actions. Kamea men do not set themselves up as a separate political body charged with the reproduction of other men, because Kamea do not understand gender in essentialized terms. The engenderment of a male form is as much dependent on women as it is on men. There are no exclusive camps in this world which are capable of their own parthogenesis because cultural distinctions are understood to be *produced* rather than merely *reproduced*. A boy is not initiated into the men's cult, so much as he is detached from an encompassing female form. Women are not incidental to the process: they furnish the ground and the motivating force against which it takes place.

I began this chapter by asking how the body might be imagined were it possible to eat for someone else. For the Kamea, as for people the world over, food is imbued with social and cosmological significance. Since dietary restrictions govern what types of food may enter the body, they furnish a means by which sociality comes to be "embodied" (Lambek 1992:248). The taboo conditions I have described speak to the fact that cultural distinctions are created on an ongoing basis against a background of similarity. Taboos do create boundaries, to be sure, but one of the things they can mark is a composite identity (cf. M. Strathern 1987). For the Kamea, bodies go through moments of containment and decontainment, and they can appear as unindividuated and ungendered cultural forms. Society is not mapped onto the body as Douglas (1970) would have it, because people do not put their efforts into building a society. Instead, they concentrate on cultivating particular relationships. The capabilities which are associated with the body – the capacity to father a child, or to furnish a container within which it grows – are what allow one to enter into particular types of social relationships. These capabilities, however, are not given in the "nature" of things, they must be cajoled, teased, and coaxed to appear. In this sense, the body exists only as it is elicited and acquires specific meanings only within certain contexts. To be able to eat for someone else is to recognize that the essence of bodily form is grounded in a process of creativity.

ACKNOWLEDGMENTS

I would like to thank Roy Wagner, Susan McKinnon, Fred Damon, Peter Metcalf, Joel Robbins, Rebecca Popenoe, Margo Smith, Bruce Koplin, the editors of this volume, and anonymous reviewers for their comments on an earlier draft of this paper. Any errors in interpretation, of course, remain my own.

NOTES

1 The term Kamea is an administrative designation only and goes wholly un-recognized by the local people themselves. Government officers use the term to refer to those speakers of the Kapau language who reside in Gulf Province and are administered from the District Office at Kaintiba. Another 23,000 Kapau-speakers reside across the border in Morobe Province.

2 More recently, several other ethnographic studies have also been undertaken of Angan peoples. J. Mimica (1981, 1988) conducted research with Yagwoia-speakers during the late 1970s, while P. Bonnemère (1993) and P. Lemmonier (1991) studied Ankave peoples during the 1980s. For further information on Angans, see also Blackwood 1939a, 1939b, 1940, 1978; Fischer 1968; Simpson 1953; Sinclair 1966; McCarthy 1964.

3 Throughout this paper, terms given in Tok Pisin will be underlined, while those given in the Kapau language will be italicized.

4 The warrior function has, of course, lapsed since pacification although the promotion of "strength" (*yannganga*) continues to be a primary aim of initiation. The Kamea told me that strength is required to clear gardens, climb pandanus trees, build houses, etc. – all of which are normatively defined as masculine activities.

5 One man likened the smell of these animals to human excreta.

6 Here, I follow Lambek (1992) who writes: "If the semantic content of the taboo elaborates who or what one is not, it is the *practice* of the taboo that substantiates who one is" (p. 248 – italics added).

7 The image of a woman confined to the house, unable to cook, collect firewood, garden, etc. is actually realized each month during a woman's menses.

8 Indeed, the tabooed food item should not even be cooked together in the same container as other food in that the smell of the interdicted game would spoil what would otherwise be acceptable food.

9 To anticipate the argument which follows, he is considered to be "female-like," but, at the same time, he lacks a woman's "containing" capacity (see below).

10 At initiation, a boy is presented with *simnga* – the traditional buttocks covering worn by adult men.

11 I do not mean to imply here that the Kamea have descent groups. Vertical sociality is conceptualised more in terms of a continuity with past generations which the Kamea describe in terms of "lines" (lain) rather than groups (see Bamford 1996, 1997; cf. Wagner 1974).

12 This is, in fact, a fairly common occurrence given that polygyny is frequent.

13 Some of my Kamea friends drew a distinction between the idea of "one-blood" and "one-line," the latter of which would include all the offspring of a given man.

14 Indeed, it could be argued that his eating habits, in part, perpetuate this "containment" – see Lambek (1992) on the performative quality of taboo.

15 Some Angan groups initiate women as well as men (see Godelier 1986, for example) but the Kamea perceive such a practice as erroneous. In terms of the argument being advanced in this chapter, it can be seen that such a practice would make little sense. Women are capable of imparting only a horizontal kind of sociality. Since a female child will be a "container" herself, she has little need to be "decontained" in contrast to her brother who will be a marker of intergenerational relations. I will have more to say on this point below.

16 I hasten to note that the situation would have been different prior to the prohibition of warfare. Until the 1960s and the founding of the government station at Kaintiba, all boys were initiated regardless of whether their mother lived or not. Promoting strength was seen to be necessary in creating an effective warrior, and initiations have this as one of their principal aims.

17 In many ways, Kamea formulations represent a complete reversal of orthodox anthropological theory. Taboo is generally seen to maintain a system of preexisting boundaries, while commensality, in the form of prolonged feeding behavior is seen to produce "substantial" connections between people (see, for example, Carsten 1995a; Weismantel 1995; A. Strathern 1974; LiPuma 1988). For the Kamea, by contrast, taboo is every bit as much about marking

off a state of unity, while feeding can create important social distinctions. This issue is taken up elsewhere in greater detail (see Bamford 1997, 1996a).

18 We are now in a position to understand what initially struck me as a peculiarity of Kamea kinship: that sister exchange, although occasionally practiced, does not cancel out bridewealth obligations. Kamea insist that simply exchanging one's sister for the sister of another man does not negate the need to make matrilateral payments. Each side to the transaction is still expected to give bridewealth, even if the items moving back and forth are only identical qualities and quantities of the same foodstuffs. Simply to exchange sisters is to exchange ungendered beings – persons who are the "one-blood" product of a previous act of procreation, but who have no capacity to move within the world as an autonomous agent. Giving brideprice to a woman's kin creates her fertility. This act of differentiation continues until there is a complete metamorphosis: the woman is pregnant with a child herself. She has moved from the ungendered state of being contained, a state summed up through the metaphor of "one-bloodedness," to being able to act as a "container" in her own right.

8 Electric vampires: Haya rumors of the commodified body

Brad Weiss

Introduction

During my field research I occasionally heard reports of "greedy" people who had made their fortunes by stealing and selling other peoples' blood. As my neighbors talked with me about such diverse matters as the number of well-stocked stores in a particular town, or the dangers of life in urban areas they often brought up rumors of blood stealing. In their accounts, the victims of blood extraction and blood selling were not of much interest. I never heard anyone claim that someone they knew, or even knew of, had been murdered by blood sellers. What was of interest was the fact that vast sums of money could be made by such blood sellers, who acquired their victims by a variety of means. As one young Haya man described this phenomenon to me:

You can see a person who has a brick house, a store, cars. And you think a year ago he was the same as me, but he hasn't done any work. How did he get these things? You know he has been selling people's blood.

Wealth in itself, in such accounts, is not a sign of wrong doing, but the perception of a sudden and inexplicable shift in fortunes can invite suspicion.

Cars, in particular, were cited in Haya rumors as objects typically acquired through such nefarious actions. While most rumors spoke of the practices of blood stealing in general terms and without reference to particular cases, the one individual I knew of who was identified as being a blood seller was reported to have purchased his Land Rover with money made from his victims' blood. Moreover, this person was said to be using his car in order to further his bloody business. Owning a car enabled him to lure unsuspecting travelers looking for a lift into his car, and then to transport his victims' blood for sale outside the borders of Tanzania. Cars, in these accounts of blood stealing, are both the quintessential objects purchased through blood selling, and a principal means of engaging in the blood trade (Pels 1992:169; White 1993a).

172

The centrality of transport and travel is another important feature of blood stealing rumors. The most elaborated reports of blood stealing concern travel to urban areas, to Bukoba the capital of the region, and especially to the town of Mwanza, a ferry's voyage across Lake Victoria. Several Haya told of *Matende*, or "Evil Doers," at work in Mwanza employing a dangerous technological apparatus to procure their victims' blood. According to one typical report:

There are houses in Mwanza where they steal people's blood. They use electricity, and your body, it dries up. They steal your blood and just toss your corpse into a big hole in the back. I have been in these houses! The front door is made of wood, and they have written "Danger, Electricity" (*Hatari: Umeme*) on it. But if you just touch it, straight away that electricity catches you and your blood is sucked out (*imevutiwa*).

In such cases I was told that blood stolen in this way could be sold to hospitals in Mwanza, Dar es Salaam, and Nairobi, to "specialists," *wataalamu*, who knew what to do with human blood.

The final "type" of rumor circulating in Kagera while I was there has to do with youth (*vijana* in Swahili, usually synonymous with *abasigazi*, "unmarried *men*," in Haya) who are, as Haya villagers say, "lost in the city" (*babula omumji*). Young men who leave their rural homes in search of work in Bukoba, Mwanza, or beyond, are often said to be "lost," but in certain stories some young men become the victims of blood stealers. In these accounts, newly urban youth are kept alive by blood sellers who feed them very well so as to fatten them up in order to extract their blood every month (see White 1990a:430), for a description of "pits" where men were kept "just like dairy cattle"). Urban areas in such reports, as well as in the rumors of blood stealing by electrocution, are places of extreme vulnerability and insidious activity, where even the apparent benefits of eating well and being well fed can become a means of destruction.

These rumors of blood stealing seem to speak to the uneasy tensions local cultural orders experience in the face of global political economic processes. The effects of commodities as forms of objectifying and displaying value, or the ongoing project of urbanization and migration, are represented in these accounts as very immediate aspects of personal experience. And yet, the precise *nature* of that experience is not as predictable, even in the face of such powerful forces as these, as one might expect. Studies of sorcery and witchfinding in other African contexts have considered the significance of such "standardized nightmares" (in Wilson's phrase) which seem to present parallel personifications of evil that also emerge under conditions of massive social transformation and dislocation (Richards 1935; Wilson 1951; Willis 1968; Auslander 1993).

While I will argue below that there are important relations between Haya and other East African visions of sorcery (*oburogi* in the Haya language) and accounts of blood stealing, I also make it clear that these relations are not isomorphic, and that blood stealing is not simply sorcery in a modern voice. Each speaks to the tensions and ambiguities of sociality and its transformations, but each does so from a distinct perspective and in a distinct voice.

What are particularly arresting and distinctive about reports of blood stealing and selling are the ways in which they clearly *conjoin* discourses of economics and physiology; they articulate the circulation of commodity forms and bodily fluids, and characterize certain qualities of monetary transaction and accumulation in the terms of physical destruction. In analyses of colonial and post-colonial encounters in Africa, the variety of these commonplace, popular experiences is certainly less well documented than the activities of, for example, state-supported development programs, international banking institutions, or biomedical epidemiological projects, entities that are typically looked to as the agents of rapid social transformation. But popular Haya experiences such as these legends and rumors are equally integral to the unfolding historical processes in which *both* local and global actors are engaged. In this chapter I explore the implications of blood stealing rumors as a particular Haya form of consciousness, and in so doing attempt to assess what they reveal about the ways in which contemporary Haya imagine and construct their *own* place in making the history of which they are a part.

Considering relations between embodied consciousness, objectifications of value, and sociocultural rupture within an integrated perspective may also permit this analysis of a local understanding of transnational transformations and processes to serve comparative purposes, as well. As Knauft points out (this volume) the body has often been assessed as an apt expression of political economic realities in Africanist accounts of resistance, embodied spirituality, and historical consciousness; while Melanesianist accounts have tended to treat embodiment in phenomenological terms, as grounds for the expression of meaning and value. My focus in this essay on embodied dimensions of commoditization has further resonances with a Melanesianist interest that has been relatively less well articulated in Africanist anthropology, namely the links between embodiment and objectification especially as they are realized in contexts of exchange and transaction (e.g. Munn 1986; Strathern 1988; Battaglia 1992; Bercovitch, this volume), and further assesses the significance of processes of exchange like commoditization in terms of their implications for bodily experience. This essay attempts to combine what I hope are the strengths of each of these approaches, and argues explicitly that politico-economic and phenomenological perspectives, an analysis of processes of embodiment and objectification, and a recognition of the forms of value at stake in commodity forms can and must be reconciled in our efforts to understand the increasingly common conditions of modernity that confront an ever wider range of sociocultural contexts.

Looking for work and leaving home

Stories of blood stealing clearly suggest that the pursuit of wealth is highly problematic in the East African context. Not only can the accumulation and display of particular forms of property be looked on with suspicion, but the very project of simply seeking to make a living, either by selling labor or engaging in trade, poses imminent dangers. To begin to comprehend these rumors and the iconic forms of evil they deploy we have to examine the ways in which the people who tell and listen to them attempt to make a living; in turn, this requires that we understand a certain history of how the Haya are situated with respect to the *places* in which such material gains are sought. The Haya who shared these stories with me all lived in agrarian communities, and were engaged to some degree with maintaining farms and fields.[1] While, the rumors they exchanged were about urban areas and forms of work that are not centered on agricultural activities, it is, nonetheless, critical to point out that these accounts of blood stealing are *not* merely exoticizing reports about the alien character of strange and remote locales told to the stable residents of familiar home regions. The people telling these stories were reporting on their own experiences in places they may have routinely traveled to, and those who listened were often equally well acquainted with these places. Even those who had never been as far as Bukoba (100 km to the north) were very much aware of the property that might be acquired through travel, as well as the means of transport that made this travel possible. Blood stealing rumors, then, despite their images of the unfamiliar, are less about the contrast between the country and the city, but rather more about their *mutual* constitution (cf. Williams 1973). Indeed, the central themes of Haya rumors suggest that between country and city there are interconnections of the most intimate sort.

As a consequence of explicit colonial divisions imposed at the Berlin Conference of 1884–5 (which split up East Africa into British and German "spheres of influence" just north of the pre-colonial Haya kingdom of Kiziba (Coulson 1982:34)) Kagera is separated from Uganda by a national border. The Haya living in this region find themselves on the margins of the Tanzanian state with respect to Dar es Salaam, rather than integrated into the flow of traffic and trade surrounding Kampala, as

Haya kingdoms were throughout the nineteenth century. Owing to political ebbs and flows in the East African community in the post-independence period, culminating in the invasion of Uganda by Tanzanian forces in 1979, the border with Uganda has been little traveled in the 1980s.

The Kagera region remains rather peripheral to the national transport system. It is possible to travel from Bukoba to Mwanza by ferry, and from Mwanza the railroad can be taken south and east to the capital Dar es Salaam. This is a two-day trip, and the third-class compartments (a colonial "survival" in spite of Tanzania's African Socialism) which are what most Haya travelers can afford are talked about not only as exceedingly uncomfortable, but also as especially dangerous. Third-class passengers are seen as easy prey for thieves and "gangsters" – *majambazi* – who ride the rails. The roads that connect Kagera to the rest of the nation are largely impassable, and there is no regular bus service that travels from Bukoba to Mwanza, which lends greater prestige and power to – but further connotes the likely hazards of – private automobile ownership.

In spite of these obstacles, Haya do travel extensively throughout East Africa. The relation between Haya peoples and urban East Africa is long standing, and extensively documented. Many older men I spoke with recalled their military service in Tanga, Kampala, and Nairobi during World War II. White has evidence of Haya women arriving in Nairobi as early as the mid-1930s (White 1990b:103). In contemporary Tanzania, many Haya routinely travel to Mwanza where goods like clothing, soap, and housewares can be acquired for resale in Haya markets. As I have argued elsewhere (Weiss 1993), Haya rural communities face increasing pressures on their farms in the form of: an increasing population that results in the ever-diminishing size of inherited plots of land; fractious relations between agnatic relations as access to these farms becomes open to processes of commoditization; the prohibitive cost of converting uninhabited land into an arable residential farm; an increasingly entrenched class structure that leads to the rapidly declining cash income generated by coffee, the principal cash crop of the region, being concentrated in the hands of fewer and fewer coffee brokers. These pressures have meant that many Haya young men and women do feel that urban life presents opportunities to seek employment or other enterprises. Factory work is occasionally available in Mwanza; those who come to either Mwanza or Bukoba with less certain prospects often make a temporary living working as "houseboys" in the homes of elites, or selling goods, especially prepared foods and similar snacks, in roadside kiosks. But in all of these cases, the stay in town, while it may last for a few years, is transitory. Traders return to market their wares, factory work is rarely long term, and those who rely on less dependable employment return home even more quickly.[2] In fact, White observes that a high rate of mobility with no attempt made to establish permanent residence in urban areas was the defining characteristic of Haya women's forms of prostitution in colonial Nairobi of the thirties and forties, a residence pattern that is widely recognized as markedly distinct from other East African women who work as prostitutes (White 1990b:19, 103ff). Haya men and women were, and continue to be, motivated to migrate to urban areas in order to acquire resources which secure and enhance their standing in rural Haya communities. Again, these patterns of mobility indicate that an array of urban experiences insert themselves profoundly into rural ways of life through the continuous actions of coming and going.

Haya efforts to seek financial gain, or employment, have given many of them direct experiences of the world beyond their natal villages; but the form of this experience is largely itinerant, and is characterized even in cases of long-term residence by rather tenuous attachments to urban locales. White's essential research on blood stealing in East and Central Africa – focusing especially on Nairobi and northern Zambia of the 1920s and 30s – has concentrated largely on the significance of blood stealing as a means of articulating this tenuous position, and disclosing disjunctures in the control of property relations and labor under colonial regimes through an idiom that rather strikingly objectifies notions of descent, inheritance, and productivity (White 1990a, 1993a, 1993b). The history of their engagement with East African urban life tells us that Haya experiences of work and property are similarly fraught with the tensions of uncertain control, and it is not surprising to find that the ways in which they describe the places where they seek such work and property are often charged with the same graphic accounts of horrific physical destruction.

While I think the connections that White elucidates between rumors of blood stealing and transforming colonial and neo-colonial constructions of property relations are absolutely essential to an understanding of these reports, I also think that the specific symbolic qualities of both the images of violence and bodily attack, as well as the concrete, experiential dimensions of property, wealth, and value, can be examined from a perspective that does not privilege economic actions and motivations. For the characteristic semantic values of material forces like money and property, labor and markets are not simply *represented* by the images embedded in these widespread discursive forms; rather, the meanings of the contemporary Haya political economy are *constituted* by the mutual construction of intimate experience *and* economic practices. My contention in this analysis is that this process of construction can be usefully examined by a careful consideration of specific modes and ways of embodiment. The phenomenological perspective I develop here considers bodiliness as the grounds for collective (and not merely individuated) action and experience. Such an approach does not regard "the body" as an artefact whose components can be made to "stand for" exterior social, cultural, and historical projects, but rather sees the bodiliness as a mode of being-in-the-world which simultaneously brings into being (i.e., constitutes) and objectifies (or symbolizes) concrete orientations to and motivations in the world (Merleau-Ponty 1962; Munn 1986). Material forms and relations like labor and property can then be examined not only as historical conditions that have effects *on* the body, but as material realities that are themselves created *through* specific embodiments of social practice.

The implications of this approach to bodiliness have significant consequences for our understanding of the images of blood sucking as symbolic forms. For example, blood, from such a perspective, is more than an *idiom* or even metaphor for addressing, debating, or representing other "underlying" realities. Instead, as we shall see, I describe blood (and other dimensions of bodiliness) as an *iconic* form, not a representation *of* some more fundamental process, but a concretely experienced substance whose specific meanings and capacities both embody but also actively inform and shape the values of a transforming political economy. Property, money, and commodities, I am suggesting, are significant features of Haya and other Africans' lives, not only because of the transformations they bring about, or because of what they *do*, but because the very meanings of property, commodities, and the like are *created* in the course of a concretely situated unfolding historical process. Stories of blood stealing and blood selling, for example, tell us that aspects of the body can literally become commodities, indeed commodities that can be reduced to the price of their constituent parts. But at the same time, these rumors indicate that for many Haya, the very process of social transformation, from the technological forms of electrical wiring and automotive transport to the institutions of biomedicine – innovations that are, of course, dependent on the kinds of property relations characteristic of the colonial and neo-colonial encounter – are concretely realized and made meaningful through their bodily effects. To put it succinctly, not only do components of Haya bodies become commodities, but the process of commoditization becomes embodied.

Circulations of blood in the body

The potentials of blood described in these stories, as an *alienable* substance to be exchanged and evaluated according to a monetary measure, certainly seems to suggest a capacity for circulation inimical to Haya notions of blood. Yet, blood is a tremendously generative fluid in Haya

models of both physiology and sociality. According to Haya understandings of circulation, blood operates in ways which are dynamic and enabling. I want to address these understandings of circulation and transaction in order to assess their relevance to the conception elaborated in
these rumors of blood as a *commodity* form, and this in turn may allow us
to appreciate precisely what kind of exchange *commodity* exchange is in
the Haya world.

Within the body, according to the physiological theories offered to me
by numerous neighbors and informants, blood is not simply a constant
volume that is only altered by traumatic intervention.[3] Rather, the quality, consistency, and volume of blood is in constant flux in an active body.
For example, Haya men and women often refer to the ability of certain
foods to "increase the blood" (Haya, *okukiza obwamba*; Swahili, *kuon-
geza damu*), or to "decrease the blood" (Haya *okuiyao*; Swahili, *kupun-
guza*). According to informants, meat, especially organ meats, leafy veg-
etables, and fish are held to increase blood, while bitter foods like black
coffee and citrus fruits will decrease blood.

Moreover, the ability of blood volume to increase and decrease is a
matter not simply of quantitative measure, but of qualitative potential.
Thus, blood content fluctuates according to the thermal properties of the
body's situation. Blood itself is considered to give heat and energy to the
body – one friend actually compared the function of blood in the body to
petrol in a car – and increases or decreases in blood volume can be gauged
by how hot or cold a person feels. For example, eating foods or engaging
in activities which Haya men and women consider particularly hot – foods
such as chili peppers or certain bitter greens, and activities like working in
direct sun or excessive sexual activity (a potential problem for newly
married couples) – are frequently cited as causes of illnesses such as
feverish chills which are characterized by a lack of blood. In the practical
logic of Haya physiology, excessive heat causes the blood to "race" (in
Haya *okuiruka*; in Swahili *kukimbia*), and "boil" (*okutagata*) which in
turn diminishes blood volume. Women's bodies, by both women's and
men's accounts, are held to have more heat than men's bodies,[4] and this
heat leads directly to blood loss in the form of menstrual flow, which is
held to be the hottest of all blood.

The thermal qualities of blood and the management of blood volume
are also of concern in relation to drinking, especially to drinking distilled
banana gin, *enkonyagi*. Drinking gin to excess is typically conceived of as a
sure way to cause the blood to race too quickly, heat up, and eventually
diminish. A Haya hangover is typically described as feverish. In order to
counteract the effects of banana gin, many Haya drink sweet, unfer-
mented banana juice (*omulamba*), or eat fatty deep-fried fish (always a

popular seller at gin-drinks). Both sugar and fat are blood building and *hot* substances that replenish the heat lost from drinking by restoring blood volume. Similarly, neighbors of mine often sat out in direct sunlight after a day of excess in order to reheat their blood-reduced bodies.

These understandings of physiology are an important dimension of a more general Haya concern with the control of heat in sociocultural processes. In particular these forms of bodiliness reveal a specific interest in the dynamic and thermodynamic qualities and potential of blood. Blood circulates within the body at variable rates. It can race ahead quickly or move slowly under certain conditions. The rate of blood circulation within the body is also intrinsically linked to a blood volume, as fast or slow blood tends to increase or decrease blood. These characteristics are further interconnected with the thermal qualities of blood as relative heat influences both speed and volume. All of these dynamic, fluctuating properties suggest that blood is a substance whose shifting form can be taken as an acutely sensitive index of wellbeing. However, what is especially critical to point out is that the condition of wellbeing represented by blood is not merely an individuated condition of the physical body. Rather, the qualitative condition of the body is generated through the interrelation of *active* persons with the material world in which they are situated. Personal wellbeing is a *product* of particular ways of interacting with other subjects and with other objects; it is *realized* through practices like work and sexuality, or eating and drinking.[5] And the qualitative and quantitative state of blood concretely and directly signifies this interactive and practical process. These Haya physiological conceptions demonstrate that blood, in both its quantitative volume and its qualitative characteristic, is iconic (perhaps even symptomatic) of the engaged character of persons and objects.[6] Blood is a tangible form that both embodies and signifies the processes through which it is produced, and is thus an icon of sociocultural practice. Moreover, blood, I would argue, is a general medium, whose precise semantic qualities are highly nuanced (hot, slow, increasing, etc.) and more immediately sensitive to changes than are, for example, longer-term processes like "growing fat" or "wasting away" that also objectify and signify a Haya subject's sense of wellbeing. In this way the condition of blood can also be taken as an index of a general sense of "feeling" good or bad on a day to day or hour to hour basis, while "growing fat" or "wasting away" signify the relatively more permanent condition of those whose fortunes are rising or falling. As a changing condition of the body itself, blood signifies the internalization of a subject's relation to the wider world in which he or she acts.

The fact that blood can be dynamically and continuously transformed within the body in ways which signify shifting relations between the body and its encompassing situation is, I would argue, integral to Haya suspicions that blood could be converted to a commoditized object. These physiological understandings tell us that rumors of blood stealing do much more than simply make metaphoric connections between profit-making and murder. These rumors in fact suggest that certain aspects of commoditization can eclipse the capacity of the body to act effectively, that is, to produce itself through engaging in productive collective activity. Moreover, given the concern with enclosure and interiority that is so crucial to Haya control of productive activity, it is significant that blood is not only removed from the body, but literally whisked away in cars. These local understandings of extraordinary exposure, extraction, and mobility, then, speak to an ominous challenge that undermines the kind of secured containment integral to viable social practice. Even those who seem to enjoy the benefits of being well fed, so strongly embedded in these sociospatial qualities, are ultimately doomed. In effect, these victims embody the kind of "worries" that Haya generally recognize can cause a person to eat abundantly without generating and demonstrating the productive values of food, without ever "growing fat." It is this capacity for effective and productive action, what amounts to a Haya bodily dimension of agency, that is indexed and experienced through blood, and therefore extracted and appropriated through blood stealing.

Power embodied and extracted

The qualitative dimensions of blood as a substance that can be transformed by food and heat, as well as a resource that must provide heat and energy in the body, point to its enabling aspects as well. Blood conditions clearly *signify* the potential of the body in the ways I have described. But these Haya accounts also indicate that blood *is* the potential of the body. This dual form of signification, the fact that blood provides a concrete index of a general bodily capacity and the fact that blood also intrinsically embodies that capacity, provides a critical connection to the commodity forms that circulate in these stories and in Haya experiences.

To begin with, it hardly seems accidental that blood should be compared with gasoline, and blood stealing should be so strongly associated with owning cars. While the suggestion was never made to me that blood could be used in place of petrol (but see Pels 1992 for precisely such explicit claims), the very point of these accusations, it seems to me, is that blood can be *converted* into gasoline when it is sold. This convertibility is essential to the activities of blood sellers, and the seemingly infinite potential to interconvert objects created by monetary values is often seen as an essential feature of commodity exchanges (Marx 1906:81ff). But this dimension of commoditization is not sufficient by itself to account for the meanings associated with transformations in processes of exchange and conversion. The fact of convertibility tells us little about the *specific* objects, or the various *forms* of conversion that stories such as these suggest are characteristic of contemporary Haya experience.

The link, for example, between transport and commodities in Africa as described in Haya accounts of paths and roads, has been much discussed in recent scholarship (Bastian n.d.; Masquelier 1992; White 1993a). These arguments focus on the connections between the space of colonial road systems, high degrees of mobility, and privatized control over the mechanisms of mobility; and the potential for commodities and capital to dislodge and transform the ways in which persons construct and control the spatial order of the worlds they inhabit. Here, I want to suggest that a further aspect of these connections can be seen in the substantive qualities of both blood and gasoline. I have argued that in Haya understandings, the power or *potency* of blood is achieved and made use of through the control and regulation of heat. The fact that blood and gasoline, as well as electricity which I will discuss later, are all hot substances is quite relevant to this commoditized nexus. In Haya experiences, buying and selling and the pursuit of money in general are hot procedures. These may involve travel to hot distant cities, or require migration to arid farmland. If, as we have seen, it is blood in the body that is especially susceptible to depletion through exposure to excessive *heat* it is not surprising to find that gasoline, cars, electricity, and money, all of which are integral to activities that are considered significantly hot, can be construed as central to the radical extraction of blood.

Beyond its substantive properties, the *form* of power and potential objectified by blood suggests further connections with these processes and experiences of commoditization. Haya statements suggest that blood is both a means of empowering the body as well as a *medium* that allows other sources of power (i.e., specific foods, or other bodily conditions) to be converted into bodily power. This characteristic poses some intriguing similarities to electricity, another technological capacity notable for its associations with blood stealing. Electricity itself certainly suggests connections with the blood depleting effects of extreme speed and heat, particularly at a moment when the Haya say that *AIDS yairuka nk'obumeme*, "AIDS is racing like electricity." There is no electrical power provided to households throughout the rural areas of the region, but many individual buildings, especially hospitals and occasionally government offices, do generate their own electrical supply. Most Haya residing in Kagera are familiar with electrical power through their encounters with institutions such as these, and places, like cities, where electricity is more apparent, although by no means pervasive. These contexts in which electricity is experienced, the actual buildings, generators, and phone lines that so tangibly *are* the State in both its colonial and neo-colonial incarnations for many Haya, make of electricity a form of power that is not only beyond the control of even elite rural people, but is also a *threat* to the control of value they can exert. For such institutions concretely embody a structure of privileged appropriation that has forcefully reconfigured the rural moral landscape.

Batteries used to operate radios, cassettes, flashlights, and the like make electricity a somewhat more pervasive and available commodity. But the effective control of electricity, especially on the scale implied by electrified blood stealing, remains elusive. The weak life of the ineffective batteries available in Tanzania (a very common topic of Haya complaints) confirms this elusive character. As a form of property, or commodity, then, electricity is very much like the automotive transport with which it is associated in popular consciousness. Both of these high-speed media are markedly privileged resources, something well beyond the means of most people, that are owned and operated only by those who can afford to procure them for themselves.

As a form of *power*, that is, as a specific potential, or capacity for effective action, electricity is often spoken of, not only as a *source* that provides power to other mechanisms, but as a *substance* which is *identified* with the products of those mechanisms. For instance, in many Haya descriptions, the radiance of electric lighting is not simply said to be produced by electricity, it actually *is* electricity. The rumors of blood stealers in Mwanza would seem to be based on such a conception of electricity, as well. Remember that in these accounts, the door to the blood stealer's house is made of wood, but when you touch it you are instantly "caught by electricity." Electricity, here, does not operate through some other mechanism; rather, it contains within itself the capacity to effect certain results. The victims, in these accounts, are not killed by electrified property, they are caught by electricity itself.

This view of electricity suggests that certain Haya understandings of substance and power are founded on notions of causality and efficacy that condense the product of a procedure into its source.[7] In this regard, electricity can be seen as a form of energy that can be both supplied to various mechanisms as well as directly experienced. Blood, as I have described it, seems to be a similar substance. It is intrinsically a form of power and capacity, one that manifests a range of different qualities; but it is also experienced as the most immediate index of the body's power, a medium in terms of which other resources (the sun, gin, red meat, etc.) can be expressed in bodily terms. As they are represented in a range of

Haya activities and discussions, electricity and blood can be seen to be similar configurations of potential. And these similarities do seem relevant to their conjunction in these stories of blood stealing. Yet, such similarities also point to the fact that blood stealing rumors are not about the easily reconciled compatibility of blood and electricity as forms of power. Indeed, they suggest that these meaningful compatibilities can provide a pathway for uneasy transformations.

Part of the significance of these transformations can be seen in the very different applications of these alternative forms of power. Electricity, for many Haya, is a form of energy that is simultaneously concrete and diffuse. It can be directly seen in electrical lighting, but it can also be encapsulated in batteries. It is a singular source of power, and yet it can serve a seemingly infinite array of mechanisms. Thus, electricity conflates singularity and multiplicity in a way which suggests the hypermutability of power. This sense of diffusion can be seen in the description of the blood sellers' building where electricity seems to pervade the entire structure of the house. In effect, those who are "caught by electricity" are ensnared in its capacity for permeable transposition. Perhaps the ultimately deceptive warning "Danger: Electricity" is meant to indicate not that electrical power is contained within, but that electricity is essentially uncontainable. Moreover, this form of uncontained permeable power identified with certain urban architectural forms is certainly at odds with Haya domestic productivity that is predicated on carefully demarcated enclosure.

In elucidating these distinctive properties I do not mean to suggest that Haya conceptions of electricity are somehow inadequate or mystified. Many of my Haya friends devised elaborate adaptors and mechanisms to use over-sized batteries in minuscule cassette players which amply demonstrated that if anyone's knowledge of electricity was inadequate it was my own. What I do mean to suggest is that the power of electricity has distinctive applications in Haya experiences, and these particularities help to shape its concrete meanings. Moreover, these distinctive possibilities indicate that, while electricity and blood may be similar *forms* of power, the contexts in which they are deployed make electricity into what might be seen as an anti-blood. Where electricity is a diffused and highly mutable source, blood is necessarily localized and absolutely specific. While the same batteries can be and often are transferred from radios to cassettes to flashlights, human blood is only *productive* in the human body.

I emphasize productive, because, of course, human blood can be powerful outside of the body. Exposure, for example, to discarded blood, or worse, the unmediated ingestion of another person's blood is a sure way to contract disease, and would almost certainly be attributed to sorcery. Haya did engage in blood-brotherhood relationships, a practice that entails the exchange of blood (*okunywana*, lit. "to drink each other"; see also Beattie 1958). Through these practices, however, Haya always stressed to me that they were creating "one blood" out of two different men, but also two different clans. The implication is that blood is not a generalizable substance that can empower different bodies, but rather that each body – like each Haya clan – is categorically *different*. Any *similarities* between them must, therefore, be carefully constructed i.e., blood-brothers must be *made* into men of "*one* blood" when they begin as two. Moreover, the physical connection that is created through blood-brotherhood is one that does not *encourage* the interchange and circulation of bodily substance, but actually creates regulations which further restrict and delimit such circulations. That is, one of the principal effects of blood-brotherhood is that it establishes exogamous prohibitions, not only for the "blood" relations of the two men who enter into blood-brotherhood, but for all members of their two clans. Marital exchanges extending to persons quite distant from the blood-brothers themselves are, thus, cut off through this exchange of blood.[8] In marked contrast to the hyper-transposability and generalizable applications of electrical power, then, blood works only within the body, and only the *specific* body in which it originates, or those who have been *made into* members of that "one" body. Indeed, according to both members of the staff at Rubya Hospital and my lay informants, Haya considered blood transfusion a threatening procedure even prior to widespread local concerns about AIDS. Thus, while the contexts of convertibility for electricity seem limitless, blood's capacity to be converted is much more narrowly defined. Attempts to *distribute* the potency of blood outside of its strictly regulated position in the body, of the sort envisioned in accounts of blood stealing itself, must result in a radical subversion of its proper effects.

Of cannibals and vampires

Thus far I have described various Haya accounts and experiences as they relate to distinctive constructions of power, in the specific sense of a potential or capacity for action. The forms of power embodied in blood, gasoline, and electricity, and the range of qualities that are interrelated through these forms reveal certain correspondences between these different substances, correspondences which suggest the appropriateness of their being brought into direct relation in blood stealing rumors. Similarities in the ways in which these substances are experienced, especially in terms of their thermodynamic potentials are recognizable. Important inversions in the experience of these dynamic substances are also evident, particularly in the ways that their distinct potentials are applied and distributed. But the semantic configuration and interpenetration of all of these forms – as when blood races like electricity, or fuels the body like petrol in a car – demonstrate the fact that they are mutually defined and redefined in the processes of on-going social changes.

The semantic features of these accounts, features which are simultaneously about power, are crucial to their contemporary expression in Haya consciousness. But these stories are not simply about the imaginative correspondence and free transposition of one symbolic substance for another. In fact, what motivates these correspondences, both establishing and organizing the specific relations between these substances, is not just blood stealing by means of cars and electricity, but the fact that blood can be sold to create wealth.

The principal means that blood stealers have of making money, according to these stories, is to sell their victims' blood to hospitals, a claim which should tell us something about local perceptions of biomedicine. Practical attitudes toward medical treatment, according to the reports of regional hospitals themselves, are skeptical, at best. One hospital estimated that only 12 percent of women in the area have their children delivered under any kind of biomedical supervision; they also estimate that the population of AIDS cases in the region is roughly six times higher than the population that ever seeks medical treatment.

The community that I lived in has a lengthy familiarity with biomedical practice. A local hospital was established by Dutch Franciscan missionaries over thirty years ago. Originally administered by the regional diocese, it has recently been named a district designate hospital, and is now subsidized by and run in conjunction with the state.[9] One of many results of this transition is that medical care and pharmaceuticals are provided free of charge to the resident population. This is a change that, in the main, has *not* been well received. Many Haya men and women made their feelings known to me on this subject. A typical complaint was: "If you go to the hospital and tell them you have malaria, what will they give you? *Vitamins!* That hospital is free, it's of no benefit at all!" Indeed, those with any means tend to seek attention at other regional hospitals that charge for their services.

Of course, the reception of biomedicine, and the ways in which its practices are articulated with or kept at a distance from indigenous systems of therapy and health management is a complex issue, with an uneven history throughout Africa and the Third World more generally (Young 1978; Janzen 1982a). And Haya experiences, from routine problems with state dispensaries to the services of increasingly expensive local healers, indicate that local interactions with biomedical health care are ambivalent at best. But the special concern many Haya express with regards to the cost of health care in relation to its benefits reveals that over the course of their on-going relations with local hospitals Haya have come to evaluate biomedical efficacy in monetary terms. In effect, the bodily experience of health acquires a price when it is mediated by the institutions of biomedicine, and this recognition certainly seems to make the understanding of blood as a valuable commodity more plausible.

The commoditization of blood as an aspect of biomedical encounters is further suggested by some of the practices that surround transfusion. Rural hospitals in Tanzania depend on surgical patients and their families to replenish their blood supplies; when, for example, a patient undergoes surgery members of the family must donate blood in amounts equivalent to that which the patient has received during hospitalization. Yet, according to members of the medical staff I spoke with, wealthier patients often attempted to spare their families the perceived risks of blood donation, and instead required their clients (e.g., small-scale traders in the informal economy who depend on wealthy patrons for capital), or in some cases simply paid poorer neighbors outright, to donate blood on their behalf. Such transactions make explicit claims about the expertise and technologies of biomedicine as forms of knowledge and practice that in many ways generate and facilitate the commoditization of bodily experience. They further articulate the control of commodity forms exemplified by these wealthy patients, with an ability to control the effects of medical procedures through the very processes of commoditization that turn one's clients and neighbors into useful resources.

I would argue, however, that the significance of bodily commoditization, especially as it is configured in the nefarious acts of stealing and selling blood, is not reducible to experiences of hospitals, medical fees, and transfusions. Indeed, it is unclear whether the practices surrounding blood donation just described are better understood as *explanations* of Haya concerns with dangerous blood sucking, or as *examples* of it – even if such practices "really" occur. To assess the implications of bodily experience for commoditization we also have to pay attention to the consequences of blood *selling*, not only for the biomedical enterprise that purportedly purchases blood, but for those who *sell* it, to begin to understand the meanings of these kinds of transaction. Recall that the wealth accumulated by reputed blood sellers seems not only extravagant, but especially mysterious. Indeed, the fact that such riches are suddenly and *inexplicably* possessed is taken as evidence of their illicit acquisition.[10] What is particularly unfathomable is the sudden *discrepancy* in wealth, the rapid accumulation of goods by those who one once knew and recognized as economic equals.

This concern with the relation of knowledge to the relative wealth of one's neighbors, along with a recognition of inexplicable rises and declines in economic fortunes, suggests important connections with another form of Haya popular consciousness, namely a concern with sorcerers (*abarogi*). Reports about the activities of sorcerers, frequently neighbors and kin, are a pervasive theme in Haya conversation. Virtually every funeral that I attended was accompanied by suspicions that death was brought on by such malevolent actors. Haya friends told me that sorcerers act out of "obstinacy" (*oluango*, lit. "refusal," from the verb *okuanga*, "to refuse"). "He doesn't like to see that you exceed him" (in Swahili, *Hataki kuona kwamba wewe unamzidi*) is a standard description of a sorcerer. "Jealousy" or "envy" are the terms anthropologists have generally used to translate African terms for the sorcerer's motivations, and these might be applied in the Haya case; but it must also be remembered that Haya sorcerers are clearly driven not by a desire to possess what others who "exceed" them possess, but rather by an ambition to destroy those others completely. No sorcerer that I heard of ever accumulated a fortune by destroying his or her victims, and wealthy people were less likely to be suspected of being sorcerers than they were of being potential victims of sorcery.

These popular rumors of both blood stealing and sorcery present icons of evil that are intimately connected with perceived economic[11] differences within the Haya community. Yet, interestingly, blood selling, according to my Haya sources, is categorically *not* the same as sorcery.[12] To begin with, we can see that blood sellers and sorcerers represent differences within a community in opposing ways. Whereas blood sellers embody an idea of sudden, inexplicable (and implicitly illicit) advantage and inequality, sorcerers always act to invert radically these very sorts of inequality. Moreover, the wealth accumulated by blood sellers is conceived of as arising from unknown and impenetrable sources, while most Haya fear that neighbors who are constantly scrutinizing their households (those who "have the evil eye," *baina ekiisho*) are likely sorcerers.[13] Blood selling is made evident by tangible *displays* of wealth, while sorcerers are obtrusive *observers* of internal household resources.

Blood selling and sorcery not only embody alternative "visions" of economic inequalities, they are characterized by alternative actions on the human body. Blood sellers, as we have seen, sell their victims' blood in order to acquire houses, cars, and the like; but sorcerers, by most Haya accounts, kill their victims in order to dig up their corpses and eat them. These distinctive forms of consumption tell us something about the ways in which the significance of property relations and economic transaction are constituted and embodied in Haya experience.

Blood sellers make use of their victims by a decomposition of their constituent *parts*.[14] The victim's blood is always thoroughly extracted and alienated from the rest of the body. This is no mere trivial observation, for the rumors themselves focus on and elaborate this aspect of the blood stealers' actions. Once the bodies are drained of blood, the victims' corpses are merely piled up in open holes, an image of chaotic death and burial that Haya find as horrific as the idea of blood stealing itself. The lost young men, kept like cattle in the city, present another image of bodily detotalization. These young men's bodies are effectively converted into transactable units – indeed, commodities – by this blood sucking operation. As Pels notes in his account of rumors of blood suckers (known as *mumiani*) in the Uluguru mountains of Tanzania, under colonial economic practices "the body became a commodity, a thing to be exchanged for an abstract value expressed in money, and a similar perspective on the body is unfolded by mumiani rumors" (Pels 1992:178). The blood of the anonymous victims of the blood stealer thereby becomes a resource, a utility that is thoroughly separable and abstracted from the context in which it is produced.

By contrast, sorcerers in the Haya context are interested in much more than the fragments of their victims' lives; they seek to encompass them completely. Death and burial in Haya communities establish a fixity and finality in personal identity. Proper burial on a family farm secures one's attachments to an enduring place, and reciprocally ensures the attachment of those who continue to live in such farms to the deceased who are buried there. It is the fully realized and anchored identity established through mortuary practices that is the sorcerer's true object. Haya descriptions of sorcerers often elaborate their techniques for exhuming newly buried bodies, and certain amulets are buried with a corpse in order to prevent this from happening. By eating their victims' corpses sorcerers finish off, in effect, the completed and total person. This form of consumption is also in keeping with the sorcerers' excessive scrutiny of their potential victims while they are alive. Sorcery establishes a thoroughgoing identification between sorcerers and their victims, an identification that proceeds from intrusive observation through exhumation and consumption of the finalized corpse.

These characteristic actions of the sorcerer reveal important correspondences (albeit in the form of inversion) to many fundamental qualities of productivity and viability that are essential to Haya domesticity. The concern with the sorcerers' invasive scrutiny and observation of the household is especially important because of the centrality of *enclosure* as an essential characteristic of domestic activities. As I describe at length elsewhere (Weiss 1996), households are defined and established as quintessentially *interior* spaces, an orientation that is made explicit in everything from house-entering rites to the daily provision and consumption of Haya meals. The nefarious acts of sorcerers also demonstrate that this spatio-temporal pattern is not only a matter of concrete forms or practical techniques, but one that is intrinsic to what I describe as Haya *sociality*, a basic orientation that Haya households and persons have toward each other. The understanding of neighbors as ever-present witnesses, carefully evaluating fluctuations in household fortunes as a most insidious threat, demonstrates how crucial (and so how fragile) are Haya attempts to establish their household as an acknowledged locus of independence, self-sufficiency, and separation from surrounding "others."

The fact that cannibalism, *eating* the dead, is the ultimate expression of this threatening agency also reveals how central the practices surrounding food consumption are to this model of domestic security. The preparation and presentation of food within the home and literally behind closed doors ensures the kind of enclosure that is essential to the viability and endurance of the household. The dramatic disinterment of a household's recently deceased members enacts a violent dislocation on a number of levels. Such an activity not only suggests the graphic and shameless exposure of eating (which in itself should be kept from view) and its consequent threat to household productivity; it also clearly portends the disruption of underlying processes of generativity that are, quite literally, deeply embedded in Haya family farms, and in particular, in the generations of ancestors that are buried in them. Haya graves and burial practices should confer stability to the land, as well as to the identity of those who inhabit it, as a landholder will "stay by the grave of his father" in order to assure the perpetuity of his father's and his own legacy for future generations (Weiss 1993). Cannibalism of this sort, then, signals a totalizing dislocation and disorientation of the household and the immediate landscape it inhabits. It is a form of undoing that is deeply rooted in (and hostile to) the practices, techniques, and spatio-temporal organization of domestic life, as well as the forms of property that sustain it.

On the other hand, blood stealers present a threat that is oriented toward a different form of property, transaction, and sociality, an orientation that is concretized in their distinct selection and use of their victims' bodies. The threat of blood stealers, for example, is not something that emerges in the context of land holding which is so powerfully implicated in the creation of generative household activities and identities. But land holding disputes are often accompanied by sorcery accusations. Blood stealers are not interested in domestic productivity, but are, instead, a model of "business" taken to its horrifically logical conclusion. Indeed, I would argue that in many respects the actions of these blood stealers challenge our "conventional" notions of "vampirism"; for vampires (at least in their Euro-American (re)incarnations), with their sexual as well as alimentary interests in their victims, and the fact that they sustain their own eternal lives, as opposed to lining their pockets, with the bodily substance of their victims, are bound up in the kinds of intimacy and destruction that are of little interest to blood stealers. It is sorcerers in East Africa who crave such an intimate invasion of the lives of their obsessively observed and (too) well-known neighbors and kin; the victims of blood stealing are largely anonymous, unattached, dislocated, and "lost" youth.[15] Yet East African blood stealers do convert their victims into transactable resources, while it is sorcerers, through their totalizing consumption, who make the very practice of transaction with others an impossibility. Thus, while blood stealers present the tangible evidence of economic success, however tainted it may be, sorcery, say many Haya, is bad for business.

Conclusions

These stories on the surface may appear to be concerned with contrasts between former ways of life and the hazards of the modern world. But they clearly address notions of power and agency, and represent forms of efficacy and potential that underlie commodities, bodies, and the actions in which they engage. In short, rumors such as these describe a series of articulations, articulations that illustrate connections between bodies and commodities, semantic values and economic transactions, rural liveli-hoods and urban travels, as well as "local" values and "global" institutions.

If we examine the contrast between blood stealers and sorcerers from the perspective of bodiliness as a grounds for action and sociality we can see that the changing social worlds in which such figures are situated inextricably *fuses* politico-economic and semantic processes. This contrast suggests, for example, that a putatively economic category like "consumption" can only be assessed by breaking it down into specific historical modalities. The concrete forms of consumption, from appropriation to accumulation to purchase, to ingestion, must then be related to the variety of practical contexts in which they are configured. These practical contexts reveal some of the ways in which the meanings of blood, heat, speed, and the like construct and define the values of commodities, while the forces of market transactions simultaneously appropriate bodily conditions and capacity.

At another level, blood stealing rumors demonstrate dialectical relations of a different sort. The contrast between blood stealing and sorcerers is not to be taken as indicative of a historical *transition* between discreet spheres of transaction or regimes of value. Blood stealers embody economic inequalities generated through skillful transactions, the very phenomena sorcerers attempt to subvert. But local understandings of sorcery have become permeated by the same forces that pervade its iconic representation as blood stealing. Indeed, many senior neighbors indicated to me that Haya sorcerers were far less likely to disinter corpses in the past – some even said the very practice of necrophageous sorcery was an entirely contemporary phenomenon – when family farms were held by their clans, and could not be bought and sold for ready cash. Sorcery, therefore, is implicated in the very same set of exchanges and institutions of commoditization, migration, and dislocation that are associated with the market transactions exploited by blood sellers. Both images of evil indicate that all such activities, land holding and migration, descent and "business," have become inextricably conjoined in the contemporary world. In contrast, then, to Pels who concludes that "the [sorcerer's] crimes take place within relations of production well understood by Luguru cash croppers, [while the blood stealer's] take place within ill understood ones" (Pels 1992:178), in Kagera, at least, the relations of production – and transaction – that provide the contexts for sorcerers and blood stealers do not reflect the absence or presence of knowledge about these relations, but rather, I would suggest, different attempts to *control* them. Remaining on the land and ensuring its perpetuity or selling off an inheritance to try and make it rich are different strategies for creating and securing value in the modern world, but each is suffused with the possibilities of commoditization, each is fraught with potential risks and conflicts – and each embodies the possibilities of historically and culturally situated orientations and practices. For the activities of sorcerers take shape in a world of money, informal economic practices, and consumer goods as surely as certain cosmopolitan businesmen traffic in blood and corpses.

ACKNOWLEDGMENTS

The research upon which this chapter is based was made possible by a Fulbright-Hays doctoral dissertation fellowship. The Tanzanian National Institute for Science and Technology (UTAFITI) enabled me to live and work in Tanzania. I am also especially grateful for the tremendous generosity of Severian and Anatolia Ndyetabula. An earlier and substantially different version of this chapter appears in my book (Weiss 1996), and I must thank Duke University Press for permission to publish this version here. This chapter has, moreover, been through a number of tellings and inscriptions and I am grateful to a wide audience for their contributions and suggestions. Notably, Luise White's work on vampires in Central Africa has evidently been influential, and her personal support has been immensely encouraging. Peter Pels kindly sent me his essay on the subject, and our discussions have been rewarding. Deborah Durham, Laurie Lewis, Adeline

Masquelier, and Misty Bastian offered important suggestions at an impromptu University of Chicago graduate student gathering where the earliest draft of this work was first presented. Jean Comaroff, Nancy Munn, and Bill Hanks contributed enormously to a clarification of the theoretical questions raised. Finally, Michael Lambek's editorial skills have been crucial to the final form that the chapter now takes. In spite of all of these laudable contributions, there are undoubtedly problems that remain, for which I take full responsibility.

NOTES

1 Just over one million Haya live in the Kagera region, located in the northwest of Tanzania. The Haya form a part of the Interlacustrine sociocultural area, that includes (among others) the Ganda and Nyoro in Uganda to the north, as well as the indigenes of Rwanda and Burundi to the west and southwest. Haya villages (*ekyaro*, sing.) in the rural areas of Kagera, the primary site of my research on which this chapter is based, are composed of a number of family farms (*ekibanja*, sing.). These farms are also places of residence, and all households occupy farmland. All of the farms within a village lie immediately adjacent to one another, so that the village as a whole is a contiguous group of households on perennially cultivated land. These residential villages are dispersed across and clearly contrast with open grassland (*orweya*). The primary products of Haya family farms are perennial tree crops, bananas that provide the edible staple and coffee that provides the principal source of money. While coffee remains the most significant source of a rapidly declining cash income in Kagera today, this cash is filtered through the Haya community in an informal economy (*biashara ndogo ndogo* in Kiswahili) of marketing local agricultural produce, fish from Lake Victoria, household commodities, and new and used textiles and clothing at local weekly markets.

2 This characterization of Haya patterns of work-related traveling does not include an important educated elite, many of whom live and work for many years in places like Dar es Salaam, London, and Chicago. Yet even in these cases, perhaps especially in these cases because of their economic capacity to do so, most Haya make concerted efforts to maintain attachments to their agrarian homes, not only by regular financial support to family members, but by actually owning and maintaining homes and farms of their own in a village.

3 Haya medical practice does call for blood letting in some instances, usually in response to the thermal conditions described below.

4 This heat comes from the greater amount of fat that Haya usually say women have. Heft is also an *aesthetically* desirable condition, especially for women, and this preference certainly inclines Haya to think of women's bodies as fatter than men's.

5 Looking at blood in this way, as a *product* of sociocultural actions and a transformation of material substance and processes, allows us to get beyond questions as to the "authentic" issues addressed in these rumors. Whether they are, for example, "really" about the body or food, alienated labor or kinship relations, becomes a moot point when bodiliness is seen as the foundational condition through which the material world and sociality and the relation between subjects and objects are constituted (cf. White 1993b: 761–7).

6 This description of blood as an icon of a subject's engagement in social action corresponds to my analysis (Weiss 1996) of "growing fat" and "wasting away," each of which I describe as iconic of the subject's wellbeing as signified by a capacity to control food (cf. Munn's (1986:17) analysis of such "qualisigns" as well).

7 I have indicated elsewhere (Weiss 1992) that Haya experiences of plastic reflect a similar understanding of the ways in which process and product are embodied in commoditized objects.

8 It is unclear to me how exactly Haya understandings of conception might be fitted to these restraints on the transmission and transaction of blood, although clearly some connections – given the exogamous prohibitions that ensue from blood-brotherhood – are implicit. Haya men and women described a fetus to me as the product of a man's and a woman's comingled sexual fluids – *amanyare* is the term for such fluids, both male and female. The fetus itself grows by being "fed" with the fluids of intercourse during the course of pregnancy; a father's attachments to his growing child are secured perinatally (both before and after birth) by his provision of food – and not blood – which either develops the fetus or feeds a nursing mother. Given the effects of food on blood described above it might be possible to speculate that masculine contributions to the "feeding" processes of gestation work to construct the blood of a father's child.

9 The physicians who work at this hospital are still all European, but the staff of medical assistants, nurses, and administrators are currently all Tanzanian.

10 Cars, especially, are seen as outwardly visible forms of wealth of ultimately unknown and unknowable acquisition and operation (see White 1993). Haya often comment that one can never be sure exactly who owns a car; it can be driven by different people, so its *control* seems open to multiple agents.

11 Here I take "economy" in a broad sense to include forms of value that are not equivalent to commodities, or even possessions. Children and fertility, for example, are attributes of a family that will characteristically incite the *oluango* of sorcerers. The economy here concerns the control of all forms of value, which the iconic forms of sorcery – and blood selling – implicitly recognize are bound up in social relations.

12 Luise White confirms this distinction. Her informants insisted that blood selling was not something carried out by sorcerers, since sorcerers "couldn't get a market for blood" (personal communication).

13 This concern with scrutiny and observation is a crucial instance of Haya understandings of vision and visibility as sensory dimensions of hierarchical control (see Weiss 1996).

14 Misty Bastian (nd) also discusses the significance of commoditization as a process of detotalization in her analyses of *juju*, or money magic, in Nigeria.

15 See Pels (1992:178–9) for a similar contrast *vis-à-vis* property and productivity between *mumiani* blood stealers and *wawanga* cannibal sorcerers in Uluguru.

Part III

From exchange to history

9   Creative possessions: spirit mediumship and millennial economy among Gebusi of Papua New Guinea

Bruce M. Knauft

In recent years, notions of power and resistance have often informed anthropological understandings of spiritual experience and embodiment. The entranced individual can be viewed as pushing against inequities bequeathed by political domination, gender, race, or age. Providing a voice for the disempowered, the possessed persona can be considered the colonial subject crying out against colonialism, the woman resisting patriarchy, the youthful agent protesting gerontocracy, the heathen subverting Christianity or Islam, or the spiritual gift economy resisting the market. In various permutations, such views are common in works on spirit possession and millenarianism in Africa and Melanesia, including classic studies such as Lanternari's *Religions of the Oppressed* (1963), Worsley's *The Trumpet Shall Sound* (1968), and Lewis's *Ecstatic Religion* (1971). More recently, local expressions and idioms of spirituality have been seen to contradict and destabilize the assumptions upon which state or Western logics of control are founded. This point has been elaborated by Michael Taussig (1987, 1993), Anna Tsing (1993), Mary Steedly (1993), and Smadar Lavie (1990), among others. As Boddy (1994:419) notes in a recent review, "most would agree that possession cults are or have become historically sensitive modes of cultural resistance."

Amid signal contributions, however, such portrayals easily partake of what Abu-Lughod (1990) calls the romance of resistance. And as Ortner (1995) has recently noted, there is a tendency for studies of resistance to be ethnographically thin rather than rich. Analogously, treatments of spiritual imagination and mimesis can be frustratingly vague at the same time that they can be suggestive and stimulating.

Viewed more phenomenologically and taken on their own terms, the aesthetics and experience of spirituality come to center stage, not as resistance or counter-hegemonic agency but as the expression of cultural meaning and sociality. Presaged by Marcel Mauss, transactional and phenomenological understandings of spirituality have proliferated in recent decades. In the Melanesian context, such perspectives resonate with the important work of Roy Wagner (1967, 1972, 1978), Edward Schieffelin (1976), Nancy Munn (1986), and, more recently, Marilyn Strathern (1988), Debbora Battaglia (1990, 1995a), Aletta Biersack (1995), and Andrew Strathern (1996), among others. In the main, these analyses tread but lightly on the consideration of power, hegemony, and resistance. Analogues from Africa cover a similarly wide ambit, including figures such as Godfrey Lienhardt, Victor Turner, James Fernandez, Michael Jackson, and Michael Lambek.

Vis-à-vis Melanesianist renderings, however, Africanist counterparts more frequently combine phenomenological or symbolic perspectives with ones that draw on critical theory and political economy. There is arguably a longer and more developed tradition of Marxist scholarship in African than in Melanesian studies, including resonance with anticolonial sentiments in African histories and politics (contrast for Melanesia, A. Strathern 1982a). The critical edge of resistance to power in embodied spirituality echoes prominently in Africanist works such as Jean Comaroff's *Body of Power, Spirit of Resistance* (1985), Jean and John Comaroff's *Of Revelation and Revolution* (1991), Peter Fry's *Spirits of Protest* (1976), David Lan's *Guns and Rain* (1985), as well as, more diversely, in Fritz Kramer's *The Red Fez* (1993), Paul Stoller's *Embodying Colonial Memories* (1995; cf. also 1989), and Janice Boddy's *Wombs and Alien Spirits* (1989), among others (see more recently, Graybill 1996; Weigert 1996).

The goal of the present chapter is not to reify differences of analytic perspective or ethnographic area so much as to articulate them. In particular, I draw on sensibilities developed in some Africanist contexts to consider innovative developments in a local genre of Melanesian spirit mediumship.[1] Melanesian spiritual and millenarian innovations commonly engage political, ethnic, or gendered inequality in the context of emergent Christianity, political rivalry, and economic aspiration. The articulation of materiality and religion through "possession" (in both its economic and its spiritual sense) is ripe for interpretation and analysis well beyond what used to be called Melanesian "cargo cults."[2] How to understand the embodiment of spirituality amid poignant inequities of post-colonial circumstance is a key issue. In the present case, I consider a new genre of spirit seance developed by a spirit medium named Wahiaw in a remote Gebusi settlement.

Spiritual context

Innovations in Gebusi spirit mediumship are thrown into relief by more general beliefs and practices.[3] In the early 1980s, the roughly 450 Gebusi were scattered in some seventeen longhouse settlements clustered in a remote corner of Papua New Guinea's Western Province. Located at the northern edge of the extensive lowland rainforest that extends from the New Guinea south coast to the foothills of the New Guinea Highlands, Gebusi life at this time was uninfluenced by Christian or missionary influence and was at the remote fringes of outside economic or administrative impact. Spirit seances occurred about once every eleven days and lasted all night.

Gebusi seances each entail up to a hundred songs sung spontaneously by the spirit familiars of an entranced spirit medium (Knauft 1985a, 1989). At the beginning of the seance, the medium relaxes in the longhouse, smokes, and induces his own spirit to leave, thus allowing spirit persons to come into his body and speak through it. The song lines of the spirits – their primary means of communication with Gebusi – are immediately chorused in resonant harmony by the assembled men of the settlement.

To ride Gebusi seance songs is to take a train of radically fragmented images: arcane, evocative, and erotic. They telescope the past, present, and future, as well as the spaces of the spirit world and those of the Gebusi landscape. Song lines do not form a connect-the-dots picture so much as a poetic collage of overlapping and resonating flashes. Subsequent images recontextualize, ironize, or eroticize previous ones. As if to collapse the Melanesian pre-modern with the academic post-modern, Gebusi seances have that license that merges obscure and arcane vocabulary with larger general themes that are ultimately predictable if not taken-for-granted by the audience.

Gebusi spirit seances foreground the lewd adventures of the medium's spirit women, who cavort in the spirit world and joke sexually with Gebusi men present. These voicings, and their chorused echo among the men, prompt banter and infectious repartee. As well as teasing each other, men joke directly back to the spirit women, who can respond with further provocations in subsequent song lines. Dialogic as well as multi-voiced, Gebusi seances are shot through with humor, play, and aesthetic creativity. As the "second voice of discourse," they are at once melodic, profoundly meaningful, funny, and arousing (cf. Bakhtin 1986:110).

In terms of gender, this deep aestheticism is dominant if not hegemonic. While women themselves are excluded from participating in the seance, the agency of the spirit woman, who forms the ideal image of female beauty and sexuality, is controlled by men; she is voiced by a male medium, echoed by the male chorus, and responded to in autocommunication between the men's chorus and their own banter. Spirit women are bold and sexy; they not only flirt with seduction, they consummate it. The fantasy ends abruptly, however, in the lives of real Gebusi women. Like their spiritual counterparts, young women are encouraged by cultural ideals to be attractive, coy, and flirtatious. These same themes are reinforced by the lascivious idioms of the spirit seance itself, which women listen to from the other side of the thin sago-leaf wall that separates their collective sleeping quarters from those of the men.[4] But Gebusi women can be beaten by brothers and with impunity by husbands if they are suspected of flirting or, especially, adultery (Cantrell n.d.). The spirit woman, in contrast, flirts and fornicates at will even as she remains the medium's spirit wife and the center of universal acclaim. Her excesses fuel men's sexual impetuousness: "I'm too horny to wait for a woman." In day to day experience, a Gebusi woman alone is considered an invitation to rape.[5]

In addition to heavy joking and homoerotic horseplay, men aroused by the spirit women may seek sexual release with a younger man or boy, who sucks him to orgasm outside the longhouse. Though most seances are not accompanied by homosexual trysts *per se*, men's homoerotic joking pervades virtually all of them. This action appropriates and redirects what Gebusi typically suggest is heterosexual desire. This move parallels in a sexual arena men's structural appropriation of female reproduction, for instance their belief that boys need to receive masculine life-force through insemination in order to achieve adult masculinity (see Knauft 1986, 1987a, 1989; cf. 1993).

Despite and indeed because of the charged context, Gebusi spirit seances also provide the fluid context – and often the sugar-coating – for serious and potentially grave spirit pronouncements that galvanize anger against sorcery suspects. Between about 1940 and 1981, virtually one-third of all adult Gebusi deaths were homicides, and the bulk of these were the execution of persons within the community suspected of sorcery.[6] These killings are legitimated and typically instigated by the pronouncements of the medium's spirits during seance inquests, including those that entail a high degree of sexual joking and repartee. In the eroticized aura of the seance, the structural tensions of sexual frustration that accompany unreciprocated marriage or other marital disputes easily inform men's collective acceptance of the sorcery target – male or female – that the medium's spirits have scapegoated for aggression. These accusations draw on gender hegemonies and appropriations; just as men appropriate the voice of the spirit woman in their singing, and just as they appropriate the spirit woman's desire in their sexual joking, so too they maintain a gendered monopoly on violence that can draw upon the energy of sexual frustration and direct it as aggression against the sorcery suspect. In short, the multivocal dialogue of the Gebusi spirit seance combines rich aestheticism with the cultural hegemony of gender domination and violent scapegoating.

Though the killing of sorcery suspects is in no sense reducible to spiritual imagery alone, this violence is effectively instigated by the sexual and social imagery of the seance (Knauft 1985a:ch.8; 1989). The structural tensions of Gebusi society revolve around the mandate for sister-exchange in marriage despite practices of kinship and social affiliation that reduce both the practical possibilities for completing such marital exchanges and the means to acknowledge or ameliorate animosity in cases of nonreciprocity. The projection of anger and the justification of aggression against a sorcery suspect are the prominent result. In the context of the spirit seance, male license becomes men's habitus. A definitive spiritual verdict, if there is one, typically appears self-evident if not taken-for-granted. This reception is predisposed by the heightened arousal and sexual tension that accompanies the event. Gebusi audiences are not dupes; to push this issue is to miss the point. Rather, there is a deep and mutual resonance between the super-conscious associations of the entranced spirit medium, the deepest and most unstated fault lines of Gebusi marital and sexual practice, and the unexpressed or inexpressible sensibilities of audience members that come out as bawdiness and aggressive displays of sexual humor. As if to hybridize Bakhtin (1986) with Gramsci (1971), the chronotope that bridges these domains is hegemonic. It is the application of this spiritual ontology to the situation at hand that the spirit medium makes explicit.

The sociological side of this shared larger reality is prominent; the seance is a public event attended by the men of the various clans in the settlement, if not the larger community. During the seance itself, they typically accept and unify around the spirits' identification and indictment of the sorcerer. Indeed, men find it difficult to discuss or confront these most serious issues in the absence of spiritual guidance; the mandate for accusing or executing a sorcery suspect almost invariably comes from the omniscient voice of the medium's spirits in seances. This voice seems obviously true in retrospect, even if it is often not predictable ahead of time.

Innovation

Gebusi seance format was altered by Wahiaw. At one level, he elaborated the festivity and entertainment of the seance while negating its divinatory and accusatory dimensions. Indeed, some of Wahiaw's most important innovations were sung spontaneously in lieu of an anticipated sorcery inquest. Instead of sorcery and revenge, Wahiaw engaged a new set of tensions that seethed just beyond the Gebusi horizon: the proliferation of trade goods, wage labor, and their conflict with Gebusi notions of kinship and exchange. These developments were poised to complicate Gebusi men's control over violence and sexuality. Among other things, they glimpse the possibility of a shift from direct male violence as a means of settling disputes over sorcery and marriage to the possibility of paying goods or money to compensate aggrieved parties. Though material compensation has been quite developed in the New Guinea Highlands and other areas of Melanesia, Gebusi have favored a person-for-person model of exchange in violence as well as marriage (Knauft 1985b; cf. A. Strathern 1971, 1982b; Godelier 1986).

Wahiaw's seances were innovative in form as well as content. Like standard seances, his new songs were sung spontaneously by his spirits and chorused line by line by the assembled men. But unlike regular seances, his story lines and characters formed a coherently evolving mythic drama. Gebusi mythic narratives (*gisagum*) are not normally "invented"; they are a stock set of stories handed down from elders to juniors in public tellings. Wahiaw created new *gisagum*, however, as spontaneously sung to him by his spirits. In effect, he altered the aesthetic genre of the seance to imbue transient spirit world images with unprecedented coherence and permanence. That these stories were not just told but were physically *embodied* by Wahiaw's spirits gave them illocutionary force and legitimacy. Wahiaw's stories were not just remembered; they were retold by audience members to others afterwards in the form of standard *gisagum*. Transformed from transient song to lasting myth, they became an enduring part of Gebusi narrative corpus.

Wahiaw's innovations are illustrated in two contrasting *gisagum* that he sung over a short period of time. In the first, Wahiaw's songs developed standard mythic themes of a handsome and upright male hero whose propriety ultimately rewards him with marriage to a beautiful young woman. Wahiaw put a poignant twist on this tale by introducing a trade-store gift between the man and his hopeful partner as a pivotal thematic element. Indigenous gifts are common between Gebusi friends and need not normally be returned. But because the trade-store good also qualifies as a new kind of personal property that is ultimately inalienable, the young woman in Wahiaw's story feels obligated to come back to the hero and give his gift back once she has been promised away in sister-exchange marriage to an ugly suitor. Her reappearance gives the hero the chance to break off her onerous marital commitment (which was never consummated), and draw her back to himself. The narrative ends with the happy reunion of the original couple.

In this *gisagum*, the anomalous status of the trade-store good as both gift and commodity provides the ambiguity of an elastic band that allows the actors to stretch their relationship apart and yet be pulled back together again. In point of fact, the hero's trade-store gift *is* an elastic – a band of stretch cord sewn into the woman's bark cape. The trick of the story is the creative use of the trade item, not as bald foreign intrusion, but as a good that can be selectively manipulated to play upon *both* the affective connection of gift-giving and the impersonal nature of commodity ownership. The narrative thus hybridizes an autonomous Western individual, who abides by the commodity contract, with what Marilyn Strathern (1988) describes as the indigenous Melanesian "dividual" – a transacted or trans-individual identity based on gifts and exchange.[7] In the process, the woman and her lover are able to subvert the rules of sister-exchange marriage and assert their nonreciprocal union without negative consequence.

Wahiaw's second *gisagum*, by contrast, marks a more radical transformation of mythic themes. The story begins with four young cousins (two boys and two girls) who are enticed down a hole by an old woman; they are kidnaped and disappear. Their parents search at length for the lost children but cannot find them; ultimately, they all give up except for the mother of the youngest girl. Eventually, she finds the hole the children have gone through. Climbing into it, she descends a cavernous underground waterfall and emerges, like Alice in Wonderland, on the other side of the millennial looking glass.

Much of the narrative takes place in this lower world – a Gebusi place of danger and notoriety. But the lower world in the narrative is a revelation of cargo. The woman finds a huge Western-style house, fully furnished, where she is welcomed by another woman. (The audience is amazed and exclaims their desire to live there, too.) After digging a few net bags of sweet potatoes,[8] the women get into the resident woman's new truck (!) and drive to the patrol post. (More exclamations by the audience.) Shaking with fear, they are admitted through a long series of rooms and doors until they enter the office of the chief Patrol Officer, who is surprisingly termed *kogway wi*, or "culture mother." The Officer is a gruff, fearsome, and yet generous benefactor with a nose as big as a house post; he swivels in his office chair all day and alternately gives orders and grants favors. To the young woman's amazement, he gives them metal patrol boxes full of clothes and money in exchange for their mere bags of sweet potatoes. (The Gebusi audience exclaims in awe.) The primordial giver of Gebusi culture has become the giver of commodities.

The women drive back to their Western house, where they count their money and try on their clothes under the light of their pressure lamp before washing with soap, eating a full meal of store-bought goods, and going to bed on a mattress with sheets under the cover of a mosquito net. (Such stuff is high fantasy for Gebusi; the audience goes wild.)

The women continue to supply the Patrol Officer with bags of sweet potatoes in return for trunks of clothes and money. When the young woman asks for her missing children, however, the Officer becomes angry; the children are under contract to work at the patrol post, and their absence is the price of the goods the woman receives in trade. The children are indentured, and the very process of earning them back ensconces their mother in the same material seductions that separate them from her. Michael Taussig's *The Devil and Commodity Fetishism* (1980) could hardly have found a better model.

Over time, the loss of familial separation works its toll on the young woman, despite her ever-increasing wealth. The Patrol Officer keeps putting her off, taking her sweet potatoes, giving her trunks of money and clothes, and writing letters that say the children's employment is not yet up. The Gebusi audience gets provoked: one man yells he would rip up the letters; another proclaims that the woman was living like in jail, even if she *did* receive clothes and money.

After years of waiting, the Patrol Officer gives the woman a letter telling her that her former husband has given her up for lost, married another woman, and started another family. As the woman reads (she has learned to read), her tears cover the letter until it disintegrates in her hands. She has lost not only her children but her upper-world husband as well. The Gebusi audience loudly laments her plight.

The next day, however, the four years of the children's contracts are up and they are returned to her. Moreover, she is given the patrol boxes full of goods and money that each of the children has received; as their faithful parent, she becomes the mother of them all. In their new truck, the four young adults and their de facto mother drive back up to the upper world. Finding their old house fallen down and the clearing covered with weeds, they set up their lawn chairs, relax, and wait for the woman's ex-husband to emerge from the bush. His former wife berates him for his unfaithfulness: How could he have given up on his wife and child? Unlike the standard narrative hero who bears privation to maintain romance (as in the first narrative), the upper-world husband has been unfaithful and must suffer the consequences. The woman then opens a final letter the Patrol Officer had given her; it invites her back down to the lower world to live. The woman and her children thus leave their natal kin and drive back down to the patrol post with all their possessions, leaving the traditional village, still impoverished, behind forever. Down below, the Patrol Officer welcomes the family back and gives them all big houses full of Western amenities. The woman's sons and daughters all marry outsiders in balanced exchange. In addition, her new sons-in-law give her huge bridewealth gifts – a practice Gebusi themselves have strongly avoided. The tale ends with a Gebusi heaven-on-earth at the patrol post, and the audience exclaims what a fine way to live that would be.

As a new kind of morality tale, Wahiaw's second narrative portrays the tension between indigenous and wage economies. What starts as kidnaping proceeds through loss, the dark alienation of wage labor, and spousal abandonment. One plumbs the deep sorrow that is pervasive in Papua New Guinea as the schism of separation between relatives in town and those in the village. This pathos is perhaps now the new "Sorrow of the Lonely" in a Papua New Guinea that is now post-colonial (cf. Schieffelin 1976). Nevertheless, all doubts are resolved and washed away as the wage economy persists in its largeness. What starts as pain ends up in millenarian luxury. By the narrative's conclusion, new families have been reconstituted, wealth abounds, and morality has been maintained. By contrast, the indigenous village has faltered in its commitments; poor and disparaged, it is left behind in the bush.

Variations on a dream

Wahiaw's two narratives of spiritual embodiment are complements – two sides of an ambiguous currency. Each recognizes the moral tension that pits the desire for Western goods against the demand for social and moral affiliation. But in the first narrative, the trade good *resolves* indigenous romance and brings it to fruition as traditional marriage within the village. It uses the propriety of the material contract to cement rather than explode this local world. In the second narrative, by contrast, wealth, contract, and family are clearly bought at the *expense* of village life.

Wahiaw's two myths embrace highly contrastive outcomes. Yet both are viable, not only aesthetically but practically, to Gebusi as they contemplate their future. As Michael Lambek (1993a:14) puts it in an African spiritual context: "varying views of the world, even different senses of what knowledge is can be held concurrently. People's attitudes to knowledge cannot be reduced to ideological formulae."[9] As Lambek (this volume) suggests, local notions that are incommensurable need not entail logical contradiction or antinomy; to the contrary, they can enrich human experience by diversifying understandings and horizons of expectation.

The logical strictures of our own theories, categories, and standards of interpretation should expand to comprehend this rich and supple complexity. These complications are not just idiomatic or significatory; they can provide the spark for importantly different courses of action. In the present case, Wahiaw's *gisagum* provide a mandate either to encompass Western goods within an indigenous morality or, as in the second narrative, radically to transform economic and social relations.

The tension between these competing desires – for communal morality and for individual wealth – is at the heart of cultural dynamics in contemporary Melanesia. This tension also informs more radical attempts at millenarian or politicospiritual transformation. In various guises, for well over a century, such poignant initiatives have bubbled and erupted in Melanesia, and they show no sign of abating. The changing cultural and economic dimensions of possession – possession in both its spiritual and its material sense – are central to such movements.

Wahiaw's second narrative goes against many dominant – some might say hegemonic – assumptions in Gebusi culture. It proposes a female hero rather than a man to triumph in the world of trade goods and wage labor (cf. Knauft in press). Western wealth is engaged not out of greed, but out of devotion to children and cousins. In addition, the exchange of persons for wealth – both the children laboring for the Patrol Officer and the grown children marrying for bridewealth – suggests change in Gebusi notions of person-for-person reciprocity. In contrast to an indigenous world that legitimates control over women in sister-exchange marriage and male violence in sorcery accusation, material exchange in Wahiaw's *gisagum* forestalls and overcomes both these negative possibilities. Tensions are resolved without recourse to either violence or male control.[10] Ultimately, then, Wahiaw mediates opposed logics of exchange while transcending the limitations of each; moral propriety and equivalence are made consistent with material wealth rather than being at odds with it.

Wahiaw's innovative challenge to both indigenous and intruding forms of power is especially remarkable given his personal circumstances. His village was extremely remote; its population had used stone axes into the mid-1960s.[11] Even by the early 1980s, out-migration and development were very slight, trade stores or schools were generally inaccessible, and no one from Wahiaw's area spoke pidgin or any other contact language. As if to cap this marginality, Wahiaw himself had long been crippled. He had to be carried laboriously to give seances in neighboring hamlets, and it is likely that he had never even seen the Nomad patrol post. Though there was an incipient development project north of Nomad in late 1981, Wahiaw's own settlement was too distant to benefit from it.[12] His extraordinary vision of wage labor, commodities, and accompanying social relations emerged from tranced visions that drew on others' fleeting accounts but had no basis in personal observation or experience.

Implications

Wahiaw's prescient awareness expands upon views of spirituality that either ignore or overweight the relevance of colonial and other hegemonies. Change is not imposed like Captain Cook, arriving like Leviathan on a self-contained island of culture. Not only is change desired poignantly, sometimes achingly, it is generated actively, sometimes almost *de novo*, from the heart of most distant cultures.

Wahiaw's *gisagum* illustrate the special potentials of embodied spiritual innovation. While divergent scenarios of social and cultural change may be talked about or fantasized, their embodiment in tranced experience gives them special performative force as well as aesthetic freedom and diversity. In this respect, spiritual embodiment provides an "intermediate zone" between projective rumination and committed social action; it mediates the creative possibilities of spiritual transformation with potentials for agency and practice.[13]

Wahiaw's spiritual expressions reveal how indigenous views of change are often more multilayered and nuanced than those of our own analyses. They articulate different voices and different opinions, not only between individuals, but within a single individual like Wahiaw over a short period of time. They illustrate the ambiguity, tension, and what Gramsci (1971:333) called the contradictory consciousness of embodying *both* sides of a material and moral problem. The implications of alternative possibilities are brought into focus and imbued with cultural force and value.

If these characterizations are basic, it remains true that many of our own perspectives on culture and hegemony fail to penetrate *the deep ambiguity and profound tension of living agents as they wrestle morally and socially with the inequities of change*. A more focused and nuanced attention to these rocky realities can encourage both an appreciation of spiritual experience and a critique of domination. It is important to retain the relativist moment that appreciates idioms without reducing them into resistance. But if we are to expose and understand inequalities, this moment needs to be matched by others that view spiritual assertions through the critical edge of cultural contestation and bodily constraint. One of our more important tasks is to climb inside these tensions to appreciate and critique alternately the richness of spiritual experience that engages inequity in the absence of easy answers.

ACKNOWLEDGMENTS

Comments on an earlier draft of this chapter from the editors, other volume contributors, and anonymous reviewers are gratefully acknowledged. All short-comings remain my own. Some of the case material presented here is considered in a different analytic context in Knauft (1996:ch.6).

NOTES

1 The theoretical positions at issue are discussed more generally in Knauft (1996).

2 See Worsley 1968; Lawrence 1964; Schwartz 1962; Burridge 1960. Lamont Lindstrom's scintillating *Cargo Cult* (1993) critiques the genealogy of Occi-dental motives that surround the notion of cargo cult as a projective Western category. As a historically material complement, Nicholas Thomas (1991) considers the Western imposition of material possessions into lives that were ostensibly Pacific. As Annette Weiner (1992) re-reminds us, it is important not just to critique our own categories of possession but to understand the potentials of theirs more fully (see also Bercovitch 1994; Robbins 1994a, 1995).

Excepting Fortune's early *Manus Religion* (1935), surprisingly, few if any full-scale monographs on Melanesian religious possession or mediumship have been published, though the increasing syncretism between indigenous and Christian beliefs makes this possibility ever more intriguing. Stephens's (1995) major recent study richly considers the internalization of spirituality in the context of Mekeo magic and sorcery.

3 Concerning Gebusi spirit mediumship, see Knauft (1985a:chs. 2, 4, 11; 1989).

4 In a sense, women are the ultimate audience of the spirit seance – its superaddressee.

5 Though Gebusi women may go off alone to attract a lover, this non-binding sexuality carries no obligation for the man and high cost to the woman. Except when they are eminently marriageable, women fear this option and guard against it. Men justify non-consensual sex by arguing that if the woman was not willing, she would not let herself be accosted while alone.

6 See Knauft 1985a:ch.5, 1987b; cf. Kelly 1993.

7 The notion of "dividuality" in intersubjective personhood first emerged in South Asian contexts (e.g. Marriott 1976; Daniel 1984).

8 Sweet potatoes are not frequently raised by Gebusi but are known to be desired by government workers.

9 Ellipses in this statement are not shown.

10 It is notable that the Patrol Officer does not attempt to engage the lone young woman sexually or make her his wife. During her long absence from her husband, the female hero in Wahiaw's second narrative is neither subject to nor solicitous of sexual advances. Even at the end of the narrative, the implicit connection between herself and the Patrol Officer is left as a platonic com-radeship.

11 In 1962, Patrol Officer Hoad (1962–3) reported that large trees were still felled by stone axes in the area of Wahiaw's hamlet.

12 In late 1981, an advance exploration team for the Chevron Oil Corporation established a base camp north of Gebusi territory. The team conducted a seismic survey for oil reserves; for this purpose, they needed transects cut across rainforest areas two days' walk north of Gebusi settlements. Much of the timber was cut with chain saws by immigrant Southeast Asian laborers, but some – perhaps for public relations reasons – was hand cut by men hired from the local area. These included some Gebusi men (as well as Bedamini, Samo, and Kubor) who were willing to walk to the base camp and work for several weeks or months away from their villages. A few Gebusi men departed for this labor and were paid about 20 kina a week; most returned home either sick or homesick within a few weeks. Wahiaw's new seance genre developed about the same time that some of these men were returning to their Gebusi settlements. His spirit innovations do not refer to these events directly, but they do resonate with its context as projected by Wahiaw, as well as with the working conditions of paid officials and their retinue at the Nomad patrol post more generally. I do not believe any of the Gebusi laborers in 1981 departed from or returned to Wahiaw's own settlement, but he knew of these developments from stories and hearsay. The actual economic impact of these developments was not particularly great, as the goods available for cash were few and the prices very high. The Chevron seismic team departed shortly thereafter, and the possibility of further work departed with them. Though similar explorations had been conducted in the early 1970s with no positive result, in the present case a large oil well was ultimately dug several years later further to the northeast. This project is separate from that described here, but news of such projects travels widely and can have significant cultural impact outside the area that is impacted most directly (e.g., Stürzenhofecker 1994).

13 This point draws on the trenchant remarks of Andrew Strathern in the conclusions to his important recent book, *Body Thoughts* (1996). Strathern (pp. 202–3) suggests that embodiment as an analytic concept is crucial for articulating and mediating our Western distinctions between self and enactment, person and practice, individual and experience, and society and action.

10　Dis-embodiment and concealment among the Atbalmin of Papua New Guinea

Eytan Bercovitch

In the early to middle 1980s I carried out research among the Atbalmin, a people who live in a remote mountainous area of Papua New Guinea. At that time, the Atbalmin had recently converted to Christianity, but they still continued to depend on indigenous social, economic, and religious practices. In the area where I lived, there was a continuous debate over whether to preserve or destroy a particularly important temple. The temple had been for generations the center of a complex system of rituals, myths, and objects from which women were largely excluded and to which men gained access only through a long series of initiation ceremonies. Many people believed that keeping the temple was a great sin which would ensure that they would burn in Hell forever. Others felt strongly that the temple was of key importance and that its destruction would endanger their lives and society.

What makes this debate among a New Guinea people relevant for the topic of this volume is that it was deeply about persons and bodies. Defenders and opponents of the Bomtem temple alike shared the view that people, individually and collectively, were at risk and needed help. The threat was expressed in terms of its negative effects on the body: grotesque Christian scenes of torture in Hell, and equally terrifying indigenous forebodings of sickness, starvation, and loss of bodily capacities. Both sides emphasized that the threat came from a concealed source that they had a special means of revealing and responding to. Yet, as I will shortly explain, the solution promised by Atbalmin Christianity and the indigenous religion also depended on concealment and bodily destruction.

Anthropologists are giving renewed attention to how people understand and relate to their social conditions through practices and images of the body (see the Introduction to this volume). These practices and images may be negative as well as positive, involving bodily harm and destruction as well as wholeness and health. As Africanists and Melanesianists know well, social conditions may be represented powerfully through beliefs in sorcery, witchcraft, and pollution. In an extreme form, this might be called *dis-embodiment:* the process by which people's bodies and bodily capacities are actually or imaginarily taken away from them, in part or in whole. Anthropologists have repeatedly shown how such concerns with dis-embodiment reflect conflict: at the level of social principles and institutions; between rival social systems; and between particular individuals.

In what follows, I will explore concepts and experiences of dis-embodiment among the Atbalmin. My analysis bears on three sets of issues that emerge in other studies but that are made especially clear in the Atbalmin case. First, I argue that by attending to concerns with dis-embodiment, we may gain insights into a common dilemma of agency: the fact that in order to preserve relationships individuals may often have to betray other relationships. Second, I will explore the uses of concealment in situations of social conflict, in order to consider the connection between concealment and dis-embodiment. This leads to the third and final point, that different forms of concealment and dis-embodiment can exist in the same society. Among the Atbalmin, there were distinct forms in everyday life, in the indigenous religion, and in the new Christian faith. All three were at issue in the struggle over the fate of the temple, and I will return to that struggle repeatedly in the following pages.

Society and reciprocity among the Atbalmin

In the early to middle 1980s, about three thousand Atbalmin lived in the Star Mountains of Papua New Guinea, very close to the border with the Indonesian province of Irian Jaya (I use the past tense not because the Atbalmin no longer exist but because my knowledge about them is based on a particular period of time).[1] Their land was rugged and heavily forested and far from any towns or government centers. The only way I found to reach the main area of Atbalmin habitation was by flying to a small dirt airstrip and then walking in for several days. I found that the Atbalmin tended to live in small settlements, averaging three or four houses and thirty people each. Several settlements were usually clustered together, separated from other clusters by distances of several hours to a day or more. I ended up living in Bomtem, an unusually large settlement with eight houses and sixty-five people. It was located two days' walk from the airstrip in a fertile valley that had ten other, smaller settlements.

Living in Bomtem, it quickly became apparent how the remote location of the Atbalmin had not kept them from the impact of external forces. The Atbalmin had been visited by government representatives beginning in the 1950s. This was mostly in the form of occasional visits by patrol officers who had to walk in ten days from Telefomin, the nearest outpost of what was then a United Nations Trust Territory administered by Australia. It was not until the time of Papua New Guinea independence in 1975 that the first airstrip was cleared among the Atbalmin. The airstrip greatly improved access to the area, and it also allowed the opening of a primary school and a one-room health clinic at the airstrip. Around the same time, a Christian mission at Telefomin (started by the Australian Baptist Missionary Society) sent Papua New Guinean pastors into the Atbalmin area. These pastors proved remarkably effective in converting people. In addition, just before my arrival, in 1981, a multibillion dollar copper and gold mine opened at Ok Tedi, a week's walk away on the other side of the Star Mountains.

Despite their contacts with all these new forces, the geographical isolation of the Atbalmin ensured that they relied largely on their indigenous economic and social practices. In the early to middle 1980s, they subsisted on swidden cultivation (with sweet potato and taro as the main crops) supplemented by hunting and gathering. The government school and aid post were too hard to reach for most of the Atbalmin including those in Bomtem. Very few men anywhere in Atbalmin had ever left the area to work for wages, a fact which the Ok Tedi mine did not change. Manufactured goods entered the area not through stores (which did not exist) but through exchange with neighboring areas. In such exchanges, money served as one form of valued object along with others, such as Nassau shells, cooked pork, bark-fiber bags, and bows and arrow.

Likewise, although the Atbalmin were increasingly aware of the importance of social relationships with new forces like the government and the Baptist mission, their everyday lives were oriented primarily around local ties of residence, kinship, and exchange. People spent most of their time with others who lived in their own or neighboring settlements. Each settlement was generally organized around a group of very close cognates, often one or more sets of actual siblings. At a higher level people affirmed their cognatic ties with members of neighboring settlements in terms of a shared membership in a broader kind of descent group. These cognatic descent groups averaged about 150 members (ranging from less than 30 to the 300 in the descent group to which Bomtem belonged), each claiming a significant territory for exclusive use by its members. The term they used for these groups, *tenum miit*, combined the word for people (*tenum*) with the word that literally meant a plant's base (*miit*). Indeed, as I came to learn, there was an underlying plant metaphor in concepualizing human collectivities: groups began with an ultimate ancestor (the plant's base) out of which subsequent generations arose and hopefully increased in number (the plant's branches and leaves).[2]

The descent groups as well as the plant metaphor were also organizing principles in the indigenous religion. Each group owned the contents of the temples in their area and sponsored initiation ceremonies, to which qualified members of other descent groups were invited.[3] Ritual elders sometimes referred to the contents of their temple by the same term as they used for descent groups, *tenum miit*. In this way, they identified the relics with their group's origin as well as with its ongoing growth and wellbeing.

Social relationships among the Atbalmin were shaped not only be cognatic descent but also by processes of exchange (*duyadamin*, "giving and receiving"). Individuals exchanged many kinds of valued objects, including shells, money, bows, clothing (both indigenous and manufactured), string bags, axes, and knives. They also constantly gave and received quantities of food to each other, including both highly valued meat and ordinary garden staples. All adults were active in exchange, though men were more active in the exchange of shells, money, and wild game while women were more active in the exchange of garden staples.

Exchanges served to create and sustain relations between individuals and groups. Exchanges of objects and persons made possible close relationships between people whose cognatic ties were distant or nonexistent. Exchanges were expected in connection with marriages and the birth of children. Exchanges were even at the heart of relationships between close cognates, who regularly gave each other food, support, and various valued things.

Reciprocity and the social basis of bodies

Significantly, the process of exchange was also used to conceptualize the bodily meaning of cognatic relationships. A fetus was formed, I was told, when semen (given by the father) combined with blood and other fluids (given by the mother) in the womb. This giving of substances led to the resemblances between children and parents; it was also the basis of a basic bodily commonality between siblings and, to a lesser extent, more distant cognates who shared an ancestor. The physical dimension of exchange, moreover, did not end with birth. A child's health and growth depended on a continual giving of food and support by the parents as well as others. When they grew up, men and women were expected to reciprocate the imbalanced flow of gifts they had received from conception onwards – including sexual fluids, food, care, and other things – by providing food and labor to those who had given birth to them and helped raise them. This reciprocal flow helped older individuals to maintain their physical health and social standing.

The theory of conception was only the most obvious example of a more general interconnection of bodies and exchanges in Atbalmin thoughts and practices. To make this clear it is necessary to add a few more details. I was told that people were composed not just of flesh (*tiil*) but also of several other components. The most important of these were the "heart/will" (*aket*), the "thought/consciousness" (*finang*), and a principle of vital force called *simik*. The latter, though invisible, was understood to be physically attached to the skin. People depended on all these components; the failure of any one would threaten bodily existence. And every one of the components could be affected by the actions of other people. People could add to or diminish another's flesh or vital force, and they could influence his or her heart or thinking in a manner that could be likewise either helpful or harmful.

For the Atbalmin reciprocal exchange was the overriding principle of human actions and the essence of morality. Through exchange, people ended up mutually strengthening each other's bodies and vital force. They also created (in part for this physical reason) a basis of shared will and thought. People emphasized that exchange was most important not as a means by which individuals pursued their own interests but rather as a process through which they could collectively create a situation of common and shared interests. This was linked, in turn, to an emphasis on openness and physical closeness, as crucial conditions not only of exchange but also of ordinary social life. People regularly commented that they should not hide anything from each other, whether their material possessions or thoughts. They said it was crucial to live very close to each other. There was a circular quality to this reasoning: those who had close relationships should live in this way, but it was precisely by living in this way that people created close relationships.

The circularity reflected a tension between social ideals and practices among the Atbalmin. As people made clear to me, a situation of reciprocal exchanges, openness, and closeness was something that required constant effort to achieve. This effort was worthwhile not just because it was morally right but because it led to better life for people individually and collectively. I was deeply impressed with how hard people worked to meet the ideals of reciprocity, closeness, and openness. They constantly shared food and other valued things. They built their houses close together and left their doorways open, making it easy for them to see and visit each other. The only exceptions were the small house which women used when menstruating and giving birth and which men never entered and the larger temple, which was forbidden to women. But these exceptions were made, men told me, to ensure that people could go on living their ordinary lives of social closeness and openness, strengthening each other's bodies and keeping each other alive. The result would be a group that became increasingly large and powerful. It would be – following the common Atbalmin metaphor of plant existence – a mass of thriving branches and leaves spreading out over its healthy base.

Hidden conflicts: sorcery and dis-embodiment

The intense quality of warmth, intimacy, and mutual good will of life in an Atbalmin settlement gave me much pleasure. But I also wondered how they could personally bear a situation of such constant physical and social closeness. I dismissed my reaction by reminding myself that cultures differ, and that what seemed to me unbearable intimacy might seem to them to be normal and desirable. Eventually it became clear to me that there was a very different side of Atbalmin life that complicated these initial impressions and explanations. They had reason to fear that the same physical conditions and social processes that created and nurtured their bodies led to the destruction of their bodies, to their dis-embodiment.

This other side of Atbalmin life was revealed to me first in concerns about death. The men and women I came to know in Bomtem and elsewhere seemed to be constantly worried about their survival, both as individuals and as a society. This was in some ways not surprising to me. The rugged Atbalmin landscape presented many physical dangers, including drowning, falling from cliffs, and being buried in landslides. There was also risk from violent quarrels between people and a high toll from diseases such as malaria, tuberculosis, and influenza. But the Atbalmin traced almost all deaths (as well as most serious injuries and sickness) not to these obvious and visible sources but to the hidden acts of those they called *biis*, whom I will translate as "sorcerers." They assumed that without such intervention few people would ever die, and most importantly that death was not an inevitable natural process.[4]

Some information about sorcery was provided to me very early, in part because of concerns that I would make an easy victim. I was repeatedly warned not to let crumbs of food I was eating fall to the ground. I was told that sorcerers took food remains or other bits of material intimately connected to the body (such as finger nails, hair and so on) and were able to use them to cause harm to all the bodily components of their victims. Flesh would waste away painfully, will and thought would became vague and unclear, and, most critically, the vital spirit (*simik*) would diminish. Having been weakened in these ways, the victim would then be finished off through an assault. Invisible to ordinary people, sorcerers could strike them with arrows or axes, push them into a river or over a cliff, or make a tree fall down on them. They then consumed them in a cannibalistic feast. Like the other acts of sorcerers, this feast was invisible, for what was consumed was the vital spirit (*simik*) rather than visible flesh. But for the Atbalmin it was very real, the final stage of a gruesome process by which people were literally dis-embodied. They were robbed of each component of their embodied existence: their will, thought, spirit, and flesh. The visible signs of this process were sickness and death, followed by the burial of the victim's wasted corpse by his or her kin.[5] All that was left was an invisible ghost or *sakbal*, an entity the Atbalmin imagined as lacking in substance and individual will.

People took many precautions to protect themselves against sorcery and death, and they urged me to do so also. They said it was crucial to hide meticulously any bits of food or other materials intimately connected to the body. They were on constant guard against sorcery assault, traveling between settlements in groups bearing bows and arrows, axes and other weapons. Despite these precautions, everyone I spoke to believed that the sorcerers would eventually kill him or her just as they would everyone else. Every major sickness or death brought these concerns to the surface and seemed to confirm them for those involved. As further evidence of this trend, people sometimes pointed out that the number of those who had once lived and died was far greater than those now alive, and that there were far more abandoned settlement sites than existing settlements.[6] Their descent group was only a small, withered remainder of what it had once been. Thus they saw sorcery not only threatening their individual bodies but also the collective body of their group (understood through the dominant metaphor of plant life). There was a real fear that in the end no Atbalmin individuals or groups would be left.

While I learned early on about these general ideas and precautions related to sorcery, it proved much harder to learn specific information about who sorcerers were or why they killed and ate people. Sorcerers, I was told, could not be seen and they had no clear motives other than their presumably evil will. But beginning after about a year of living in Bomtem I began to hear more detailed accounts. People proved to have very definite ideas about how sorcerers were ordinary people who sought to avenge grudges. I was shocked to discover that they suspected specific neighbors and even close relatives of carrying out cannibalistic murders for reasons as seemingly minor as failing to reciprocate a small gift. They always told me these details in confidence for fear of angering the persons in question and provoking their sorcery.

These disclosures changed my understandings of Atbalmin social life profoundly. I came to see that below the surface appearance of openness, closeness, and good will lay another level of unspoken conflicts and grudges. This was the level at which suspicions (and possibly realities) of sorcery thrived. The metaphor of concealed depths was a central idiom in use by the people involved. They regularly made a distinction between what they called *fitap*, "in plain sight," and what they called *uwap*, "hidden" or more literally "covered up." All of this fitted well with the important metaphor of plant life, to the extent that a plant's real basis lies underground. It became clear that people took it for granted that much of what existed or occurred in plain sight could only be understood in terms of what could not be seen, in many cases through intentional concealment ("covering up" was one of the main terms). There was a strong moral dimension to this fact. Concealment was wrong, not just because of the harm it caused directly but also because it supported other kinds of wrong, whether a greedy desire not to share something or an old grudge. Sorcery was at once the worst kind of concealment and dire proof of the harm that other kinds of concealment fostered.

The Atbalmin I came to know thus approached their social lives in terms of an opposition between something right and visible and something wrong and hidden. This opposition involved two different ways of thinking of their society as well as of persons and bodies. In its positive and visible side, the focus was on embodiment. Social life involved mutual exchange and support through which individuals acted as good human persons to help sustain each other's bodily health. But people also recognized a negative and hidden side that was tied to dis-embodiment. Society, according to this view, was a conflicted process, in which people wished and actively sought to exclude others and cause them harm. At its worst, as conceptualized through sorcery, social life led self-destructively to individuals killing others and consuming their bodies. Everyone seemed to agree that this was wrong. They constantly affirmed that people would all die if they did not learn to live differently, to live as they should.

Dis-embodiment and social process

How and why were people unable to live as they believed and said they should? People often suggested that their problems were due largely to the selfishness and evil of a recalcitrant minority. They complained that some people were unwilling to share what they had, jealous of the possessions of others, easy to anger and unable to forgive. Indeed, anyone who acted in these ways was more likely to be suspected of covertly practicing sorcery. This seemed to suggest the possibility of solving the problem by eliminating the limited set of people who were sorcerers.

It became increasingly clear to me, however, that the problems ascribed to sorcerers were linked to basic conditions of Atbalmin life. Individuals regularly found themselves in situations where they had to choose between conflicting demands, so that no matter what they did would be seen in some way to be wrong. This had much to do with the way that Atbalmin initiated and sustained social relationships through delayed exchange of gifts. The individuals I knew had many outstanding obligations to reciprocate past gifts. As a result, when they tried to reciprocate one obligation, they risked being seen as neglecting obligations to many others. This would have negative consequences for both giver and receiver, both of whom would be resented by those who had been neglected. For this reason, people often tried to keep exchanges hidden from those not involved. But this had the opposite effect of increasing people's suspicion of ongoing deception and provoking their anger if the deception was revealed. In this way, people's efforts to be good friends paradoxically fostered exclusion, concealment, and conflict – precisely the conditions that the Atbalmin linked to sorcery.[7] The process of embodiment was inextricably connected to its opposite, what I call dis-embodiment.

A further source of conflicts was the emergence of several different sets of external forces on Atbalmin life. Christianity, for example, involved many demands on people's time and labor. The pastors and local Christian leaders told them not to work on Sundays but come to church and then rest for the remainder of the day. They expected them to maintain the church hut and the pastor's house, and to provide the pastor with food. The pastors demanded that people forsake aspects of their lives that they valued, such as polygamous marriage, the accumulation of wealth, and, as I will explain in more detail later, the indigenous religion. Besides Christianity, the government and mine were also linked with conflicting demands. Older men and women criticized the tendency of younger men to leave for visits to the mine at Ok Tedi or the government outpost at Telefomin, at times when they were needed to help with gardening and hunting. There was resentment when men left to carry loads for government patrols and returned with money which they did not share with those who had been forced to make up for their lost work.

The conflicts the Atbalmin experienced in relation to Christianity, the government, and the mine were exacerbated by the local emphasis on exchange. Whether in terms of new contexts or of indigenous ones, people faced the problem that creating and maintaining some relationships proved destructive of other relationships. And this problem was cast very much in terms of a dilemma of reciprocal exchange: that to give to one ongoing relationship meant neglecting another.[8]

The temple debate: alternate forms of dis-embodiment and concealment

A concern with the dangers of hidden conflict and sorcery suffused almost every aspect of Atbalmin life. The openness and closeness that I enjoyed (but also at times felt suffocated by) in their everyday life was in part a desperate attempt to avoid destruction. In the context of each death or serious sickness people expressed a deep sense of inadequacy, bordering on despair about the underlying conditions and eventual prospects of their social lives. It was a fear focused on the body – both their individual bodies and the collective (plant-like) body of their descent group.

This grim view of the difficulty of resolving these problems using indigenous means had much to do with the rapid adoption of Christianity among the Atbalmin. Though Christianity in one sense contributed to the conflicted quality of their life, it also and more prominently offered itself as a solution to conflict and death. The pastors had come with the "good news" that people could have eternal life. During the period that I carried out research, this theme remained a focus of the weekly Sunday services which were led by a pastor or one of the more devout local converts. The sermons were held in a settlement an hour's walk from Bomtem where a pastor sometimes lived (most of the time he was away in his home area near Telefomin). The sermons also made clear how the possibility of eternal life had a terrible as well as a good side. Only those who had converted and became truly good would enjoy endless happiness in a realm called Heaven. Those who had not converted and who did wrong would go to Hell where they would "burn forever like a roasting sweet potato" – a kind of bodily harm that was worse than anything in the ordinary world, even sorcery.

The pastors had also introduced a set of new terms and concepts to understand these new realities, all of which were derived from Tok Pisin (the pidgin language that few Atbalmin knew but that has become the prevalent language of wider communication in Papua New Guinea). I have already mentioned *laip* (for eternal life, or the soul), Heaven and Hell. Another crucial term was sin, to refer to wrongs that people did. The pastors mentioned many kinds of sin: fighting, stealing, lying, deceiving, or insulting others; being greedy, selfish, and envious; and lusting after others. Above all they emphasized sorcery. Sin, they explained, was like a heavy burden that people carried and which would lead, after their death in a scene of judgment before God, to their punishment in Hell. Sin had originated with a figure called Satan. Satan was a master of concealment, who rarely showed himself directly but rather influenced people from within themselves, particularly through the desires of their own body.

The pastors had also revealed a number of positive entities. They spoke of God, the Holy Spirit and Jesus. God, they explained was a being who lived in the sky and who was invisible but sought to reveal Himself rather than conceal or deceive like Satan. God was said to be "like the wind." He sent an equally invisible, wind-like Holy Spirit to help people with their problems and to resist the powers of Satan. He also had once sent a son called Jesus to live with people. Jesus had made a kind of exchange, his life for that of humans, making it possible for people to escape the burden of their sins and gain eternal happiness in Heaven. For the Atbalmin, perhaps the most dramatic disclosure of the pastors was that Jesus would soon be returning to bring the world to an end. Everyone would die, but those who had truthfully converted would be reborn, embodied anew in a different and better world.[9]

The promised return of Jesus added to a sense of urgency that shaped Atbalmin life throughout the period I carried out research. At almost every Sunday service, the pastor or a local Christian leader warned people that they had to struggle to place their complete *bilip* ("belief," another introduced term) in Christianity. People were expected to confess and renounce their past sins and to commit themselves to live according to the way of God and Jesus. They warned them that many of them did not have complete belief and, even worse, that they continued to do sin through their thoughts and body. "You only pretend to be Christians," the pastor and his followers frequently said, "but you do evil in hidden ways. Stop hiding it, confess it, and stop it forever!"

Most of the practices and concepts of Atbalmin Christianity are likely to seem familiar to those with a knowledge or experience of Christianity in any form. I have described them at some length because of a significant parallel between the themes stressed by Atbalmin Christianity and major concerns of indigenous life. Particularly notable is how both stressed an opposition between a realm of openness and good will with a reality of concealment, conflict, and destruction. This parallel is due partly to the nature of the form of Christianity brought by the pastors, an Australian Baptist sect which emphasized concealment and deception as the core meaning of sin and Satan. It is a theme that runs deeply in many branches of Christianity. Some scholars have traced it back to the conditions of internal social conflicts between and among Jews and early Christians in the era in which the New Testament was written (cf. Pagels 1995).

But Atbalmin Christianity also reflected the influence of indigenous factors. It was probably significant that the pastors came from neighboring groups who had much the same set of social conditions as the Atbalmin (Jorgensen 1981a, 1981b; Robbins 1995). It was certainly significant that Christianity was sustained by strong local involvement. In any case, Atbalmin Christianity drew deeply on people's association of concealment with the conflicts that divided them and, through that, with sorcery and death. It disclosed a set of new concepts and entities that promised a possible way out of these problems (especially God, Jesus, and the Holy Spirit who had superiority over Satan and human evil). Most importantly, it provided a concept of eternal life that was opposed to the earthly body but which served, in key ways, to allow people to imagine a continuation of their personal existence (an embodiment even if in another kind of body) beyond the present world and its certainty of death (and dis-embodiment).

Atbalmin Christianity's opposition to concealment undoubtedly helped it gain such quick and broad support from all segments of the population. But this opposition to concealment also led to one of the main areas of contention between Christianity and indigenous life, one which at once drew some people to it and strained many other people's loyalties. For Atbalmin Christianity attacked concealment not only in everyday life, but also in another form that was not usually associated with it, that of indigenous religion. The pastors and local Christian leaders saw a direct link between secular concealment and the systematic way that indigenous sacred rituals, narratives, and objects were kept hidden from the uninitiated. They cast indigenous religious concealments and revelations as an evil deception. It was the way that Satan insinuated himself into people, into their minds and bodies. The pastors and many others were particularly concerned about the continuing existence of the temple at Bomtem, which had for several generations been the most important one in the Atbalmin area. "You only pretend to be Christians," they warned, "but you still continue covertly to worship a false god."

People in Bomtem and neighboring settlements talked about these warnings and argued about what they should do. I noticed that the most vehement critics of the temple were usually in their twenties or younger and that many of them were women. The chief defenders were often older men. But for the purposes of present analysis, what was more important was the fact that most people seemed to be genuinely ambivalent. I was struck by how even the men most devoted to the temple never challenged the main tenets of Christianity, the pastor, and his supporters. They emphasized that they were as much converts as anyone else and that they accepted the ideas of Christianity. They thought it was very possible that Jesus would return soon to end the world. They shared a distaste for almost all the everyday evils that the Christian leaders condemned and like them associated these wrongs with concealment and sorcery. But, as defenders of the temple emphasized, and most others agreed, there were important differences between the concealments of the indigenous religion and the hidden wrongdoings of everyday life. Any concealment in the indigenous religion was meant not to harm people but to help them, in ways crucial to their most crucial bodily wellbeing. Without its help, they said, hunting would fail and the gardens would not produce crops. People would become weak, small, and sterile. The descent group, too, would grow smaller and weaken. Many of the supporters of the temple longed for a kind of reconciliation with Christianity, such as possible use of prayers to Jesus in temple rituals.

The debate over the temple continued through much of my fieldwork. There were a number of occasions when it seemed that the pastor and the most devout Christian supporters were about to prevail. This was particularly the case during March and April 1985 when a number of women were possessed by what was believed to be the Holy Spirit and used this special authority to support the Christian side. One of these women said she personally was going to lead a group up to the temple to destroy it. For days, I waited with others in Bomtem for this event to occur. Kupsep, the 62-year-old man who was the leader of the settlement and the chief caretaker of the temple, said bitterly but with a certain resignation, "Let them come and take everything out [of the temple] and cast it into the forest. Let us all die of hunger."

Rival religions, common concerns

The struggle over the fate of the temple was disturbing for the Atbalmin individuals whom I knew. They felt it was dangerous to keep the temple but also dangerous to dismantle it. Either course of action would very likely cause harm, resulting in the bodily suffering of individuals and the decline of their communities and descent groups. I found myself caught uncomfortably in the midst of this debate. Despite my occasional attendance at Christian services, I was known to support the continuing existence of the temple and, more generally, to have a great interest in the indigenous religion. I heard that some people regarded my presence and my work as a problem.[10]

But, for purposes of understanding Atbalmin social life, the debate about the temple proved very revealing for me. It forced me to think about the relation between Christianity and the indigenous religion and to become aware of striking parallels between the two religious systems in a way that helped me understand both systems better.

The first parallel was how both Christianity and the indigenous religion were constituted in contrast to a realm of ordinary social conflicts that imperiled human bodily existence. This was dramatically evident in Christianity, with its frequent attacks on evil deeds, sorcery, and other divisive aspects of life. By contrast, an opposition to everyday conflict was more an implicit than an explicit theme of the indigenous religion. All hostilities had to be ended during periods of rituals. During their initiation ceremonies boys were given moral warnings to stop their ongoing habits of theft, disobedience, and everyday concealment. Most importantly, the indigenous religion offered specific ritual means to enhance people's embodied wellbeing. It was aimed against tendencies toward individual and collective decline and destruction, tendencies that were perceived to lie within ordinary human bodies and everyday social life. The ritual leader, in these indigenous terms at least, was the reverse of the sorcerer.

The second parallel between Christianity and the indigenous religion was how they were both organized around concealment and dis-embodiment, but in a manner that opposed and ultimately worked to reverse what occurred in ordinary life. The importance of concealment was perhaps more obvious in the case of the indigenous religion, with its multiple levels of initiation to a hidden body of sacred things and words.[11] Christianity, however, was presented in much the same way as a process of disclosure of otherwise hidden truths. Concealment in Christianity was also a fundamental principle of sacred matters. This was the case not just in terms of the negative instance of Satan but also in the positive reality of a God who acted on people from an invisible heavenly realm. There was also an emphasis on concealment that seemed more indigenous in origin. Many told me that they had heard that there was a special "deep" version of the Bible, using the same Atbalmin term (*uwap*) that they would have used for a deep part of their own indigenous sacred accounts. This hidden Bible, they said, was different from the one carried by the pastors and used by them at Sunday services. It contained passages that revealed underlying connections between the figures and incidents in the Bible and in the indigenous religion. Either the pastors were concealing their knowledge for some reason or, what was more likely, this hidden Bible had never been shown to them by the real experts at the Mission headquarters at Telefomin.

In the case of dis-embodiment, the more obvious case was Christianity, with its vision of sinners tortured and burning in Hell, of people's impending death and spiritual rebirth, of Jesus's death on the cross and his gift of his blood for human redemption. In Atbalmin Christianity, as in many other forms, the body was deeply opposed to the real basis of existence (the Soul, or "laip" as the Atbalmin knew it) and the destruction of the body was the precondition of resurrection. A more subtle form of dis-embodiment was demanded by Christianity in terms of the necessity of renouncing bodily pleasures and desires. The converted had to become pure in a manner that opposed aspects of themselves connected with the "flesh" (and also, of course, Satan).

But, as I learned, images and practices of bodily destruction also lay at the heart of the indigenous religion. Kept inside the temple were the bones of wild animals caught by hunters on ritual and other occasions. There were also string bags filled with sacred relics, including human bones. A prominent part of the rituals of the indigenous religion involved the dismembering and display of parts of animals and, on very rare but important occasions, parts of humans.[12] I found similar themes important also in indigenous religious narratives known only to initiates. These linked many aspects of the social and natural world to an ancient killing, dismemberment, or other kind of bodily destruction carried out by a divinity (upon an animal, human, or other divinity). Finally, in the course of their initiations, boys were subject to a great many physical assaults; ritual leaders told me this was essential for the efficacy of the initiations. In this way, in the rituals as well as in the narratives and objects of the indigenous religion, the destruction of the body was linked to creation and renewal in ways that had fundamental similarities with Christian ideas.

Agency, concealment, and dis-embodiment

It has long been recognized by anthropologists, often through pioneering work in Africa, that sorcery and witchcraft beliefs are tied to conflict. It has become clear that conflict can exist not only between individuals or groups but also within people's consciousness and subjectivity. Certain predictable forms of conflict can emerge from incompatible principles within a social system or the confrontation between social systems. Concerns with dis-embodiment – of living bodies captured, weakened, or killed by spirits – have been linked not only with these kinds of conflicts but also with attempts to mediate or redress them.

The Melanesian case I have focused on here points to all these kinds of conflict. The case also highlights the importance of another kind of conflict that has been less commonly recognized. This emerges not so much from incompatible social principles as from a dilemma in the most seemingly coherent principle of all: building human relationships through reciprocal exchanges. Such a dilemma is arguably quite common, though it may be more dramatically evident in some cases than others.[13]

Among the Atbalmin, the process of being a good person and friend meant being a bad person and betraying someone else. I have explained how this dilemma had roots in indigenous life but also was supported by the emergent effects of external forces. The dilemma had profound implications for human agency, for it meant that effective social action was at once creative and destructive, right and wrong.[14] People related to this basic contradiction (or, more accurately, the multiplicity of particular conflicts that it resulted in) through concealment and dis-embodiment. Concealment was a means of avoiding the dilemma that only made it worse, and it was identified with the essence of the problem. This conflicted and concealed social reality was understood in terms of dis-embodiment. As I have noted, this understanding was articulated especially in beliefs about sorcery. The indigenous religion and Christianity drew on the same themes but also transformed them.[15]

The Atbalmin's predicament is worth comparing with recent work by Melanesianists on the relational basis of social identity. These works have made clear that, in many Melanesian societies, people think and act as if persons are from the start a product of relationships (involving exchanges of food and valuables, as well as spirits or bodily substances) rather than being individuals first who enter into relationships. The fact that persons are the product of many social relationships means that persons can encompass many individual and collective identities, and that these may be differently highlighted depending on context. This leads to Roy Wagner's emphasis on how different relational identities can be "elicited" (e.g., 1974, 1986) and to Marilyn Strathern's insistence that the Melanesian person should be seen as a "dividual" (e.g., 1988). For both these theorists, such a reality means that different aspects of social existence are alternately hidden and revealed.[16]

The present analysis highlights an important consequence of such a social reality. Among the Atbalmin, I suggest, there was a multiplicity of social relationships and identities, due both to indigenous factors and external forces. This multiplicity was associated with situations of conflicts and perceived betrayals, in people's sense that they were at odds with their friends and with themselves. Concealment and disclosure were not only an expression of the larger social and cultural situation, but also intentional strategies and moral problems.[17] Ultimately, concealment became linked with this primary dilemma of life: by trying to build social relationships and strengthen their bodies through reciprocal exchanges people also destroyed their relationships and endangered their bodies. Sickness, death, and other kinds of physical destruction served as a constant proof and reminder of the terrible consequences of this perceived state of affairs.

By keeping this predicament of agency in mind, it becomes possible to evaluate better the parallels between Atbalmin Christianity and indigenous religion. Both were organized critically around a very similar operation. They turned a profound dilemma into what appeared to be the uniquely effective means of resolution, in large part by a transformation of the forms of concealment and dis-embodiment with which the dilemma was most deeply identified. In the practices and beliefs of Atbalmin Christianity and indigenous religion there was an inversion which occurred in everyday life. Instead of the usual pattern of selective concealment by individuals in particular relationships, they imposed collectively shared disclosures and concealments. They reversed the meaning of dis-embodiment articulated through sorcery beliefs. Instead of bodily destruction being an effect of conflicts between individuals it became a source of positive consequences for people individually and collectively. In the indigenous religion, bodily health and social wellbeing was linked to rituals involving the killing and dismemberment of animals and the physical punishment of humans. In Atbalmin Christianity the physical destruction of Jesus was the essential precondition for freeing humans from their sinful nature and sufferings – both associated with their bodies. Jesus's sacrifice became the model of a profound renunciation by humans of their bodily needs and desires, as a basis for their eventually receiving a new and better existence in Heaven. In many respects, Jesus served as model of the Christian persons as anti-sorcerers, who would preserve life through bodily renunciation instead of taking life to satisfy bodily needs. I have suggested that a similar anti-sorcery role was exercised, though in a more implicit way, by the indigenous ritual leaders.[18]

More generally, the transformation of concealment and dis-embodiment in the indigenous religion and Christianity was linked with the possibility of a different kind of agency, one which would have positive effects without negative consequence. In this respect, they paralleled what people tried unsuccessfully to achieve through ordinary practices of concealment and disclosure. I would argue that people's belief that Christianity and the indigenous religion could succeed where ordinary practices failed depended crucially on their sense that they involved a very different kind of concealment and disclosure. This was not just a matter of conceptual support, but also a recognition of the social conditions of agency. It was deeply evident among the Atbalmin that concealment and disclosure were uniquely powerful means of creating and altering relationships between people.

I do not have space here to consider how far Christianity and the indigenous religion in fact constituted a different context of agency or created different social relationships. If I were to do so I would have to consider some important differences as well as parallels between Christianity and the indigenous religion. But it is important before closing that I do address one possible misunderstanding of what I have said. I am not suggesting, in a kind of neo-functional way, that Christianity and the indigenous religion should be seen as solving the problems of society or individuals. For, in fact, few people seriously believed that Christianity and the indigenous religion could end their problems. The indigenous religion emphasized that no matter how much it might help, it could not in the long run keep people from being destroyed. Atbalmin Christianity had, in some ways, an even more dismal view. It made clear that being Christian would never be enough; that people were by nature sinful and would continue to do evil and suffer from it. The present world, it warned, would soon end in a terrible cataclysm of fires and earthquakes. After the apocalypse, most people would roast in Hell for eternity.

Yet people regarded the limitations of Christianity and the indigenous religion as further proof of their special efficacy and necessity. Viewing Atbalmin Christianity and the indigenous religion as inadequate solutions does not do justice to the way they emerged from but also opposed the conflicts of everyday life. More importantly, it obscures recognition of how among the Atbalmin certain kinds of dilemmas were an essential part of agency and social life.

Attention to dis-embodiment and concealment works to highlight the importance of these dilemmas. It not only helps the process of analysis but also illuminates how agents can have a complex awareness of their difficult and mortal relation to their society. In addition, it reveals how people may possess alternative ways of understanding and responding to their conflict-ridden lives, marked by somewhat different forms of concealment and dis-embodiment. Evidence on these points can be found in writings by anthropologists in many other parts of the world.[19]

Finally, attention to concealment and dis-embodiment illuminates a creative and unfinished aspect of social life. Social life in many settings involves an ongoing struggle of people to live together in the face of conflicting and contradictory social principles and opposing personal ties. This struggle is expressed in particular debates, such as the one I observed about the fate of the temple. In that debate, people wrestled with the problems of their social lives as well as the rivalry between two religions, an indigenous ritual system and a local Christianity. Concealment and dis-embodiment figured centrally in the debate. They were essential problems that people faced in everyday life; but they were also – in their different forms in the two religions – essential principles that could help people.

The fate of the temple was still uncertain at the time my fieldwork ended in December 1985. When I left, I expected to return again soon, but a serious injury made me unable to negotiate the rugged trails of the Atbalmin area. I often try to imagine what I will find when I am able to return. I suspect that the opponents of the temple eventually prevailed.

But I expect to find people still fiercely arguing with each other and themselves about sorcery and, more generally, about how to understand and respond to the conflicts and contradictions that sustain but also threaten their social existence.[20] I expect to find them concerned in various different ways with concealment and dis-embodiment.

ACKNOWLEDGMENTS

This paper is based on three and a half years' research among the Atbalmin of Papua New Guinea between August 1981 and December 1985. My research was funded by the Fulbright-Hays program of the U.S. Dept. of Education and the National Science Foundation. I would also like to thank the Institute of Papua New Guinea Studies and the West Sepik Provincial Government. This chapter benefited from the comments and advice of many people, but especially Kirin Narayan, Hanna M. Bercovitch, Sacvan Bercovitch, Gilbert Herdt, Dan Jorgensen, Bruce Knauft, Michael Lambek, Andrew Strathern, and Marilyn Strathern. My colleagues Talal Asad, Donald Carter, Niloofar Haeri, Gillian Feeley-Harnik, Sidney Mintz, Susan Reed, Michel-Rolph Trouillot, and Katherine Verdery provided additional intellectual inspiration.

NOTES

1 Using the past tense may lead to certain misunderstandings. But these seem less serious than the dangers of a fictional "ethnographic present."
2 It is interesting that the Atbalmin model the "social body" on the form of a plant rather than on that of a human. Some anthropologists seem to take the primacy of a human body archetype almost for granted (e.g., Douglas 1966: 115).
3 Similar social and cultural forms (including the plant metaphor) are found in groups neighboring the Atbalmin, who speak languages of the Mountain Ok family and who share much in common with each other. Many of these societies have received previous anthropological attention, including the Baktaman (Barth 1975), Bimin-Kuskusmin (Poole 1976, 1981b), Faiwolmin (Jones 1980), Mianmin (Gardner 1980, 1987; Morren 1986), and Telefolmin (Brumbaugh 1980; Jorgensen 1981a, 1981b, 1984, 1990).
4 Though I translate it here as "sorcery," the Atbalmin term *biis* actually encompasses the meaning of both "sorcery" and "witchcraft" as commonly used by anthropologists. For a more detailed discussion of Atbalmin *biis* beliefs see Bercovitch 1989; for discussions of closely related understandings of sorcery and witchcraft in neighboring Mountain Ok societies see Barth 1975, Jones 1980, Jorgensen 1981a, and Poole 1981b.
5 In former times, they had placed bodies in caves and on platforms in trees.
6 My own research pointed in a different direction. In my three years among the Atbalmin, the total population of Bomtem and the other settlements in its valley steadily rose. I calculated an average increase of about 2.5 percent per year, a rate that would lead to doubling in about thirty years. But when I pointed out to people how there were more births than deaths, this did not

make much of an impression on them. Their grim view reflected the pivotal assumption that death was not natural and also perhaps their memory of an earlier period of depopulation, especially severe in the 1960s, when the Atbalmin found themselves subject to new diseases in connection with increasing contacts with Europeans and neighboring New Guinean peoples.

7 I provide here only a bare outline of the dilemmas of exchange among the Atbalmin. I provide a more detailed discussion elsewhere (Bercovitch 1994).

8 Such understandings have much to do with how the Atbalmin continued to rely mainly on indigenous forms of production and exchange into the 1980s. A shift to significant dependence on wage labor would probably alter the situation, as it seems to be doing in groups not too far from the Atbalmin who have become far more involved with the Ok Tedi mine (see Jorgensen 1981b).

9 According to some, there would first be a new world on earth, a version of the common Christian idea of the Millennium. Joel Robbins has documented these influences among the Urapmin, a neighboring group and the group which many Atbalmin pastors came from. He argues (1994b) that through the medium of word of mouth as well as cassette tapes the Urapmin were following some of the latest developments in global fundamentalist Christian theology.

10 People were also concerned that I was not a Christian. I am Jewish by birth though non-practicing. I mentioned this early on in my fieldwork, without understanding the importance it might take on.

11 Concealment was central to the indigenous religion in several ways. On the one hand, the sacred rituals, objects, and narratives had to be kept hidden from those who were not adequately initiated. Those who transgressed such rules would undermine the efficacy of the sacred practices and also bring harm to themselves and others. But, on the other hand, I found that concealment had a kind of value in its own right. Rituals were filled with actions meant not only to deceive novices but also to make them aware that they were being deceived. Likewise, the actions recounted in sacred narratives often took the form of a series of deceptions and counter-deceptions by the various characters.

12 Michael Lambek has suggested to me that the preparation and placement of bones and relics in the temple might be seen in more positive terms, as a kind of preservation. This is a valid point, with the qualification that what was preserved always had to be killed and dismembered first as a condition for its efficacy and thus its reason for preservation. The bones were never a whole entity but a part that had been detached from the original source, which in turn was no longer a "body." Thus, to take a particularly relevant example, the preserved forearm of a deceased man who had been a great hunter was no longer in any significant sense a continuation of that individual as a whole person even in a spirit sense. It only preserved some spiritual efficacy that would help other men hunt more as he had done.

13 The intensity of the dilemma of reciprocity among the Atbalmin seems to be shared by the societies immediately surrounding the Atbalmin, which are generally called the Mountain Ok. Anthropologists who have carried out research in these societies have noted the oppressive, conflictive, and destructive meanings of reciprocity (Barth 1975; Jones 1980; Jorgensen 1981a, 1981b, 1984). My analysis has drawn on this previous work but also seeks to

extend it in two main ways. First, I conceptualize the problem in terms of a dilemma of agency. Second, I focus more attention on the relation between the concealment of everyday life (and its indigenous recognition through sorcery beliefs) and the concealment of indigenous religion and Christianity.

14 There was no way out of this problem, since people had to exchange and they would accomplish nothing in the way of maintaining friendship if they did nothing that might be resented by others.

15 By emphasizing the dilemma inherent in gift exchange, I do not mean to suggest this was the only source of conflict among the Atbalmin in the early to middle 1980s. People also found themselves caught between contradictory obligations and ties based on gender, age, differing ways of defining ties through shifting residence and cognatic kinship, and several emergent contexts of social meanings and practices (along with Christianity, the Atbalmin were becoming increasingly involved with emergent contexts of the nation and government, capitalism, and a millenarian movement in Irian Jaya). However, I see the dilemma inherent in creating social relations through exchange as particularly central for the Atbalmin. This is because, as I noted before, other kinds of conflicts could and did appear as variations of it.

16 My discussion of these trends in Melanesian anthropology is oversimplified. Wagner and Strathern each develop their arguments in terms of a larger set of issues about social and symbolic processes of collectivizing and differentiating. In these terms, my focus on dilemmas of exchange might be linked to how an act of exchange can have different qualities of differentiation and collectivization, depending on whether it is understood from the vantage point of participants or of those excluded. I further suggest that agents have a recognition of this complicating reality. To prevent possible misunderstanding, I would like to make clear that this recognition is not merely a matter of "individual" thought or immediate "experience" but is always mediated by social and symbolic forms. The recognition is linked, as I have tried to show, to concepts and practices of concealment and dis-embodiment, as developed differently in sorcery beliefs and in Christianity and the indigenous religion. My argument invites a comparison with Wagner's concept of "obviation" that I cannot pursue here.

17 This is true whether or not one prefers to conceive of the social and cultural situation as a unified system or as a volatile mixture of indigenous forms and emergent forces.

18 To a lesser degree, all participation in rituals carried this same anti-sorcery function, putting people in the position of acting to preserve rather than destroy their social lives. For reasons of space, I cannot further pursue this suggestion that Christianity and the indigenous religion were alternate anti-sorcery systems. This would be especially easy to do with Atbalmin Christianity. The pastors and local Christian leaders often emphasized this theme, and there were cases where they actually attempted to reveal sorcerers and stop their actions. The Atbalmin and other Melanesian cases invite comparison with the "anti-witchcraft" movements that have been described in Africa.

19 This is particularly clear in writings that focus on sickness and curing, witchcraft and sorcery, spirits and possession, social dramas, hidden exchange, and veiled speech (Apter 1991; Boddy 1989; Brenneis 1984; Comaroff 1985;

Feeley-Harnik 1984, 1989; Gilsenan 1976; Hertzfeld 1985; Jones 1980; Jorgensen 1981a, 1981b, 1984, 1990; Knauft 1985a; Lambek 1992; Munn 1986; Murphy 1990; Piot 1993; Scheper-Hughes 1992; A. Strathern 1975, 1989; Taussig 1980, 1987; Turner 1957, 1967). These reveal dilemmas linked to particular social systems as well as to situations where people live at the conjuncture of different social systems.

20 Debates of a comparable kind happened before people adopted Christianity. I gathered evidence that the ritual system had existed in a context of ongoing disagreements about both when and how to carry out rituals. Older ritual experts acknowledged that specific forms of the indigenous religion had been adopted from other groups and / or innovated locally (even as they insisted that there was ultimately a single sacred source underlying any human history or innovations).

11 Melpa and Nuer ideas of life and death: the rebirth of a comparison

Andrew J. Strathern and Pamela J. Stewart

In this chapter we assist in resuscitating a comparison lost to anthropology for some time, the axis of comparison between Africa and Melanesia. We move from a narrative exposition of our theme of compensation and exchange among the Melpa of Papua New Guinea to a more general rendering of its underlying logical components, then we detail the colonial impact on compensation payments in the Melpa case, and finally we specifically compare Melpa materials with those on the Nuer people of the Sudan, described long ago by Evans-Pritchard (1940, 1951, 1956), and more recently by Sharon Hutchinson (1996).

Our Melanesia / Africa comparison has a double historical dimension. The first relates to the 1960s when Evans-Pritchard's model of Nuer social structure was initially taken as the blueprint for studies of "lineage systems" in the New Guinea Highlands and then in short terms rejected after the work of Barnes (1962). The second dimension belongs to the 1990s, when Hutchinson's study of the Nuer enables us to establish cultural correspondences and differences between the Melpa and the Nuer across a range of variables through its engagement with the topic of this volume, bodies and persons, or more accurately the embodiment of sociality.

Equivalence and substitution

What is a life worth? In the course of their history the peoples of the New Guinea Highlands elaborated a series of answers to this question. In the simplest of answers, a life is worth another life, in the sense that the killing of a person demanded a retaliatory killing. The implications of such a rule for the overall social organization varied in accordance with the specificity of the rule's application: whether, that is, a close relative of the killer must be killed, or only the killer himself; whether killings by witchcraft and sorcery were included along with overt physical violence; whether the deliberate provocation of allied groups could be encompassed by killing one of their members so as to induce internecine strife, and so on.

More elaborated answers depended on the idea of substitution as a successor to the norm of equivalence: pigs and shell wealth became acceptable compensation for the taking of a life, thus halting the practice of revenge killing. In the elaboration developed by the Mount Hagen or Melpa people such compensation payments were over time converted into reciprocal exchanges of wealth between groups, in which the original life that was taken was further objectified, as it was not only substituted for by wealth but replaced as the central object of concern by the "game" of the exchange of wealth. This was a development which had begun already in pre-colonial times but accelerated rapidly from the 1930s onward in response to both pacification and the introduction of large numbers of valuable pearl shells by colonial administrators and entrepreneurs.

That such shells are a kind of sublimated substitute for pork can be seen clearly in the verbal expression, always accompanied by a gesture of pointing toward the mouth, that older men made in the 1960s when referring to occasions when they would receive shells in such ceremonies: *akop nondopa nuimin*, "soon we shall eat," they would say. Indeed we can trace a series of correspondences and transformations here. In speaking of the rationale for compensation generally men conventionally would say to their enemies who had killed one of their number in warfare: "You killed our man, but you did not really eat him or enjoy anything. So here we are giving back to you his bone, so that you in return may make the man-head payment to us." This statement was made in conjunction with handing over a number of cooked sides of pork for actual consumption by the other side. The imaginary baseline was the idea that the enemy would kill someone of one's own clan and eat his body. The Melpa people were not cannibals, reserving their attribution of this propensity for sky-beings known as Tei Wamb and subsequently transferring this to European outsiders (who happened to be light-skinned as were the Tei Wamb and to have arrived from the sky in aeroplanes). Cannibalism for them is an activity appropriate to spirits, not to human beings like themselves ("planted people," as they say, *mbowamb*).

In an inverse modality of this phraseology between enemies, the Melpa also expressed the need to pay allies for their losses in warfare. "The owners of the fight" (*el pukl wuö*) had to pay wealth to the ally (*kui wuö*, the dead man) because they had "taken and eaten" the life of the ally. In accordance with this logic the ally could be envisaged as saying to the fight owner that "you have not killed our man, but you have taken and eaten him, therefore you must pay for this." Otherwise, the eating would be an act of stealing, as any unreciprocal act is. "Eating" an ally's life is in this way like an adulterous sexual relationship, also described as "going around stealing food and eating it," thus requiring compensation to be paid "to tie up the woman's apron."

This prime imaginary value of the body – as meat to be eaten – was, then, notionally transmuted by the Melpa into the substitutive value of pork, and the pork was labeled as the "man's bone" (*wuö ombil*), where "bone" refers to the extremities (hands, arms, legs, feet) of the body and is consonant with the fact that it was the sides of pork containing the front and back legs of the pigs that were ceremonially laid out for this prestation. The "bone" in this case is also notionally of less value than the "head," and the recipients of the man-bone payment would then be obliged to make a much larger prestation in return, consisting of live whole pigs which would stand as the "man's head." The head is synonymous with the victim's identity and individuality, and while the rest of his body can be represented by sides of pork, his whole personality can be represented only by whole live pigs. The body/person amalgam is thus the model for the structure of obligatory gift-giving which follows a killing in warfare. Parts of a pig's body can stand for parts of the human victim, but the victim's totality, itself spoken of metonymically as his head, can be substituted for only by a whole living animal.

The transformations we are tracing here are therefore: human victim for consumption → parts of pigs/whole pigs → valuable pearl shells. Already at the point where living pigs are given the consumption involved is not literal, and with shells the objectification of consumption is made complete, while language usage reveals the trajectory involved.

Shells, pigs, and sacrifice

Shells and pigs in the pre-colonial political economy belonged to a restricted sphere of exchange. They could be converted into each other but neither could be exchanged directly for foodstuffs as such, and exchanges of pigs and shells were never of a simple trading kind: combinations of shells and pork might be given, for example, for a delayed return of eight or ten shells. In this way one-to-one exchange rates of pigs and shells were never enunciated. Exchanges were encapsulated within the prestigious sphere of compensation payments and the competitive *moka* exchanges elaborated out of these or constructed separately from them (A. J. Strathern 1971). In the compensation payments for deaths there was also no simple rate of payment of the kind "one death = x pigs and y shells." Rather, the assumption was that a killing generated a whole series of payments, leading into reciprocal exchanges which would re-create friendly relations between the networks of individuals and groups involved. The object was therefore not to establish what a life was worth and acquit a killing by paying for it, but rather to transform hostility into friendship. Pigs and shells became the substitutes or equivalents for the person, but no scales of values for the person were rigidly created. Although undoubtedly the death of an important leader might call for a more immediate, concerted, and massive attempt to pay compensation for his killing, this also did not mean that a scale was created. Rather, it was recognized that the hostility to be averted was greater. Worth was rated along political lines, and more wealth was needed to overcome the problem of hostility. The size of compensation payments was related to the probability of war ensuing if the payment was considered unsatisfactory by the recipients. A generous payment, on the other hand, could elicit the evolution of a unilateral gift into a flow of reciprocal exchanges over time until the original death was forgotten and pigs were simply given "along the road" (*kng nombuklal*), that is, on the lines of existing partnerships. At this point, pigs ceased to be substitutes for human life and achieved, like shells, the states of pure signs of relationship or pure items of exchange.

Here again, however, the ritual actions performed at the occasions of transfer of the pigs continued to encode the original contexts of sacrifice and consumption which underlay the axis of compensation. In the transformative formula we have adduced, the first step was the substitution of *cooked pork* for a human life, and every act of cooking pork is essentially also a sacrifice. The pork offered to the kinsfolk of a dead man was thus also intended for the ghost of the dead man himself, and for this it had to be cooked, so that the smell of it (*tindeklem*) could be appreciated by the disembodied spirit. This original sacrificial aspect of pigs was preserved in the ceremonial phrases used by donors and recipients. An orator walked down the line of pigs tethered to stakes at intervals along the length of a ceremonial ground and called out the name of a big-man on the receiving side, adding *oa rok' kui-o*, "kill and steam-cook this one." A representative of the big-man followed, adding faithfully after each announcement *oa rop kuimb-o*, "this one I will kill and steam-cook." The sequence was always followed, yet almost invariably the pigs were led away and *not* sacrificed, but reinvested in further exchanges.

We see here the remnants of a ritual promise to dedicate pigs as sacrifices, preserved at the verbal level but ignored in practice. In a further elaboration certain pigs were kept back from the initial line-up and brought onto the ceremonial ground in a triumphant stampede only at the last moment. They were then tethered to a very large stake (*nde olka*) decorated with flowers and rubbed with charcoal and pig-fat at the head of the ceremonial ground, and orators gathered to make speeches over them. While the orators spoke the pigs were supposed to lie quietly with their tethering ropes intertwined, peacefully waiting to be killed. If they were noisy and fought, this was an omen that peaceful relations between the groups of the donors and recipients would not prevail. Each pig had privately been promised to a particular recipient, although donors collectively denied this and declared that they were all surprise gifts. Every one of these pigs had to be killed and consumed shortly after being given away. In this way the original context of sacrifice was reintroduced into these occasions, and we speculate further that the act of tethering a pig to a stake at the ceremonial ground originally meant that it was marked for sacrifice. When this meaning was removed from the action of lining up pigs for a *moka* gift, it was reinstated with the *olka* stake ritual.

The account given so far reveals some dimensions of the cultural logic that underpinned Melpa historical practices, up to and including colonial times in the 1960s when the area was under Australian administration. The efflorescence of ceremonial exchange, as has often been pointed out (e.g. Feil 1987), was greatly facilitated by the imposition of colonial peace, and in turn it also extended the peace into widening spheres of interaction between local groups. The local meanings, however, derived from a limited set of equations or comparisons between spheres of action that can be set out in a more explicit manner.

Melpa models of the person and sociality

We have been discussing the progressive substitution of forms of wealth for human life in Melpa exchanges. These partial substitutions depend on an indigenous model of what human life is, how it comes into being and is sustained, and what happens to it at death. We need, therefore, to outline a model of the person seen in these terms, which is provided in Figure 11.1.

What we are labeling "body" here does not have a single corresponding term in the Melpa language, but it signifies the part of the person that is formed through substances possessing "strength" or "grease" (*kopong*).

The two spheres from which *kopong* arise are: (1) the mixture of female blood and male semen that combine to produce a fetus and (2) the nurturing substances, breast milk and food.

The *min* (spirit) comes directly from the ancestors, entering into the body during gestation, while *noman* (mind) develops after birth through the socializing influences of kin and primarily through the ability to speak. The person is therefore a complex amalgam of substances and influence. The ancestors also give power to the living to transmit their substances (i.e. semen and female blood) in reproduction, and living kin provide the framework in which breast milk and food are transmitted to the child. At death the *min* is separated from the body and reenters the spirit world as it

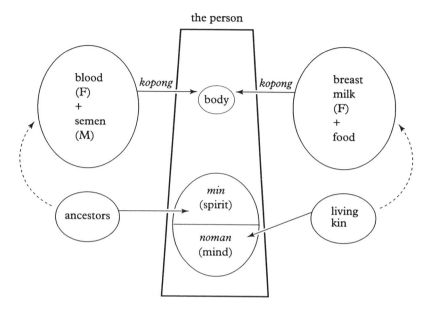

Fig. 11.1 A Melpa model of the person

does also temporarily in dreams, while the *noman* as an unique attribute of the individual person comes to an end. A person is a product of the efforts of the living and the dead and also contributes uniquely during a lifetime through the development of the *noman*. What is paid for in compensations, therefore, is the loss of this amalgam which demands its replacement through various forms of substitution, since an exact re-placement is impossible. Through compensation life force becomes re-producible as a result of transactional equivalences which are set up. Figure 11.2 summarizes a model of these equivalences.

Figure 11.2 introduces sexuality into our model in order to indicate the tripartite character of the relationships involved. The substitutive prin-ciple is shown both in bridewealth and in homicide payments, and these can be regarded as in this context homologous with each other, since a compensation payment can be used to finance a bridewealth. What links the elements together is a covert linkage between killing and sexual intercourse as well as a linkage between sexual intercourse and eating. The terms used for sexual activity are *ronom* (he strikes) for the action of the male and *nonom* (she eats) for the action of the female. Taken together they form a single complex action. In the construction of sociality these equivalences are used to create differentiations. Those who kill must not

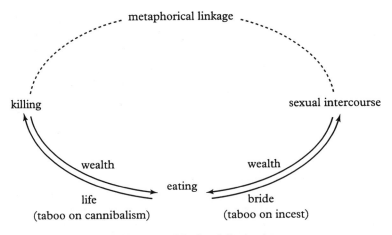

Fig. 11.2 A Melpa model of sociality/exchange

also eat their victim's body even if they consume the victim's life; and they must compensate the victim's kin by providing them with wealth to "eat." In the sphere of sexuality incest is prohibited by the rule that men may not "eat" their sisters. Instead they must give them away (transfer life-giving power) and "eat" wealth in return. The whole figure therefore represents the fundamental operations by which Melpa sociality is constructed as a kind of doubled version of the incest taboo that Lévi-Strauss saw as the universal move from nature to culture (not that "nature" and "culture" as Western categories are here implicated as such: it is rather how sociality is imaged as being created out of opposite precursors).

If we look at Figures 11.1 and 11.2 together we see that Figure 11.2 takes three actions of a concrete, embodied kind (killing, eating, sexual intercourse) and uses these to express the basic substitutive logic of *exchanges*. These actions also enter into Figure 11.1, since substances are employed to make the person by means of sexual intercourse and eating, while death is also implicitly present through the element of the ancestors, who are seen as able to kill their descendants as well as to provide them with the power to create life.

Transactions with ancestors (or more generally dead spirits) are in fact integral to the processes of substitution for life and the creation of new life that we have been discussing. The *min* of a person who has been killed seeks revenge, both by itself and by giving power to those of its living kin who attempt to avenge the death. It can be partially appeased by the gift of animals in compensation and their slaughter in sacrifice, although in principle it is not fully satisfied with these. Compensation then has an aspect of sacrifice in it. Analogously, some of the bridewealth pigs paid for a woman should be killed in sacrifice to her dead kin so that they will not withhold her fertility. If a woman does prove barren or does not give birth to sons, special sacrifices may be called for, perhaps to her dead father's spirit who may be annoyed at a lack of payment of bridewealth or a failure to kill pigs in sacrifice earlier. In both contexts, then, of killing and fertility, sacrifice is integral to the process of sociality and exchange that ensures the reproduction or reconstitution of social relationships. This conjunction between sacrifice to spirits and exchange among the living constitutes one axis of a comparison between the Melpa and the Nuer people of the Sudan which we pursue on p. 243.

Overall, we can see that the model of the person and the model of sociality or exchange map onto each other through the triad of embodied actions and their use as basic images of actions of exchange. Body, person, and exchange are therefore linked together. Put otherwise, exchange embodies the person. We return next to the context of historical practice.

Colonial commoditization and after

When Europeans began trading with the Melpa people from the 1930s onward, one of the first things they did was to destroy the indigenous spheres of exchange by directly purchasing both vegetable foodstuffs and pigs directly with shell valuables. The immediate effects were twofold: one was that the privileged access through elite networks which big-men had maintained in relation to shells was at once broken; the second was that the people were bound to the suppliers of shells in new relations of dependency. Wealth was commodified and social relations were colonialized in a single moment of exchange. A pig became worth x shells, leaving room for fluctuations in its value over time. It is evident that since pigs and shells began their "symbolic careers" as substitutes for the human person (in the sense of "life," and therefore as payments for deaths), and still carried this meaning for the people, the value of human life was also at this historical moment implicitly commodified. This implication, however, did not immediately become apparent. The Melpa took the shell wealth and used it in all their exchanges, whose social range and size they now expanded but whose essential meanings they preserved. These meanings were closely related to the themes of fertility and reproduction that we have been examining here.

In the pre-colonial period pearl shells intended for exchange were suspended in netbags which were attached at two sites along the length of a carrying pole. The netbag is symbolically equated with the female womb while the pearl shell symbolizes the male element as well as standing as an equivalent or substitute for the person generally in Hagen culture (see A. J. Strathern 1979 on shells as "male" wealth). Women use netbags to carry produce, piglets, and infants. These bags convey multiple sets of meanings that bear on notions of the body, the skin, reproduction, nurturance, and female versus male social capacities.

When shell-laden netbags were brought into the dancing grounds the "male" wealth was enclosed by the "female" netbag, thereby presenting a composite of the genders as a symbolic representation of the importance of the male / female amalgamation essential for the reproduction of life. We can also see the shells as like children enclosed in the netbags as children are carried by their mothers.

Eventually, shells became extremely plentiful. Gifts became so large that the items were unwieldy and difficult to carry from place to place. Pearl shells were mounted on large boards made from the resin of the *kilt* or *elua* trees, both trees with bright purple blossoms on which parrakeets delight to feed, an image of wealth coming into the men's house of the big-man, and these boards made the shells bulky and more difficult to transport. They were no longer carried in netbags. Before a presentation the boards had to be sprinkled over with fresh red ocher (a marker of health, life, and wealth akin to human blood), and then laid out carefully in a row. Hundreds of such shells were now given away on a single occasion as opposed to only a few in pre-colonial times. At a certain point in the 1960s men decided to switch from shells to introduced cash (A. J. Strathern 1979). Already, early in 1964, Engk, then a young man, of the Tipuka Kitepi clan held up a pearl shell and said "These shells have come to us from the white man. We used to think they were real wealth. Now some of us have been to the urban areas on the coast and we know that the shell is like a husk which the white man discards after he has removed from it the animal to eat or the real pearl inside. It is what the white man used to throw away, yet he brought it to us and we thought it was real wealth. Now we are not so sure and we are about to give these things up but still we hold on to them."

By the 1970s shells had routinely been dropped from the *moka* with a corresponding loss of symbolic meanings. Australian money was originally introduced into *moka* by young men, who spent much time using it in competitive card games against one another and switched from cards to ceremonial exchange. An initial gift in *moka* now became known as a "bet" which would later elicit a "prize" as the larger return gift. The increment involved was described as "profit" or "win-money." The ethic of the capitalist market-place had thus penetrated linguistically into the heart of prestige-bearing activities.

In the 1980s effects of commoditization were felt clearly in two ways. First, compensation payments in money began to vary according to the status of persons in the new capitalist economic and political order. Second, and co-variantly, compensation payments sometimes became unilateral, once and for all acquittals, not leading to reciprocal exchanges. These two changes contributed subsequently to a worsening of violent conflicts, to an expansion of the range of such conflicts, and to a retreat from the principle of compensation back to the principle of retaliatory killing, bringing the evolutionary trends in the social system full circle. The effects of capitalism were therefore exactly contrary to the intentions of those who originally introduced it as a new economic system. Instead of rendering the people more and more amenable to state control they led to a progressive resistance to such control and to a return to earlier ways of settling disputes by killings and counter-killings. This trend was halted in 1995 only by the introduction of Christian themes into the mediation processes between groups.

At the deepest level, we are arguing, the historical situation was a product of commoditization, issuing in the partial commoditization of persons. In the pre-colonial social system, violence was always the ultimate sanction of relations between groups and individuals not tied closely together by kinship or affinity. In certain contexts, physical violence was an automatic reaction to provocation, as much an intrinsic expression of group identity as a calculated strategy of reprisal. In this context it was linked to the concept of *popokl*, deep-seated anger or frustration, which, if not revealed or acted upon, will result in the sickness of the person who experiences it.

Between those categories of persons who were defined mutually as *el parka wamb*, "Raggiana Bird of Paradise people," or major traditional enemies, a permanent state of *popokl* was expected to hold, and large-scale compensations were not held between them. Raping of women in warfare and the mutilation or burning of the bodies of male enemies at the boundaries of their territories marked this basic attitude to the body of such enemies: the practice was to destroy them, spoil them, render them worthless, and thus insult their living kin. Between "minor enemies," however, it was expected that compensation would be paid for killings and reparations made to allies who gave assistance in fights. Intermarriage took place between these minor enemy / ally categories, there was a sharing of "blood" as a bodily substance between them and an arena in which transactional exchanges of wealth as substitutes for blood were preserved. Within this sphere, then, human life gained its value, and that value was defined socially, as an expression of the value of the ties that bound persons together. The value was thus communalistic and founded on the embodiment of sociality.

In colonial times this sphere of sociality was extended to pockets of previous major enemies, via intermarriage and the alliance-seeking activities of big-men. Pre-colonial practices preserved their meaning, stretched into a larger arena, and supported by pacification and an influx of shell wealth. The Melpa remained in control of their own definitions of the value of life because shell wealth operated only within their own system, even if it came from outside and even if the new supply of shells came from colonial sources. With the shift to money, accelerated around the time of Papua New Guinea's national independence in 1975, this local independence was eroded. Shells were abandoned when the people's attention shifted to money as a scarce valuable, and at the same time people were drawn increasingly into activities that could secure for them a monetary income. Coffee grown on clan land gave that land also a monetary dimension and thus gave a new meaning to old acts of destruction in warfare: enemies concentrated on slashing down coffee trees and hacking trade-stores to pieces as well as the earlier practice of burning down dwelling houses. With the introduction of education, younger men entered the nexus of business and politics, funneling cash back into their home areas as a means of building political factions to secure election to positions in the introduced governmental system, an arena previously suppressed in colonial times. Money became a dominant component in *moka* gifts between allies, but transactions in it between major enemies halted, along with the regrowth of political competition between them. Such political blocs became the basis for the major factions in the new parliamentary political system. The colonial expansion of the pre-colonial system fell to pieces. Major battles which took place in the latter half of the 1980s occurred between political enemies and were deeply exacerbated by the introduction of guns, making it possible to kill many people and to do so without even knowing who they were. The scale of these killings further made it difficult even to contemplate making compensation payments to cover them. The preconditions for these processes of kaleidoscopic change were set in hand in colonial times. The commoditization of land and wealth sharpened oppositions between enemies, and the inflated "rates" of compensation produced a breakdown in the flow of payments. Whereas the substitution of exchange for violence in the 1960s was able to produce an aura of security, in the 1990s people felt much more vulnerable in their bodies, especially with the advent of guns (A. J. Strathern 1992). Violence began again to define the edges of identity, impairing the substitution of wealth for killing, and defining an expanded arena of killing, while at other times compensations attained a factitious or cargoistically inflated value in monetary terms. The use of Christian themes as a means of ritually controlling these events was a further development out of the fluidity and confusion of political processes which accelerated in the 1980s.

Melpa and Nuer: dimensions of a comparison

When social anthropologists first began in the 1950s onward to work in the Highlands of Papua New Guinea they were faced with the problem of how to relate their studies to work done elsewhere. By historical chance the "African models" developed by Evans-Pritchard and Fortes were prominent at the time and were both strongly espoused (e.g. Meggitt 1965) and strongly rejected (Barnes 1962) as guides to understanding the populous polysegmentary groupings found from east to west in these highland areas. The debate has been more and more resolved by regarding the highlands cases, or even cases in Melanesia as a whole, in their own terms and by implication, if not explication, different from "Africa."

The trend has been challenged more than once already. Holy, for example, introduced the Melanesian "big-man" model into his discussion of Nuer political organization (Holy 1979). Roger Keesing made an illuminating comparison between the Tallensi of Ghana studied by Fortes and ancestral shrines and kinds of descent among the Kwaio of Malaita (Keesing 1970; Fortes 1945, 1949). Raymond Kelly has divided his attention between the analysis of materials on the Nuer and on the Etoro of New Guinea (Kelly 1977, 1985, 1993). In his closely argued book on the Nuer Kelly in fact makes a specific comparison between the Tsembaga Maring of Papua New Guinea as described by Rappaport (1967) and the Nuer, pointing out that among the Maring self-regulative processes such as pig-killing festivals appear to have had negative feedback effects in ecological terms, whereas with the Nuer predatory territorial expansion of grazing areas for cattle in time led eventually to a further need for expansion and so induced positive feedback over time after an initial negative feedback (Kelly 1985:236–42). We cannot pursue here a detailed triangulation between the Nuer, the Maring, and the Melpa, but briefly note that among Melpa there was no clear ritual regulation of pig populations or of territorial expansion; but whereas among the Nuer competition for grazing led to actual appropriation of land, among Melpa intergroup competition was deflected into the symbolic sphere of competition for prestige through *moka* exchange. The Melpa therefore took a different evolutionary pathway, lying in between the Maring, with their stable patterns of warfare and pig-kills, and the Nuer with their continuous territorial expansion. A triangulation of this kind shows us in another arena the merits of comparisons between African and Melanesian cases. We continue this tradition of crossing over between the two geographical domains by looking at some further direct comparisons between the Melpa and the Nuer. When we step outside the narrowly defined arena of the original African models of segmentary descent and into the wider dimensions of cultural ideas about practices in the spheres of killing, sexuality, eating, and compensation, as elaborated by Hutchinson (1996), we find that the axis of comparison is suddenly enlivened. The comparisons are facilitated by the emergence in anthropology of discussions regarding personhood and embodiment that can be used to make clear linkages between Nuer and Melpa ideas of the body and the person. Hutchinson's study also enables a historical comparison to be made, since she traces changes among the Nuer from the 1930s through to the 1990s in a trajectory of colonial and post-colonial history that can be set alongside our account of the history of Melpa compensation practices and their vicissitudes. The most powerful and obvious reason for comparing the Melpa to the Nuer is that both peoples have historically used animals as the symbolic substitutes or equivalents of aspects of human life, resulting in a structure of sacrifice plus compensation through which sociality is mediated. Both also have drawn comparisons between bloodwealth for killings and bridewealth for the transfer of reproductive power between persons. Both stress the importance of ramifying ties of "blood" between persons related through females, counterposed to agnatic ties mediated through cattle themselves in the Nuer case and notions of semen or "grease" (*kopong*) among Melpa. These symbolic objectifications fit with equations made between sexuality and killing and between sexuality and eating. We could consider such ideas as central foci out of which similarities in practices can be seen as growing. Equally we can discern differences. The Nuer did not develop competitive reciprocal exchanges between groups as the Melpa did. The Melpa did not develop the idea of collective pollution (*nueer*) arising out of the transfer of a victim's blood into the body of the killer as the Nuer did. Nuer cattle objectify the person even more than do Melpa pigs, as can be seen from the practices of ghost marriage, woman to woman marriage, and the encompassing statements "cattle beget children" or "we eat our children" (i.e. the food or wealth they bring to parents). Melpa male leaders do not self-identify with their livestock as Nuer leaders do, who are described as "the bulls of the camp." Instead Melpa big-men are described as "holding all the ropes" of pigs for sacrifice or as "the central post" in a communal men's house at the head of a ceremonial ground used for making exchanges. The reception of money and guns into Nuer and Melpa social life also shows certain parallels and differences. The Nuer have had guns longer and have given them more positive moral associations, lifting them up in praise songs as they traditionally do in lifting up their arms to represent oxen horns, and Melpa regard money more positively than do the Nuer, even giving it a new sacred status in contexts of illness when collections of cash are made to buy pigs and sacrifice these for sick persons. Such differences, deriving from historical experience, show that we are dealing with those creative local manifestations that Brad Weiss has also insisted on in his study of the Haya (Weiss 1996 and this volume), as well as with processes that incorporate global influences into themselves. Both Nuer and Melpa have experienced extensive influence from Christian missions also. Hutchinson reports that Protestant religion narrowed the scope of Nuer religious behavior through its prohibition on cattle sacrifice during the 1980s. Among Melpa such effects were felt from the 1930s on; but by the 1990s as we have noted they were adapting Christianity to their own uses in assisting them to mediate homicide disputes.

The identification between cattle and people is made clear by both Evans-Pritchard and Hutchinson. "In sacrificial and exchange contexts cattle were considered direct extensions of the human person" (Hutchinson 1996:60, citing also Evans-Pritchard 1956:248ff.). "The cow creates the person" was a statement often made to Hutchinson (*ibid.*). Hutchinson also points out that this identification gave people a greater sense of mastery over their world through sacrifices for sickness, and through the use of cows to marry wives to the name of a person killed, and as "the conflict resolvers par excellence" (p. 61). She goes on to say that this identification worked most to the advantage of cattle-wealthy men and most in the service of male control over reproduction and so "cattle were in a very real sense the currency of power among men" (p. 62). In these contexts one could practically insert "pigs" for "cows" in order to generate statements applicable to the Melpa. She also adds that identification did not mean cattle and people were equally valued. A bride was worth more than the cattle given for her. A blood feud was said never to end and cattle given in it were used mostly to marry a ghost wife so that "she would bear a son who would someday avenge his father's blood with that of the enemy" (p. 61, citing also Evans-Pritchard 1940:155). Further gifts of bridewealth were expected to flow back along paths of matrilateral kinship.

Quite strikingly both Melpa and Nuer use a terminology of the body to refer to feud. As we have seen, the Melpa refer to an initiatory gift in settling a feud as "bone." The "bone" is the dead man who lies between the groups. In giving the "bone" back in the form of wealth they are asking for a larger payment in return. The Nuer also refer to a feud as a "bone," meaning here both the dead person and the fact that a feud endures for a long time, it does not go away easily. "Bone" is in some contexts a synonym for "male" strength among both the Melpa and Nuer and is thereby implicitly contrasted with flesh / blood which is seen in certain ways to be "female." This correspondence of ideas sets the scene for a further set of comparisons.

In Evans-Pritchard's time the payment of bloodwealth to settle a feud was restricted to relations within what he called the tribe or largest named grouping, and its actual transfer was always subject to negotiations. The imperative to pay it sprang from the fear of communal *nueer* pollution, and the earth-priest had to release from the killer the blood of his victim which had mystically entered him, thereafter negotiating the bloodwealth. Among Melpa, similarly, blood compensation was not made between major enemies but only between minor enemies cum allies who were usually intratribal. But there was no equivalent of *nueer* as a concept of communal pollution. The imperative to pay was simply fear of retaliation or loss of an ally's support. There was no "ghost-wife" custom either. The spirit of a victim killed in war was thought to demand revenge and to reside in the piled up netbags (womb-equivalents, as we have noted) worn by his widow on her head; but this custom had fallen into disuse by the 1960s. The practice of transcending compensation by turning it into *moka* exchange in colonial times probably brought this about. The victim was "immortalized" not by his own symbolic reproduction but by the reproduction of social relations between the groups at large. Big-men doubtless played an important part in this transformation.

The Anglo-Egyptian colonial government among the Nuer altered the direct relationship between bloodwealth and bridewealth by increasing the size of the former in an attempt to discourage killings, and by specifying exact amounts to be paid. In classic fashion they altered a flexible and adjusted situation to one that was rigid and imbalanced. This did not happen among the Melpa. The Australian authorities did not regulate the size of payments of bloodwealth, although the indigenous Local Government Councils set up in the 1960s tried to reduce the amounts of bridewealth given without linking their actions to the sizes of compensation payments being made at this time. The colonial power did later express disapproval that so much wealth was tied up in exchanges, failing to see that these exchanges subsidized their own efforts at social control. It was not until the 1980s that special Trouble Committees were set up to take over from big-men the role of negotiating homicide payments in a post-colonial context. Interestingly, Evans-Pritchard seems to have been consulted by the British District Commissioner in Nuerland. A comparable use of anthropologists did not occur among the Melpa, among whom compensation therefore took its own pathway.

The reception of money into the social system further shows some differences, as we have noted. In both Nuer and Melpa history the colonial power deliberately brought the people into the nexus of money, markets, and labor as a part of its project. Among Nuer, government agents traded for cattle, used in an export trade, and cash was substituted for cattle as head tax. Gradually cattle and money became convertible, though money was seen as lacking "life" and as able to pass secretly between people. Money lacks blood, breath, and awareness, the three elements that define both humans and cows in Nuer eyes (Hutchinson 1996:80). In so far as cattle were obtained with money and then used in sacrifice or exchange they in effect became hybrid categories, as Hutchinson argues, although money obtained from demeaning work such as emptying latrines could not be used to obtain cattle, and a conceptual barrier was maintained between money and blood. For the Melpa, as we have seen, hybridization prevailed, but in this process money also became partly sacralized, largely through its use in *moka* by substituting it for shells. Patterns of difference and similarity also show in the history of guns and their relationship to wealth and personhood. The Nuer were a dominant, expansive people, whose men were and are proud to be warriors and have been for many years involved in a harsh civil war. Guns are more important to them than to the Melpa, and they have had them longer. But one effect of killings by guns among them has its parallel in Melpa history. Bullets kill indiscriminately, in large numbers, and often the killer cannot be identified. For the Nuer this led to dilemmas with their concepts of blood-pollution. When guns were used more frequently during the early 1980s in eastern Nuerland they led to the abandonment of battle lines and the adoption of ambushing tactics just as happened with the Melpa. The powers of earth priests declined (after they had already been undercut by the British) and the Sudanese People's Liberation Army proposed that considerations of *nueer* be set aside in the context of a "government war." The scale and context of killings also made bloodwealth payments impossible to manage, and so altered the "individuality" of deaths by killing as well as denying the "immortality" obtained through ghost-marriage. We have already seen briefly how essentially the same problems halted the processes of compensation payments among Melpa. Cultural logics, always changing, were mired in a new technology of force, and elements of personhood altered accordingly. To lift themselves out of a severe impasse the Melpa have begun to adapt Christianity to their own ends; while one of the Nuer's dilemmas is that the narrow version of Christianity offered them gives them no basis in its present form to deal with their needs for sacrifices (for parallels to this among the Huli of the Papua New Guinea Highlands see Frankel 1986).

Cattle and pigs: blood ties and gender

Cattle amongst the Nuer and pigs amongst the Melpa can both be seen in a similar light in terms of being exchange wealth and playing a central role in structuring social relations. Various differences exist in the ways that the person is identified with these animals. Some of these differences may be partially explained by environmental variation. The Nuer being a pastoral transhumant people equate personhood more closely with their cattle than the Melpa who are sedentary and identify personhood both with their pigs and with their land that is the source of food for both pigs and people. Cattle are also similar to humans in their gestation period, as the Nuer note (Hutchinson 1996:78), while pigs multiply more swiftly and present no analogs to human social structure other than purely in terms of fertility itself.

For the Nuer the social circulation of cattle is seen to take precedence over that of human blood in structuring interpersonal relationships. For Nuer men, personhood and sociality were intimately linked to the circulation of cattle which is equivalent to a flow of blood in social value. Nuer say that "cattle, like people, have blood," meaning that "cattle and people are capable of a parallel extension of vitality across the generations," as Hutchinson puts it (1996:78, citing also Evans-Pritchard 1951:97).

In tracing agnatic descent, cattle transfer took precedence over the flow of human blood and assured a man heirs. His cattle could be used to negotiate political alliances through exchange and to supplicate the Divinity through sacrifice (Hutchinson 1996:170). The extreme identification of men with cattle has led in the Nuer case to an objectification of their role in social relations that goes beyond that of the pig in Hagen. The statement "pigs beget children" would be intelligible to the Melpa, but it is not what they do say. They stress rather the necessity to *have* pigs in order to *be* a person.

For Nuer women, the association with cattle is partly through the use of the animals as food. The women milk the cows, churn the butter, and cook the meat. An intimate relationship existed between Nuer women and their cows. A menstruating woman was prohibited from drinking a cow's milk or stepping over a cow's tethering line in case these acts might endanger the cow's health or produce infertility in the cow (p. 171). Hutchinson argues that Nuer women were more closely associated with symbolic linkages between blood and food (p. 160). Unlike paternity, maternity bonds were also constructed through a direct, substantive contribution of uterine blood to the child or its equivalent, breast milk (p. 171). The same is true for the Melpa, among whom blood (*mema*) ties are traced through women directly. Pigs, however, among Melpa, are associated as closely with women as with men, and are sometimes spoken of as women's "children" because they are reared by the women. This usage indicates one basis for Melpa women's further claim that they are in a sense transactors in, not just producers for, the *moka* exchanges, since "women list exchanges which have involved their herd as *moka* which *they* have made" (M. Strathern 1972:151). They recognize that their active role here is pursued conjointly with their husbands but nevertheless express their own agency within the partnership. It would be interesting to know if Nuer women make similar claims regarding cattle, but Hutchinson does not appear to mention this; rather she implies that women are in general excluded from full participation in the realm of cattle-transfers (Hutchinson 1996:61). We may still wonder if Nuer men and women might maintain different versions of what happens. Further, among the Melpa it is the "grease" of pigs, not their blood, that symbolically links them to both sexes. For the Nuer blood is regarded as being generated from food and food from blood. Blood and food are sources of human vitality. Acts of sharing food create and affirm lasting bonds of "kinship" between men and women. At a boy's initiation "blood-brotherhood" is forged between age-mates. Through the sharing of food the expectation of exogamy and communal peace is maintained as represented by the statement, "Once we have eaten together we should not marry each other's daughters nor kill one another" (Hutchinson 1996:165). A similar type of bond is found among the Melpa, through the practice of sharing food and adopting the name of the food as a food-name between a pair of people. Food-name ties are ties of shared substance paralleling those of kinship and expressing ties of friendship that can endure even after another form of relationship, such as affinity, is abrogated. Brad Weiss (1996) in his chapter on "A moral gastronomy" among the Haya, has written extensively on ideas of this sort that closely resemble both Melpa and Nuer notions, for example the idea that bodily conditions are the visible results of concealed processes, the metaphorical equivalence of sexuality and eating, the equation of expressions of hunger with a lack of control, all of which could probably be mirrored by ethnographic materials from many parts of the world, but which fit very neatly into an Africa / Melanesia nexus (Weiss 1996:137–49). Haya, like the Nuer, also use blood as a productive symbolic element, because of its flow within the body (Weiss 1996:207ff.). With the Nuer the equation between blood and food is very clear. A Nuer man might refer to his harvest as "my blood," and when sons would bring fish back home the parents would say "we eat our children" (p. 164). Also, when a daughter was married the parents would say that she is "eaten" in referring to the milk and meat of the bridewealth cattle (p. 164).

Melpa and Nuer models of the person

In comparing the Melpa model of the person (Figure 11.1) with the Nuer concepts of personhood we can see the pivotal role that blood plays. For the Nuer conception occurs through the merger of male and female blood flows, and the broader definition of blood includes semen and milk and even sweat (Hutchinson 1996:74–5). Hutchinson states further that the "mysterious merger" is "forged by the life-creating powers of Divinity." Breast-feeding a child is the determinant of maternity and the feeding of children is a duty that falls to the mother. Both are forms of nurturance that sustain the development of the person. The life of a person consists of two other components in addition to blood: *yieeg*, vitality (breath) and *tiiy*, awareness. Like the Melpa concept of *noman*, *yieeg* ceases to exist at the time of death; while *tiiy* (translated as "soul" by Evans-Pritchard 1956:155), like the Melpa concept of the *min*, is held to survive death. On the other hand *tiiy* in most respects corresponds to *noman* in the sense of "awareness," while *yieeg* is similar to *min* in the sense of "breath, life." Regardless of this we find that the person is made up of "material" and "immaterial" elements in both cases. Of the three elements among the Nuer (blood, *yieeg*, and *tiiy*), blood is the substance that produces fluidity in social relations. The expansion, fusion, and dissipation of kin groups are defined in terms of blood flow. Adulthood is reached by females when the blood of their first childbirth flows and by males at the flow of blood that occurs during the male initiation ceremony.

Blood has the potential to pollute individuals or entire communities through transgressions such as homicide, incest, and adultery. That blood flow should be kept in balance within the society can be observed through the examples in which blood was manipulated in ways to promote wellbeing such as letting blood from both humans and cattle. Specific blood flows arise as acts of blood-vengeance. In addition, cattle sacrifices and exchanges frequently achieve the goals of equilibrating blood flows.

In general, it appears that blood is a dominant symbol for the Nuer to a greater extent than for the Melpa. Blood integrates, while also separating, the spheres of livestock, exchanges, and kinship relations among the Nuer in much the same way as the concept of "grease," *kopong*, does among Melpa, for whom it applies both to the human bodily substances of semen and milk, to vegetable food, and to pork. Blood for the Nuer seems also to stand for the whole flow of exchange relations, encapsulated in the two related spheres of bridewealth and bloodwealth that are also important for the Melpa (see Figure 11.2). (On similar ideas of exchange and flow in Rwanda see Taylor 1992.) The basic proposition of "wealth for life" which informs the Melpa system appears in a more direct form among the Nuer as "a wife for a life," mediated through wealth. While, therefore, we find many significant differences between the two cases, at both the level of ideas and the level of practices, in their most fundamental propositions they are at one with each other. Indeed, since "blood" for the Nuer includes semen as *kopong* does for the Melpa, we may say that these apparently discrete concepts in fact considerably overlap.

Envoi: why the Nuer and the Melpa?

In concluding we take a look at the kinds of comparisons we have been making and how it has come to be opportune to make them. Our exposition of a Nuer / Melpa comparison could hardly have been possible without Hutchinson's Nuer ethnography coming to hand. Melanesianists have tended to make comparisons between cases within Melanesia itself, or at most the Pacific, with occasional forays into eastern Indonesia, and recently Amazonia. The axis of Africa / Melanesia was effectively broken through the trends set in the 1960s and a concentration on exchange as the principle underlying Melanesian sociality. A great many ethnographies were produced first on the basis of the exchange model, and second on the basis of gendered ideas about personhood. One effect of this Melanesian ethnography, in turn, was that it influenced anthropological theorizing generally, as anthropologists turned to the analysis of gender and personhood in different parts of the world. While conditions for fieldwork in Melanesia also remained reasonably favorable, those for work in many parts of post-colonial Africa became more adverse. A great deal of important work continued to be done in Africa and to contribute to emerging themes such as personhood and embodiment (e.g. Stoller 1995; Jackson 1989). But the numbers of Africanist monographs do seem to have decreased while those on Melanesia have increased. New Africanist ethnographies such as those by Hutchinson (1996) and Weiss (1996) have been able to draw on analytical trends that have been enriched by Melanesianist writings and have depended on shared theoretical sources, such as phenomenology and practice theory (e.g. Merleau-Ponty and Bourdieu). The somewhat paradoxical result is that these new Africanist works make their subjects much more obviously comparable to the Melanesians as portrayed since the 1980s than heretofore. Africa in the ethnographies of the 1990s looks much more like Melanesia, then, than it did in the 1960s. As a further result, we have been able to benefit from this trend, to reimport Nuer models back to the Melpa and trade with them, setting up an exchange that was first refused more than thirty years ago. The encouraging conclusion is that, like blood and "grease," theories flow and may do so in unpredictable and interesting directions over time, renewing channels that were blocked and opening out others not previously envisioned. *Vive la comparaison!*

12   Afterword: embodying ethnography

Janice Boddy

Entering upon this discussion is like sitting down to a sumptuous meal: one is faced with such abundance that it is difficult to know where to start. I propose, therefore, to nibble, proceeding somewhat eclectically from thought to thought as the palate leads. What follows is offered in the spirit of exchange: by consuming these essays and engaging them my aim is to fortify existing relationships and to elicit rather than define. Headings do not signal discrete jumps in fare, but convocations in the flow.

On comparing

Readers will surely have noticed that the ethnography presented here pays meticulous heed to detail, its authors refusing to disdain the prosaic but plumbing it for keys to understanding instead. The subtlety with which cultural logics are parsed and bodily practices explored distinguishes this work from the sweeping statements and grand generalizations of earlier comparative projects. Absent too are the static "structures" on which past correlations between Africa and Melanesia were made to hinge. Where such ventures reduced ethnographic descriptions to artifactual common coin, minted from investigations in one place and circulated to humanity as a whole, contributors here ground themselves in positioned practices, persons, relationships, and ideas. They deploy images of movement and fluidity, accenting process, indeterminacy, fluxes and flows, sociality and relatedness instead of formal rules, and above all, practice – the active engagement of persons in their worlds – over categorical essence. Through such radical specificity more refined and nuanced comparison now proceeds.

Ironically, the "bare" fact that societies everywhere are comprised of bodies/persons seems to have liberated us from reductive abstraction while enabling us to get on with comparing all the same. This is hardly, as Moore (1993a:279) points out, a simple return to "biology." Works in this volume eschew Western presumptions that the body is inherently presocial, proceeding instead from a recognition of the body's constructedness: the premise that one's physical existence from the moment of birth, if not before, is subject to interventions so pervasive and patently banal that the prospect of any unmediated experience is moot. In the words of feminist Elizabeth Grosz, "human biology must be *always already cultural*, in order for culture to have any effect on it" (1987:7, original emphasis). Adopting "the body" as the ground for *cultural* comparison requires us to confront ideological distinctions between culture and nature in our thought, and allows us to query naturalistic assumptions – about kinship, for example – that have vexed even feminist accounts (Collier and Yanagisako 1987). The point is not to fix a new typology of social forms. Rather, as Lambek (ch. 5) suggests, by revealing disparities among ways of being and acting in the world, it is to contextualize our thought. And, I would add, to criticize it.

But that critical edge requires prudence to maintain. In a recent review (Boddy 1995) I suggested that in emphasizing embodiedness – how conventions are "made body," inform one's dispositional alignment in the world – we paradoxically displace the commonsense wisdom that "culture" consists in assumptions which people tacitly "share." However cultural and mindful bodies may be, to the extent that they are singular entities, embodiment is a singular process. This is so despite its being shaped by aggregate discourse and coordinated and constrained by the orientations of relevant others. For scholars trained in Western traditions, there thus exists a potential for slippage between the singularity of embodiment and the ideology of individualism,[1] akin to that between an analytical model of gender as constructed difference and the popular (and ideological) view that culture builds upon a natural divide. With very little effort, the distinctions collapse and slide towards "biology," nature recalcitrant and self-contained. The prospect of unintended essentialisms infiltrating discussions of embodiment ought to give us pause. Surely, however socially grounded they are (e.g. Csordas 1994), the notion warrants our mistrust.

This volume marks an important advance in thinking about embodiment and personhood, not least because several contributors scrutinize those concepts' foundations and assess their potential utility (see also A. J. Strathern 1996). The highly specific ways that persons are embodied and bodies personified warn against responding uncritically to embodiment's intuitive appeal. It is not surprising that a latent presence in a number of chapters is Marilyn Strathern's (1988) ethnographic exposé of Western and Melanesian knowledge practices – *The Gender of the Gift*. Two issues at least are stirred by this materialization: the first concerns the limits of comparison, the second the relevance of a distinction between dividuals and individuals which is the hallmark of that work. The issues are closely related and weave through the discussion below.

The Gender of the Gift is, in part, an organized confrontation between Western commodity logic and the logic of Melanesian gift exchange, designed to bring to light the distinctive ways that bodies and persons are contoured in each through a broad-ranging comparison of the anthropological literature on Melanesia. But in the dualism: commodity-versus-gift, "commodity," the dominant medium of exchange in the West, is presupposed, while "gift" is construed as that which is not-commodity, defined as the counter-image of "commodity" in commodity terms. Their difference is thus hardly natural or presocial, but a "controlled fiction" (1988:6) or heuristic, and M. Strathern insists the distinctions she reveals remain rooted in Western metaphysics.[2] The ways that Western scholars describe non-Western realities are always compromised, and we must regularly call such compromises to conscious attention lest we be drawn into making what, from our respondents' perspectives, are misplaced reifications. Thought is culturally configured; that configuration is not shed through engagement with alternative conventions, though it may be challenged and enlarged (1988 *passim*).

We do well to bear the caution in mind. Comparison, as the editors note, is implicit in all ethnographic endeavors, for one's intellectual home supplies the ground against which the integrity of the foreign can and will be gauged. Moreover, Western constructs inform anthropological thought, often inflecting ethnographic analyses with a logic in which things – products, property, bodies, individuals, social categories – appear to have immanent value while the relationships that comprise them remain hidden from view. True, paradigms have shifted and more processual accounts, like those in the present volume, now prevail. And this shift owes much to our increasingly self-critical engagement with peoples whose lives do not map readily onto our own. Yet as M. Strathern's critique sometimes startlingly reveals, unwarranted commodity thinking can still catch us unawares, intruding into otherwise culturally sensitive analyses when we least expect it. At minimum it constitutes a force to resist. Thus, Lambek's careful deliberation on the distinction between body and mind, arguing for recognition of incommensurabilities among phenomena embraced by these terms, implicitly acknowledges the platform of commensurability from and against which he writes.

There are further constraints on comparative ventures: not only do anthropologists' "home" societies supply the original backdrop to their work, but their foundational field experiences tacitly filter both subsequent researches and future engagements with ethnographic texts. In reading about Melanesia or sub-Saharan Africa, for instance, I constantly tack between my understandings of the Sudanese people with whom I lived and the case at hand, with Western constructs constant if silent partners in my thoughts. Triangulations like those Strathern and Stewart perform in their treatment of Melpa and Nuer embodiment (ch. 11) do not intersect on a horizontal plane, but in an implicitly ordered matrix whose connections are impossible to disengage, had one the mind to try. Indeed, I would hazard that it is precisely by making such tenuous and emergent but implicitly prioritized links (prioritized thematically as well as ethnographically) that one's own data and others' gain focus and depth. The ways that papers in this volume play off and against each other reveal the fruitfulness of comparison for sharpening our grasp of what is local in local contexts and what, as a number of authors note, is relative in relativity. The nuances of Vezo embodied personhood are dramatically clarified through the contrasts with Austronesian and African societies Astuti marshalls to think through Vezo statements about themselves (ch. 2; 1995a).

Embodying persons

In a footnote to his chapter, LiPuma (ch. 3, n. 7) performs a virtuoso decomposition of the objectified academic conference paper into the rhetorics of gift exchange, suggesting, *en passant*, that no ethnography is insular, non-comparative, immune to the entanglements and influences of others' professional efforts. The presence of others' work inside our own is recessed from view, confined in citations and notes that allow the individuality of the author to emerge intact. To extend, but also precede his theme, the suppression of others' effects is an acquired disposition. Students newly returned from the field may endure months of post-partum restiveness, consumed by an anxiety of influence. This transient yet paralyzing affliction is born of one's profound implication in the lives of others, teachers and texts no less, perhaps, than informants. It is heightened by the challenges to personhood that fieldwork inevitably provokes. The inability to objectify when required, coupled with the fear of having to make "an original contribution," provokes a crisis of agency – of individuation.

For Marilyn Strathern, Western and Melanesian epistemologies predicate bodies and persons in strikingly different ways. Without belaboring well-established arguments, where emphasis in the West is on stable, coherent, intentional subjects – unique and autonomous individuals housed in unique and autonomous bodies – emphasis in Melanesia is on "dividuals" (M. Strathern 1988, following Marriott 1976 on India). Dividual persons are construed as unstable products of the relationships (exchanges, encompassments) and the material influences they embody, including bodily substances variously transmitted between them. As Bamford has ably illustrated within (ch. 7), such persons are at once multiple or composite, and divisible, or subject to contextual separations of their parts. Taken more generally, dividuality emphasizes the relational quality of personhood salient where kinship and sociality are key. For Africanists, phrases describing the "embeddedness" or "knottedness" of persons in social relations (e.g. Boddy 1989; Devisch ch. 6; also Corin ch. 4; Weiss ch. 8) express a similar idea, though styles of "dividuality" and individuality are no doubt culturally specific.

LiPuma refines these insights. Where M. Strathern foregrounded ideology, proposing that societies differ depending on which of the two facets is ideologically elaborated and which is masked or assumed, he foregrounds practice, arguing that people everywhere operate both dividually (as repositories of relationships) and individually (as loci of agency, judgment, and intent). His point is echoed by Corin, citing literature from both Africa and Melanesia to make her case. These are *modalities* or aspects of persons, as in the example of students above; they are not fixed categories. Pragmatically speaking, persons in the West are no more the full-blown individuals of its discourse than living Melanesians are thoroughly and transparently dividual. LiPuma cogently observes that a transcultural "individuality-in-practice" is our entry into other social worlds; without it, anthropological fieldwork could not take place. Certainly our own idioms of dividuality, submerged like the kinship they mark, facilitate our comprehension of its more elaborated forms elsewhere. Our commonsense notion that talents or proclivities are "in the blood," passed from parent to child or circulated among kin, captures the point; moreover, as in Melanesia, such influences on or in another, though anticipated, are only affirmed after the fact. Body parts in the West can also "personify" relationships, as in, "she has her father's eyes." But if the two modalities everywhere coexist at a practical or even folk theoretical level, they are also likely to be opposed from the perspective of ideologies.[3] Hence *both* the statutory immorality of Maring sorcery and the reputed rise in sorcery practice with the advance of modernity's political and economic forms. In short, while LiPuma is plainly correct, so too is M. Strathern, whose project to relativize our own metaphors challenges us to labor against their constraints as we think and write. And this is precisely what LiPuma has done. LiPuma's "subversion" of M. Strathern's "subversion" is a barter of standpoints underlining the problems that can arise when indigenous tenets are taken for ideal types.

So far we have distinguished two senses in which a concept of "individual" emerges in the essays here: as the integral, possessive individual of

Western ideology, and the transcultural, practical individual of everyday life. There is, I think, at least one more. Several of the authors describe situations in which persons are temporarily detached from the conventions of their world and afforded the possibility for reflexive thought or more opportune reattachment. To some extent this accords with Dumont's notion of the individual as "renouncer" (1985; Corin ch. 4), so long as its temporal dimension is not overlooked. Under certain conditions (ritual, trauma, colonial intrusion, indeed fieldwork), one's normative personhood may be suspended, as it were, put in abeyance by challenges – planned or unintended – to the routine reciprocity of perspectives characteristic of social life. This is not a process of dividuals dissolving into self-contained, autonomous entities, or being split into component (e.g. gendered) parts in relation to their social complementaries. Rather, it is a temporary resituation or momentary transcendence of ideologically informed personhood, impelled by ritual or social upheaval or both. And in such moments, as Corin suggests, the coordinates of the person are made explicit. Although the process implies disengagement from the quotidian world, this is always a partial displacement, subject to conventions and not solipsistic; moreover, it is never an escape to nowhere, but to another somewhere. It is at once a separation from and engagement with alterity, a portal opening onto influences or entities beyond the routinely experienced world. Through it, a person may be empowered by the perspective of another.

The articles on spirit possession and mediumship by Knauft, Lambek, and Corin speak to these issues in various ways. Possession can be thought of as non-representational meaningful practice that carries the potential to foster representational "competence" – distanciation or reflexive individuality. Spirits do not signify so much as actualize meanings that their hosts embody and convey. As bodily conduits for embodiedness that they themselves are not, and know to be separate from "themselves," the possessed enact a double distanciation; this is most evident in, but by no means limited to possession trance, when the personified body no longer instantiates a normative habitus and its performative habitus suspends realization of embodied personhood. Yet these different persons and bodies are synchronously implicated in the mimetic event. To the extent that someone is perpetually influenced by *multiple* foreign or historically antecedent spirits, as in the Sudanese Zar (Boddy 1989) and the northern Sakalava possession that Lambek (ch. 5) describes, she contains and embodies alternative dividualities – two composite and divisible "persons" respectively produced via protean relationships with spirits and other human selves. Spirits may relate to their hosts directly, by inducing bodily effects: dreams, visions, other sensations including illness and pain. In some cases, those possessed may recall their more formal encounters with spirits in trance (Boddy 1989; Steedly 1993); in others, mediation by third parties may be required (Lambek 1981, 1993a). In either case, spirits become increasingly objectified for the host and audience alike, and as they do, so do the persons they embody. Yet spirits are invariably proximate, within. The shift is one of scale: from composite persons whose constitutive "parts" are selectively emphasized in different social contexts, to composite dividuals whose constituent *persons*, composites themselves, are selectively active and recessed. This complex interplay between distinctive persons housed in a single material body creates a potential for "absence" or detachment of body from person that is productive of reflexivity – as when the French sailor spirit reflects on the limited artistic skills of his host, Ali, in Lambek's piece, or when "Ali" speaks of Madagascar as a nation from the standpoint of a partial outsider. The possessed does not extricate himself from relationships with spirits and other humans, he contextualizes them and thus implicitly, himself.[4] Importantly, possession can also elicit reciprocal distanciations in those who witness or participate in the event.

Such moments supply conditions for creativity and innovation whose consequences may far exceed ritual space and time, as Knauft (ch. 9) clearly shows. The Gebusi medium, Wahiaw, at once coordinates understandings among the men who attend spirit seances, and is a conduit for his spirit women's authoritative words. When these spirits, working through his body, sing narrative songs that do not belong to the recognized corpus but are newly invented instead, they / he transform seances from sorcery inquests that often result in killing, into controlled assays with modernity that do not. Given his and his spirits' established authority and the legitimacy of the seance itself, Wahiaw can dramatically refocus the tensions of sister-exchange addressed by the rite, and induce his audience to explore the problematics and potential outcomes of impending and ambivalently desired social change. At minimum the spirits appear to endorse the substitution of gift exchange for revenge killing, a move some Highlands groups undertook decades before (Strathern and Stewart, ch. 11).

In the Zebola cult of Zaire, a limited decentering of the embedded self is facilitated by the presence of an external power, the spirit of a deceased Mongo woman of unspecified relationship to the initiate's matrilineage, who has invaded the initiate's body to protect against her suffering an illness that others have caused (Corin ch. 4). The illness, which thus preexists the possession, is generally attributable to the malevolence of closely related kin or their retaliation for a breach of sociality on her part. In Africa, at least, both the ruptures and the remedies are often inflected by gender. Fractured embodied relationships have bodily consequences; the Zebola initiate's spirit reveals the coordinates of her person that have been subject to stress and are responsible for her affliction. The spirit enables "her" to address family members from a position that is not wholly external to herself (the spirit is possibly family too), but is not the fulcrum of her network of kin. And the comments "she" makes on others' conduct of their lives have consequences for them as well as for the initiate herself. Thus, the individuation accomplished by Zebola ritual, Corin notes, does not reject the conventional world but reworks the possessed's belongingness in it.

What Zebola clearly demonstrates is the downside to "dividual" personhood: persons at the mercy of each other's capacities and good will, or hard pressed to meet their expectations. The obligations and demands of kin might well conflict, and it can be difficult to manage responsibilities to the dead and living alike. The point is central to Bercovitch's discussion of sorcery among the Atbalmin of New Guinea (ch. 10). There the numerous exchanges through which relationships are made, and bodies materially produced and sustained, require judicious management. Sorcery is the province of those who hold grudges, whose wrath is provoked by reciprocity that is neglected or put off. Faced with the practical impossibility of discharging their extensive obligations while fearful of being ensorcelled if they do not, the Atbalmin live in close if precarious intimacy, open to neighbors' inspection yet secretive all the same. Melanesian tensions between dividuality and individuality are expressed, as LiPuma also observed, in contrasts between transparent and clandestine acts. Virtually all deaths are attributed to sorcery, which effects a progressive "dis-embodiment," a telling decomposition of the socially embodied self.

It is important to note that Atbalmin, like Gebusi or Mongo, are aware of their existential contradictions and seek the means to limit them. As is true everywhere, Atbalmin conventions are being encompassed and transformed by commodity logic, if less through trade than through Baptist Christianity. Bercovitch argues that the exogenous religion is persuasive precisely in so far as its reformulations of evil and death speak to prior concerns. Still, one wonders what effects pastoral messages about "autonomous" individuals responsible for their own salvations might have. What difference does it make when Christianity precedes commodity trade rather than accompanies or succeeds it? And it is intriguing that the new religion has attracted younger women. Is their agency otherwise more curtailed than men's? Are they more likely to be thought individualistic? Moreover, in the disjunction of beliefs lies space for creativity: several women converts became possessed by the Holy Spirit and "used this special authority to support the Christian side" (p. 222) in debates over dismantling the local temple.

Devisch's intricate study of a Yaka curing rite recalls us to the entanglements of relational personhood and its non-representational embeddedness in the world. By non-representational I mean the sense in which persons do not stand apart from surrounding bodies, objects, spaces, through a logic of separation that distinguishes material from non-material, inert or inherently meaningless from intelligible or symbolic, indeed, nature from culture, other from self, body from mind (e.g. Bordo 1993). If, as Mitchell (1991) observes, an ontological distinction between physical reality and its representations informs the metaphysics of capitalist modernity, where "representation is the non-material, non-physical dimension of intelligibility" (Mitchell 1991:xiii), then the reification of this convention may well inure us to the effects of others on ourselves (eliciting LiPuma's admonitions). And make it more challenging, therefore, to appreciate the depth of others' immersion. I am not, of course, suggesting that representational thought is a preserve of the capitalist West: far from it, as the discussion of spirit possession makes clear. But where personhood is culturally configured primarily through its constitutive relationships, it would be foolish to assume that its performative subtleties can be grasped by uncritically invoking our static analytical dichotomies.

Yaka, and the Sudanese villagers with whom I worked, and I think most of the peoples discussed in this book, espouse a broadly *ecological* notion of embodiment that includes the world beyond the body's edge. For Yaka, Devisch notes, "to become a person is to be connected, bonded and tied into, and with, those multiple forms of reproduction and exchange that give form to the Yaka universe" (p. 130). The body's skin is an interface, its orifices sites of transaction with other people and the world. Yaka identity takes shape as a "knot," "in a weaving of superimposed layers" of multi-relational spheres (*ibid.*). It is crucial to balance the interrelations that compose the person, lest illness should result when one is knotted too tightly to the uterine sources of life or too loosely to agnatic sociality. The images of tying, knotting, binding, are recursive, resolving into other images whose meanings lie in the logic of their coherence, their knottedness. The therapeutic initiation Devisch describes works in complex ways to "re-source" the person, taking her back to the prehuman point of emergence and reweaving her vital relationships; this happens gradually, by encouraging a profound identification with condensed anthropomorphic images. Devisch is clear that the person's revitalization does not merely confirm prior identifications; she is also invited to explore, in a more reflexive or "representational" way: "to keep open a window of disbelief" (p. 154) that is, like all windows, limited by its frame.

The image of ecology is particularly well suited to the Vezo (ch. 2) of coastal Madagascar, for whom identity is literally grounded in the place where they live and the marks their bodies acquire in wresting a living from the sea. Vezo-ness *is*, says Astuti, no more or less than Vezo *do*. But this radically performative, non-essentialist, transactional dimension of personhood is only part of the story, for it is evanescent, confined to the span of one's natural life. The dead, who no longer enact Vezo-ness, are not Vezo. When entombed a person's identity is transformed: permanently fixed in place and kind. Tombs are sites where descent groups are forged, for death contracts the cognatic possibilities of life to a single affiliative strand. Still, for all its singularity, Vezo-ness seems comparable to other forms of personhood discussed in this book: for it too is relational, embodied through reciprocal exchanges with the "person" of the sea.

At the outset of Vezo life is another fixed point, sex, which for Vezo is an essential capacity that portends the personhood one might achieve. Gender, like Vezo-ness in general, is performative and negotiable. While Astuti provocatively suggests that adult Vezo are thus "ungendered," it is not obvious from her account how bodily signs of reproduction are accommodated to this view. If what is crucial about performance is its indeterminacy, do not the inevitabilities of pregnancy, menstruation, and birth pose existential dilemmas for Vezo notions of identity? Astuti's distinctions between flexible and fixed dimensions of personhood, gender, and sex chafe against the "nature / culture" shibboleth that feminists have struggled to retire (e.g. Collier and Yanagisako 1987; Moore 1993b). And, since Vezo have no obligation to be coherent on our terms, my questions may be irrelevant, and evidence that the sex-role model of gender is still alive and well in academe.

Flourishing too is the distinction between body and mind, no matter how we restrain or transcend it. Should we seek to dissolve the opposition or deploy it? Is it particular solely to Western thought and the impediment to understanding we have come to believe? Lambek (ch. 5) argues the dualism is common, "everywhere transcended in practice yet everywhere present, in some form or another, in thought" (p. 105). His empirical standpoint is one that I share: researching spirit possession, one cannot help but be struck by the imaginative skill with which spirits distinguish themselves from the bodies in whom they appear. Further, as discussed above, learning to distance may be therapeutic. Bearing this in mind, I want to extend Lambek's observation in a preliminary way. However heretical it may seem, perhaps a distinction between body and mind is not just universal in thought; perhaps it is also imperative for health. This goes back to my argument (1988, 1989) about how the Zar cult in northern Sudan guides women in cultivating a distanced perspective on their lives when such distance is everywhere else abridged. Women's bodies are continuously identified with a coherent vision of moral fertility, first through traumatic childhood circumcision, then in manifold contexts from the transcendent to the expressly mundane. Possession rituals address illnesses linked to blood, the source of a woman's fertility which spirits are said to have "tied up" or "seized." Alternatively spirits may have "loosened" her blood and induced miscarriage. Much like the cures that Corin and Devisch describe, possession rituals proceed to resituate the afflicted and induce her to resituate herself through imaginative engagement and bodily practice. I suggested that Zar is associated with problems of embodiment – of over-embodiment to be precise – problems in which fertility incarnate is not realized through successful birth.

In teaching it has been helpful to compare this to Susan Bordo's analysis of anorexia nervosa and bulimia in Western societies (1993). Bordo links eating disorders to historically profound cultural distinctions between the material and the ideal, body and mind or spirit, in which the physical body is regarded as alien, not-self. In Augustine's formulation, the body is a cage that confines and limits; it is "the enemy," the locus of all that threatens our attempts at control (Bordo 1993:144). Sex maps onto this model, as Ortner (1974) described: the female body – fleshy, menstrual, sexual, reproductive – is ambivalently trapped in repudiated nature, and becomes both source and ineluctable evidence of woman's subordination. In this context, the very materiality of the female body is a problem for female personhood: from the perspective of mind, as Lambek notes, body and mind are incommensurable.

In anorectics, embodiment of the body's alienness is especially pronounced: they experience not only hunger but other physical sensations – pain, cold, heat – as invasive, originating from outside the self (Bruch 1973:254), much like spirits are experienced in Zar. Self-mastery, the triumph of mind, is achieved by denying sensation; refusing to eat becomes an act of creation, mind dictating to nature, actively producing the body's design, and experiencing in the process the (ultimately self-defeating) satisfaction of material transcendence.

From childhood on, women are schooled to contemporary versions of this mind–body aesthetic through television, film, other public media, and peers; yet relatively few go on to develop full-blown anorexia. But its symptoms illustrate commonplace patterns writ large. Here dramatically personified are the politics of female restraint, an ideal of thinness that women are enjoined to enforce in themselves. Profound mimetic internalization of impossibly slim "normality" – as of perfect fertility in Sudan

– grants the person little space, little distance from which to critique. Should the embodied aesthetic contradict her body she feels compelled by her growing dysphoria to achieve their accord. Thus, like acknowledging possession illness in Sudan, refusing or limiting one's food is a therapeutic endeavor (Boddy 1997). If therapeutic from the anorectic's perspective, however, it sows seeds of a more dangerous affliction from another: by becoming, as it were, "all mind," the very existence of the person is at risk. One difference between possession and anorexia may be that the West has no curing rites adequate to the cultural complexities of the condition, which, by working to offset conventional embodiment through counter-mimesis as in Zar, might cultivate a healthier distance between "body" and "mind."

What health means in this context would, I assume, depend in part on the conventions of personhood, and whether the sufferer is reattuned to the situation that made her ill or enabled to critique and conceivably change it. The definition of health is a political matter, and it is important to ask whose interests it might serve.

Personifying bodies

In their discussion of how wealth became a substitute for human life in Melpa exchange, Strathern and Stewart (ch. 11) counsel the need for "an indigenous model of what human life is, how it comes into being and is sustained, and what happens to it at death" (p. 236). The phrase pithily captures what ought to be significant to any ethnographic endeavor. But as Moore (1993b:198) points out, there has been a tendency in the past to relegate such theories to the domain of "procreation beliefs" whenever they threaten our commonsense (anthropological) model of the relationship between gender and sex. This insulates them from the wider social concerns with which they indubitably belong, while preserving the presocial "givenness" of sex undefiled. Embodiment offers a means to avoid such pitfalls and transcend entrenched ideologies. It enables us to deploy Foucault's insight that "sex" is an artifact of a discourse whose conventions can be specified, rather than a prior unity and universal causal principle (Foucault 1990:154). At last, *pace* Delaney (1986), perhaps the virgin birth debate can be put to rest.

In many Melanesian and African societies, dividual and relational forms of personhood seem inextricable from conventional understandings of how bodies form from the bodies of others. Bodies encompass and expel one another, corporeal substances move between them. Movement may be continual or episodic as contexts and cultures ordain. Such bodies are composites, not inherently unique or autonomous entities. Internal differences may be more relevant and nuanced than external ones, and internal composition may shift with the ebbs and flows of a person's life. Parts may be detached, substances fortified or depleted. In these cases bodies do not express the relations through which they are formed, so much as realize them. Although there are parallels between the two regions covered by this book, there are also telling differences, and I will try to adduce some below.

Bamford's discussion of Kamea food taboos emphasizes the performative dimension of Melanesian transactional embodiment (ch. 7). For the Kamea, taboos not only maintain categorical distinctions, they are an important means to create them, to fashion differences within a field of essential similarity. A boy is regarded as being contained by his mother's body even after birth; more, he is described as "female-like" and dresses the part. But their identity is incomplete and, in certain respects, transitional. Thus, the boy avoids certain foods prior to initiation because not to do so would adversely affect his mother's health. Once he has been initiated the taboo is reversed; henceforth his mother must avoid those foods he forewent as a child. Only then is he fully "de-contained" and, being made separate, gendered. He is now able to wed, to enter into a relationship and elicit the containment capacities of another. Bamford describes the cycle as one of enchainment, premised on cultivating specific relationships over time, not contributing to a broad notion of "society." Yet she notes that continuity with past generations adheres in the male line, and maternal siblings are linked in a lateral, non-transmissible "blood" relationship for having been born of the same womb. Thus food taboos abet the creation of distinct maternal generations as well as genders, and it is unclear from Bamford's account how this plays out in Kamea life: guiding potential marriages, perhaps? I note this because of a vague similarity between Kamea lateral relations and those in northern Sudan, touched on below.

The focus on circulation in Bamford's account as well as on gendered forms of relatedness calls to mind examples of Melanesian societies where bodily substances necessary for life are considered limited in quantity or finite, not generated by each "biological unit" afresh. As substances circulate through relationships, their qualities affect the bodily/spiritual constitutions of partners to the exchange. Among the Hua (Meigs 1984), blood, for instance, carries pollution but also contributes to growth. Plentiful in women, it is the fluid they impart to offspring in the womb. Its effects are also transferred by contact, as in coitus. It can be fortified by consuming foods that share its qualities (e.g., red, juicy), but too great a concentration in the body can be dangerous to others and oneself. Over the course of her life a woman rids herself of blood and thus its attendant pollution; a post-menopausal woman who has born three or more children is sufficiently depleted, hence pure, that she is entitled to be initiated into the "men's cult." A man begins adulthood in a state of purity but is increasingly polluted through contact as he matures; as such he becomes a source of contamination to others.[5]

The example of Etoro (Kelly 1993) enlarges the discussion. Here bodies are composites of bone, derived from paternal semen, and flesh, derived from maternal blood; *hame*, or spiritual life force, is also carried in semen. At birth both sexes have sufficient semen / *hame* to sustain life, but men's is progressively weakened as they transmit it to others: children they father, boys they ritually inseminate and so enable to become fathers themselves, female sexual partners. As women do not transmit semen but merely convey it, heterosexual relations are circumscribed: when they do not lead to conception, *hame* is lost. Through the circulation of semen between kin groups, affinal relations are corporealized, for ideally a youth's inseminator is his sister's future husband. Thus, a man and his brother-in-law share semen, gifted by the former for the reproductive capacity of the latter's sister. From the perspective of a child, semen / *hame* is shared with father and with mother's brother, who also shares the child's maternal flesh and blood (Kelly 1993:162).

In Melanesia embodied capacities and constraints are composite and mutable, forever becoming in relation to others, as Bercovitch (ch. 10) and Strathern and Stewart (ch. 11) attest. In Poole's (1981a) analysis of Bimin-Kuskusmin, no fewer than four principal substances are transmitted over the generations and transformed, weakened, or sustained according to the relationships they effect. A child receives contributions of venous or "red" blood from both mother and father; this is made up of blood from the eight agnatic groups from which their grandparents derived. Each "strand" is imparted to offspring in progressively attenuated form once it passes through a female link, until the third generation who can no longer transmit it at all. Those with whom one shares venous blood are one's exogamous kindred. Members of one's kindred with whom one shares undiluted venous blood, blood that is strengthened by the dual spirit entity contained and transmitted through semen, are one's agnates.[6] Father's semen forms the body's hard, enduring parts – bone and sinew – whereas mother's father's semen, transformed in mother's body into womb fluids and milk (i.e. semen in "female" form), becomes the child's soft, fleshy parts. Menstrual, "black" blood is transmitted solely through females to both daughters and sons. Thus, Bimin-Kuskusmin embody aspects of one another in multiple and overlapping ways: one's body is a corporeal history of past relationships that contain potentials for the present and provide direction for future sociality. What each parent contributes to the fetus is itself a partible composite separated from the larger partible composite of which he or she is formed. And as elsewhere in Melanesia, these aspects of the person can be strengthened or diminished by consuming certain foods.

I want to juxtapose the above Melanesian ideas to some issues arising in my own research among Muslim villagers in Hofriyat, northern Sudan. To me, whose perspective is rooted in Africa, and Islamic Africa at that, the tension or momentum in much of Melanesian exchange consists in the positive value of *extending* sociality, paired with the recognition that extension cannot be endlessly unlimited or uncontained. Here Bercovitch's discussion of Atbalmin openness and secrecy comes to mind. Hofriyati corporeal logic contrasts with Melanesian forms less in idiom than in practice. Readers should not suppose that Hofriyat is in some sense archetypal for "Africa"; indeed it is not. There are, however, some family resemblances among African cultures in the ways that bodily substances are configured.

Hofriyati say that a child's bones and sinew (hard parts) are formed from the semen or "seed" of its father, while its flesh and blood (soft parts) are formed from its mother's blood (cf. Holy 1991:48 on the Berti of Darfur). Venous and menstrual blood do not differ in kind, but in *time*: the "red" blood that circulates in the body and pools in the womb as the source of a woman's fertility turns "black" when its potential is extinguished. This shift from red to black blood is, I think, metonymical of a comprehensive temporal orientation – a view of the human life span as well as of generational relatedness – that is fused with a concern for maintaining vitality less through extensive or enchained exchange, than through conservation, maintenance of internal balance, and intensification of prior embodied relationships.

Children's bodies are composites of male and female substance: I use gender terms advisedly, as gender becomes an increasingly fixed identity as the child matures, such that mothers who transmit their blood are more fully female / feminine than their young daughters, and fathers who transmit semen more fully male / masculine than their young sons. More to the point, I am fairly sure that Hofriyati do not conceptualize gender as the elaboration of precultural biological difference (hence the slashes between terms above), for biological sex is only fully created by human hand, that is, through male and female circumcision. Circumcision reduces physical manifestations of the child's inherent androgyny: to remove the clitoris and labia is to remove male body parts in female form, while to remove the foreskin is to remove a female body part in male form. The infibulated female body is "closed," its blood is bound within; the male body is opened, untied. The operations are said to make the children marriageable. They capacitate their bodies for procreation, producing a lack in one that only the other can meet, but not in any crude physical way (Hofriyati are well aware that uncircumcised people reproduce). Rather, they endow their bodies with moral and social consequence and align them in the world. Borrowing a Melanesianist idiom, they create difference in order to create a relationship.

Children are circumcised when they have become minimally "reasonable" (*'agil*/*'agila*), between the ages of about six and nine. *'Agl* is a dimension of "mind," its social dimension, as distinguished from *nafs*, which means both physical life force and self, all that which is not oriented to others. To become *'agila* is to become socially aware: able to anticipate others' needs and acts and respond in appropriate ways, to internalize and demonstrate the reciprocity of perspectives that is the basis of human sociality. Once circumcised, boys and girls lead relatively segregated lives and their complementary dispositions mature. Continuous imaginative and material engagement with humanly ordered spaces, objects, processes, and other persons ensures their progressive implication – or, to invoke a Yaka idiom well known to Sudanese, their "knottedness" – in the world.

Circumcision reduces androgyny, but by no means erases it. It refines paternal and maternal contributions, differentiating them by sorting between bodies capable of conferring them to others. Paternal and maternal substance joined in a human body part company over the generations, for only women transmit blood, only men transmit seed. More, they become increasingly disconnected inside the body with age: the body "dries up" as it matures, skin cedes its moisture, red blood in the womb loses its fecundity, flesh no longer adheres firmly to bones but becomes slack, withers, and ultimately, with death, decays. The bones alone remain. Maternal connection is ephemeral, paternal connection enduring. As the paternal skeleton structures the body, patrilineality structures relationships through time; indeed, the rigid appendages of the body – foot, calf, thigh – are levels of patrilineal affiliation. Maternal relations supply the tissue that binds the village's skeletal descent groups, providing integument that eventually must yield to entropy –unless, that is, entropy can be averted by endogamy, as it should.

If the body is a microcosm of social relationships, the village is a body writ large, whose bones are bound by the successive intramarriages of its women and men. The elusive yet ideal union joins the offspring of brothers *who are also the offspring of sisters* – bilateral parallel cousins – whose grandfathers are brothers, or grandmothers sisters. Such couples' internal constitution is precisely the same – they are social and physical "clones," derived from the same paternal and maternal sources. Their children will thus be exact internal replicas of themselves. Exemplary marriages are in practice rare (1:50 in Hofriyat); still, they provide a measure by which people can gauge the suitability of partners whose moral and physical bodies are less co-present in their own. When sisters marry into different patrilines, people remember; their offspring are classed as "children of maternal aunts." But this limited extension of relationship is subject to intensification and containment over time, in that the co-subsantiality of the children of maternal aunts provides a basis for marriages among their descendants in the next. Bodily substances cycle continuously through the village body, its differentiated bones bound and re-bound by flesh and blood that maternal connection provides. Blood is thus conserved in the village body much as it is bound in the body of a circumcised girl.

Considering Hofriyati relatedness from the perspective of embodiment reveals entanglements and convolutions quite distant from Melanesian forms. Hofriyati accent condensing exchange, intensifying sociality, and repelling temporal (and moral) dissolution by using present and past to create the possibility of relationships one or more generations hence. To summarize villagers as "patrilineal" would leave much that is important about their lives unsaid. It should not go unremarked that my information came more often through women's words than men's. Yet I do not think that the emphasis on maternal connection was solely women's elaboration, for it was a man who first alerted me to how marriages are made through the children of maternal aunts.

Beyond this, by focusing on embodiment finer distinctions can be drawn among forms of thought and organization within the Islamic world: in rural Turkey, for instance, father's semen provides the spark of life that is nurtured in mother's womb, much as soil nurtures planted seed without contributing to its basic identity. Reproduction is thus monogenetic; to veil and control women is to fence off fertile agnatic fields, and to guarantee the essence of that which is planted within (Delaney 1991). For Hofriyati, reproduction unites paternal and maternal "essence," while circumcision ensures the physical and moral continuity of both.

Within Africa, on the other hand, Somalis and northern Sudanese practice similar forms of circumcision and share a number of idioms through which sociality is expressed. Yet the meanings of these operations do not fully coincide. As in Hofriyat, Somali children are androgynous composites that genital operations later refine (Talle 1993:84–6). Relationships formed through (male) bone are "hard," strong, and lasting, while those formed through (female) blood are "soft," pliable, and ramifying, as are the body parts that they create. Both sexes inherit their "hard" body parts and agnatic identity from their fathers, but girls, suggests Talle (p.104), must have that ascription reconfirmed through circumcision (not also boys?). Talle notes that the stitching of the vaginal opening "ties" a girl to her natal patriline. The operation confers on her body the "seal of agnation" – making her genital area hard, like the penis and other male body parts.[7] Moreover, "the constructed genital 'resembles' the male organ by its straight scar / seam and small orifice at the lower end" (Talle 1993:97). Interestingly, most Somalis are exogamous, lineage endogamy being neither preferred nor proscribed, but less common than marriages between distinct patrilines and different locales.[8] A woman's scar is mnemonic of her enduring identity as female agnate; marriage loosens but does not fundamentally refashion that bond: in being opened by her husband's penis,[9] she is only provisionally re-tied to her husband's group.

Despite shared themes, and even what appear to be similar practices, Hofriyati corporeal logic differs from Somali in subtle yet crucial ways. Hofriyati understandings were no doubt tempered in the crucible of historical interaction between their exogenous "patrilineal" Arab and indigenous "matrilineal" Nubian antecedents. This history is cryptically captured in local myth as a game between a powerful man (a sultan's son) and a wiley woman (an ostrich-like virgin associated with the Nile), that results in an exchange of seed and blood (cf. Boddy 1989:75–88). It is perhaps not surprising that realizations of "blood" in Hofriyat resemble those in parts of sub-Saharan Africa, where blood flows between bodies or circulates among them; has qualities whose relative internal balance is indexical of bodily / social / moral health and age; and can be depleted through the intervention of extraneous agents like spirits or sorcerers, and otherwise jeopardized or conserved (e.g. Weiss, ch. 8; Lan 1985). Such themes occur in Melanesia too, as Strathern and Stewart (ch. 11) affirm.

Comparing Melpa and Nuer, peoples from the two regions for whom animals could substitute for human "blood" through exchange, Strathern and Stewart explore the problems of structuring human relationships once animals and "blood" have been drawn into crude communion with money, inanimate, utterly depersonalized medium that it is. For Nuer, the blood of cattle and people is "one," capable of extending vitality over the generations in parallel ways. Bonds of maternity are direct, unmediated transfers of bodily substance – blood and milk – that connect mothers and children in continuous mutual relationship, ties that are the strongest of all in Nuer life (Hutchinson 1996:179). From men's perspective, however, cattle, not women, produce children; a man's reproductive potential is merged with that of his agnatic kinsmen and vested in the ancestral herd on which he and they rely to obtain wives, thence daughters and sons. Male fertility is "corporate" or communal, inseparable from that of the patriline and the herd (p.62). Money's role in Nuer sociality is ambivalent and contextually differentiated, sometimes being put to work in support of these vital truths, sometimes undermining them, and sometimes entering into hybrid categories like "the cattle of money" and "the money of cattle," a point I return to below. Nuer's increasing acceptance of currency has, Hutchinson notes, contributed to a profound reevaluation of the place of cattle in their lives that entails no less than a reassessment of what it means to be themselves (1996, ch. 2).

The enigmatic "East-African cattle-complex" beloved of introductory texts takes on fresh meaning when viewed in terms of embodiment and dividual exchange. The close relationship between Nuer and their herds is not only metaphoric and symbiotic, an identification between discrete classes of entities mutually engaged, but speaks to their deeper, participatory, metonymic, and material implication in each others' lives. It transects "species" boundaries such that the blood of one can be transformed into the blood of the other, as with cattle given in compensation, for the fertility of wives, or consumed in whole or part as food. The point is echoed and extended in Broch-Due's (1993) sophisticated language-based analysis of personhood among the Turkana of north-west Kenya, a brief consideration of which leads us back to the essays at hand.

Turkana, like Nuer, are cattle pastoralists. Cattle and humans are linked materially and imaginatively in a plethora of ways, not least having to do with procreation and sociality. A child and a calf are analogous in that both arise from the same essential sources: grass and water, semen and clotted blood. These sources are at once recursive images of each other, and serial transformations in a shared alimentary, hence nutritive process: humans and animals are continuous (Broch-Due 1993:54). The body is neither bounded and unitary, but permeable and plural, a "cognatic collage of blood streams" (p.76), containing and sharing bodily substance with all collateral kin four generations back. Descent is but one path among those that create the composite person. The term for kindred means "like bodies"; yet these are not necessarily composed of the same maternal and paternal substance. Their likeness derives too from living with and off the animals that circulate within this group (*ibid.*). Food forms vital links among people, and between them and the surrounding world. The qualities of foods a pregnant woman eats have a formative effect on her future child, and must be kept in balance; they are continuous with the qualities of semen and clotted blood from which the fetus was formed. Foods, tastes, and other sensations, items of clothing and adornment, parts of the body, states-of-being and their transformations from wet to dry, prone to erect, open to closed, all of these and more, condense multiple interpenetrating meanings that animate the person's continuous, fluctuating involvement in the world. The body is a micro-cosmic landscape of persons, artifacts, cattle, plants; the seasonal land-scape is a socially differentiated, macrophysiological body turned inside out (Broch-Due 1993).

A view of the person as composite, multiply sourced, and constituted through reciprocal engagement in a recursively meaningful world is not uncommon in Africa. Prevalent too are many of the processes through which that engagement is experienced and expressed. Yet its forms are specific and historically supple. Weiss's examination of how tensions surrounding social and economic transformation among the Haya of Tanzania "are concretely realized and made meaningful through their bodily effects" provides a case in point (ch. 8). For Haya, blood circula-ting in the physical body is both indexical of relative health and enabling, the force of human agency. Its dynamic qualities – its variable volume, heat, and speed – are affected by, and signify internalization of, the wider world in which the person acts. As such, blood is subject to continuous evaluation and control by managing what one does and eats. Rumors about blood stealing index a disruption to the circulatory balance of Haya capacity, a capacity put, through wage labor and urban migration, to productive ends that may subvert blood's proper effects.[10] Alienated, commoditized blood is thus a hybrid form, like Nuer "cattle of money." It captures people's ambivalent engagement in an emergent relational ecology: Haya, as Weiss notes, are in fact embodying the commodity form even as they question the morality of alienated exchange. Impersonal, commoditized, state-controlled substances that circulate and enable – i.e. petrol and electricity – are now *compared* to blood. As such they constitute each other in Haya moral imagination, challenging and enlarg-ing it as they do. The possibility of buying and selling blood, ordinarily productive only when contained in the body, implies the reconfiguration of corporeal sociality rather than its dissolution (as sought by sorcerers). The petrol-powered automobile that whisks away blood presents an arresting image: iconic of the human body of commodity exchange, the canonical individual encased in a skin of steel, mobilized and connected to others by deanimated "blood."

Haya concepts of blood bear a striking resemblance to those of north-ern Sudanese: both emphasize the fluid's fluctuating indexical and en-abling qualities and its productive capacity when enclosed in the body, contained. In both societies, for example, people eat certain foods in order to increase their volume of blood and temper its flow. So the formal correspondences Haya adduce between blood and electricity and the specific differences these also entail (i.e. electricity is diffuse, transmutable, able to drain the body dry) may shed light on something I found puzzling in my work on the Zar: the spirit called Electricity. Zar spirits are all held to "steal" or "seize" blood, here the (female) blood of reproduction. Invariably they are analogues of human foreigners who have impinged on villagers' world at some time in the last two centuries. But women have trouble classifying Electricity: sometimes it is a European spirit, sometimes a *Sahar*, or "sorcerer," otherwise identified as Azande. What sorcerers, including Electricity, share are abilities to pass through obstacles and metamorphose at will. They are the most dangerous of spirits, the hardest to bargain with (so as to restore one's health), and the most frightening by far to entertain. For Hofriyati women, Electricity is an alien personified power whose circulatory effects on the body are uncannily like those of electric power on Haya blood; I wonder if they elucidate similar existential dilemmas?

Le digestif

Weiss (pers. com.) has drawn an intriguing parallel between the reported effects of electric vampires among the Haya, and an experience of the body known (but not [yet] biomedically legitimated) as "environmental illness" in the West. Environmental illness is seen as a failure of the body's immune system to shield it from the debilitating effects of an industrialized world; living too close to power lines is a salient cause. He notes, "In both cases, what makes the person viable (a strong 'self,' or a well-fed, temperate body) is most vulnerable to attack."[11] And in both cases commodities and commodified powers are embodied in self-transforming ways. Yet the trajectories of these processes are basically opposed: where Haya bodies index a normative process of engagement with the world stopped short, Western bodies register a normative defence against the world transgressed. Here, then, is Western personhood performatively defined: created, like Vezo identity, through the body's interaction with its milieu, but unlike Vezo identity, created by repelling that world and asserting the body's presocial essence. The embattled integral body sheltering bravely within its fortress / skin, protected by a specialized army of combat-ready warrior cells (cf. Martin 1994), is none other than the atomic age Western individual in physiological form.

The essays in this volume demonstrate the impossibility of divorcing body from person, embodiment from relationship, relationship from history and environment in ethnographic work. The virtue of their comparative efforts is to unsettle deeply embodied suppositions not only about and within ourselves, but also about those with whom we, as anthropologists and intruders of other ilk, ply our trade.

NOTES

1 This ideology is, of course, associated with a specific constellation of ideas surrounding the body's unity and agency in Western societies. Neither the presence nor the absence of ideological individualism rules out other forms of individuality or subjectivity in a given society. LiPuma's discussion (ch. 3) and my own (below) take up that point from slightly different angles. For more on the issue, see Cohen (1994).

2 For recent works concerning the gift/commodity argument, see Thomas (1991) and Carrier (1995).

3 The point might be extended by considering one Western context in which dividuality is not, on the face of it, submerged: this is in military training, designed to forge a disparate group of youths into a single physical unit such that each becomes willing to sacrifice himself for the rest. Once the trappings of recruits' individuality are shorn away, they are bound together by rigorous physical drill and often marked off by hazing rituals in which bodily substances like blood and feces are "shared"; the result is "dividuality" tellingly embedded within a composite but integral individual – one body, one mind.

4 The closest analogy from my own experience to what Sudanese women say happens to them through the Zar, i.e. "we see things differently," is what happens when I am absorbed in a novel of complex ideas and fully drawn characters that is impossible to put down. There is a sense of loss when you at last close the book and also a sense of having been profoundly affected, indeed changed, by it. The experience adds to one's resources for living, but the specific changes to one's life may be impossible to articulate. The book or the possession experience enriches the person. It does not always or necessarily have an instrumental effect.

5 I have tried to avoid replicating Meigs's suggestion that the sexes change genders over time, as this suggests a shift from one whole identity to another that seems debatable in light of her evidence. For criticisms see Moore (1994: 23–4); M. Strathern (1988:105–7).

6 The vitality of agnatic blood imparted by a woman diminishes because women transmit semen in indirect ways, i.e. transformed into fertile fluids that do not contain this spirit entity (Poole 1981a:131).

7 The hardness of the infibulated vulva was often noted by my Somali informant, Aman (Aman, Barnes and Boddy 1994), in contrast to descriptions from Sudanese who emphasized smoothness and (en)closure. The idiom of tying is common in both societies, but has different emphases in each.

8 Though according to Talle (1993:94) lineage endogamy has increased of late.

9 While this is not the only means used to open an infibulated woman's orifice, it is, I was told, the only honorable way among Somali men.

10 This is reminiscent of "fat-stealing" rumors in the Andes, where body fat is believed to be extracted, typically from indigenous youth, and sold in coastal (European-associated) cities for use in producing cosmetics. It is only the rich who ornament their bodies with commercial cosmetics, who thus wear the transformed bodies of Indians as a mark of their class on their skins.

11 Personal communication, March 7, 1997.

Bibliography

Abu-Lughod, Lila 1990. The romance of resistance: tracing transformations of power through Bedouin women. *American Ethnologist* 17:41–55.

Allibert, Claude 1994. Les Sekatse de Flacourt: réflexion sur un comportement. Déviance ou contournement social? *Cahiers Ethnologiques* (Presses Universitaires de Bordeaux), 22(16):106–21.

Aman, Virginia Lee Barnes and Janice Boddy 1994. *Aman: The Story of a Somali Girl*. London: Bloomsbury.

Antze, Paul and Michael Lambek, eds. 1996. *Tense Past: Cultural Essays in Trauma and Memory*. New York and London: Routledge.

Anzieu, D. 1974. Le Moi-peau. *Nouvelle Revue de Psychanalyse* 9:195–208.

1985. *Le Moi-peau*. Paris: Dunod.

Appadurai, Arjun 1988. Putting hierarchy in its place. *Cultural Anthropology* 3:36–49.

Appiah, Kwame Anthony 1992. *In My Father's House: Africa in the Philosophy of Culture*. Oxford: Oxford University Press.

Apter, A. 1991. The embodiment of paradox: Yoruba kingship and female power. *Cultural Anthropology* 6(2):212–30.

Ardener, Shirley 1975. Sexual insult and female militancy. In S. Ardener, ed., *Perceiving Women*. London: Dent/Malaby, pp.29–53.

Astuti, Rita 1993. Food for pregnancy. Procreation, marriage and images of gender among the Vezo of western Madagascar. *Social Anthropology. The Journal of the European Association of Social Anthropologists* 1(3):1–14.

1995a. *People of the Sea: Identity and Descent among the Vezo of Madagascar*. Cambridge: Cambridge University Press.

1995b. "The Vezo are not a kind of people." Identity, difference and "ethnicity" among a fishing people of western Madagascar. *American Ethnologist* 22(3):464–82.

Atkinson, Jane M. 1990. How gender makes a difference in Wana society. In J. M. Atkinson and S. Errington, eds., *Power and Difference: Gender in Island Southeast Asia*, Stanford: Stanford University Press, pp. 59–93.

Auslander, Mark 1993. "Open the Wombs!": the symbolic politics of modern Ngoni witchfinding. In John Comaroff and Jean Comaroff, eds., *Modernity and its Malcontents*. Chicago: University of Chicago Press, pp. 167–92.

Babcock, B. A. 1978. *The Reversible World*. Ithaca and New York: Cornell University Press.

Bakhtin, Mikhail M. 1986. *Speech Genres and Other Late Essays*. Austin: University of Texas Press.

274

Balandier, G. 1965. *Au Royaume de Kongo: du XVIe au XVIIIe siècle.* Paris: Hachette.

Bamford, S. 1996a. Insubstantial identities: locating meaning where the flow of bodily substance stops. Paper presented at the Canadian Anthropological Society Meetings, May 1996.

1996b. The family tree: giving new meanings to an old concept. Paper presented at the American Anthropological Society Meetings, November 1996.

1997. The containment of gender: embodied sociality among a South Angan people. Ph.D. dissertation: The University of Virginia.

Barnes, J. A. 1962. African models in the New Guinea Highlands. *Man* 62:5–9.

Barth, F. 1975. *Ritual and Knowledge among the Baktaman of New Guinea.* New Haven: Yale University Press.

Bastian, Misty n.d. "My head was too strong!" Body parts and money magic in Nigerian popular discourse. Unpublished paper.

Bastide, R. 1973. Le principe d'individuation (contribution à une philosophie africaine). In Centre national de la recherche scientifique, ed., *La Notion de personne en Afrique noire.* Paris: Editions du CNRS, pp. 33–43.

Battaglia, Debbora 1990. *On the Bones of the Serpent: Person, Memory, and Mortality in Sabarl Island Society.* Chicago: University of Chicago Press.

1992. The body in the gift: memory and forgetting in Sabarl mortuary exchange. *American Ethnologist* 19:3–18.

1995a. On practical nostalgia: self-prospecting among urban Trobrianders. In Debbora Battaglia, ed., *Rhetorics of Self-Making.* Berkeley: University of California Press, pp. 77–96.

1995b. Fear of selfing in the American cultural imaginary or "You are never alone with a clone." *American Anthropologist* 97(4): 672–8.

Beattie, John 1958. The blood pact in Bunyoro. *African Studies* 17:198–203.

Belo, Jane 1949. *Bali: Rangda and Barong.* Monographs of the American Ethnological Society 16. Seattle and London: University of Washington Press.

Bercovitch, E. 1989. Mortal insights: victim and witch in the Nalumin imagination. In G. Herdt and M. Stephen, eds., *Varieties of the Religious Imagination in New Guinea.* New Brunswick, NJ: Rutgers University Press, pp. 122–59.

1994. The agent in the gift: hidden exchange in inner New Guinea. *Cultural Anthropology* 9(4):498–536.

Berger, Peter and Thomas Luckmann 1966. *The Social Construction of Reality.* Garden City, NY: Doubleday.

Bernstein, Richard 1983. *Beyond Objectivism and Relativism: Science, Hermeneutics, and Praxis.* Philadelphia: University of Pennsylvania Press.

Besnier, Niko 1996. Heteroglossic discourses on Nukulaelae spirits. In Jeannette Mageo and Alan Howard, eds., *Spirits in Culture, History and Mind.* New York: Routledge, pp. 75–97.

Biersack, Aletta 1991. Prisoners of Time. In Aletta Biersack, ed., *Clio in Oceania.* Washington, DC: Smithsonian Institution Press, pp. 231–95.

1995. Heterosexual meanings: society, economy, and gender among Ipilis. In Aletta Biersack, ed., *Papuan Borderlands: Huli, Duna, and Ipili Perspectives on the Papua New Guinea Highlands.* Ann Arbor: University of Michigan Press, pp. 231–63.

1996. Word made flesh: religion, the economy, and the body in the Papua New Guinea Highlands. *History of Religions* 36(2):85–111.

Binswanger, L. 1947. Der fall Jürg zünd. Studien zum Schizophrenieproblem. II. Studie. Schweiz. Archiv. J. Neur. u. Psych., LVI, LVII & LIX.

Blackwood, B. 1939a. Life on the Upper Watut, New Guinea. *Geographical Journal* 94 (1):11–28.

1939b. Folk stories of a Stone Age people in New Guinea. *Folklore* 1(3): 209–42.

1940. Use of plants among the Kukukuku of south east central New Guinea. *Proceedings of the Sixth Pacific Science Conference, Berkeley* vol. 4, pp. 111–26.

1978. *The Kukukuku of the Upper Watut.* Edited from her published articles and unpublished fieldnotes with an introduction by C. R. Hallpike. Pitt Rivers Museum. Monograph Series 3. University of Oxford.

Bloch, Maurice 1992. *Prey into Hunter: The Politics of Religious Experience.* Cambridge: Cambridge University Press.

1993. Zafimaniry birth and kinship theory. *Social Anthropology. The Journal of the European Association of Social Anthropologists* 1a:119–32.

Boddy, Janice 1988. Spirits and selves in northern Sudan: the cultural therapeutics of possession and trance. *American Ethnologist* 15(1): 4–27.

1989. *Wombs and Alien Spirits: Women, Men, and the Zar Cult in Northern Sudan.* Madison: University of Wisconsin Press.

1994. Spirit possession revisited: beyond instrumentality. *Annual Review of Anthropology* 24:407–34.

1995. The body nearer the self. Review essay. *American Anthropologist* 97(1):134–7.

1997. Violence embodied? Female circumcision, gender politics, and cultural aesthetics. In R. Dobash and R. Dobash, eds., *Rethinking Violence Against Women.* London: Sage.

Bonnemère, P. 1993. Maternal nurturing substance and paternal spirit: the making of a South Angan sociality. *Oceania* 64(2):159–86.

Bordo, Susan 1993. *Unbearable Weight: Feminism, Western Culture, and the Body.* Berkeley: University of California Press.

Bourdieu, Pierre 1977. *Outline of a Theory of Practice,* trans. Richard Nice. Cambridge: Cambridge University Press.

1984. *Distinction.* Cambridge, MA: Harvard University Press.

1990. *The Logic of Practice,* trans. Richard Nice. Cambridge: Polity Press.

Bourgeois, A. 1978–9. Mbwoolu sculpture of the Yaka. *African Arts* 12(3):58–61; 96.

Brenneis, Donald 1984. Straight talk and sweet talk: political discourse in an occasionally egalitarian society. In Donald Brenneis and Fred Myers, eds., *Dangerous Words: Language and Politics in the Pacific.* New York: New York University Press, pp. 69–84.

Brightman, R. 1995. Forget culture: replacement, transcendence, relexification. *Cultural Anthropology* 10(4):509–46.

Broch-Due, Vigdis 1993. Making meaning out of matter: perceptions of sex, gender and bodies among the Turkana. In V. Broch-Due, Ingrid Rudie and Tone Bleie, eds., *Carved Flesh, Cast Selves: Gendered Symbols and Social*

Practices. Oxford: Berg, pp. 53–82.

Bruch, Hilde 1973. *Eating Disorders*. New York: Basic Books.

Brumbaugh, R. 1981. A secret cult in the West Sepik Highlands. Doctoral dissertation, State University of New York at Stony Brook.

Buakasa, Tulu Kia Mpansu 1973. *L'impensé du discours: kindoki et nkisi en pays kongo du Zaïre*. Kinshasa: Presses universitaires du Zaire.

Burridge, Kenelm O. L. 1960. *Mambu: A Melanesian Millennium*. London: Methuen.

Busby, Cecilia 1997a. Of marriage and marriageability: gender and Dravidian kinship. *Journal of the Royal Anthropological Institute*. 3(1): 21–42.

  1997b. Permeable and partible persons: a comparative analysis of gender and body in south India and Melanesia. *Journal of the Royal Anthropological Institute*, 3(2): 261–78.

Butler, Judith 1990. *Gender Trouble: Feminism and the Subversion of Identity*. New York and London: Routledge.

Cantrell, Eileen M. n.d. Gebusi gender relations. Ph.D. dissertation in progress. Department of Anthropology, University of Michigan, Ann Arbor.

Carrier, James G. 1995. *Gifts and Commodities: Exchange and Western Capitalism since 1700*. London: Routledge.

Carrithers, Michael *et al.* 1985. *The Category of the Person: Anthropology, Philosophy, History*. Cambridge: Cambridge University Press.

Carsten, Janet 1992. The process of childbirth and becoming related among Malays in Pulau Langkawi. In Göran Aijmer, ed., *Coming into Existence: Birth and Metaphors of Birth*. Gothenburg, Sweden: Institute for Advanced Studies in Social Anthropology, pp.20–46.

  1995a. The substance of kinship and the heat of the hearth: feeding, personhood, and relatedness among Malays in Pulau Langkawi. *American Ethnologist* 22(2): 223–41.

  1995b. Different ways to make a difference: gender in Southeast Asia. Paper presented at the Association of Southeast Asian Studies UK Conference, University College, Durham, 1995.

Cartry, M. 1973. Introduction. In Centre national de la recherche scientifique, ed., *La Notion de personne en Afrique noire*. Paris: Editions du CNRS, pp. 33–43.

Centre national de la recherche scientifique, ed. 1973. *La Notion de personne en Afrique noire*. Paris: Editions du CNRS.

Cohen, Anthony P. 1994. *Self Consciousness: An Alternative Anthropology of Identity*. London: Routledge.

Collier, Jane F. and Sylvia J. Yanagisako, eds. 1987. *Gender and Kinship: Essays toward a Unified Analysis*. Stanford: Stanford University Press.

Collomb, H. 1965. Assistance psychiatrique en Afrique (expérience sénégalaise). *Psychopathologie Africaine* 1(1):11–84.

Comaroff, Jean 1985. *Body of Power, Spirit of Resistance: The Culture and History of a South African People*. Chicago: University of Chicago Press.

  1992a. Bodily reform as historical practice. In John and Jean Comaroff, eds., *Ethnography and the Historical Imagination*. Boulder, CO: Westview, pp. 69–91.

1992b. Medicine, colonialism, and the black body. In John and Jean Comaroff, eds., *Ethnography and the Historical Imagination*. Boulder, CO: Westview, pp. 215–33.

Comaroff, Jean and John Comaroff 1991. *Of Revelation and Revolution: Christianity, Colonialism, and Consciousness in South Africa*. Chicago: University of Chicago Press.

Comaroff, Jean and John Comaroff, eds. 1993. *Modernity and Its Malcontents: Ritual and Power in Postcolonial Africa*. Chicago: University of Chicago Press.

Connerton, Paul 1989. *How Societies Remember*. Cambridge: Cambridge University Press.

Corin, E. 1979. A possession psychotherapy in an urban setting: Zebola in Kinshasa. *Social Sciences and Medicine* 13b:327–38.

1981. Possession féminine et structure de pouvoir dans les sociétés zairoises. *Culture* 1(1):31–40.

1985. La question du sujet dans les thérapies de possession. *Psychoanalyse* 3:53–66.

1995. Meaning games at the margins: the cultural centrality of subordinated structures. In G. Bibeau and E. Corin, eds., *Beyond Textuality: Asceticism and Violence in Anthropological Interpretation*. Approaches to Semiotics Series, Berlin: Mouton de Gruyter Publ., pp. 173–92.

Corin, E. and G. Bibeau 1975 . De la forme culturelle au vécu des troubles psychiques en Afrique. *Africa* 45:280–315.

Coulson, Andrew 1982. *Tanzania: A Political Economy*. Oxford: Clarendon Press.

Crapanzano, V. 1977. Introduction. In V. Crapanzano and V. Garrisson, eds., *Case Studies in Spirit Possession*. New York: John Wiley and Sons, pp. 1–40.

Csordas, T. J. 1990. Embodiment as a paradigm for anthropology. *Ethos* 18:5–47.

1994. The body as representation and being-in-the-world. Introduction to *Embodiment and Experience: The Existential Ground of Culture and Self*. Cambridge: Cambridge University Press, pp. 1–24.

Damasio, Antonio 1994. *Descartes' Error: Emotion, Reason, and the Human Brain*. New York: G. P. Putnam Press.

Daniel, E. Valentine 1984. *Fluid Signs: Being a Person the Tamil Way*. Berkeley: University of California Press.

David-Menard, M. *et al*. 1987. *Les Identifications: confrontation de la clinique et de la théorie de Freud à Lacan*. Paris: Denoël.

De Beir, L. 1975. *Religion et magie des Bayaka*. St. Augustin-Bonn: Anthropos Institut.

De Boeck, Filip 1991. Therapeutic efficacy and consensus among the Aluund of southwestern Zaire. *Africa* 61:159–85.

1994. Of trees and kings: politics and metaphor among the Aluund of southwestern Zaire. *American Ethnologist* 21(3):451–73.

Delaney, Carol 1986. The meaning of paternity and the virgin birth debate. *Man* 21: 494–513.

1991. *The Seed and the Soil: Gender and Cosmology in Turkish Village Society*. Berkeley: University of California Press.

Derrida, J. 1967. La parole soufflée. In J. Derrida, ed., *L'Ecriture et la différence*. Paris: Edition du Seuil, pp. 253–92.

Devisch, R. 1988. From equal to better: investing the chief among the Northern Yaka of Zaire. *Africa* 58:261–90.

1990. The therapist and the source of healing among the Yaka of Zaire. *Culture, Medicine and Psychiatry* 14(2):213–36.

1991. Mediumistic divination among the Northern Yaka of Zaire: etiology and ways of knowing. In P. Peek, ed., *African Divination Systems: Ways of Knowing*. Bloomington: Indiana University Press, pp. 112–35.

1993a. *Weaving the Threads of Life:the Khita Gyn-eco-logical Healing Cult among the Yaka of Zaire*. Chicago: The University of Chicago Press.

1993b. Soigner l'affect en remodelant le corps en milieu Yaka. *Anthropologie et Sociétés* 17(1–2):215–37.

Douglas, Mary 1966. *Purity and Danger: An Analysis of Concepts of Pollution and Taboo*. London: Routledge and Kegan Paul.

1970. *Natural Symbols: Explorations in Cosmology*. New York: Pantheon Books (Random House).

1979 (1989). Taboo. In A. Lehmann and J. Myers, eds., *Magic, Witchcraft, and Religion*. Mountain View, CA: Mayfield Publishing Co., pp. 64–8.

Dumont, L. 1985. A modified view of our origins: the Christian beginnings of modern individualism. In M. Carrithers, S. Collins and S. Lukes, eds., *The Category of the Person*. Cambridge: Cambridge University Press, pp. 93–122 (French publication 1938; trans. W.D. Halls).

Errington, Shelly 1990. Recasting sex, gender, and power. A theoretical and regional overview. In J. M. Atkinson and S. Errington, eds., *Power and Difference: Gender in Island Southeast Asia*. Stanford: Stanford University Press, pp. 1–58.

Evans-Pritchard, E. E. 1940. *The Nuer: A Description of the Modes of Livelihood and Political Institutions of a Nilotic People*. Oxford: Clarendon Press.

1951. *Kinship and Marriage among the Nuer*. Oxford: Clarendon Press.

1956. *Nuer Religion*. Oxford: Clarendon Press.

Fardon, Richard 1990. General introduction. In R. Fardon, ed., *Localizing Strategies: Regional Traditions of Ethnographic Writing*. Edinburgh: Scottish Academic Press; Washington: Smithsonian Institution Press, pp. 1–35.

Fardon, Richard, ed. 1990. *Localizing Strategies: Regional Traditions of Ethnographic Writing*. Edinburgh: Scottish Academic Press; Washington: Smithsonian Institution Press.

Featherstone, Mike 1990. The body in consumer culture. In Mike Featherstone *et al.*, eds., *The Body: Social Process and Cultural Theory*. London: Sage Publications, pp. 170–96.

Feeley-Harnik, G. 1984. The political economy of death: communication and change in Malagasy colonial history. *American Ethnologist* 11:1–19.

1989. Cloth and the creation of ancestors in Madagascar. In A. Weiner and J. Schneider, eds., *Cloth and Human Experience*. Washington, DC: Smithsonian Institution Press, pp. 73–116.

Feil, D. K. 1987. *The Evolution of Papua New Guinea Highlands Societies*. Cambridge: Cambridge University Press.

Feyerabend, Paul 1975. *Against Method: Outline of an Anarchistic Theory of Knowledge*. London: NLB.

Fischer, H. 1968. *Die Negwa: Eine Papua-Gruppe Im Wandel.* Munich: Klaus Renner Verlag.

Florence, J. 1987. Les identifications. In M. David-Ménard *et al.*, *Les Identifications: confrontation de la clinique et de la théorie de Freud à Lacan.* Paris: Denoël, pp. 149–87.

Fortes, M. 1945. *The Dynamics of Clanship among the Tallensi.* Oxford: Oxford University Press.

1949. *The Web of Kinship among the Tallensi.* Oxford: Oxford University Press.

1966. Totem and taboo. Presidential Address, 1966. *Proceedings of the Royal Anthropological Institute*:5–22.

1983. Problems of identity and person. In Anita Jacobson-Widding, ed., *Identity: Personal and Socio-Cultural.* Stockholm: Almqvist and Wiksell, pp. 389–401.

Fortune, Reo F. 1935. *Manus Religion: An Ethnological Study of the Manus Natives of the Admiralty Islands.* American Philosophical Society Memoirs 3. Philadelphia.

Foster, Robert 1993. Bodies, commodities, and the nation-state in Papua New Guinea. Paper presented at the University of Chicago, Department of Anthropology Conference on Culturalism, Nationalism, and Transnationalism, 1–2 November, 1993.

1992. Take care of public telephones: moral education and the nation-state formation in Papua New Guinea. *Public Culture* 4:31–45.

1995. Print advertisements and nation making in metropolitan Papua New Guinea. In R. Foster, ed., *Nation Making: Emergent Identities in Postcolonial Melanesia.* Ann Arbor: University of Michigan Press, pp. 151–84.

Foucault, Michel 1990. *The History of Sexuality.* Vol. 1: *An Introduction.* New York: Vintage.

Fox, James J. 1987. The house as a type of social organization on the island of Roti. In C. Macdonald, ed., *De la Hutte au palais: sociétés "à maison" en Asie du Sud-Est insulaire.* Paris: CNRS, pp.171–8.

Frankel, S. 1986. *The Huli Response to Illness.* Cambridge: Cambridge University Press.

Fry, Peter 1976. *Spirits of Protest: Spirit Mediums and the Articulation of Consensus among the Zezuru of Southern Rhodesia (Zimbabwe).* Cambridge: Cambridge University Press.

Gadamer, Hans-Georg 1975 [1960]. *Truth and Method.* New York: Crossroad.

1986. *The Idea of the Good in Platonic-Aristotelian Philosophy.* Trans. and Intro. by P. Christopher Smith. New Haven: Yale University Press.

Gardner, D. 1980. Cult ritual and social organization among the Mianmin. Doctoral thesis, Australian National University.

1987. Spirits and conceptions of agency among the Mianmin of Papua New Guinea. *Oceania* 57:161–77.

Geertz, Clifford 1973. The growth of culture and the evolution of mind. In C. Geertz, ed., *The Interpretation of Cultures.* New York: Basic Books, pp. 55–84.

Gell, A. 1979. Reflections on a cut finger: taboo in the Umeda conception of the self. In R. H. Hook, ed., *Fantasy and Symbol: Studies in Anthropological Interpretation.* London: Academic Press, pp. 133–48.

Gilsenan, M. 1976. Lying, honor and contradiction. In Bruce Kapferer, ed., *Transaction and Meaning: Directions in the Anthropology of Exchange and Symbolic Behavior.* Philadelphia: Institute for the Study of Human Issues, pp. 191–219.

Godelier, M. 1982. Social hierarchies among the Baruya of New Guinea. In A. Strathern, ed., *Inequality in New Guinea Highlands Societies.* New York: Cambridge University Press, pp. 3–34.

1986. *The Making of Great Men: Male Domination and Power among the New Guinea Baruya.* Cambridge: Cambridge University Press.

Godelier, Maurice and Marilyn Strathern, eds., 1991. *Big-Men and Great-Men: Personifications of Power in Melanesia.* Cambridge: Cambridge University Press.

Gramsci, Antonio 1971. *Selections from the Prison Notebooks of Antonio Gramsci,* ed. Quintin Hoare and Geoffrey Nowell Smith. London: Lawrence and Wishart.

Graybill, Lyn S. 1996. *Religion and Resistance Politics in South Africa.* Westport, CT: Praeger.

Grosz, Elizabeth 1987. Notes towards a corporeal feminism. *Australian Feminist Studies* 5 (Summer):1–16.

Gyekye, Kwame 1995. *An Essay on African Philosophical Thought: The Akan Conceptual Scheme.* Revised edition. Philadelphia: Temple University Press.

Hacking, Ian 1996. Memoro-politics, trauma, and the soul. In Paul Antze and Michael Lambek, eds., *Tense Past: Cultural Essays in Trauma and Memory.* New York: Routledge, pp. 67–87.

Havelock, Eric A. 1963. *Preface to Plato.* Oxford: Basil Blackwell.

Herdt, G. 1981. *Guardians of the Flutes: Idioms of Masculinity.* New York: McGraw Hill.

Herdt, G., ed. 1982. *Rituals of Manhood.* Berkeley: University of California Press.

1984. *Ritualized Homosexuality in Melanesia.* Berkeley: University of California Press.

1987. *The Sambia: Ritual and Gender in New Guinea.* New York: Holt, Rinehart and Winston.

Héritier-Izard, F. 1973. Univers féminin et destin individuel chez les Samo. In Centre national de la recherche scientifique, ed., *La Notion de personne en Afrique noire,* Paris: Edition du CNRS, pp. 243–54.

Hertzfeld, M. 1985. *The Poetics of Manhood: Contest and Identity in a Cretan Mountain Village.* Princeton: Princeton University Press.

Hoad, Richard A. 1962–3. Patrol Report No. 1. Nomad Sub-District Office, Western Province, Territory of Papua New Guinea.

Hobart, Mark 1987. Summer's days and salad days: the coming of age of anthropology? In L. Holy, ed., *Comparative Anthropology.* Oxford: Basil Blackwell, pp. 22–51.

Holland, D. and A. Kipnis 1994. Metaphors for embarrassment and stories of exposure. The not-so-egocentric self in American culture. *Ethos* 22(3): 316–42.

Holy, Ladislav 1979. Nuer politics. In L. Holy, ed. *Segmentary Lineage Systems Reconsidered.* The Queen's University Papers in Social Anthropology 4.

Belfast: Department of Social Anthropology, The Queen's University, pp. 23–48.

1987. Description, generalization and comparison: two paradigms. Introduction to *Comparative Anthropology*. Oxford: Basil Blackwell, pp. 1–21.

1991. *Religion and Custom in a Muslim Society: The Berti of Sudan*. Cambridge: Cambridge University Press.

Howell, Signe and Marit Melhuus 1993. The study of kinship; the study of the person; a study of gender. In T. del Valle, ed., *Gendered Anthropology*. London and New York: Routledge, pp. 38–53.

Howes, David 1991. *The Varieties of Sensory Experience: A Sourcebook in the Anthropology of the Senses*. Toronto: University of Toronto Press.

Huber, H.1956. Magical statuettes and their accessories among the Eastern Bayaka and their neighbors. *Anthropos* 51:265–90.

Huntington, Richard 1988. *Gender and Social Structure in Madagascar*. Bloomington: Indiana University Press.

Hutchinson, Sharon E. 1996. *Nuer Dilemmas: Coping with Money, War, and the State*. Berkeley: University of California Press.

Isaacs, Harold R. 1975. Basic group identity: the idols of the tribe. In Nathan Glazer and Daniel P. Moynihan, eds., *Ethnicity: Theory and Experience*. Cambridge, MA: Harvard University Press, pp.29–52.

Iteanu, André 1988. The concept of the person and the ritual system: an Orokaiva view. *Man* 25:35–53.

Ivy, Marilyn 1995. *Discourses of the Vanishing: Modernity, Phantasm, Japan*. Chicago: University of Chicago Press.

Jackson, Michael 1989. *Paths toward a Clearing: Radical Empiricism and Ethnographic Inquiry*. Bloomington: Indiana University Press.

Jackson, Michael, ed. 1996. *Things As They Are: New Directions in Phenomenological Anthropology*. Bloomington: Indiana University Press.

James, Wendy 1989. Some African notions of the person reconsidered. Unpublished paper presented to the 1989 Satterthwaite Colloquium on Ritual and Religion in Africa.

Janzen, John 1982a. *The Quest for Therapy in Lower Zaire*. Berkeley: University of California Press.

1982b. *Lemba 1650–1930: A Drum of Affliction in Africa and the New World*. New York: Garland.

1991. Doing *Ngoma*: a dominant trope in African religion and healing. *Journal of Religion in Africa* 21:291–308.

Jara, R. and N. Spaduccini 1989. Introduction: allegorizing the New World. In R. Jara and N. Spaduccini, eds., *1492–1992: Re/Discovering Colonial Writing*. Minneapolis: University of Minnesota Press, pp. 9–50.

Johnson, Mark 1987. *The Body in the Mind: The Bodily Basis of Meaning, Imagination, and Reason*. Chicago: University of Chicago Press.

Jones, B. 1980. Consuming society: food and illness among the Failwolmin. Doctoral dissertation, University of Virginia.

Jorgensen, D. 1981a. Taro and arrows: order, entropy and religion among the Telefolmin. Doctoral dissertation, University of British Columbia.

1981b. Life on the fringe: history and society in Telefolmin. In R. Gordon, ed.,

The Plight of Peripheral People in Papua New Guinea. Cambridge, MA: Cultural Survival, pp. 59–79.

1984. The clear and the hidden: person, self and suicide among the Telefolmin of Papua New Guinea. *Omega* 14:113–26.

1988. Nurturing, killing and the flow of life: the logic of Telefol food rules. Paper prepared for the working session on the power of food, presented at the Association for Social Anthropology in Oceania meetings 1988.

1990. Secrecy's turns. *Canberra Anthropology* 13(1):40–7.

Josephides, Lisette 1991. Metaphors, metathemes, and the construction of sociality: a critique of the new Melanesian ethnography. *Man* 26:145–61.

Karim, Wazir Jahan 1995a. Introduction: genderising anthropology in Southeast Asia. In W. J. Karim, ed., *"Male" and "Female" in Developing Southeast Asia*. Oxford and Washington DC: Berg, pp. 11–34.

1995b. Bilateralism and gender in Southeast Asia. In W. J. Karim, ed., *"Male" and "Female" in Developing Southeast Asia*. Oxford and Washington DC: Berg, pp. 35–74.

Keesing, R. 1970. Shrines, ancestors, and cognatic descent: the Kwaio and Tallensi. *American Anthropologist* 72:755–75.

Kelly, Raymond C. 1977. *Etoro Social Structure: A Study in Structural Contradiction*. Ann Arbor: University of Michigan Press.

1985. *The Nuer Conquest: The Structure and Development of an Expansionist System*. Ann Arbor: University of Michigan Press.

1993. *Constructing Inequality: The Fabrication of a Hierarchy of Virtue Among the Etoro*. Ann Arbor: University of Michigan Press.

Knauft, Bruce M. 1985a. *Good Company and Violence: Sorcery and Social Action in a Lowland New Guinea Society*. Berkeley: University of California Press.

1985b. Ritual form and permutation in New Guinea: implications of symbolic process for sociopolitical evolution. *American Ethnologist* 12:321–40.

1986. Text and social practice: narrative "longing" and bisexuality among the Gebusi of New Guinea. *Ethos* 14:252–81.

1987a. Homosexuality in Melanesia. *The Journal of Psychoanalytic Anthropology* 10:155–91.

1987b. Reconsidering violence in simple human societies: homicide among the Gebusi of New Guinea. *Current Anthropology* 28:457–500.

1989. Imagery, pronouncement, and the aesthetics of reception in Gebusi spirit mediumship. In Gilbert H. Herdt and Michele Stephen, eds., *The Religious Imagination in New Guinea*. New Brunswick, NJ: Rutgers University Press, pp. 67–98.

1993. *South Coast New Guinea Cultures: History, Comparison, Dialectic*. Cambridge: Cambridge University Press.

1996. *Genealogies for the Present in Cultural Anthropology*. New York: Routledge.

in press. Gender identity, modernity, and political economy in Melanesia and Amazonia. *Journal of the Royal Anthropological Institute* (incorporating *Man*).

Kramer, Fritz 1993. *The Red Fez: Art and Spirit Possession in Africa*, trans. M. R. Green. London: Verso.

Kristéva, J. 1987. Le réel de l'identification. In M. David-Ménard *et al.*, *Les*

Identifications: confrontation de la clinique et de la théorie de Freud à Lacan. Paris: Denoël, pp. 47–83.

Kuhn, Thomas 1970. *The Structure of Scientific Revolutions.* Chicago: University of Chicago Press.

Kulick, Don 1992. *Language Shift and Cultural Reproduction.* Cambridge: Cambridge University Press.

Kwame, Safro, ed., 1995. *Readings in African Philosophy: An Akan Collection.* Lanham, MD: University Press of America.

Lacan, J. 1966. Fonctions et champ de la parole et du langage en psychanalyse. *Ecrits.* Paris: Editions du Seuil, pp. 237–322.

Lakoff, George and Mark Johnson 1980. *Metaphors We Live By.* Chicago: University of Chicago Press.

Lambek, Michael 1981. *Human Spirits: A Cultural Account of Trance in Mayotte.* Cambridge: Cambridge University Press.

1989. Rationalization or resistance? Examples from rural Africa. Paper presented to the AAA annual meeting.

1991. Tryin' to make it real, but compared to what? In M. Lambek, ed., *From Method to Modesty: Essays on Thinking and Making Ethnography Now.* Special section of *Culture* 11(1–2):43–52.

1992. Taboo as cultural practice among Malagasy speakers. *Man* 27(2):245–66.

1993a. *Knowledge and Practice in Mayotte: Local Discourses of Islam, Sorcery, and Spirit Possession.* Toronto: University of Toronto Press.

1993b. Cultivating critical distance: oracles and the politics of voice. *Political and Legal Anthropology Review* 16(2):9–18.

1995. Choking on the Quran and Other Consuming Parables from the western Indian Ocean Front. In Wendy James, ed., *The Pursuit of Certainty: Religious and Cultural Formulations.* London: Routledge, pp. 258–81.

in press. The Sakalava Poiesis of History. Forthcoming in *American Ethnologist.*

Lan, David 1985. *Guns and Rain: Guerillas and Spirit Mediums in Zimbabwe.* Berkeley: University of California Press.

Lanternari, Vittorio 1963. *The Religions of the Oppressed: A Study of Modern Messianic Cults.* New York: Knopf.

Laqueur, Thomas 1990. *Making Sex: Body and Gender from the Greeks to Freud.* Cambridge, Mass.: Harvard University Press.

Lavie, Smadar 1990. *The Poetics of Military Occupation: Mzeina Allegories of Bedouin Identity Under Israeli and Egyptian Rule.* Berkeley: University of California Press.

Lawrence, Peter 1964. *Road Belong Cargo: A Study of the Cargo Cult in the Southern Madang District, New Guinea.* New York: Humanities Press.

Leach, E. 1964. Anthropological Aspects of Language: Animal Categories and Verbal Abuse. In E. H. Lenneberg, ed., *New Directions in the Study of Language.* Cambridge, Mass: Massachusetts Institute of Technology Press, pp.23–63.

Leenhardt, M. 1947. *Do kamo: la personne et le mythe dans le monde mélanésien.* Paris: Gallimard.

Leenhardt, Maurice 1979 [1947]. *Do Kamo: Person and Myth in a Melanesian World,* trans. Basia Miller Gulati. Chicago: University of Chicago Press.

Lemonnier, P. 1991. From great men to big men: peace, substitution and competition in the Highlands of New Guinea. In M. Godelier and M. Strathern, eds., *Big Men and Great Men: Personifications of Power in Melanesia.* Cambridge: Cambridge University Press, pp. 7–27.

Lévi-Strauss, Claude 1969 [1949]. *The Elementary Structures of Kinship,* trans. J. H. Bell, J. H. von Sturmer and R. Needham. Boston: Beacon Press.

1963 [1962]. *Totemism,* trans. R. Needham. Boston: Beacon Press.

1963 [1958]. *Structural Anthropology,* trans. Clare Jacobson and Brooke Grundfest Schoepf. New York: Basic Books.

1966 [1962]. *The Savage Mind.* Chicago: University of Chicago Press.

1971. *L'Homme nu.* Paris: Plon.

1972. Structuralism and ecology. *Barnard Alumnae* (Spring 1972), pp. 6–14.

Lewis, Ioan M. 1971. *Ecstatic Religion: An Anthropological Study of Shamanism and Spirit Possession.* Harmondsworth: Penguin.

Lienhardt, G. 1985. Self: public, private. Some African representations. In M. Carrithers, S. Collins and S. Lukes, eds., *The Category of the Person.* Cambridge: Cambridge University Press, pp. 141–55.

Lima, M. 1971. *Fonctions sociologiques des figurines de culte Hamba dans la société et dans la culture Tshokwe (Angola).* Luanda: Instituto de Investigaçao cientifica de Angola.

Lindstrom, Lamont 1993. *Cargo Cult: Strange Stories of Desire from Melanesia and Beyond.* Honolulu: University of Hawaii Press.

Linnekin, Jocelyn and Lin Poyer, eds., 1990. *Cultural Identity and Ethnicity in the Pacific.* Honolulu: University of Hawaii Press.

LiPuma, Edward 1988. *The Gift of Kinship: Structure and Practice in Maring Social Organization.* Cambridge: Cambridge University Press.

1989. Modernity and medicine among the Maring. In Stephen Frankel and G. Lewis, eds., *A Continuing Trial of Treatment: Medical Pluralism in Papua New Guinea.* Boston: Kluwer Academic Publishers, pp. 295–310.

1990. The terms of change: linguistic mediation and reaffiliation among the Maring. *The Journal of the Polynesian Society* 99:93–121.

1994. The sorcery of words and evidence of speech in Maring justice. *Ethnology* 33:1–17.

1995. Nationalism and national culture in Oceania. In R. Foster, ed., *Nation Making: Emergent Identities in Postcolonial Melanesia.* Ann Arbor: University of Michigan Press, pp. 33–70.

1996. What is democracy in the age of encompassment? Paper presented at the conference, Beyond Civil Society: Democratization and Globalization. Chicago Humanities Institute, February 23–25, 1996.

LiPuma, Edward and Sarah Meltzoff 1989. Towards a theory of culture and class: an Iberian example. *American Ethnologist* 16:313–34.

Lock, M. 1993. Cultivating the body: anthropology and the epistemologies of bodily practice and knowledge. *Annual Review of Anthropology* 22:133–55.

Lock, Margaret and Nancy Scheper-Hughes 1987. The mindful body. *Medical Anthropology Quarterly* 1(1):6–41.

Lutz, Catherine 1988. *Unnatural Emotions: Everyday Sentiments on a Micronesian Atoll and their Challenge to Western Theory.* Chicago: University of Chicago Press.

McCarthy, J. K. 1964. *Patrol into Yesterday*. London: Angus and Robertson Ltd.

MacCormack, Carol and Marilyn Strathern, eds. 1980. *Nature, Culture and Gender*. Cambridge: Cambridge University Press.

Macintyre, Martha 1989. The triumph of the *susu*. Mortuary exchanges on Tubetube. In F. H. Damon and R. Wagner, eds., *Death Rituals and Life in the Societies of the Kula Ring*. DeKalb: Northern Illinois University Press, pp. 133–52.

Mageo, Jeannette and Alan Howard, eds. 1996. *Spirits in Culture, History, and Mind*. New York: Routledge.

Maldiney, H. 1973. *Regard parole espace*. Lausanne: Editions l'Age d'Homme.

Marriott, McKim 1976. Hindu transactions: diversity without dualism. In Bruce Kapferer, ed., *Transaction and Meaning: Directions in the Anthropology of Exchange and Symbolic Behavior*. Philadelphia: Institute for the Study of Human Issues, pp. 109–42.

Martin, Emily 1987 [1992]. *The Woman in the Body: A Cultural Analysis of Reproduction*. Boston: Beacon Press.

    1994. *Flexible Bodies: Tracking Immunity in American Culture from the Days of Polio to the Age of AIDS*. Boston: Beacon Press.

Marx, Karl 1906. *Capital: A Critique of Political Economy*. New York: Charles H. Kerr and Co.

Masquelier, Adeline 1992. Encounter with a road sign: machines, bodies and commodities in the imagination of a Mawri healer. *Visual Anthropology Review* 8:56–69.

Mathieu, Nicole-Claude 1991. Identité sexuelle / sexuée / de sexe? Trois modes de conceptualization du rapport entre sexe et genre. In *L'Anatomie politique: catégorisations et idéologies du sexe*. Paris: Côté-femmes Editions, pp. 227–266.

Mauss, Marcel 1967. *The Gift*. New York: Norton [original 1925].

    1979a. Body techniques. In M. Mauss *Sociology and Psychology: Essays*, trans. Ben Brewster. London: Routledge and Kegan Paul, pp. 95–123.

    1979b. A category of the human mind: the notion of person, the notion of self. In M. Mauss *Sociology and Psychology: Essays*, trans. Ben Brewster. London: Routledge and Kegan Paul, pp. 57–94.

    1985. A category of the human mind: the notion of person, the notion of self. In M. Carrithers, S. Collins and S. Lukes, eds., *The Category of the Person*. Cambridge: Cambridge University Press, pp. 1–25.

Meggitt, M. J. 1965. *The Lineage System of the Mae Enga of New Guinea*. New York: Barnes and Noble.

Meigs, Anna 1984. *Food, Sex and Pollution: A New Guinea Religion*. New Brunswick, NJ: Rutgers University Press.

Merleau-Ponty, Maurice 1962. *The Phenomenology of Perception*. London: Routledge and Kegan Paul.

Middleton, Karen 1996. How Karembola men become mothers. Paper presented at the conference Boundaries and Identities, University of Edinburgh, 24–26 October 1996.

Mimica, J. 1981. Omalyce: an ethnography of the Ikwaye view of the cosmos. Unpublished Ph.D. thesis. Australian National University. Canberra.

    1988. *Intimations of Infinity: The Cultural Meanings of the Iqwaye Counting and*

Number System. Oxford: Berg Publishers.

Missenard, A. and Y. Gutierrez 1989. Etre ou ne pas être en groupe. Essai clinique sur le négatif. In A. Missenard, ed., *Le Négatif: figures et modalités*. Paris: Dunod, pp. 55–77.

Mitchell, Timothy 1991. *Colonising Egypt*. Berkeley: University of California Press.

Moore, Henrietta L. 1993a. Epilogue. In V. Broch-Due, Ingrid Rudie and Tone Bleie, eds., *Carved Flesh, Cast Selves: Gendered Symbols and Social Practices*. Oxford: Berg, pp. 279–82.

1993b. The differences within and the differences between. In Teresa del Valle, ed., *Gendered Anthropology*. London: Routledge, pp. 193–204.

1994. *A Passion for Difference: Essays in Anthropology and Gender*. Cambridge: Polity Press.

Morren, G. 1986. *The Miyanmin: Human Ecology of a Papua New Guinea Society*. Ann Arbor: UMI Research Press.

Morris, Brian 1994. *The Anthropology of the Self*. London: Pluto.

Morris, Rosalind C. 1995. All made up: performance theory and the new anthropology of sex and gender. *Annual Review of Anthropology* 24:567–92.

Mosko, Mark 1983. Conception, de-conception and social structure in Bush Mekeo culture. *Mankind* 14(1):24–32.

1992. Motherless sons: "divine kings" and "partible persons" in Melanesia and Polynesia. *Man* 27:693–717.

Munn, Nancy 1986. *The Fame of Gawa*. Cambridge: Cambridge University Press.

Murphy, Robert 1987. *The Body Silent*. New York: Henry Holt.

Murphy, W. 1990. Creating the appearance of consensus in Mende political discourse. *American Anthropologist* 92:25–41.

Novack, Cynthia J. 1995. The body's endeavors as cultural practices. In Susan Leigh Foster, ed., *Choreographing History*. Bloomington: Indiana University Press, pp. 177–84.

Obeyesekere, G. 1995. British cannibals: contemplation of an event in the death and resurrection of James Cook, explorer. In G. Bibeau and E. Corin, eds., *Beyond Textuality: Asceticism and Violence in Anthropological Interpretation*. Berlin: Mouton de Gruyter, pp. 145–70.

Ortigues, E., M.-C. Ortigues, A. Zempleni, and J. Zempleni 1968. Psychologie clinique et ethnologie (Sénégal). *Bulletin de Psychologie*, 211 (15–19) (Special Issue): 950–8.

Ortigues, M.-C., P. Martino, and H. Collomb 1967. L'utilisation des données culturelles dans un cas de bouffée délirante. *Psychopathologie Africaine* 3 (1):121–47.

Ortigues, M.-C. and E. Ortigues 1973. *Oedipe africain*. Paris: Plon.

Ortner, Sherry B. 1974. Is female to male as nature is to culture? In Michelle Rosaldo and Louise Lamphere, eds., *Woman, Culture, and Society*. Stanford: Stanford University Press, pp. 67–87.

1995. Resistance and the problem of ethnographic refusal. *Comparative Studies in Society and History* 37:173–93.

Overing, Joanna 1987. Translation as a creative process: the power of a name. In L. Holy, ed., *Comparative Anthropology*. Oxford: Basil Blackwell, pp. 70–87.

Pagels, E. 1995. *The Origin of Satan*. New York: Random House.

Parry, Jonathan 1989. The end of the body. In Michel Feher, ed., *Fragments for a History of the Human Body*, Vol. 2. New York: Zone Books, pp. 490–517.

Peel, J. D. Y. 1987. History, culture, and the comparative method: a West African puzzle. In L. Holy, ed., *Comparative Anthropology*. Oxford: Basil Blackwell, pp. 88–118.

Pels, Peter 1992. Mumiani: the white vampires, a neo-diffusionist analysis of rumor. *Etnofoor* 5(1–2):165–87.

Pels, Peter and Rijk van Dijk, 1995. Contested authorities and the politics of perception: deconstructing the study of religion in Africa. Paper presented to the Department of Anthropology, University of Toronto, Nov. 3, 1995.

Piault, C., ed. 1975. *Prophétique et thérapeutique: Albert Atcho et la communauté de Bregbo*. Paris: Collection Savoir, Hermann.

Piot, C. 1993. Secrecy, ambiguity and the everyday in Kabre culture. *American Anthropologist* 95:353–70.

Poole, Fitz John Porter 1976. The Ais Am: an introduction to male initiation ritual among the Bimin-Kuskusmin of the West Sepik District, Papua New Guinea. Doctoral dissertation, Cornell University.

1981a. Transforming "natural" woman: female ritual leaders and gender ideology among the Bimin-Kuskusmin. In S. B. Ortner and H. Whitehead, eds., *Sexual Meanings*. Cambridge: Cambridge University Press, pp. 116–65.

1981b. Tamam: ideological and sociological configurations of "witchcraft" among the Bimin-Kuskusmin. In M. Zelenietz and S. Lindenbaum, eds., *Sorcery and Social Change in Melanesia*. *Social Analysis* 8, special issue, pp. 58–76.

Postone, Moishe 1986. *Towards a Reconstruction of the Marxian Culture of Modernity*. Chicago: Working Papers and Proceedings of the Center for Psychosocial Studies 3.

1993. *Time, Labor, and Social Domination*. Cambridge: Cambridge University Press.

Rappaport, Roy A. 1967. *Pigs for the Ancestors*. New Haven: Yale University Press.

1979. The obvious aspects of ritual. In R. Rappaport, ed., *Ecology, Meaning, and Religion*. Richmond: North Atlantic Books, pp. 173–221.

Richards, Audrey 1935. A modern movement of witchfinders. *Africa* 8(4):448–61.

Ricoeur, P. 1988 [1985]. *Time and Narrative*, Vol. 3, trans. Kathleen McLaughlin and David Pellaver. Chicago: University of Chicago Press.

1992. *Oneself as Another*, trans. Kathleen Blamey. Chicago: University of Chicago Press.

Riebe, Inge 1987. Kalam witchcraft: an historical perspective. In Michele Stephen, ed., *Sorcerer and Witch in Melanesia*. New Brunswick: Rutgers University Press, pp. 211–48.

Robbins, Joel 1994a. Christianity and desire among the Urapmin of Papua New Guinea. Paper presented at the Annual Meetings of the American Anthropological Association, Atlanta, GA, 1994.

1994b. Missions without frontiers: Western apocalypticism, revelation, and Christian temporality among the Urapmin of Papua New Guinea. Paper presented at the Annual Conference of the Canadian Anthropology Society, 1994.

1995. Dispossessing the spirits: Christian transformations of desire and ecology among the Urapmin of Papua New Guinea. *Ethnology* 34:211–24.

Rorty, Richard 1980. *Philosophy and the Mirror of Nature*. Princeton: Princeton University Press.

Ruel, Malcolm 1997. *Belief, Ritual, and the Securing of Life*. Leiden: Brill.

Sahlins, Marshall 1976a. *The Use and Abuse of Biology*. Ann Arbor: University of Michigan Press.

1976b. *Culture and Practical Reason*. Chicago: University of Chicago Press.

Samuel, Geoffrey 1990. *Mind, Body, and Culture: Anthropology and the Biological Interface*. Cambridge: Cambridge University Press.

Scheper-Hughes, N. 1992. *Death without Weeping*. Berkeley: University of California Press.

Schieffelin, Edward 1976. *The Sorrow of the Lonely and the Burning of the Dancers*. New York: St. Martins Press.

Schwartz, Theodore 1962. *The Paliau Movement in the Admiralty Islands, 1946–1954*. Anthropological Papers of the American Museum of Natural History 49, pt. 2. New York.

Searle, John 1997. Consciousness and the philosophers. Review of *The Conscious Mind* by David J. Chalmers. *New York Review of Books* 44(4):43–50.

Shaffer, Jerome 1967. Mind–body problem. *The Encyclopedia of Philosophy*. New York: Macmillan.

Shilling, Chris 1993. *The Body and Social Theory*. London: Sage.

Shweder, R. A. 1990. Cultural psychology. What is it? In J. W. Stigler, R.A. Shweder and G. Herdt, eds., *Cultural Psychology: Essays on Comparative Human Development*. Cambridge: Cambridge University Press, pp. 1–43.

Shweder, R. A. and E. J. Bourne 1991. Does the concept of the person vary cross-culturally? In R. A. Shweder, ed., *Thinking Through Cultures: Expeditions in Cultural Psychology*. Cambridge, MA: Harvard University Press, pp. 113–55.

Simpson, C. 1953. *Adam With Arrows*. Sydney: Angus and Robertson.

Sinclair, J. 1966. *Behind the Ranges*. London and New York: Cambridge University Press, and Melbourne University Press.

Smith, Michael French 1994. *Hard Times on Kairiru Island: Poverty, Development, and Morality in a Papua New Guinea Village*. Honolulu: University of Hawaii Press.

Smythies, John R. and John Beloff, eds. 1989. *The Case for Dualism*. Charlottesville: University of Virginia Press.

Stallybrass, Peter and Allon White 1986. *The Politics and Poetics of Transgression*. London: Methuen.

Steedly, Mary M. 1993. *Hanging without a Rope: Narrative Experience in Colonial and Postcolonial Karoland*. Princeton: Princeton University Press.

Stephen, Michele 1995. *A'aisa's Gifts: A Study of Magic and the Self*. Berkeley: University of California Press.

Stolcke, Verena 1993. Is sex to gender as race is to ethnicity? In T. del Valle, ed., *Gendered Anthropology*. London and New York: Routledge, pp. 17–37.

Stoller, Paul 1989. *Fusion of the Worlds: An Ethnography of Possession among the Songhay of Niger.* Chicago: University of Chicago Press.

　1995. *Embodying Colonial Memories: Spirit Possession, Power, and the Hauka in West Africa.* New York and London: Routledge.

Strathern, Andrew J. 1971. *The Rope of Moka: Big Men and Ceremonial Exchange in Mount Hagen, New Guinea.* Cambridge: Cambridge University Press.

　1974. Kinship, descent, and locality: some New Guinea examples. In J. Goody, ed., *The Character of Kinship.* Cambridge: Cambridge University Press, pp. 21–33.

　1975. Veiled speech in Mount Hagen. In M. Bloch, ed., *Political Language and Oratory in Traditional Society.* London: Academic Press, pp. 185–203.

　1979. Gender, ideology, and money in Mount Hagen. *Man* (n.s.) 14:530–48.

　1982a. Two waves of African models in the New Guinea Highlands. In Andrew J. Strathern, ed., *Inequality in New Guinea Highlands Societies.* Cambridge: Cambridge University Press, pp. 35–49.

　1982b. Witchcraft, greed, cannibalism, and death: some related themes from the New Guinea Highlands. In Maurice Bloch and Jonathan Parry, eds., *Death and the Regeneration of Life.* Cambridge: Cambridge University Press, pp. 111–33.

　1984. *A Line of Power.* London: Tavistock.

　1989. Melpa dream interpretation and the concept of hidden truth. *Ethnology* 28:301–15.

　1992. Let the bow go down. In R. Ferguson and N. Whitehead, eds., *War in the Tribal Zone.* Santa Fe: School of American Research Press, pp. 229–50.

　1993. Big-man, great-man, leader: the link of ritual power. *Journal de la Société des Océanistes* 1993(2):145–58.

　1994. Keeping the body in mind. *Social Anthropology,* Journal of the European Association of Social Anthropologists 2(1):43–53.

　1996. *Body Thoughts.* Ann Arbor: University of Michigan Press.

Strathern, Andrew and Pamela J. Stewart in press. Seeking personhood: anthropological accounts and local concepts in Mount Hagen, Papua New Guinea. *Oceania.*

Strathern, Marilyn 1972. *Women in Between.* London: Seminar Press.

　1988. *The Gender of the Gift: Problems with Women and Problems with Society in Melanesia.* Berkeley: University of California Press.

　1990. Negative strategies in Melanesia. In R. Fardon, ed., *Localizing Strategies.* Edinburgh: Scottish Academic Press and Washington: Smithsonian Institution Press, pp. 204–16.

　1993. Making incomplete. In V. Broch-Due, I. Rudie and T. Bleie, eds., *Carved Flesh, Cast Selves: Gendered Symbols and Social Practices.* Oxford: Berg, pp. 41–51.

Stürzenhofecker, Gabriele 1994. Visions of a landscape: Duna premeditations on ecological change. *Canberra Anthropology* 17:27–47.

Sylvain, Renée Jackson, n.d. To build a fire. Unpublished paper, Deptartment of Anthropology, University of Toronto.

Talle, Aud 1993. Transforming women into "pure" agnates: aspects of female infibulation in Somalia. In V. Broch-Due, I. Rudie and T. Bleie, eds., *Carved*

Flesh, Cast Selves: Gendered Symbols and Social Practices. Oxford: Berg, pp. 83–107.

Tambiah, S. 1969 [1985]. Animals are good to think and good to prohibit. In S. Tambiah, ed., *Culture, Thought, and Social Action.* Cambridge, MA: Harvard University Press, pp. 169–211.

1990. *Magic, Science, Religion, and the Scope of Rationality.* Cambridge: Cambridge University Press.

Taussig, Michael 1980. *The Devil and Commodity Fetishism in South America.* Chapel Hill: University of North Carolina Press.

1987. *Shamanism, Colonialism, and the Wild Man: A Study in Terror and Healing.* Chicago: University of Chicago Press.

1993. *Mimesis and Alterity: A Particular History of the Senses.* New York: Routledge.

Taylor, Charles 1989. *Sources of the Self: The Making of Modern Identity.* Cambridge, MA: Harvard University Press.

Taylor, Christopher 1992. *Milk, Honey, and Money: Changing Concepts in Rwandan Healing.* Washington: Smithsonian Institution Press.

Tellenbach, H. 1983 [1968]. *Goût et atmosphère,* trans. Jean Amsler. Paris: Presses Universitaires de France.

Thomas, Nicholas 1991. *Entangled Objects: Exchange, Material Culture, and Colonialism in the Pacific.* Cambridge, MA: Harvard University Press.

Tsing, Anna L. 1993. *In the Realm of the Diamond Queen: Marginality in an Out-of-the-way Place.* Princeton: Princeton University Press.

Turner, T. S. 1980. The social skin. In J. Cherfas and R. Lewin, eds., *Not Work Alone.* London: Temple Smith, pp. 112–40.

1995. Social body and embodied subject: bodiliness, subjectivity, and sociality among the Kayapo. *Cultural Anthropology* 10(2):143–70.

Turner, V. 1957. *Schism and Continuity in an African Society.* Manchester: Manchester University Press.

1967. *The Forest of Symbols.* Ithaca: Cornell University Press.

1968. *The Drums of Affliction. A Study of Religious Processes among the Ndembu of Zambia.* Oxford: Clarendon.

1978. Comments and conclusions. In B. A. Babcock, ed., *The Reversible World: Symbolic Inversion in Art and Society.* Ithaca and London: Cornell University Press, pp. 276–96.

Van Wing, J. 1959. *Etudes Bakongo I & II.* Louvain: Desclée de Brouwer.

Vorbichler, A. 1957. Fetischismus und Hexerei. *Kongo-Overzee* 23(1–2):35–57.

Wachterhauser, Brice, ed., 1986. *Hermeneutics and Modern Philosophy.* Albany: SUNY Press.

Wagner, Roy 1967. *The Curse of Souw.* Chicago: University of Chicago Press.

1972. *Habu.* Chicago: University of Chicago Press.

1974. Are there social groups in the New Guinea Highlands? In M. Leaf, ed., *Frontiers of Anthropology: An Introduction To Anthropological Thinking.* New York: D. Van Nostrand, pp. 95–122.

1975. *The Invention of Culture.* Englewood Cliffs, NJ: Prentice Hall. Revised and expanded edition, 1981. Chicago: The University of Chicago Press.

1977. Analogic kinship: a daribi example. *American Ethnologist,* pp. 623–42.

1978. *Lethal Speech*. Chicago: University of Chicago Press.

1986. *Asiwinarong: Ethos, Image, and Social Power among the Usen Barok of New Ireland*. Princeton: Princeton University Press.

1987. Taboo. M. Eliade, ed., *The Encyclopedia of Religion*, Vol. 14. New York: Macmillan.

Weigert, Stephen L. 1996. *Traditional Religion and Guerilla Warfare in Modern Africa*. New York: St. Martin's Press.

Weiner, Annette B. 1992. *Inalienable Possessions: The Paradox of Keeping-While-Giving*. Berkeley: University of California Press.

Weiner, James F. 1991. *The Empty Place: Poetry, Space, and Being among the Foi of Papua New Guinea*. Bloomington: Indiana University Press.

Weismantel, M. 1995. Making kin: kinship theory and Zumbagua adoptions. *American Ethnologist* 22:685–704.

Weiss, Brad 1992. Plastic teeth extraction: the iconography of Haya gastro-sexual affliction. *American Ethnologist* 19(3):538–552.

1993. Buying her grave: money, movement, and AIDS in northwest Tanzania. *Africa*, 63(1):19–35.

1996. *The Making and Unmaking of the Haya Lived World: Consumption and Commoditization in Everyday Practice*. Durham, NC: Duke University Press.

Werbner, Richard 1989. *Ritual Passage, Sacred Journey*. Washington: Smithsonian Institution Press.

White, G. M. and J. Kirkpatrick, eds. 1985. *Person, Self and Experience: Exploring Pacific Ethnopsychologies*. Berkeley: University of California Press.

White, Luise 1990a. Bodily fluids and usufruct: controlling property in Nairobi, 1917–1939. *Canadian Journal of African Studies* 24:418–38.

1990b. *The Comforts of Home: Prostitution in Colonial Nairobi*. Chicago: University of Chicago Press.

1993a. Cars out of place: vampires, technology and labor in East and Central Africa, *Representations* 43:27–50.

1993b. Vampire priests of Central Africa: African debates about labor and religion in colonial northern Zambia. *Comparative Studies in Society and History* 20:746–72.

Whitehead, Harriet 1981. The bow and the burden strap: a new look at institutionalized homosexuality in native North America. In S. B. Ortner and H. Whitehead, eds., *Sexual Meanings: The Cultural Construction of Gender and Sexuality*. Cambridge: Cambridge University Press, pp. 80–115.

Williams, Raymond 1973. *The Country and the City*. New York: Oxford University Press.

Willis, Roy 1968. Kamcape: an anti-sorcery movement in S.W. Tanzania. *Africa* 38(1):1–15.

Wilson, Monica 1951. Witch-beliefs and social structure. *American Journal of Sociology* 56:307–13.

Winnicott, D. W. 1971. *Playing and Society*. London: Tavistock.

Worsley, Peter 1968. *The Trumpet Shall Sound: A Study of "Cargo" Cults in Melanesia*, 2nd edn. New York: Schocken.

Yanagisako, Silvia Y. and Jane F. Collier 1987. Toward a unified analysis of kinship and gender. In J. F. Collier and S. J. Yanagisako, eds., *Gender and*

Kinship: Essays toward a Unified Analysis. Stanford: Stanford University Press, pp. 14–50.

Yoder S. 1981. Knowledge of illness and medicine among Cokwe of Zaire. *Social Science and Medicine* 15:237–46.

Young, Allan 1978. Modes of production of medical knowledge. *Medical Anthropology* 2:97–122.

Zavala, I. M. 1989. Representing the colonial subject. In R. Jara and N. Spadaccini, eds., *1492–1992: Re / Discovering Colonial Writing.* Minneapolis: University of Minnesota Press, pp. 323–48.

Zempleni, A. 1977. From symptom to sacrifice: the story of Khady Fall. In V. Crapanzano and V. Garrison, eds., *Case Studies in Spirit Possession.* New York: John Wiley and Sons, pp. 87–140.

1987. Des êtres sacrificiels. In M. Cartry, ed., *Sous le masque de l'animal: essais sur le sacrifice en Afrique noir.* Paris, Bibliothèque de l'Ecole des Hautes Etudes: Presses Universitaires de France, pp. 267–317.

Index